DATE DUE

AR 27 '98			
MY 18 '98			
MY 15 '99			
JE 6 '00			
OC 2 '03			
DE '03			
DE 8 '03			
AP '04			

DEMCO 38-296

JAPANESE CHILDREARING

CULTURE AND HUMAN DEVELOPMENT
A Guilford Series

Sara Harkness
Charles M. Super
Editors

JAPANESE CHILDREARING:
TWO GENERATIONS OF SCHOLARSHIP
David W. Shwalb and Barbara J. Shwalb, Editors

PARENTS' CULTURAL BELIEF SYSTEMS:
THEIR ORIGINS, EXPRESSIONS, AND CONSEQUENCES
Sara Harkness and Charles M. Super, Editors

CULTURE AND ATTACHMENT:
PERCEPTIONS OF THE CHILD IN CONTEXT
Robin L. Harwood, Joan G. Miller, and Nydia Luccia Irizarry

SIBLINGS IN SOUTH ASIA:
BROTHERS AND SISTERS IN CULTURAL CONTEXT
Charles W. Nuckolls, Editor

Japanese Childrearing
Two Generations of Scholarship

David W. Shwalb
Barbara J. Shwalb

Editors

Foreword by Takeo Doi

THE GUILFORD PRESS
New York   London

© 1996 The Guilford Press
A Division of Guilford Publications, Inc.
72 Spring Street, New York, NY 10012

Printed in the United States of America

This book is printed on acid-free paper.

Last digit is print number: 9   8   7   6   5   4   3   2   1

Library of Congress Cataloging-in-Publication Data
Japanese childrearing : two generations of scholarship / edited by
    David W. Shwalb and Barbara J. Shwalb.
        p.   cm.—(Culture and human development)
    Includes bibliographical references and index.
    ISBN 1-57230-081-7
    1. Child rearing—Japan.   2. Child development—Japan.
    3. Children—Japan—Social conditions.   I. Shwalb, David W.
    II. Shwalb, Barbara J.   III. Series.
    HQ792.J3J39   1996
    305.23′0952—dc20   96-15169
                                                            CIP

To our five children

About the Editors

David W. Shwalb is Associate Professor in the Department of International Studies of Koryo Women's College, Nagoya. He received his B.A. from Oberlin College, and an M.A. and Ph.D. from the University of Michigan Developmental Psychology Program. He began learning the Japanese language in 1974, on the GLCA Japan Study Program at Waseda University, and conducted doctoral research at Tokyo University in 1982 under a Fulbright fellowship. Dr. Shwalb also visited over a hundred schools in Hiroshima Prefecture as a Japanese Ministry of Education Fellow in 1977–1978. He has published on various aspects of Japanese socialization in family and school contexts, and his current projects include studies of fathering, abacus juku education, *tatemae/honne* (social cognition), cooperation/competition, and temperament.

Barbara J. Shwalb has been Associate Professor in the Department of Languages at Nagoya Shoka University since 1992. She received a B.S. in English from Southeast Missouri State College. After five years of public school teaching, two in high school and three in elementary school, she returned there to earn the M.A.T. and the M.A. in psychology. In 1978, she was awarded a full four-year scholarship to the University of Michigan's Combined Doctoral Program in Education and Psychology. While there, she worked at the Center for Research on Learning and Teaching, which led to support from the Japanese Ministry of Education for dissertation research at Tokyo University. She joined the University of Utah's Department of Educational Studies as Assistant Professor in 1986 and completed her Ph.D. in 1987. In her research and writing Dr. Shwalb has tried to integrate learning with individual, group, and national culture issues.

Barbara and David Shwalb have five children.

Contributors

Hiroshi Azuma is Professor of Developmental Psychology at Shira-yuri College, and Professor Emeritus at the University of Tokyo. He received his bachelor's degree in psychology at Tokyo University, and his doctorate in psychology at the University of Illinois. Founder and President of the Japanese Society of Developmental Psychology, Dr. Azuma has been an active member of numerous international organizations and editorial boards. His research specializations include educational and developmental psychology.

Shing-Jen Chen is Associate Professor of Developmental Psychology on the Faculty of Education of Hokkaido University. Born in Taiwan in 1946, he graduated from the National Cheng-chi University and served in the military. He received a Diploma (B. Litt.) in social anthropology from the University of Oxford, an M.Ed. in child psychology from Hiroshima University, and a doctorate in developmental psychology from Hokkaido University. In addition to interests in cross-cultural developmental psychology, he now does research on the development of infant crying. Dr. Chen lives in Sapporo with his pediatrician wife and three children.

George A. De Vos is Professor Emeritus of Psychological Anthropology at the University of California at Berkeley. A proponent of the multidisciplinary approach, he is a product of a period at the University of Chicago (where he received his Ph.D. in psychology in 1951) when it was possible to range variously in pursuit of knowledge within fields now designated separately as sociology, anthropology, and psychology. Dr. De Vos has also worked as a clinical psychologist, and has published fifteen books, including *Socialization for Achievement* (1972), *Religion and Family in East Asia* (1986), *Ethnic Identity* (1975), *Heritage of Endurance* (1984), *Koreans in Japan* (1984), and *Social Cohesion and Alienation: The United States and Japan* (1992).

Takeo Doi is a Consultant at St. Luke's International Hospital, Tokyo. Formerly Professor of Mental Health and Psychiatry at the University of Tokyo, Dr. Doi received his M.D. in 1942. He is the author of several books, including *Anatomy of Dependence* (1973, translated from the original *Amae no kozo*) and *Anatomy of Self* (1986, translated from *Omote to ura*).

Regina J. Garrick works independently on several Japan-related projects, near Chicago, Illinois. She received her doctorate from Tokyo University's Faculty of Medicine, where she specialized in mental health. Dr. Garrick lived in Japan for eight years, where she taught in Japanese universities and corporations. She has conducted clinical work in Japanese on mental health, and as a principal investigator has interviewed Japanese delinquent girls, and never-married middle-aged Japanese women. She has taught history of medicine at the University of California at San Francisco, and is a former Associate Director of the Japan Society of Northern California.

Per F. Gjerde is Associate Professor of Developmental Psychology, and Director of the Developmental Ph.D. program at the University of California at Santa Cruz. He received his Cand. Psychol. degree in clinical psychology from the University of Bergen, Norway, in 1976, and his Ph.D. in personality psychology from the University of California at Berkeley in 1984. In 1986 he was Visiting Research Fellow at the University of Tokyo. His interests include longitudinal research on personality, developmental psychopathology with emphasis on depression, attachment patterns in young adults, and cultural influences on development.

Hiroko Hara is Professor at the Institute of Women's Studies at Ochanomizu University. She received her B.A. (1957) and M.A. (1959) from the University of Tokyo, and her Ph.D. in anthropology (1964) from Bryn Mawr College. She has served as the President of the Japanese Society of Ethnology, and as chairperson of the International Group for the Study of Women. Her work covers life course and gender analysis in a cross-cultural perspective. Dr. Hara has conducted fieldwork in Japanese villages and cities, Canada (Hare Indians), and Indonesia.

Susan D. Holloway is Visiting Associate Professor of Education at Harvard University, and from 1983 to 1993 was a faculty member at the University of Maryland. She received her doctorate from the

Stanford University School of Education in 1983. While at Stanford, she became involved in the Hess–Azuma–Kashiwagi research, and since then has continued to conduct research on early childhood socialization and education in Japan and America. She is completing a study of Japanese and American teachers' beliefs about motivating children to achieve in mathematics, and is beginning a project on the role of individualization in Japanese early childhood education.

Betty B. Lanham is Emeritus Professor of Anthropology at Indiana University of Pennsylvania. She received her Ph.D. from Syracuse in 1962. Her specialization has been in culture and personality, with a concentration on processes of childrearing and development. She has also published on folktales, ethics, social change, and emotional expression and restraint in Japan and the United States. Dr. Lanham conducted fieldwork in Japan and in Guyana, South America, at intervals from 1951 through 1985.

Catherine Lewis is a Research Psychologist and Adjunct Associate Professor at the University of California, San Francisco, and Director of Formative Research, Developmental Studies Center, Oakland, California. She graduated from Radcliffe College in 1972, and received a Ph.D. in developmental psychology from Stanford University in 1979. Recipient of the Japanese Ministry of Education's Japanese speech award, and author of *Educating Hearts and Minds: Reflections on Japanese Preschool and Elementary Education* (1995), Dr. Lewis has lived and worked in Japan for three years. She is the mother of two young children.

Sandra Machida is Professor of Psychology at California State University, Chico, and Director of Policy Studies on Youth and the Family at CSUC. She received her Ph.D. in child development and early education from the Department of Psychological Studies in Education at Stanford University. Dr. Machida was a Research Associate from 1979 to 1980 at the University of Tokyo (working with Hiroshi Azuma) and a Visiting Scholar in the Educational Psychology Department at Keio University in 1992. In addition to her interests in children's development in Japan, she has authored articles on family daycare, early education intervention programs, and family and school factors associated with school achievement.

Mieko Minagawa is Associate Professor at Jumonji Junior College of Saitama, Japan. She received her B.A. and M.A. in education from

Ochanomizu University. She specializes in the study of children and families, especially the culture and history of Japanese families based on diaries written in the 17th–19th centuries. Her publications include "Images of Women and Children in the Edo Period" (1985), "Japanische Kindheit seit 1600" (with Hiroko Hara, 1986), and "Child Rearing and the Family in Tokugawa Japan" (1985).

Masahiko Minami is a lecturer at the University of Massachusetts, Lowell. He received his Ed.M. and Ed.D. in human development and psychology from Harvard University, and his B.A. from Kyoto University. His interests include developmental psychology and psychosociolinguistics, with an emphasis on cross-cultural comparisons of language development. He recently coedited a volume, *Language Issues in Literacy and Bilingual/Multicultural Education.* Mr. Minami has also contributed book chapters covering Asian narratives, East Asian students' experiences in U.S. classrooms, and childcare quality in Japan.

Carmi Schooler is Acting Chief of the Laboratory of Socioenvironmental Studies of the National Institute of Mental Health. He received his B.A. in psychology as well as philosophy and history from Hamilton College and his Ph.D. in social psychology from New York University. Much of his research has aimed at explaining social-class differences in psychological functioning in terms of the effects of occupational conditions. His research in Japan involves replicating his U.S. occupational studies as well as comparative historical studies and empirical research on women's roles. Other research involves psychological experiments examining basic cognitive processes in normal and abnormal individuals throughout the life course.

Nancy Shand is a Senior Research Anthropologist at the Menninger Foundation, Topeka, Kansas, and has taught anthropology at the University of Utah and the University of Kansas. She received her bachelor's degree in anthropology and intellectual history from Northwestern University, her master's in anthropology and sociology from the University of North Carolina, and her doctorate in anthropology from the University of Kansas. In addition to her studies of Japan, Dr. Shand has conducted fieldwork in Lebanon, India, Algeria, Egypt, Sweden, and inner-city Chicago.

Curtis A. Vaughn works as a consultant to primary intervention programs, with the West Contra Costa Unified School District, and has been a school psychologist for nine years with multiethnic populations in the San Francisco Bay Area. After receiving his B.S. in psychology from Virginia Commonwealth University in 1972, he worked in the U.S. Army for two years as a Personnel Psychologist. He received his master's and doctoral degrees in school and educational psychology at the University of California at Berkeley. His research on Japanese and American adolescents has focused on cognitive independence and achievement motivation. As a visiting scholar at Keio University in 1990–1991 he lectured on school psychology practices.

Ezra F. Vogel is Henry Ford II Professor of the Social Sciences at Harvard University. After graduating from Ohio Wesleyan in 1950 and serving two years in the U.S. Army, he studied sociology in the Department of Social Relations at Harvard, receiving his Ph.D. in 1958. He was Chairman of the Harvard Undergraduate Concentration in East Asian Studies from its inception in 1972 until 1991, and currently teaches courses on communist Chinese society, Japanese society, and industrial East Asia. He is now studying Japan's world role and has traveled to some 30 countries in 1991 to conduct interviews on this topic.

Suzanne Hall Vogel is Senior Clinical Social Work Supervisor in the Mental Health Service of Harvard University's Health Service, and maintains a private practice of psychotherapy. She holds a B.A. from the University of Texas, an M.A. in sociology from Northeastern University, and an M.S.W. in psychiatric social work from the Simmons College School of Social Work. Since 1989, she has been spending six weeks a year doing teaching and consultation at Hasegawa Hospital, Tokyo. She has written various articles on Japanese women's roles, family life, and mental health.

Merry White is Professor of Sociology at Boston University, and Associate in Research at the Harvard Edwin D. Reischauer Institute of Japanese Studies. She is a graduate of Harvard College and recipient of master's and doctoral degrees from Harvard University. She has been a consultant to a wide range of educational and corporate institutions, and to the U.S. Congress. Her research has focused on Japanese education, internalization, family and social issues. Recent publications include *The Japanese Educational Challenge: A Commitment to Children* (1987), *The Japanese Overseas* (1988), and *The Material Child: Coming of Age in Japan and America* (1993).

Foreword

It is a great honor and pleasure to be asked to write a foreword to *Japanese Childrearing*. I think the editors asked me to do so because I am acquainted with all the contributors. As a matter of fact, I have met all the authors of the seven leading chapters. We belong to the same generation, having become professionally active in the early 1950s. Although I never engaged in rigorous research myself, being an M.D. and primarily a clinician, our paths often crossed in the past precisely because of my cross-cultural interest, aroused by my study in the United States in the 1950s.

I think a few words are called for to explain my close relationship to William Caudill, whose pioneering studies of Japanese childrearing are well summarized by Carmi Schooler in the present volume. I had the good fortune to be introduced to Caudill when he first visited Japan in 1954, and at once became his consultant and colleague. This relationship continued until his untimely death in 1971. We used to discuss many things about Japanese culture, and he showed great interest in, among other things, my developing ideas on *amae,* which I interpreted as something that characterizes interpersonal relationships in Japan. Since the word may not be familiar to many readers, let me explain it briefly. It signifies indulgent dependency, primarily indicating what an infant feels when it seeks its mother, though *amae* can be applied to an adult who is supposed to entertain a similar feeling of being emotionally close to another. Understood in this way, the psychology of *amae* is not confined to the Japanese, yet the word is Japanese and the existence of such a word and its related rich vocabulary may well be indicative of Japanese culture.

In my opinion it was Caudill's interest in *amae* and its possible roots in childhood that induced him in his later years to study Japanese childrearing closely. It was he who offered me the first opportunity to present my ideas on *amae* in English, by inviting me to speak at a symposium on culture and personality that he organized and chaired at the Tenth Pacific Congress in 1961. The paper I read then, "*Amae:* A Key Concept for Understanding Japanese Personality Structure," later became widely known among those interested in Japanese studies. I might add that it was also Caudill who introduced the Vogels to me when they first came to Japan in 1958, thus contributing to the enduring, fruitful relationship that has since developed between us.

I hope it will not be considered improper to begin this foreword by emphasizing my personal relations with some of the authors; rather, it may be very significant. I do so because it seems to me that all the chapters in this volume, though they differ in methodology and object of study, converge on one point: the overwhelming importance of personal relations in Japan. One may say that what they each study and describe are, after all, the different aspects of personal relations in Japan. For instance, Carmi Schooler points out, citing the work of Caudill and others, that Japanese childrearing tends to strengthen the mother–infant bond, which undoubtedly sets the pattern for subsequent personal relations. George A. DeVos calls attention to the cultivation of social sensitivity that characterizes Japanese behavior on various levels. Betty Lanham found it remarkable that Japanese parents insist on always making the children understand the "whys" in disciplining them. And Suzanne Vogel's chapter is especially interesting in stating that the understanding of *amae* was instrumental in orienting her in the process of mingling with the Japanese families, who became the object of her conjoint study with Ezra Vogel.

I think the preceding examples clarify what I meant by the statement that all the chapters included here evaluate and describe personal relations in Japan in one way or another. But I wonder if this inclusive viewpoint is acceptable to all the contributors. Some might argue about the advisability of comprehending all the different studies by one and the same concept; I would maintain that it is advisable to do so because one can then compare and even integrate them. All the same, it is also possible to contend that personal relations should be no less important in Western societies. I agree, but I maintain that there is a certain quality to Japanese personal relations, and that quality corresponds to what I named *amae*. To avoid misunderstanding, let me repeat what I said above: The psychology of *amae* is not confined to the Japanese. It can be understood by the non-Japanese, though it would be expressed differently in English, depending upon the situation to which it refers. But *amae* as something ubiquitous in personal relations is peculiarly Japanese, and it may be defined as the implicit common expectation of apparent readiness between people to please and serve each other.

Again, I am not saying that such expectations may never be encountered in Western societies. They are encountered, but only on rare occasions, and perhaps only in special personal relations for that matter. I think this fact must be related to the lack of a word like *amae* in European languages. There is no need for such a word, and thus no corresponding concept, no social recognition. In other words, one might just as well have said that *amae* simply does not exist there. That is what I felt keenly when I first lived in the United States. So one can say that I discovered the importance of *amae* only by living abroad, that is to say, only when and where it was missing. The concept of *amae* thus became the cornerstone of my psychiatric and psychoanalytic studies. Incidentally, this fact of appreciating one's own culture while living in another culture is very interesting, and should underlie all cross-cultural studies. One may even state that in studying a different culture one really studies one's own culture in absentia. I would naturally like to ask the American contributors to this volume what they learned about their own culture by studying Japanese culture.

Needless to say, I have enjoyed reading all the chapters presented here and have been very stimulated by them. I sincerely hope that the excitement I have had will be shared by all the readers of the present volume. I assure you that it will be useful not only to non-Japanese people who are curious to know what makes the Japanese tick, but also to the Japanese who want to have a more objective perspective about themselves or simply to know how they have been observed. Finally, I hope that knowing about the Japanese will also encourage readers to reflect upon the culture into which they were born and with which they have lived to this day.

TAKEO DOI
St. Luke's International Hospital
Tokyo

Preface

This book is a tribute to the wisdom of our seniors. It is a "thank you" to the social scientists from the generation before ours, who pioneered the study of Japanese childrearing and socialization. The senior contributors to this volume, all born before World War II, have insights and perspectives attainable only from a lifetime of experiences. They understand Japanese socialization processes and childrearing more deeply than we do, and this book is their forum.

In 1996 we have access to a vast research literature on child development that did not exist for the previous generation. There were almost no Japanese developmental psychologists when De Vos (Chapter 4) began studying socialization in 1947, but there is now a Japanese Association of Developmental Psychology, which has over 1,200 members and publishes a quarterly research journal. Thus, one now has the luxury of a large and expanding database. As a result, Nancy Shand (Chapter 15) could relate her 1980s infancy data to recent findings on prenatal influences. But such knowledge was unavailable to Caudill and Schooler (Chapter 8) when they studied mother–infant interaction in the 1960s. In this sense we as scientists have more information than did our mentors. But do we understand more?

As Western social scientists we are trained to assume that scientific understanding inevitably progresses, and to value "hard data" and research technology. Because of such beliefs, and also bound by personal vanity and narrow training, some in our post-World War II generation look back smugly and view past research with 20/20 hindsight. Concerning Japanese socialization, critiques of "classic" research are common, although the original scholars are no longer alive to defend their work. For instance, ethnographic accounts by Embree (1939) and Benedict (1946) of normative Japanese childhood are relegated to the status of historical markers, that is, baselines from which to measure change. But are 1996 data any less a reflection of contemporary historical influences? Interpretations of Japanese parent–child relations by Gorer (1943) and LaBarre (1945) are now cited merely as examples of Freudian bias. But is research today any less tainted by current ideologies? Even quality empirical postwar research studies, the focus of this volume, may be accorded a scientific emeritus status upon the retirement of the scholar.

The context of Japanese childrearing has changed during the postwar era. Nowadays, Japan has the world's lowest infant mortality rate, and the world's highest longevity (life expectancy now averages 76.25 years for males and 82.51 years for females, as compared with 63.60 for males and 67.75 for females in 1955). Indeed, change has been rapid, but to look at older research as simply "the past" is to lose sight of its true value. To learn from our predecessors we try to read their work with open minds and avoid "kiss-of-death" reactions like "interesting, but mainly from a historical perspective." And we try to be honest about our own theoretical biases—for instance, that cross-generational continuity rather than change best characterizes Japanese childrearing and socialization. We have concluded that "motherhood is extolled as a morally virtuous and socially significant profession" (D. Shwalb, B. Shwalb, Sukemune, & Tatsumoto, 1992, p. 341). Yet a century ago Alice Bacon made a very similar point about Japanese mothers. She wrote that childhood and family socialization centered around the mother, and that a woman's life was "one of perfect devotion to her children; she is their willing slave" (Bacon, 1891, p. 86). This example shows that "new" observations concerning childrearing and socialization may not actually be new.

This volume is an attempt to establish continuity with past researchers. The format of the book is simple. Following each chapter by a senior scholar is a reaction chapter by a "junior" author. We asked senior scholars to look back at their lifework and derive what they now believe is its enduring value. Reaction chapter authors were to comment on the implications of the senior chapters for the understanding of culture, child development, and childrearing and socialization, as well as for a future research agenda.

We challenge scholars in other subfields of developmental psychology, Japanese Studies, and other fields to edit similar retrospective volumes. To misquote a familiar source, we must learn from the past in order that we not repeat the same research, make the same scholarly mistakes, or write books that have already been written.

ACKNOWLEDGMENTS

As Takeo Doi stated in his foreword, personal relationships are of "overwhelming importance" in Japan. Whether or not research conducted in Japan is unusually dependent on human networks, we always find it difficult to keep acknowledgments within space limitations. Whatever we two understand about Japanese childrearing and socialization is credited to those named below.

We first acknowledge the senior contributors to this volume. Their accomplishments made our work possible, and our request to define their lifework must have been a difficult task. We acknowledge the contributions of the reaction chapter writers, all of whom are now advancing the study of culture and development. We look forward a generation from now to reading their own retrospects. Next, we thank the series editors, Sara Harkness and Charles Super, for their patience, support, and wisdom. We believe their lifework will continue to open ethnocentric eyes. Appreciation is also expressed to Seymour Weingarten, Jeannie Tang, Andrea Amadio, Andrea Sargent, and Keisha Simmons at The Guilford Press, as well as to Jeanne Ford, copy-editor, for their skillful guidance.

Gratitude is also due to our mentors and colleagues. As undergraduates we were encouraged to become scholars by our teachers, including John Thompson, James Kodera, Fred Snyder, and Doug Atwood. At graduate school, the University of Michigan, we were inspired by many, including Bill McKeachie, Jim and Chen-Lin Kulik, Bill Morse, Harold Stevenson, Jacque Eccles, and Michael Lamb. As professionals we received further encouragement from Herbert Walberg, Mark Jones, and Ralph Reynolds. We are also indebted to Hiroshi Azuma, Seisoh Sukemune, Katsuhiko Takeda, Jun Nakazawa, Kiyoshi Asakawa, Junichi Shoji, Masao Tashiro, Koji Murata, and many others who have made possible our research in Japan. Finally, support from Koryo Women's College, Nagoya Shoka University, Westminster College of Salt Lake City, and the University of Utah is acknowledged.

Long-term friendships deepened our personal understanding of the Japanese. The kindness of the Tanaka, Miyake, and Bunden families of Tokyo, the Omoto, Hirakoshi, Kayano, and Hamaoka families of Hiroshima, and the Yamada and Sugie families of Nagoya has allowed us to feel at home in Japan. And the wisdom and care of our children's school teachers (Hisashi Ogino, Atsuo Matsukawa, and Kazumichi Yoneyama at Motomachi Primary School, Tokyo; Noriko Murai, Taeko Kimura, Minori Harada, Noriko Furukawa, and Yoshito Tsukamoto at Hirabari Primary School, Nagoya; and Hiroki Sugimoto at Nanzan International Middle School) have enriched all of our lives.

Our children, Lori, Connie, Becky, Davy, and Debbie, raised us as parents, and through their eyes we learned about childhood and education in Japan. They and all of our family, including our brothers and sisters, Fran, Tom, Laura, and Steve (Nichols) and Gene, Robert, and Edith (Shwalb), our grandchildren (Courtney, Meagan, Kayla and Alexis), Claude Woods, and our parents Jean Woods, Tom Nichols, and Richard and Sylvia Shwalb, showed us that family is more important than work. To quote Benedict (1946, p. 115), "One never repays one ten-thousandth of (this) *on* [indebtedness]."

DAVID W. SHWALB
BARBARA J. SHWALB

REFERENCES

Bacon, A. M. (1891). *Japanese girls and women.* Boston: Houghton Mifflin.

Benedict, R. (1946). *The chrysanthemum and the sword.* Boston: Houghton Mifflin.

Embree, J. F. (1939). *Suye Mura: A Japanese village.* Chicago: University of Chicago Press.

Gorer, G. (1943). Themes in Japanese culture. *Transactions of the New York Academy of Science,* Series F, 106–124.

LaBarre, W. (1945). Some observations on character structures in the Orient: The Japanese. *Psychiatry, 8,* 319–342.

Shwalb, D. W., Shwalb, B. J., Sukemune, S., & Tatsumoto, S. (1992). Japanese nonmaternal child care: Past, present and future. In M. E. Lamb, K. J. Sternberg, C.-P. Hwang, & A. G. Broberg (Eds.), *Child care in context: Cross-cultural perspectives* (pp. 331–353). Hillsdale, NJ: Erlbaum.

Contents

JAPANESE CHILDREARING

CHAPTER 1

Introduction
Looking Back

David W. Shwalb
Barbara J. Shwalb

Americans have reported on Japanese childrearing and socialization for over a century. During this period, however, academic disciplines, research methods, and the focus of research have changed significantly. This book examines past and present research on social development among the Japanese, and then considers framing research issues for the future. The book is mainly about Japanese culture, but also illustrates the general value of studying cultural influences on development.

GOALS OF THE BOOK

Our primary goal was to have several senior scholars share their insights on Japanese childrearing and socialization. Their work has been reviewed elsewhere by anthropologists, Japanese area specialists, and psychologists (Chen & Miyake, 1986; Lebra, 1976). Unfortunately, most reviews tend to simplify a scholar's lifework and relate it mainly to the reviewer's thesis. For example, in Rosenberger's *Japanese Sense of Self* (1992), De Vos's voluminous work is capsulized in about 200 words, and his view of the Japanese self is criticized because it "appears to Westerners as negative and self-defeating . . . [and] . . . loses sight of the positive value that Japanese give to relationships of both spontaneity and obligation in adult life" (p. 6). Readers are left wondering how De Vos would respond to this characterization of his work. One may likewise wonder what Benedict would have thought about the praise and criticisms of her 1946 work, published both in and outside of Japan (e.g., De Vos,

1973; Hamaguchi, 1993; Hara & Wagatsuma, 1974). Would Caudill have conceded to critics that his "naked-eye/stop watch observation methods" (Shand, Chapter 15, p. 264) of mother–infant interactions were unreliable? And would Gorer (1943/1962) have altered his psychoanalytic view of Japanese personality after 50 years of hostile attacks on his single article?

In a sense this volume was organized too late, because Ruth Benedict, William Caudill, Hiroshi Wagatsuma, Robert Hess, Edward Norbeck, and many others with important ideas about Japanese childrearing or socialization have passed away. Yet new researchers have carried on in their tradition. Our reaction chapter writers represent a younger generation, and the second goal of this book was to present their work as the most recent international scholarship on social development in Japan.

A third goal was to suggest the implications of past and current research for future studies. We asked the senior contributors, "What do you think is the enduring value of your work?" And each reaction chapter writer was asked to make concrete suggestions for new research, based on the legacy of the senior scholars. In the last chapter ("Conclusions: Looking Ahead") we will build from their ideas a set of research issues for the next generation.

We also asked the senior contributors to recall their scholarly evolution and early cross-cultural experiences. Such background information may clarify the social and intellectual context of their research. It is also of interest to know what it was like to study Japanese socialization and to be a cross-cultural researcher in their generation. As observed respectively by Suzanne Vogel and Hiroshi Azuma (Chapters 10 and 13), research reflects both the intellectual and personal growth of a scholar. We want readers to know about the growth of the scholars contributing to this volume.

Our final goal was to show how the study of culture and development advances scientific understanding between cultures. The research reviewed here was mainly by Americans; perhaps due to academic and funding conditions, the U.S. emphasis reflects the fact that most cross-cultural research has been conducted by Americans. But why focus on a relatively small American-based research literature, when a larger database has been accumulated by native Japanese scholars? Scanning recent editions of the Japanese *Jidoshinrigaku no Shimpo (Annual Review of Japanese Child Psychology),* for instance, we found references to 117 Japanese-language articles on "Infant Development and Family Relations" (Morishita, 1988), 173 articles on "Development of Interpersonal Relations" (Endo, 1989), and 139 articles on "Social Networks" (Ogino, 1992). Might it be more useful for Western readers to become acquainted with Japanese research that is inaccessible because of the language barrier? We are concerned about the intellectual trade imbalance, wherein Japanese scholars import American theory and research, while American scholars are seldom exposed to quality Japanese contributions. Surely the database and new concepts derived from Japanese research would advance Euro-American-centered social science. In a subsequent volume we plan to introduce some of these contributions.

Yet research by Westerners in settings like Japan is necessary for both the international field of developmental psychology and the field within Japan. As Hara and Minagawa (Chapter 2) note, it is natural to take aspects of one's native culture for granted, so that a comparative "outsider's view" is often illuminating. Doi, in the Foreword, writes that research by Westerners can be useful "to the Japanese who want to have a more objective perspective about themselves." American observers of Japan are no *more* objective than are native Japanese, since every observer is biased by cultural and personal background. But research by an outsider or a bi-cultural Japanese scholar provides a valuable *alternative* perspective. Chen (Chapter 3) notes that Japanese psychologists, striving to be objective scientists, may be particularly blind to cultural influences. If this is true, Japanese researchers' findings may widen the international database, but research on Japanese children by Americans may be relatively more valuable to those interested in the influence of culture on development.

CHANGES IN RESEARCH ON THE JAPANESE

Lanham and Garrick (Chapter 6) summarize the earliest American writings on Japanese socialization, so here we will introduce only a few sources. The first English-language accounts of Japanese social development were by Westerners (e.g., Hearn, 1904) who lived in Japan for extended periods during the Meiji era (1868–1912). Embree's (1939) ethnography of a mountain village *(Suye Mura)* was the first systematic and social scientific study relevant here, but his discussion of childhood socialization in the chapter "The Life History of the Individual" was not the main focus of his work.

During World War II Americans collected Japanese data from second- and thirdhand sources. Writers including Gorer (1943/1962) used the then-prevailing Freudian viewpoint to trace Japanese modal personality to early and strict toilet training and weaning. Also a wartime study, Benedict's (1946) *The Chrysanthemum and the Sword* included a chapter on childrearing and the life cycle ("The Child Learns"). We agree with Plath's (1987) comments about Benedict's work, that as young scholars we are "blinded by the glitter of personal experience," and that while we have the convenience of collecting our data within Japan (as Benedict could not), "from her distance she was able to perceive a pattern I'd been missing because I was too close to it" (p. 7).

Following World War II, non-Japanese researchers again conducted field work in Japan, and several works were published in the 1950s. One genre of this research, by sociologists and anthropologists, consisted of ethnographic descriptions documenting childrearing techniques as an aspect of village life (Beardsley & Ward, 1959; J. Maretzki & H. Maretzki, 1963; E. Norbeck & M. Norbeck, 1956). The second genre of postwar research, the focus of this volume, was more psychological in nature.

Writings on Japanese childrearing and socialization thus changed often during the past century. Their course went from anecdotal reports to ethnographic descriptions, to indirect Freudian analyses, back again to ethnographies, toward systematic, comparative, and quantitative and developmental approaches, and finally in some cases back yet again to recent ethnographies. Our earlier information on socialization was gleaned from general descriptions of Japanese culture, while research on Japanese children today focuses on specific issues such as social development and education.

PREVIEW OF CHAPTERS

The book chapters are arranged chronologically, with the exception of the Hara and Minagawa chapter, which is presented first because it provides historical background for reading the other chapters. Japanese studies by the senior contributors, born before World War II, began, respectively, between 1947 (De Vos) and 1975 (Shand). A commentary by a junior scholar follows each senior scholar's chapter.

Hiroko Hara and Mieko Minagawa (Chapter 2) suggest that (1) the historical, social, and physical context of Japanese childhood have changed significantly between the feudal and modern eras, and (2) traditional Japanese belief systems continue to impact on parental thinking about children. In reaction to their chapter, Shing-Jen Chen (Chapter 3) offers alternative interpretations of the

Hara–Minagawa data, and updates readers on contemporary issues concerning Japanese childhood.

George De Vos (Chapter 4) highlights "psychocultural continuities" in a review of his work that began in a multidisciplinary team studying personality among Japanese-Americans released from wartime internment camps. His chapter is mainly concerned with continuities in achievement motivation, family socialization, and the adaptation of minorities. Curtis Vaughn (Chapter 5) shows that De Vos's work is not yet completed. He has tested many of De Vos's hypotheses in studies of adolescents.

Betty Lanham (Chapter 6, coauthored with Regina J. Garrick) is cited most often for her questionnaire surveys on Japanese childrearing in the 1950s. Her research was important as the first statistical account of Japanese socialization and childrearing. She advanced this area of research by refuting the speculation of Freudian observers that Japanese parents were nonpunitive, overly strict in toilet training, and so forth. Lanham also anticipated 30 years in advance experimental findings that Japanese parental facial expressions impact on infant socioemotional development (e.g., Miyake, Chen, & Campos, 1985). Catherine Lewis's commentary (Chapter 7) focuses on continuities and discontinuities, comparing the issues that concerned Lanham in the 1950s with those of interest today.

Carmi Schooler (Chapter 8) presents a firsthand story and interpretation of the work of his collaborator, the late William Caudill. Caudill's 1960s investigations were among the first cross-cultural studies of development, and his work showed the impact of cultural values on mother–infant communication. Following Caudill's death, Schooler's work has concerned women's roles and the psychological effects of work environments on men and women. Susan D. Holloway and Masahiko Minami (Chapter 9) indicate why the Caudill and Schooler data are still valuable for our general understanding of culture and childrearing.

Ezra and Suzanne Vogel first became known to researchers on Japanese childhood for their collaboration, published as *Japan's New Middle Class* (E. Vogel, 1963/1992). This book introduced Western readers to the families of the emergent Japanese "professional housewife" and white collar "salary-man," whose lifestyles and relationships became the norm in modern Japan. In tracing her work from the time of that collaboration, Suzanne Hall Vogel (Chapter 10) sees her own evolution as a clinician and a scholar as inseparable from her development as a person. Her retrospect is relevant to the study of culture and development because it shows how we researchers may confuse changes in society or children with changes within ourselves. Ezra A. Vogel's chapter (Chapter 11) is of interest as a memoir of how social scientists in his generation became cross-cultural or Japan specialists. Merry White's comments (Chapter 12) relate the Vogels' findings to the context of Japanese families in the 1990s.

Hiroshi Azuma (Chapter 13) discusses his growth as a cross-cultural scholar, and in particular his collaboration from 1971 with Robert Hess on a study of the cognitive socialization of Japanese and American children. Theirs was among the first developmental studies of Japanese children to be published in the West (Dickson, Hess, Miyake, & Azuma, 1979), and the Hess–Azuma collaboration remains a model of equal partnership in cross-national collaboration. It showed that young Japanese and American children are socialized for different approaches toward school and achievement. Sandra Machida, in her reaction (Chapter 14), reviews the extensive publications resulting from the Hess–Azuma data, which she asserts contributed to the research literature and theories concerning several developmental issues.

Finally, Nancy Shand (Chapter 15) summarizes the most recent findings from her longitudinal research on mother–child communication, a collaboration with Yorio Kosawa. They found distinct differences in temperament (e.g., activity level) between their American and Japanese samples of newborn infants, and sought through follow-up data collection to compare these children and their mothers throughout the 1st year of life and at age 10. Per Gjerde (Chapter 16) discusses Shand's progress report as a rare example of longitudinal comparative research on human development and suggests several implications of her work for future longitudinal studies.

LOOKING BACK

There are two ways to read the work of scholars from previous generations. Those who take the first and unproductive approach focus on alleged weaknesses such as reliance on outdated or discarded methods, data analyses, or theories. From this viewpoint, one may criticize a researcher for using questionnaires, being too descriptive, or being too Freudian. A second and more constructive approach is to acknowledge that past research was conducted by competent scholars who operated with the tools and ideas available in their day. In the 1950s there was no "International Year of the Family" or "Year of the Child"—that is, there was less public attention given to child development issues. Certainly very little thought was given in that generation, outside of anthropology, to the impact of culture on child development.

The senior contributors were truly pioneers and mentors, and so the tone of the reaction chapter writers tends to be respectful. This should not be mistaken as a noncritical view—a constructive critical approach derives that which is valuable from research. We and the other junior contributors know from our experiences in Japan that the senior scholars were very wise concerning Japanese childrearing and socialization. With the help of the reaction chapter writers, readers may also understand how their insights into culture and children transcend the generations. The future of the field of culture and development will be brighter if we appreciate the work of our seniors.

REFERENCES

Beardsley, R., & Ward, R. (1959). *Village Japan.* Chicago: University of Chicago Press.

Benedict, R. (1946). *The chrysanthemum and the sword.* Boston: Houghton Mifflin.

Chen, S., & Miyake, K. (1986). Japanese studies of infant development. In H. Stevenson, H. Azuma, & K. Hakuta (Eds.), *Child development and education in Japan* (pp. 135–146). New York: Freeman.

De Vos, G. A. (1973). *Socialization for achievement: Essays on the cultural psychology of the Japanese.* Berkeley: University of California Press.

Dickson, W. P., Hess, R. D., Miyake, N., & Azuma, H. (1979). Referential communication accuracy between mother and child as a predictor of cognitive development in the United States and Japan. *Child Development, 50,* 53–59.

Embree, J. F. (1939). *Suye Mura: A Japanese village.* Chicago: University of Chicago Press.

Endo, J. (1989). Taijin kankei no hattatsu [Development of interpersonal relations]. *Jidoshinrigaku no Shimpo [Annual Review of Japanese Child Psychology], 28,* 223–253.

Gorer, G. (1962). Themes in Japanese culture. In B. Silberman (Ed.), *Japanese character and culture: A book of selected readings* (pp. 308–324). Tucson: University of Arizona Press. (Original work published 1943)

Hamaguchi, E. (1993). *Nihongata moderu to wa nanka: Kokusaika jidai ni okeru meritto to demeritto [What is the "Japanese model"?: Its merits and demerits in the age of internationalization].* Tokyo: Shinjusha.

Hara, H., & Wagatsuma, H. (1974). *Shitsuke [Japanese ways of childrearing].* Tokyo: Kohbundo.

Hearn, L. (1904). *Japan: An attempt at interpretation*. New York: Macmillan.

Lebra, T. S. (1976). *Japanese patterns of behavior*. Honolulu: University of Hawaii Press.

Maretzki, T. W., & Maretzki, H. (1963). *Taira: An Okinawan village*. Cambridge, MA: Harvard University Press.

Miyake, K., Chen, S.-J., & Campos, J. J. (1985). Infant temperament, mother's mode of interaction, and attachment. In I. Bretherton & E. Waters (Eds.), Growing points in attachment theory and research. *Monographs of the Society for Research in Child Development, 50*(Serial No. 209), 267–297.

Morishita, M. (1988). Nyuyoji no hattatsu to kazoku kankei [Infant development and family relations]. *Jidoshinrigaku no Shimpo [Annual Review of Japanese Child Psychology], 27,* 184–211.

Norbeck, E., & Norbeck, M. (1956). Child training in a Japanese fishing community. In D. Haring (Ed.), *Personal character and cultural milieu* (pp. 651–673). Syracuse, NY: Syracuse University Press.

Ogino, M. (1992). Social networks. *Jidoshinrigaku no Shimpo [Annual Review of Japanese Child Psychology], 31,* 159–185.

Plath, D. W. (1987). *Notes on a case of the scholar's itch*. Symposium paper presented at the annual meetings of the American Anthropological Association, Chicago.

Rosenberger, N. R. (1992). *Japanese sense of self*. New York: Cambridge University Press.

Vogel, E. F. (1992). *Japan's new middle class*. Berkeley: University of California Press. (Original work published 1963)

From Productive Dependents to Precious Guests
Historical Changes in Japanese Children

Hiroko Hara
Mieko Minagawa

BACKGROUND

Child development is influenced by changing societal conditions and events, so a historical perspective on childhood is essential. This volume looks back at seven different research programs that began between the 1950s and 1970s, while Japan was undergoing rapid social change. During this generation the Japanese people experienced a decline in the proportion of the agricultural population, a decline in the use of domestic servants and housemaids, land reform, increases in the public's standard of living, a growing high school and college attendance ratio, the emergence of the white-collar "salary-man" lifestyle, and the development of informal schooling such as *juku*. We must consider how Japanese childhood evolved prior to and during these decades, because changes in children's environments and experiences probably impacted on the research described in this book.

The goal of this chapter is *not* to reinterpret the research of the other contributors to this volume; we leave it to the readers to decide how research data has reflected changing social conditions. But in looking back on previous studies, we question first whether findings from past generations would be replicated today. For example, Betty Lanham (Chapter 6, this volume) conducted surveys about childrearing in Wakayama Prefecture in the early 1950s, when Japan was still recovering from the devastation of World War II. Few of the 6- and 7-year-old children whom she studied went on to attend college, but today many of them are the parents of college students who lived through "examination hell" as teens. In addition, the physical environment of the city where she conducted her fieldwork has changed completely since the early 1950s. Finally, the thinking and expectations of parents, including fathers (Hara, 1993), have shifted in the past generation. Given such changes, how do Lanham's data help us nowadays to understand childrearing in Japan? The relationship between historical change and research findings or interpretations is even clearer when we consider the cultural descriptions of Ruth Benedict (1946). Her depiction of the daily life of Japanese children is completely out of touch with childhood experiences in 1996 Japan. Further, her ideas of modal personality and national character are now obsolete within the field of anthropology. Yet I still assign the reading of *The Chrysanthemum and the Sword* to my students. Finally, we can assume that historical factors are currently influencing the latest research data on Japanese child development in the 1990s. Certainly the world of Japanese children continues to evolve, and perhaps the milieu of Japanese child development will change even more in the next 40 years than it did between the generations discussed in this book.

In this chapter we will describe the changing context of Japanese childhood, from the 17th through the 20th centuries. Below we will document how, despite significant changes in the experiences of children and families, basic Japanese values and beliefs concerning childrearing and human development have remained constant.

Our Own Interests in the History of Childhood

I (Hara) first got interested in anthropology at the age of 12, when I repatriated from Seoul, Korea, to Fukuoka (Kyushu) in January 1946. I underwent various culture shocks and began to ponder the issues of ethnicity, social class, and socialization processes in different cultures and societies. I have studied historical changes in Japanese thinking about childrearing since the 1950s, when I was an undergraduate and master's student in cultural anthropology at Tokyo University. As an undergraduate, I was fortunate to participate in fieldwork in various parts of Japan, including Kaida Village

(Nagano Prefecture), where I conducted the fieldwork for my bachelor's and master's theses on *Children and Culture*. At the same time, I had the good fortune to work with anthropologist Takao Sofue and psychologist Akira Hoshino in 1957, when they returned from their studies in the United States. Also while at Tokyo University, I took courses given in English by John Pelzel, William Caudill, Gordon Bowles, and others.

At that point I decided to study in the United States, to get more sophisticated anthropological training and in order to conduct fieldwork in arctic and subarctic areas. In the United States (1959–1964) I first studied at the University of Pittsburgh, where I took a seminar on psychoanalysis from Charlotte Babcock, who had analyzed Takeo Doi and William Caudill. I then did my doctoral training at Bryn Mawr College, and wrote my thesis in 1964 on the Hare Indians. From my vantage point in the United States, I also became greatly interested in the changes occurring in the lives of Japanese children. During that period I worked with Hiroshi Wagatsuma, then a professor at the University of Pittsburgh. My long-term association with Wagatsuma grew into a collaboration on a 1974 monograph titled *Shitsuke (Japanese Ways of Childrearing;* Hara & Wagatsuma, 1974). In this book we analyzed how Japanese childhood was studied both by Japanese and American social scientists between 1950 and 1970. The crucial difference we found in comparing the thinking of Japanese and American scholars was in how maturity was viewed in relation to independence. Westerners associated maturity with becoming an independent individual, while Japanese assumed that a mature person knows when, how, and on whom to be dependent or not to be dependent. In other words, Japanese words like *amaeru, amaenai, amaesaseru,* and *amaesenai* are the criteria for maturity. A person who tries to be independent or "overindependent" does not know how to *amaeru.* Also included in this work were accounts of what ordinary people and professionals thought about children, throughout Japanese history. Some of the historical outline that follows is drawn from *Shitsuke,* which was never translated into English because Wagatsuma died before we could translate it.

The second author of this chapter (Minagawa) has studied children's lives as depicted in two sets of diaries written by lower-rank *samurai* over a 10-year period during the late Tokugawa era (Minagawa, 1985). Minagawa has studied aspects of the lives of children, including play, eating, reading, clothing, and health, based on 1839–1848 materials from Kuwana City (Mie Prefecture). These materials help us to understand childhood in the premodern era. Our collaboration (e.g., Hara & Minagawa, 1986) began when Minagawa was a doctoral student at Ochanomizu University.

The Field of Childhood History in Japan

In Japan, the history of childhood has recently been studied by scholars in the fields of education, child studies, sociology, ethnology, and folk studies. Historical studies in the early 20th century were summarized by sociologist Sakurai (1941), and the most significant and groundbreaking 20th century work on this subject was carried out by Dr. Yanagida Kunio (1874–1962) and the *Kyodokai* (Study Group on Local History and Life). For example, Yanagida and his associates conducted a nationwide survey in 1935 on customs and beliefs concerning childbirth and childrearing (Onshi-Zaidan Boshi Aiikukai, 1935, 1975; Yanagida, 1949). Most of their informants were born in the late 19th or early 20th century, and their reports were based on memories of childhood. These accounts provide us with information about 19th-century Japanese childhood, as passed down from informants' parents and grandparents. Yanagida's research employed more direct methods than the previous work of historians, who depended on written and dated sources. Although these retrospective data were at times second- or thirdhand, Yanagida and his followers shed new light on traditional Japanese thinking and its relation to actual childrearing practices. Indeed, he established a new field of study in Japan (Kawada, 1993).

After World War II, scholars resumed the study of children's play, welfare, and education, reconstructing various aspects of childhood from a historical perspective. One writer, K. Ishikawa (1948), made a major contribution to the historical study of education in his *Waga Kuni ni okeru Jidoh-kan no Hattatsu (Development of Views on Childhood in Japan)*. In this book he dealt with a variety of documents from the 11th–19th centuries, focusing mainly on the educational and disciplinary techniques of upper-class *samurai*. Another landmark publication was the 24-volume *Encyclopedia of Childhood for Children* (Heibonsha, 1956–1957). This work included historical coverage of various aspects of children's lives by specialists from many fields.

In the 1960s, historical research was influenced by demographic and economic developments within Japanese society. At this time, the population had become urbanized and the number of children per family was dropping. Children began to spend more time watching television or attending afterschool learning activities, and had less and less free time to play among themselves, or to experiment with physical objects. Japanese began to worry about the deterioration of childhood experiences and indeed about the future of childhood, so books on childcare and child growth became very popular. In *Shitsuke* (Hara & Wagatsuma, 1974), we reexamined the findings of Yanagida's group, in light of research by contemporary Japanese and American anthropologists. This book revealed the belief systems behind Japanese childrearing since the 1868 Meiji Restoration (the date usually given as the beginning of Japan's modern era), as influenced by geographic, socioeconomic, historical, and individual factors. Subsequently, M. Ishikawa and his colleagues (1977) edited the seven-volume *Nihon Kodomo no Rekishi (History of Japanese Childhood)*, the most extensive effort of its kind in Japan, covering the millennia from the Neolithic Jomon period to the present. A final landmark publication was the 1980 Japanese translation of Aries's (1960) *L'enfant et la Vie Familiale sous l'Ancien Régime*. This book stimulated wider interest in the history of childhood in the disciplines of philosophy, education, and child development (e.g., Kojima, 1986).

Although there were scholars in Japan who had been writing on the social history of childhood, such as Hiroshi Takai, their works did not draw attention until the 1980s. Takai's work, discovered only after his death in 1979, was particularly notable. Takai (1991) described processes of mental and psychological development among merchant-class boys and girls in the Tempo era (1830–1844).

PREMODERN JAPANESE CHILDREARING VIEWS AND PRACTICES
Belief in the Supernatural

Various sources are available from which we can formulate ideas about post-1600 Japanese views on childhood, but it is more difficult to do so for the period prior to 1600. According to the Yanagida group, the Japanese of the 19th and 20th century believed that a child is closely related to *kami* (supernatural beings or spirits) until the 7th birthday. Other sources indicate that this belief may have originated before the 10th century. In various Shinto ceremonies children under 7 years old were traditionally given important roles as mediators between the sacred and profane worlds (T. Iwamoto, 1956). If a child died before age 7, the body was treated differently from that of an older child, since the soul could return immediately to the other world and prepare for rebirth. Because of such beliefs, a deceased infant's body might be buried under the floor of one's house, at road crossings, or at village borders. These burial customs in effect allowed the soul of the deceased to stay near one's home and guard the remaining family members. Such customs seemed to have persisted even after the Meiji Restoration, despite changes in beliefs associated with Buddhism. In the context of such traditional beliefs children under 7 are often indulged, and are still treated by some with respect and even awe. Indulgence of children's wishes has long been viewed ethnocentrically by Western-ers as "spoiling" (Bird, 1880/1973). But according to the traditional Japanese viewpoint, an inherently pure and sin-free child is gradu-ally corrupted by the adult world. So actual spoiling results from contamination by adults rather than from indulgence.

Another practice influenced by the association of young chil-dren with the supernatural world was *mabiki*, or infanticide (Chiba & Ohtsu, 1983; Takahashi, 1936). Infanticide of baby girls, the physically deformed, one of twins, or babies born in a bad ca-lendrical year was not traditionally considered murder. Rather it was seen as a sending back of the soul to the otherworld for a better rebirth (Tsuboi, 1971). This view influences Japanese popu-lar beliefs about abortion even today, as an aborted fetus is thought to return from this world to the spirit world of *kami*. Many people do not feel that abortion terminates the life of a fetus, but rather that it puts off the life of the fetus, who will be born at a later time. The soul is thought to be eternal and can be born in a human shape at any time.

Thus, the Japanese have long believed that children develop not only in the hands of parents, family, and neighbors, but also under the protection of supernatural beings. Buddhism, Confu-cianism, Taoism, Christianity, and modern science have intermin-gled in various degrees to influence this Japanese thinking about childhood since 1600. However, archaic feelings toward supernatu-ral beings seem to have continued throughout history to strongly affect Japanese ideas about childhood and child development. Later we shall see that this influence persisted well into Japan's modern era.

Family and Childhood in the Tokugawa Era (1600–1867)

During the feudal Tokugawa (Edo) era, there was a dramatic expansion of publishing activity, including books on childrearing.

It was common to read guidebooks throughout Japan, as the literacy rate was high across social strata (Dore, 1965). For instance, the *Onna-Chohhohki-Taisei* (*Detailed Handbook of Everyday Life and Rituals for Women;* Kusada, 1692), which advised women how to behave during pregnancy, was read widely. Children's medicine emerged as a specialty in the 17th century, and one medical doctor (Kazuki, 1703) published a six-volume work, *Shohni Hitsuyo Sodate-Gusa (Guidebook for Childrearing).* This series, which discussed children from birth through 10 years of age, is thought to be the first publication of its kind. It was common in this era to visit pediatricians, who made diagnoses and prescribed medicine.

One Tokugawa era belief that persists to some degree even today was *taikyo,* which refers to teaching and disciplining a child even before birth (Meishin Chohsa-Kyohgikai, 1949; Ogata, 1946). Japanese believed that a mother's thoughts, feelings, and actions during pregnancy were transmitted to the fetus and continued to influence a child's character, health, and abilities after birth. Mothers therefore were told to provide a healthy environment for the fetus by being industrious and kind to others, and by avoiding painful or stressful experiences (e.g., funerals). It is still assumed today that mothers are responsible for providing a good prenatal environment, and this belief is transmitted across generations within the family and by professionals.

Upper-class Tokugawa women married earlier and bore more children than women from lower social strata. This was both because they were compelled to bear sons to succeed in the family line *(ie),* and because wet nurses were available to help raise the children. Infanticide was practiced widely in rural areas to control the numbers of children; induced abortions were conducted at first only in urban areas, because more doctors were available to urban women. However, abortions gradually became common in rural areas as well during the Tokugawa period. In this era high infant mortality rates were recorded for Japanese of all social strata (Matsuda, 1978). Due to these rates and the practice of infanticide (Kitoh, 1978), rural families in the Tokugawa period averaged only three or four children. Comparable data are not available for urban families.

The major causes of death among infants and children were smallpox, measles, and other infectious diseases (Minagawa, 1985; Suda, 1973). Interestingly, smallpox was viewed at this time as a rite of passage, reflecting beliefs in the supernatural. Rituals including prayers and magic were conducted to treat smallpox *(Hohsoh e-shuh,* n.d.), and were also held at the time of recovery (Kazuki, 1703). In contrast, people thought that other ailments, including measles or eczema, were caused by the spiritual pollution or inappropriate behavior of the mother, depending on the severity or frequency of symptoms (Minagawa, 1985).

Despite beliefs that babies and children were assisted by deities, we have evidence that mothers were considered to be the primary caregivers (Yamakawa, 1943). Wet nurses *(uba)*, babysitters *(komori)*, and foster families reared the children of some wealthy families (Wada, 1912), but Confucian scholars of this era advocated motherhood as a key feminine virtue. Descriptions of Tokugawa era childrearing depicted a close and physical mother–child relationship (Minagawa, 1985), and mothers were said to be sensitive to the most subtle signals of their babies and children. Further evidence of the traditional value placed on motherhood are revealed in analyses of Japanese folktales by psychiatrist Kawai (1982), who found a trust in women's wisdom and strength to be a major theme in such materials.

The roles and responsibilities of children varied according to social standing within the four hierarchical classes of feudal Japanese society (in order of higher status: *samurai*/warrior—10% of the population; agricultural—80%; artisan and merchant—together 10% of the population). Higher-rank *samurai* boys were expected to master the military and literary arts and codes of etiquette (Yamakawa, 1943), while children of lower *samurai* helped with parents' side jobs. In the agricultural strata, one was considered to be an adult upon entering the labor force at about age 15, and children from ages 7 to 14 were expected to help in farming or household chores (Takeuchi, 1941). Within the merchant and artisan classes, children took care of their younger siblings and helped with household chores. Boys in these latter two classes were hired as apprentices at about age 10. When they reached ages 17 or 18, they went through a ceremony called *gempuku,* after which they began to work for wages (Kitagawa, 19th c.).

Birth order also had an important influence on the lives of Tokugawa Era children. Those designated as family heirs (usually first sons) were treated differently from others. If a family had only daughters, a man could be allowed to marry into the family as a son-in law (Matsuo, 1980). Thus, adoption was a possible life path for some second and third sons, and some unmarriageable later-born sons were destined to be dependent on their older brothers.

Japanese since the late 12th century have generally considered the first seven years of life as the first half of childhood. The second half of childhood was most often said to last until ages 14 or 15

(Yuhki, 1977). Thus, most 15-year-olds in the Tokugawa era already filled adult roles, working for their parents or employers. Only since the 1960s, with the dramatic population decrease in the agrarian sector, have most teenage youth tended to stay at school rather than work.

Dore (1965) estimated that by the late Tokugawa period about 40% of Japanese boys and about 10% of Japanese girls received some kind of formal education outside the home. Under the feudal regime, the *terakoya* school (schools within temples or private homes) provided a single-sex classroom education for children of different social strata, and in some cases employed women teachers. Standard textbooks, teaching manuals, and beginner-level picture books were published, and various curricula for teaching how to read, write, and calculate appeared throughout Japan.

Play, work, discipline, and education were woven together in children's lives, reflecting Tokugawa era beliefs about the nature of childhood. Generally, childrearing and formal education practices were flexible, and depended on the character, ability, and life circumstances of each child and family. In both education and discipline, the overall philosophy was to "let children learn" rather than to "teach children" (Hara, 1979). Following this approach, children learned the skills needed for their adult occupations gradually, by playfully repeating various bodily motions and verbal behaviors. This aspect of Tokugawa era children's lives is inferred from the various materials collected by Yanagida and his group during the late Meiji and the Taisho eras, and suggested that people correlated playful imitation with effective learning.

The simple belief that children's postures and states of mind are interwoven throughout development weakened to some extent in modern Japan, as industrialization and the educational system changed the nature of childhood experiences. Yet basic Tokugawa era attitudes toward children and various childrearing customs persisted, despite the social upheavals of the Meiji Restoration and World War II.

CHILDHOOD IN THE MODERN ERA (SINCE 1868)

Demographics

In Japan, reliable data on fertility rates are available only for after 1920. The gross reproductive rate (number of children a woman bears between ages 15 and 49) was 4.24 in 1920, 5.11 in 1925, 4.71 in 1930, 4.11 in 1940, 3.65 in 1950, 2.00 in 1960, 2.13 in 1970, 1.75

in 1980, and under 1.5 in 1992 (D. Shwalb, B. Shwalb, Sukemune, & Tatsumoto, 1992). Especially since 1960, most women
have given birth mainly between ages 25 and 35. During most of
the modern era, there has been no correlation between parents'
educational background and the number of children per couple
(Kawabe, 1981).

The infant mortality rate, while lower than in the Tokugawa
period, was relatively high between 1900 and 1920 and reached
18.9% in 1918. Although vaccinations against illnesses including
smallpox had been introduced, and the government Bureau of
Medical Affairs fought vigorously against epidemical diseases, many
children died in epidemics between 1885 and 1908 (Mohri, 1972).
Since 1920, the infant mortality rate decreased due to improve-
ments in sanitary conditions, nutrition, and birth control, so that
Japan now has the lowest infant mortality rate of any modern society (D. Shwalb et al., 1992).

In contrast to the sharp drop of infant deaths from infectious
diseases, accidental deaths have not decreased as rapidly since
World War II (Koizumi, 1984). The major causes of death in 1976
for children less than 1 year old were accidental suffocation (73%),
traffic accidents (6%), falling down (5%), and fires (4%). For ages
1–4 the main causes were traffic accidents (52%) and drowning
(43%), and for ages 5–14 they were also traffic accidents (70%)
and drowning (29%). Such rankings have remained consistent up
into the 1990s.

Three other trends in the era following World War II have
been toward increasing numbers of children with allergies, meta-
bolic disorders (e.g., diabetes), and other conditions (e.g., Down
syndrome). Stated very simply, due to changes in demographics
and health conditions, Japanese people today learn how to live with
unhealthy or handicapped infants and children, instead of enduring (as their parents did) the early deaths of infants and children.

Childrearing Views and Practices

During the 1970s, the desirable size of the Japanese family changed
significantly. The ideal number of children per family was three
between 1945 and 1971, according to public opinion surveys taken
every 2 years by the *Mainichi* newspaper. But a shift occurred from
1973, as 47.6% of wives considered two children as ideal and 40.7%
called three the ideal. In all subsequent surveys, the two-child ideal
has pervaded Japanese wives' responses (Kuroda, 1977). In addition, parents' reasons for restricting family size have changed since

World War II. According to the 1950 *Mainichi* survey, basic necessities of life such as food, clothing, and housing were cited most often as the reasons for limiting family size (by 43.8% of wives), followed by the children's health and education (38.9%), and protecting the mother's health (31.4%). In 1969 and 1979 surveys, the desire to give children a good education and protection of the mother's health assumed greater importance. Conversely, economic necessities were cited by only 21.4% of mothers in 1969 and by 20.3% in 1979.

Japanese views on childrearing also changed during the modern era, and three general views have been observable during the past century. The first view considered children to be human resources for the development of the nation. From this perspective a big, strong, and healthy physique was of greatest value. The second view to emerge incorporated a Western and humanistic philosophy of childhood and emphasized such things as human rights for children. The third view consisted of devotion and tolerance toward babies and children, a mentality that grew out of the thinking typical of the Tokugawa era. In our view, these three different belief systems have been woven together in various ways during the past century. Next we will describe several events, episodes, and actions that reflected contemporary and traditional Japanese beliefs about children.

Many private and civic leaders have actively promoted child development in the 20th century. One example of such an activity was the *Akambo Tenrankai* (Annual Baby Exhibition), first sponsored in Tokyo in 1913 by the present-day Mitsukoshi Department Store. It was proposed by educator Nishiyama Tetsuji (T. Nishiyama, 1918), who studied the physical condition and health circumstances of the most robust babies among the 300–400 babies who were brought to each exhibition. Nishiyama also studied the childrearing practices and health of their mothers, and found that most of the prizewinners were fed mother's milk on a timed schedule and were lightly dressed (even though the prevalent value then was to dress babies heavily). Of the 137 prizewinners between 1915 and 1917, only 32 were girls. Sponsored by newspapers, pharmaceutical companies, and powdered milk companies to promote the "right way" of childrearing, such healthy-baby contests advocated raising big and strong children.

In 1918 the *San-iku-kai* (Niwa, 1972), a consultation center for pregnant women and mothers of infants, was established by a group of Christian couples who included medical doctors and midwives. Their goal was to provide information and technical services free of charge to low-income city dwellers, reflecting a humanistic and Western philosophy toward children. The *San-iku-kai* organization gradually expanded its activities and built a maternity hospital, daycare center, and infant home, and still runs several general hospitals and homes for the elderly in Tokyo and other cities. Many other civic organizations were founded between 1868 and 1920 to improve infant/child welfare, but most of these efforts were short-lived (Namae, 1923).

The government has also actively promoted child health and welfare over the past century. For instance, it exerted various controls that changed Japanese childbirth practices, beginning in the Meiji era. Immediately after the Meiji Restoration, the government prohibited both the sale of abortion-inducing drugs and the handling of abortions by midwives. In 1872 it decreed that people should not consider women's bleeding after childbirth as spiritual pollution, as had long been a popular belief. New regulations for becoming midwives were issued in 1899, and by 1935 all midwives were registered. The physical location of childbirth also changed completely in the modern era, particularly since the 1960s. In 1935 most babies were born in private homes, but by 1960 (the succeeding generation) about half of births took place in hospitals. At that time, 53% of births in large cities were at hospitals, compared with only 27% outside these cities. A campaign by public health officials instructed the public that hospitals were much cleaner than private homes. Word of the impressive effects of antibiotics spread rapidly, and the public reacted so quickly, that soon home births were rare even in rural areas. In fact, by 1970 96.1% of all births nationwide were at hospitals (Ministry of Health and Welfare, 1980). All of these practices and trends reflected the government's desire to use modern science to promote the welfare of children.

Another example of government involvement in the lives of children was the establishment in 1934 of the Onshi-Zaidan Boshi Aiikukai (Imperial Gift Foundation for Maternal and Children's Health and Welfare), to commemorate the birth of Prince Akihito, who is now Japan's emperor. This institute undertook nationwide surveys between 1935 and 1938 concerning geographic and socioeconomic factors related to infant mortality and nutrition. It also standardized checklists of physical and mental growth processes for pediatric examinations (Ushijima, 1938) and carried out nationwide surveys about childrearing customs, beliefs (Onshi-Zaidan Boshi Aiikukai, 1975), and practices (Yamashita, 1943). This foundation organized an extension network of public health nurses in many villages (1,000 in 1944), mobilizing midwives and nurses in each village. Nurses visited farm families in person to improve nutrition and sanitary conditions for children, and the foundation today continues its outreach programs in rural Japan.

In 1943 the wartime Health Ministry began to issue a *Nin-Sampu-Techo (Maternity Notebook)* to pregnant women, who registered for medical checkups and extra rations of clothing, food, and supplies. This intervention was intended to foster healthy human resources to serve the nation at war. The *Nin-Sampu-Techo* was similar to a notebook called *Kainin Kakiage-cho (Registration List of Pregnancies)* utilized in the Tokugawa era by local lords at times of population or labor shortage. After the war the Child Welfare Act and Health Center Law were enacted in 1947, and based on these laws the *Boshi Techo (Mother–Child Health Record Book)* was first issued in 1966. This booklet is now distributed by local governments, and in it women record the test results of their pregnancy checkups. It also includes records of the baby's physical condition, and progress in vocal, motor, and social abilities. The *Boshi Techo* serves as a record book for immunizations and child growth until the age of six. Again we can see here a strong involvement of the modern Japanese government in growth and development of children.

As a result of these governmental and civic activities, the public's conscious efforts, and rising standards of living and nutrition, children's physiques have changed remarkably over the past generation. Around 1960, the weight and size of Japanese babies began to increase both in rural and urban areas. Ironically, the physical strength of these school children has deteriorated since that same time. Thus, the long-standing motto, "big is beautiful" had to end. This switch in thinking was symbolized by the 1978 cessation of the annual contests for healthy and well-built school children, which had reflected the view of children as a national resource. From that time the new message may have become "small is beautiful."

Folk Beliefs about Children in the Modern Era

As we have seen, both the modern Japanese government and civic leaders have advocated new ways of childbirth and childrearing throughout the 20th century. Their directives and activities have of course changed the lives of children, but many parents still have retained some traditional childrearing beliefs and practices that were passed down from the Tokugawa period. For instance, after the end of World War II, the government tried to establish an educational system based on "scientific knowledge" and to discard "superstition." To accomplish this the Education Ministry organized a consortium called *Meishinchosa Kyogikai* (Committee on Folk Belief Studies) in 1946, to conduct research on superstition (Meishinchosha Kyohgikai, 1949).

But the government failed to destroy "superstition," and many folk beliefs still exist in postwar Japan. In fact, some beliefs have probably increased in their influence since World War II. For instance, before the postwar introduction of new birth control techniques, a baby was considered to be a gift from one of the gods in the Shinto pantheon. Even nowadays help is sought from supernatural powers to secure an easy delivery and healthy baby. In the 5th month of pregnancy many women still visit a shrine or temple to pray for an easy delivery and a healthy child. And in the 1st month of a baby's life, parents and/or grandmothers still take the infant to a shrine to report the birth and to thank the gods. Such customs have been practiced in various parts of Japan since the 18th century.

Looking at the preceding example, one might say that families simply practice rituals without believing in their actual impact on child development. But in 1906 and 1966, the Japanese experienced two surprising episodes that proved more directly the pervasive influence of Japanese folk beliefs. In each of these years the birthrate dropped significantly, followed by sharp increases the following years (Kohsei-shoh Daijin Kamboh Tohkei Chohsa-bu, 1968). These years were called *hinoeuma* (the year of the horse, and the solar element of fire), in a sexagenary cycle that combines a cycle of twelve animals with a cycle of five solar/lunar elements. The Japanese have believed for centuries that women born in the year of *hinoeuma* are strong-minded, are a hindrance to their husband's occupation, do not make good housewives, and outlive their husbands. Prior to the 1786 and 1846 *hinoeuma* years, the government told people to ignore this superstition, and to raise daughters born those years like any girls. But coincidentally a total eclipse in 1786 and successive fires and floods in Edo/Tokyo convinced people of the power of *hinoeuma* (Otsuka, 1800). The number of babies born in 1906 dropped by 4% compared with the previous year, but the decrease in 1966 was by a remarkable 25.4%. In the 1960s, modern birth control techniques combined with traditional beliefs, and families limited births in fear of *hinoeuma* girls. In addition, about 2% of the girls actually born in December 1966 were registered as born in January 1967, to avoid the stigma of *hinoeuma* (Murai, 1968).

Another example of the modern power of folk beliefs concerns abortions. In the 1970s there was a great increase in the number of small statues erected at Buddhist temples, to pacify the souls of aborted fetuses. But the impact of folk beliefs was not restricted to spiritual matters; ethnotheories have also found their way into modern Japanese medical practices. In 1964, Michio Matsuda (1908–), Japan's most famous pediatrician, published a popular book called *Nihon-shiki Ikuji-hoh (Japanese Ways of Childrearing)* and recommended some traditional ways of childbearing based on "grammas' wisdom." This book had a significant impact because a medical authority representing Western science advocated at least some degree of reliance on folk beliefs. Thus, folk wisdom continues to play an important role in Japanese child development.

Modern Trends in Human Relations

As mentioned above, the numbers of children in Japanese families have decreased, especially since World War II. Specifically, the proportion of families with only one or two children has been increasing for over 40 years. Today's children therefore have fewer siblings with whom to share opinions, secrets, feelings, or activities. Living with various siblings can enrich a child's perspective and insights concerning human existence, yet, on the other hand, children can now expect more concentrated attention from parents and grandparents. Also, in comparison with Japanese children 35 years ago, children today are better dressed and fed, and are surrounded by an abundance of toys. For instance, when they begin elementary school at age six, children are often given an individual study desk at home. By contrast, most children in the previous generation shared toys and rooms with their siblings, and did their homework at the family dining table.

Parents of several children can develop a different perspective on each child. This perspective itself functions as a socializing agent for parents, and deepens their insights into the breadth of human individuality. With fewer children, Japanese parents are deprived of this broadening experience, and may tend to expect too much from each child. Of course, there are individual differences in sibling relationships, but we believe that Japanese society needs a new mentality to overcome the current experiential deprivation of both children and parents.

Relationships between children and grandparents, aunts, uncles, neighbors, and fathers have also changed in modern Japan. For example, the number of coresiding aunts and uncles has decreased remarkably since 1950. Although as recently as 1971, 75%

Experiential deprivation: Two-year-old brother and infant sister entertain themselves on a fourth-floor apartment balcony, Nagoya, 1995. Courtesy of David Shwalb.

of people over the age of 65 still lived with one of their children and his or her family, that proportion is now under 40%. Grand-parents had traditionally served as playmates, caregivers, and gener-ous sources of money for children, but most parents and grandpar-ents alike now consider discipline to be the exclusive responsibility of the mother.

Many contemporary Japanese adults over the age of 40 (born before 1945) recall that as children they had a close relationship with one or two elderly neighbors. Although this type of neighbor–child relationship has not completely disappeared, it is now rare. Perhaps people now believe that neighbors should not intrude upon the parents' childrearing domain.

Until about the 1920s, many fathers gave initial occupational training to their young sons, even though sons eventually left home for an education or apprenticeship. This teaching aspect of the paternal role has gradually disappeared as the father has become separated at his workplace from family life, and companion-like fathers have become more typical over the past 50 years (Hara, 1993). These days fathers enjoy playing or taking baths with their preschool children, or going for drives with older sons and daughters. Increasing numbers of fathers also help with the care of infants and toddlers, yet most parents still consider childrearing to be the mother's job. Japanese mothers now have increased amounts of free time due to the mechanization of housekeeping and smaller family size, and they invest much of this time in their children.

In our view, many aspects of Japanese affective socialization go back well over 400 years in history, and have changed little despite changes in children's life experiences. This emotional socialization is now given predominantly by mothers, because grandparents, siblings, aunts, uncles, neighbors, and fathers have retreated from children's lives since World War II. The Japanese view of motherhood, held at least since the Tokugawa period, remains that a woman is only a full person after bearing and rearing a child. Mothers are believed to love their children instinctively, and it is assumed that nobody else can love a child as much as the mother.

Within the historical context of the intensified mother–child relationship, it is ironic that increasing numbers of mothers feel their own children are not attractive or enjoyable. According to research sponsored by the Prime Minister's Office, some of these mothers also admit a distaste for touching their babies, due to feelings of revulsion. Japanese women who did not like children may have existed throughout history, but the role expectations of motherhood may have blinded them to their aversion. Or perhaps other members of the family once assisted in childcare, which is now more exclusively the mother's responsibility. A final possibility is that modern women's work outside the home, which is often trivial (Hara, 1984) and unfulfilling, may cause Japanese mothers to feel more trapped than ever when at home. So mothers who display an overt disgust toward babies may be viewed as warning signals to the wider society.

THE PRESENT AND FUTURE OF JAPANESE CHILDHOOD

Changes during the past century have in effect extended the length of childhood and increased children's economic and physical dependence on their parents (Hara & Wagatsuma, 1974; Naka, 1977). Even 40 years ago, 57% of middle school graduates did not continue their schooling, since many had to earn money or help with their parents' work. In the early 1950s, when several American anthropologists were beginning their fieldwork in Japan, children were thought to be disciplined through exposure to the "severe winds" of society outside the family. Nowadays high school education (ages 15–17) is universal though not compulsory, and despite their earlier and greater physical development many young people remain financially dependent on parents into young adulthood.

Traditional Japanese culture has emphasized harmonious relationships within and between groups, and childhood socialization has always stressed this spirit of interdependence. As a result, independence training has not been a major aspect of Japanese childrearing. Before the 1970s the desire of youth for independence was fulfilled or challenged from age 15, when teens went to work. But in the 1990s many young people repress or even abandon their desire for independence. Others remain extremely ambivalent toward independence well into adulthood. The future world outside the family will probably require young people to balance independence and interdependence, which may require an adjustment of the Japanese socialization process regarding independence training.

Until they are 8 or 9 years old, contemporary Japanese children seem to look forward to growing up. After that age, however, many children verbally express a lack of desire to grow old. Suicide attempts among teenagers have been increasing, although the numbers of such cases are still small. Perhaps the feeling that affluent modern life is empty may account for these trends, as well as increasing incidences of teenage prostitution and drug addiction. So now when pediatricians treat a child for diarrhea, they first ask if the child likes school or is happy at home, rather than asking what he or she has eaten. This reflects the current difficulty facing childhood socialization at home and school. Since 1982, a majority of married women have been employed, mostly away from home. As a result, the Japanese also now face the necessity of finding new means of childcare at home and in the community.

As a whole, the problems of infant mortality, nutrition, and mass education have been solved in modern Japan. But future problem-solving energy must be concentrated on children's mental health and on creating a challenging environment conducive to healthy child development. As social scientists, we must anticipate how childhood in Japan will change in the future. Ideally, this chapter has provided a historical perspective from which we can face that future.

ACKNOWLEDGMENTS

We wish to thank the editors, Barbara and David Shwalb, for their assistance in the preparation of this chapter, and Takako Fukuda for her comments on an earlier draft.

REFERENCES

Aries, P. (1960). *L'enfant et la vie familiale sous l'ancien régime*. Paris: Librairie Plan.

Benedict, R. F. (1946). *The chrysanthemum and the sword*. Boston: Houghton Mifflin.

Bird, I. L. (1973). *Unbeaten tracks in Japan*. Rutland, VT: Tuttle. (Original work published 1880)

Chiba, T., & Ohtsu, T. (1983). *Mabiki to mizuko [Infanticide and induced abortion]*. Tokyo: Shadanhohjin Nohson Gyoson Bunka Kyohkai.

Dore, R. (1965). *Education in Tokugawa Japan*. Berkeley: University of California Press.

Hara, H. (1979). *Kodomo no bunka-jinruigaku [Cultural anthropology of children]*. Tokyo: Shohbun-sha.

Hara, H. (1984). The status of women. In *Population of Japan* (Country monograph series, No. 11, pp. 230–248). Bangkok: United Nations Economic and Social Commission for Asia and the Pacific.

Hara, H. (1993). Bunka no naka no chichioya: Bunkajinruigaku-teki shiten kara [Fathers within cultures: A social anthropological perspective]. In K. Kashiwagi (Ed.), *Chichiova no hattatsu shinrigaku [The developmental psychology of the father]* (pp. 152–177). Tokyo: Kawashima Shoten.

Hara, H., & Minagawa, M. (1986). Japanische Kindheit seit 1600 [Japanese childhood since 1600]. In J. Martin & A. Nitschke (Eds.), *Zur Sozialgeschichte der Kindheit [The socialization of children]* (pp. 113–189). Freiburg, Germany: Karl Alber.

Hara, H., & Wagatsuma, H. (1974). *Shitsuke [Japanese ways of childrearing]*. Tokyo: Kohbundoh.

Heibonsha, (1956–1957). *Jidoh hyakka jiten [Encyclopedia of childhood for children]* (24 vols.). Tokyo: Heibonsha.

Hohsoh e-shuh [Collection of pictures that had the power to protect people against smallpox]. (n.d.). Publisher unknown.

Ishikawa, K. (1948). *Waga kuni ni okeru jidoh-kan no hattatsu [Development of views on childhood in Japan]*. Tokyo: Shinrei-sha.

Ishikawa, M., Kami, S., Naoe, H., Naka, A., Nogaki, Y., Kuki, Y., & Yuki, R.

(Eds.). (1977). *Nihon kodomo no rekishi [History of Japanese childhood]*. Tokyo: Iwanami Shoten.

Iwamoto, T. (1956). *Shinto girei ni okeru yoji no ichi [The role of children in Shinto rituals]*. Tokyo: Heibonsha.

Kawabe, H. (1981). Sezen ni okeru chuto kyoiku no hukyu to shussei-ryoku to no kankei [Educational development and fertility in pre-war Japan. *Jinkoh Mondai-Kenkyu [Journal of Population Problems], 158*. Tokyo: Institute of Population Problems, Ministry of Health and Welfare.

Kawada, M. (1993). *The origin of ethnography in Japan: Yanagita Kunio and his times* (T. Kishida-Ellis, Trans.). London: Kegan Paul

Kawai, H. (1982). *Mukashi-banashi to Nihon-jin no kokoro [The Japanese mind revealed in folktales]*. Tokyo: Iwanami Shoten.

Kazuki, G. (1703). *Shohni hitsuyoh sodategusa [A guide book for childrearing]*. (Copies available from author)

Kitagawa, M. (19th c.). *Morisada manko—Rui-juh Kinsei fuzokushi [Morisada's miscellaneous essays—History of everyday life in the Tokugawa period]*. (Copies available from author)

Kitoh, H. (1978). Tokugawa jidai nohson no jinkoh saiseisan kohzoh [Structure of population reproduction in a farming village during the Tokugawa Period]. *Mita Gakkai Zasshi, 71*(4), 613–624.

Koizumi, A. (1984). Population and health development. In *Population of Japan* (Country monograph series, No. 11, pp. 187–199). Bangkok: United Nations Economic and Social Commission for Asia and the Pacific.

Kojima, H. (1986). Japanese concepts of child development from the mid-17th to mid-19th century. *International Journal of Behavioral Development, 9*, 315–329.

Kohsei-sho Daijin Kamboh Tohkei Chohsa-bu. (1968). *Showa 41 nen no shussei genshoh ni tsuite [On the decrease of the birthrate in 1966]*. Tokyo: Author.

Kuroda, T. (1977). Fertility: Retrospect and prospect. In *Fertility and family planning in Japan*. Tokyo: Japanese Organization for International Cooperation in Family Planning.

Kusada, S. (1692). *Onna choho-ki-taisei [Detailed handbook of everyday life and rituals for women]*. (Copies available from author)

Matsuda, M. (1964). *Nihon-shiki ikuji-hoh [Japanese ways of childrearing]*. Tokyo: Kohdansha.

Matsuda, T. (1978). *Ichi-daimyohke no keizu-kakochoh yori no tohkeiteki kansatsu [Statistical observation of geneaology and registry of the dead of a* daimyo *family in the Tokugawa period]*. Tokyo: Kohdansha.

Matsuo, M. (1980). Kinsei buke no kon-in yohshi to jisan-kin [Marriage, adoption and dowry among samurai families in the Tokugawa period]. *Gakushu-in Shigaku, 16*.

Meishinchohsa kyohgikai. (Ed.). (1949). *Nihon no zokushin [Japanese folk beliefs]* (2 vols). Tokyo: Gihoh-do.

Minagawa, M. (1985). Kuwana-nikki, Kashiwazaki-nikki ni arawareta ko-domo no yamai [Childhood diseases as revealed in Kuwana and Kashiwazaki diaries]. In M. Honda, M. Minagawa, & M. Morishita (Eds.), *Watashitachi no Edo [How we look at Edo/Tokyo]* (pp. 144–166). Tokyo: Shinyoh-sha.

Ministry of Health and Welfare (1980). *Boshi eisei no shu naru tohkei [Statistics relating to maternal and child health in Japan].* Tokyo: Author.

Mohri, T. (1972). *Gendai shohni hoken shi [History of infant public health in modern Japan].* Tokyo: Domesu Shuppan.

Murai, T. (1968). Hinoeuma soh-kessan [On the birthrate in the hinoeuma year]. *Kohsei no shihyoh [Index of Social Welfare], 15*(5).

Naka, A. (1977). Fukoku kyohei-ka no kodomo [Children under the national policy for wealth and military strength]. In *Nihon kodomo no rekishi [History of Japanese childhood]* (Vol 8). Tokyo: Daiichi-hohki shuppan.

Namae, T. (1923). *Shakai jinkoh kohyoh [Outline of social welfare activities].* Publisher unknown. (Copies available from author)

Nishiyama, M. (1972). *Edo chohnin no kenkyuh [A study of merchants in Edo/Tokyo].* Tokyo: Yoshikawa kohbun kan.

Nishiyama, T. (1918). *Akanboh no kenkyuh [A study of babies].* Tokyo: Nanboku-sha Shuppan.

Niwa, N. (1972). *San-iku-kai gojuhnen-shi [Fifty years of San-ikukai].* Tokyo: Shakai Fukushi Hohjin San-ikukai.

Ogata, H. (1946). *Nihon no taikyoh [Japanese teaching and disciplining of a child while it is in mother's womb].* Tokyo: Aoba Shoboh.

Onshi-Zaidan Boshi Aiikukai (1935). *Aiiku chohsa shiryoh [Survey materials of childrearing],* Series 1. Tokyo: Author.

Onshi-Zaidan Boshi Aiikukai (1975). *Nihon san-iku shuhzoku shiryo shuhsei [Nationwide survey reports on customs and beliefs on childbirth and childrearing].* Tokyo: Dai-ichi-hohki.

Otsuka, Y. (1800). *Sohgo zuihitsu [Sogo essays].* Publisher unknown.

Sakurai, S. (1941). *Nihon jidoh seikatsu-shi [An introduction to the history of Japanese childhood].* Tokyo: Nikkoh Shoin.

Shwalb, D. W., Shwalb, B. J., Sukemune, S., & Tatsumoto, S. (1992). Japanese maternal childcare: Past, present and future. In M. Lamb, K. Sternberg, C.-F. Huang, & P. A. Broberg (Eds.), *Childcare in context* (pp. 331–353). Hillsdale, NJ: Erlbaum.

Suda, K. (1973). *Hida O. jiin kako-choh no kenkyuh [A study on the registry of the dead recorded at O. temple of Hida Province].* Publisher unknown.

Takahashi, B. (1936). *Datai mabiki no kenkyuh [Studies on induced abortion and infanticide].* Tokyo: Zaidan Hohjin Chuoh Shakaijigyoh Kyohkai Shakai Jigyoh Kenkyuhjo.

Takai, M. (1991). *Tempoki shonenshojo no kyoyokeiseikatshi no kenku [Studies on the mental and psychological growing processes of boys and girls in the Tempo period].* Gunma City: Gunma University Bulletin.

Takeuchi, T. (1941). *Shinshuh Higashi Chikuma-gun Hongoh-mura ni okeru* kodomo no shuhdan seikatsu [Group activities of children in Hongo village in Nagano Prefecture]. Tokyo: Antique Museum.

Tsuboi, H. (1971). Nihon o shiru jiten [Encyclopedia of Japanese everyday life]. Tokyo: Shakai shisoh sha.

Ushijima, Y. (1938). Nyuhyohji seishin hattatsu kijun [Standards for mental development in infancy and childhood]. Tokyo: Aiiku Kenkyuhjo.

Wada, H. (1912). Rekishi-joh ni okeru uba no seiryoku [Political influence of wet nurses in Japanese history]. Kokugakuin Zasshi, 18(1).

Yamakawa, K. (1943). Buke no josei [Women in samurai families]. Tokyo: Iwanami Shoten.

Yamashita, T. (1943). Nyuhyohji hoiku hohhoh chohsa [Survey on childrearing methods in infancy and childhood]. Tokyo: Aiiku Kenkyuhjo.

Yanagida, K. (1949). Bunrui jidoh goi [Classified glossary of infantile words]. Tokyo: San-ichi Shoboh.

Yuhki, R. (1977). Ranse no kodomo [Children of the Middle Ages]. Tokyo: Dai-ichi Hohki Shuppan.

CHAPTER 3

Are Japanese Young Children among the Gods?

Shing-Jen Chen

In pointing out the importance of a historical perspective for the understanding of children, Hara and Minagawa enumerate several social changes that took place in Japan between the 1950s and 1970s. They mention the decrease of the agricultural population, disappearance of domestic servants and housemaids, land reform, increase in living standards, increase in high school attendance rate, emergence of the "salary-man" class, and the mushrooming of "cram schools" or *juku* (after-school private supplemental classes). Indeed, these are among the elements of an emergent new Japan, and it is unthinkable that they would not have effects on child development or childrearing. Many of the changes the authors mentioned are, however, universal phenomena, found in all industrialized countries. What may be of great interest to many readers, especially the non-Japanese, is a characterization of *Japanese* responses to social changes. Through an examination of Japanese responses and their impact on children and childrearing, both the traditional Japanese context and the emerging scene can be seen in sharper contrast.

I am a Chinese person from Taiwan who has lived in Japan for the last 19 years. My current specialty is infant developmental psychology. My additional interests in the cultural and historical aspects of Japanese childrearing stem from my earlier background in social anthropology, which I studied for several years in England. I came across the "culture and personality" literature then, although the dominant approach at Oxford during the early 1970s was influenced more by the French sociological tradition and British structural–functionalism. I found the culture and personality approach refreshing, as I became interested in behavioral development in different societies. However, when I came to Japan in 1975 to do my fieldwork, instead of pursuing cultural and personality research, I was drawn first into the field of child psychology, and then into infant developmental studies. While teaching and doing research in developmental psychology, I have maintained an interest in anthropology. As a result of my participation in a project that involved cross-national comparisons of infant–mother attachment (Miyake, Chen, & Campos, 1985), I have had the opportunity to think and write about cultural aspects of human development (Chen & Takahashi, 1987).

To many mainstream psychologists, developmental psychologists included, culture is either an irrelevant bias to be processed out or, at best, just another variable (Valsiner, 1987). Unfortunately, in my opinion, this viewpoint is even more prevalent in Japan than elsewhere. Furthermore, in Japan, developmental psychology, or psychology in general, has remained a relatively isolated field until recently. A primary reason for this situation is the lack of interaction between psychologists and researchers in other related fields (e.g., anthropology, sociology). In the Japanese academic world there is pressure to stay within one's traditional area of study and to avoid crossing disciplinary boundaries. This is partly due to the traditional attitude toward scholarship, which emphasizes and values expertise in one narrow field rather than overall erudition. Another reason is the relative detachment of scholarship (especially the humanities and social sciences) from real-life concerns in Japan, which leads to isolationism on the part of scholars. The last reason is that psychological and developmental research in Japan tends to mimic that of the West (especially that of North America) of an earlier time, when relatively little interdisciplinary research was conducted. This tendency both psychology in general and in developmental psychology in particular is perhaps even stronger than in other social science fields, because Japanese psychologists tend to consider their science superior to those of other disciplines (see Chen, 1992).

As a result, developmental psychologists do not pay serious attention to the work of researchers in other fields. For example, because their work on childrearing is considered more anthropological than psychological, scholars such as Hara and Wagatsuma (1974) have received little attention from developmental psychologists. Judging mainly from professional publications, most Japanese developmental psychologists, with precious few exceptions, appear to lack knowledge of current thinking outside their specialties. Thus, a mentality in which culture and history are understood as not only legitimate but indeed essential elements for the study of human development has yet to appear. One condition that will help foster a wider perspective is the encouragement of more inter-action among researchers in related fields. Recent years have seen a few pioneering examples (e.g., Kojima, 1989; Minoura, 1990), but more such work is needed. In sum, there has been minimal ap-preciation by Japanese developmental psychologists of either cul-tural or historical influences. The chapter by Hara and Minagawa therefore represents an unusual and enlightened perspective on child development in Japan.

In this commentary, I will discuss a few selected aspects of the history of Japanese child development. I will suggest alternative in-terpretations for some cultural practices discussed by Hara and Mi-nagawa. In some cases I will elaborate their points further, and I will also indicate some directions for future research.

TRADITIONAL JAPANESE ATTITUDES TOWARD YOUNG CHILDREN

The saying that until the age of 7 children are among the gods *(nanatsu mae wa kami no uchi)* has been evoked by Japanese writers as evidence of a belief in the supernatural quality of children in Japanese society. Hara and Minagawa discuss two customs as exam-ples to support this view. They first mention the premodern Japa-nese practice of burying a dead infant under the floor of the house, at road crossings or at village borders. Here the authors' implicit contrast is between attitudes and feelings toward the dead body of the infant and that of the adult. They emphasize the Japanese feel-ing of wanting to stay closer to the infant even after death, and the belief that the soul of the dead infant would serve as the guardian of the family. Hara and Minagawa note that children under 7 "are still treated by some with respect and even awe" (p. 14). It is true that the Japanese are said to treat their children with greater care (see Hendry, 1986, and Alcock, 1863/1963, for, respectively, a mod-ern and a historical assessment by foreign observers). But current concerns about the rights or plight of Japanese children also show that despite any special attitudes toward children the society once may have entertained, in modern Japan, when social and economic conditions are poor, the children feel the pinch first. Infanticide *(mabiki)*, which Hara and Minagawa mention, mother–child forced double suicide *(oyako murishinchu)*, and child abuse are a few examples. Even in the materially affluent present, quite a number of children (23.1% in 1991; see Nippon Seikatsu Kyodokumiai Rengokai, 1993) have to eat their meals alone *(koshoku)*. Traditional attitudes alone are no guarantee of the better treatment of children in a modern society.

The traditional view that infanticide and abortion were not thought of as murder by the Japanese is also presented as evidence of a Japanese belief in the connection of children under age 7 to the supernatural. This alleged belief may have justified behavior that otherwise would have induced more guilt feelings among practitioners and families. However, the fact that in the 1970s "there was a great increase in the number of small statues erected at Buddhist temples, to pacify the souls of aborted fetuses" (p. 23), is not evidence that children today remain "among the gods." The modern increase in abortions suggests not so much the continuation of traditional beliefs in modern time as the result of permissive attitudes toward sexual behavior, especially among adolescents, in present-day Japan. Surveys (Koseisho, 1985; Ishihama, 1989) also suggest an increase in teenage abortions. Traditional authoritarian family control has weakened since about the end of World War II, and as children have become more independent from their parents, unplanned pregnancy is more likely to lead to abortion, especially for teenagers. While the establishment of the small statues reflects the continuation of a Buddhist practice related to spiritual redemption, it does not indicate the continuation of a belief in the special god-like nature of young children.

According to Sakamoto (1985), a religious historian, the custom of erecting a statue to pacify the soul of an aborted child (called *mizuko kuyo*) is a fairly recent practice. In some old documents the miscarried or prematurely born dead infant was called *suiji* (water baby) and was treated differently from the dead body of an ordinary adult. Sakamoto holds the view that the fate of a child under 7 is not under human control and that the child cannot attain Buddhahood after death. Therefore, such children do not deserve an adult-like funerals. Another view, presented by folklore scholars, maintains that the dead body of a young child was treated differently because it was believed that by not treating it as that of an adult, the soul of the child could be saved from having to travel to the Western Land of Purity, and would be reborn quickly (Chiba & Otsu, 1983, p. 24). These young children were often buried at the entrance to the village cemetery, or in the bor-

Statue of the Goddess of Mercy (Kannon) in a *mizuko* shrine in downtown Sapporo City (Hokkaido), 1994. Courtesy of Shing-Jen Chen.

der area between villages (see Chiba & Otsu, 1983, for more details). These unattended souls were then believed to roam about in this world rather than returning to the realm of gods, and to cause trouble to humans. Sakamoto suggests that this may have reflected a change in attitudes toward young children in Japanese society, although he does not tell when this change occurred in Japanese history. Sakamoto's interpretations imply a view of children opposite to that indicated by Hara and Minagawa, namely, that children under 7 were traditionally considered not to be fully human. I would venture that these seemingly conflicting views (calling young children "among the gods" vs. "not fully human") reflect the Japanese *tatemae/honne* distinction (Doi, 1973). To call children "subhuman" would be considered too harsh and pitiful. Therefore, children would be labeled in Japanese as the opposite of subhuman, that is, "among the gods." In other words, the saying that children under 7 are "among the gods" is actually a euphemism based on *tatemae*, a choice of words that would not upset human feelings.

Furthermore, as Hara and Minagawa point out several times, the drastic social changes after World War II altered much of the traditional life of Japanese society. Changing attitudes toward children are a result of this upheaval. In considering the implications of sociohistorical changes on child development, attention also must be directed to the sociological and psychological conditions of children. As the authors note, attitudes and feelings probably reflected traditional uncertainty about children's health and survival in the first few years of life. Since conditions have improved greatly during recent decades, it is doubtful that parental attitudes and feelings have the same supporting conditions as before. Indeed, Hara and Minagawa mention that recently some mothers "display an overt disgust toward babies" (p. 25). Although it is unknown whether such revulsion occurred in the past, the authors seem to suggest that it is a recent phenomenon to be "viewed as warning signals to the wider society" (p. 25). In any event, it seems reasonable to say that Japanese adults today probably do not feel that children under 7 are "among the gods" (Shwalb & Chen, 1996). What then is the current image of young children in Japanese society? A more satisfactory answer will have to come from research relating to parents' anxiety over the children's life, death, and future, and to other sociological and psychological factors.

In addition, while a historical description of attitudes toward children in Japanese society is of great interest, many readers would want to know how attitudes have changed or have continued into modern time. Future writing on this subject will benefit from a comparative approach, both among Japanese subcultures and across cultures. From the point of view of geographical proximity and historical–intellectual connections, I would suggest comparisons with societies such as those of China, Korea, and Vietnam, all of which have long been influenced by Confucianism. An ideal study in this area would combine comparative, historical, sociological, and psychological approaches.

MATURITY AND *AMAE*

Another significant topic discussed by Hara and Minagawa concerns the goals of childrearing and socialization. These authors maintain that the definition of maturity distinguishes Japanese from American parental thinking. They point out that Westerners consider independence the most important feature of a mature individual, while the Japanese criterion is to be dependent in a sophisticated manner, so to speak (i.e., to know "when, how, and on whom to be dependent or not to be dependent," p. 11). I should first note here that while Hara and Minagawa begin their discussion focusing on the views of Japanese and American social scientists, they soon generalize and refer to their subjects as "Westerners" and "Japanese."

Although these views reflect some general tendencies in the societies being compared, the contrast can be misleading because it is too simplistic a picture. While it seems true that socialization in Japanese society places great emphasis on harmonious relationships within and between groups (see Lewis, Chapter 7, this volume), it is also true that independence is necessary for personality development in Japan. For example, Japanese parents encourage their children to do things by themselves by calling the child *onii-chan* or *onee-chan* (older brother or older sister), by teasing children who insist on having things done for them by their parents (e.g., to be carried when the child is old enough to walk by him- or herself), or by shaming children for being "like a baby." Similarly, despite an emphasis on independence in Western-style socialization, the stubbornly isolated individualist is not accepted as mature. Such a Western child tends to find fewer friends and more severe psychological stress in time of difficulty. Thus, the difference lies not so much in the kind of theme (independence vs. dependence) as in the way it is reinforced. For example, the Japanese tend to offer young children a status in the proximal zone of development (Vygotsky, 1978), such as calling a young child "elder brother."

The terms *onii-chan* or *onee-chan* are endearment terms usually used in addressing persons belonging to the same generation as the speaker but older in age. However, when used by a Japanese parent or other socialization agent to young children, they have the effect of reminding the child that he or she is expected to behave in a more sophisticated manner. Their use aims to encourage socioemotional development by raising the young children's aspirations.

Another example of the Japanese application of this Vygotskian concept is Japanese parents (or teachers) telling children to prepare themselves to "think and act" like persons 1 year or one grade older. Although not necessarily providing very concrete behavioral examples, a Japanese socialization agent would encourage the child, at the beginning of a new year or the end of a semester, to behave like a person in the next target stage of development.

According to one view deriving from Vygotsky's (1978) concept of the proximal zone of development, human development is a process by which individuals become interdependent in different degrees (Valsiner, 1987). We are social animals by nature, and no one can be completely independent; even the state of independence supposedly held as the goal of Western socialization should be understood as interdependence in degree (Valsiner, 1987). In this sense, cultural differences regarding independence and maturity are a matter of degree rather than type.

There is another aspect of independence–dependence that has seldom been noted by writers on this topic. Compared with Western societies, and in addition to what has been said above concerning Japanese socialization for independence, among Japanese there exists a strong tendency to anticipate dependency and to support dependency. For example, when Japanese first graders enter school every April 1, for about 1 week the oldest children in the school (sixth graders) are encouraged to go to school earlier than usual, so that they have time to assist and to accompany the first graders in their transition to school life. As explained by school administrators, many first graders are leaving home by themselves for the first time, and may feel lonely or find the new environment frightening, so it is good for them to depend on the nurturant sixth graders (Chen, 1996). To not only anticipate but also accept the dependence of the very young and to socialize nurturance in the older children is a typical Japanese attitude in socialization. Entering schools seems to be one of the important rituals for modern Japanese. Many Japanese parents, especially mothers, accompany their university student children on their first day on campus, an event long remembered in many autobiographies and other books. It is this coexistence of double messages that seems to be a Japanese characteristic. It is possible that when compared with many Western societies, the emphasis in Japanese society for dependence is relatively much stronger than the emphasis on independence.

On a comparative note, my personal impression of adult attitudes toward socialization in Taiwan is that in Chinese society (at least the Southern Chinese type, to which most Taiwanese trace their cultural origins) attitudes are similar to those in Western societies—that is, little psychological support is provided for dependence. Chinese adults I have known differ from Japanese adults, who appreciate and value children in their own right, empathize with young children's susceptibility to loneliness, and cosset their young children. The Chinese adult attitude leads to little effort to relieve children's helplessness, which is seen as a human condition that parents expect children to outgrow quickly on their own strength (Chen, 1966).

Although the origins of differential emphases in socialization has been attributed to history, ecology, mode of production, and temperament, attempts to spell out causal relations have not been successful. The future direction of socialization goals, in light of the social changes occurring at several levels, is an important topic for future research. For instance, recent attempts to reevaluate the concept of *amae* seem to have attracted the interest of a growing audience in Japan and of Western scholars (Johnson, 1993). One direction of research is illustrated by the attempts to reanalyze the semantics of the term *amae* and to make a distinction between a theoretical and an ordinary usage of it. (Taketomo, 1988; Sakurai, 1987; Nakayama, 1992) which, ideally, will provide a foundation for future research. From the developmental point of view, *amae* can be studied by observing and analyzing the behavior of the young infants with their caregivers and siblings. An observational study of young infants' developing "theory of mind" (Dunn, 1988), or studies on maternal teasing behavior (Reddy, 1991) may provide useful hints for the future study of *amae*.

EDUCATIONAL CREDENTIALISM AND ITS FUTURE

In discussing modern childhood, Hara and Minagawa refer to demographic and survey data, and point out the sharp drop in the number of children in the 1970s. They also discuss the results of surveys on the reasons for limiting family size. They claim that as Japanese society places great emphasis on the prestige of one's school (educational credentialism—*gakurekishakai*), parental investment in children's education has become a heavy burden. Together with limited time available for children and the need to protect maternal health, the need to invest money in order to secure better credentials for one's children is said to have led to reduced numbers of children in modern Japan.

In addition to the weight given to the prestige of children's schools, the emphasis on educational credentials has led parents to send their children to different kinds of schools or classes for various skills or cultivations, such as calligraphy, sports, music, English conversation, and extra lessons in school subjects, in the hope that these activities will prepare their children for the future. Parents also believe that they themselves lack the time and capability to teach their own children these things. Whatever the skills, so long as they are popular and promising, many Japanese parents feel obligated to obtain the learning opportunity for their children, even if they do not expect their children to pursue the activity in the future. Many businesses are capitalizing on this psychology of the parents. Further, adults are also becoming more active in the pursuit of leisure, so, ironically, many Japanese parents today are interacting less with their reduced numbers of children.

The smallness of the number of children in a family is cited in relation to various problems. For example, because of the small family size, many children have only one sibling or none. This often leads to what Hara and Minagawa term "experiential deprivation" (p. 23), in that lack of sibling relationships has resulted in a generation of children who grow up unable to interact with peers. This problem was perhaps unforseen when earlier generations of Japanese parents decided to limit family size. New research should begin soon on the effects of small family size, or deprivation of sibling relationships, on the development of social skills and personality.

Even with fewer children per family, life in the modern cities where most Japanese live has created many undesirable conditions for children. For example, according to several surveys (e.g., Adachi, 1983; Nippon Seikatsu Kyodokumiai Rengokai, 1993) more than 23% of primary school children eat their breakfast by themselves. This is mainly because family members have different schedules; many parents commute over an hour to work, and children attend several lessons or activities after school. According to one recent survey carried out in Tokyo, 43% of students from primary schools and high schools said they did not talk with their fathers at home; 18% reported not talking with their mothers ("Father, come home earlier and play with me!", January 28, 1994). We do not know if children in the past talked more or less with their parents than do their modern counterparts. What is more important for future research is to discern the reasons for this lack of communication and interaction between children and parents. The data available do not reveal whether the children themselves consider this situation a misfortune or a blessing, or how much of a relationship is desirable.

Recently, the Japanese Ministry of Health and Welfare announced the establishment in large cities of a program to tackle the problem of children abuse by providing telephone counseling and professional helpers ("Child abuse not to be tolerated: Expert counselors to be appointed," March 23, 1994). According to the Ministry's information, the number of consultations concerning child abuse has been increasing since 1990, when the Ministry started sponsoring child abuse counseling (from 1,101 cases for 1990 to 1,372 cases in 1992, for the entire country). The government's analysis indicates that this tendency, most prominent in big cities, is the result of nuclearization of family, the absence of close relatives who can advise on childrearing, and the decrease in the number of children, which deprives would-be parents of the chance to know children (i.e., their siblings) before they actually become parents.

THE CHALLENGE OF A NEW WORLD

One purpose of a historical examination is to gain insight as we prepare for the future. This seems implicit in Hara and Minagawa's view that "historical factors are currently influencing the latest research data on Japanese child development in the 1990s" (p. 10), and that "we must anticipate how childhood in Japan will change in the future" (p. 27). Indeed, all cultures socialize their children for a future no one can predict clearly. This requires us to rely on past traditions and experience, but rapid change sometimes calls for a drastic change of thinking that defies tradition. The value of a tradition may lie in how effectively it provides the new generation with skills and models for dealing with the future. One new situation that will face Japanese society in the 21st century—is the larger world role expected of today's younger generation. In view of this situation, I want to point out one aspect of childrearing that has received very little attention from social scientists in Japan. It is the future direction of childrearing to prepare the succeeding generation of Japanese for their role as citizens of the world, rather than simply as Japanese within Japan. A successful response to this challenge, one important key for the future of Japan, requires more positive and creative strategies in childrearing and socialization. As an Asian, I am anxious to see what models emerge for a new generation of international-minded Japanese. How will they form more constructive attitudes toward other countries and other human beings? The study of Japanese childrearing and socialization may hold the key to preparation of the new international Japanese citizen.

REFERENCES

Adachi, M. (1983). *Naze hitoride taberuno [Why are you eating alone?]*. Tokyo: NHK Shuppankai.

Alcock, R. (1863/1963). *Taikun no miyako [The capital of the tycoon: A narrative of a three years' residence in Japan* by K. Yamaguchi]. Tokyo: Iwanami Shoten.

Chen, S.-J. (1992). *Bunkajinruigaku kara no shisa [The relevance of cultural anthropology to developmental psychology]*. Tokyo: Fukumura Shuppan.

Chen, S.-J., & Takahashi, Y. (1987). Cross-cultural comparison of mother–infant relationship in Japan and the United States: A critical review. *Japanese Psychological Review, 31*(1), 101–111.

Chen, S.-J. (1996). Positive childishness: Images of childhood in Japan. In C. P. Hwang, M. E. Lamb, & I. E. Siegel (Eds.), *Images of childhood* (pp. 113–126). Hillsdale, NJ: Erlbaum.

Chiba, T., & Otsu, T. (1983). *Mabiki to mizuko: Kosodate no fokuroa [Infanticide and the aborted child: Childrearing folklore]*. Tokyo: Nosangyoson Bunka Kyoukai.

Child abuse not to be tolerated: Expert counselors to be appointed [Kodomo e no gyakutai yurusanu: Senmon no sohdan' in secchi]. (1994, March 23, morning edition). *Asahi Shinbun Asahi Newspaper,* p. 35.

Doi, T. (1973). *The anatomy of dependence.* New York: Kodansha International. (*Amae no kozo,* Japanese text, published in 1966)

Dunn, J. (1988). *The beginnings of social understanding.* Oxford: Basil Blackwell.

Father, come home earlier and play with me! [Otohsan, hayaku kaette issho ni asoboh]. (1994, January 28, evening edition). *Asahi Shinbun Asahi Newspaper,* p. 2.

Hara, H., & Wagatsuma, H. (1974). *Shitsuke [Japanese ways of childrearing]*. Tokyo: Kohbundoh.

Hendry, J. (1987). *Becoming Japanese.* Manchester: Manchester University Press.

Ishihama, A. (1989). *Seino herusu kea 2: Judaino ninshin to chuzetsu [Sex health care: Vol. 2. Pregnancy and abortion of teenagers]*. Osaka: Medica Shuppan.

Johnson, F. A. (1993). *Dependency and Japanese socialization: Psychoanalytic and anthropological investigations into amae.* New York: New York University Press.

Kojima, H. *Kosodate no dento wo tazunete [Exploring the Japanese tradition of childrearing]*. Tokyo: Shinyosha.

Koseisho [Ministry of Health and Welfare]. (1985). *Kokumin eisei no doko [Trends of national health].* Tokyo: Koseisho.

Minoura, Y. (1970). *Bunka no nakano kodomo [Children in cultural context].* Tokyo: Tokyo University Press.

Miyake, K., Chen, S.-J., & Campos, J. J. (1985). Infant temperament, mother's mode of interaction, and attachment in Japan: An interim report. In I. Bretherton & E. Waters (Eds.), Growing points of attachment theory and research. *Monographs of the Society for Research in Child Development, 50*(Serial No. 209), 276–297.

Nakayama, O. (1992). An analysis of *amae* based on primary bodily sensation. In A. Hoshino (Ed.), *Current state of cross-cultural relation research* (pp. 257–259). Tokyo: Kaneko Shobo.

Nakayama, O. (1993). *Kizuna no shinri [Psychology of bonding].* Tokyo: Takarajima sha.

Nippon Seikatsu Kyodokumiai Rengokai. (1993). *Kodomo no koshoku [Children eating alone].* Tokyo: Iwanami Shoten.

Reddy, V. (1991). Playing with others' expectations: Teasing and mucking about in the first year. In A. Whiten (Ed.), *Natural theories of mind: Evolution, development and simulation of everyday mindreading* (pp. 143–158). Oxford: Basil Blackwell.

Sakamoto, K. (1985). Mizuko. In *Heibonsha daihyakka* (Vol. 14) *[Heibonsha encyclopedia].* Tokyo: Heibonsha.

Sakurai, T. (1987, November). Amae no kozo no kozo [The anatomy of the anatomy of dependence]. *Hon, 12*(11), 46–52.

Shwalb, D. W., & Chen, S.-J. (1996). Sacred or selfish? A Survey of Japanese parents' images of children. *RCCCD Annual Report, 18,* 33–44.

Taketomo, Y. (1988). Meta gengo toshiteno amae [Amae as meta-language]. *Shiso, 768,* 122–155.

Valsiner, J. (1987). *Culture and the development of children's action: A cultural–historical theory of developmental psychology.* New York: Wiley.

Vygotsky, L. S. (1978). *Mind in society.* Cambridge: Harvard University Press.

CHAPTER 4

Psychocultural Continuities in Japanese Social Motivation

George A. De Vos

THEORETICAL CONTENTIONS AND RESEARCH ACTIVITIES: 1947–1987

As a social scientist I have observed both continuities and changes in the Japanese and in Japanese society since the end of World War II. In my own research with the Japanese that started in 1947, I have been more concerned with the psychological or motivational continuities of Japanese behavior than in studying the considerable changes taking place in organizational structures, or the notable changes in material well-being that characterize an almost completely urbanized society. Such an approach has been due more to my need as a social scientist to specialize in some specific form of empirical work than to an assumption of any priority of psychological determinants over social structural determinants in explaining continuity in Japanese cultural patterns. My contention has always been that a psychological dimension cannot be ignored or slighted in understanding either continuity of culture patterns or the dynamics of social change (De Vos & Tsuda, 1996).

While recognizing the usefulness of interviewing or sustained observation in anthropology and survey methods in sociology, I have been a continuous advocate of projective psychological tests and other related quantifiable devices to conduct systematic comparisons of thinking patterns, interpersonal attitudes, and motivational features of cross-cultural behavior. There are too few social scientists, including psychologists themselves, who are equipped adequately by their university training in the proficient use of systematic psychological methods in the comparative study of social groups. This is true despite the fact that knowledge of the psychological level is absolutely essential to any understanding of culture or peculiarities in the functioning of social groups in political and economic arenas or in daily life.

Among Americans doing research in Japan, very little use is made even today of the considerable psychological research done by Japanese (De Vos, 1994a). Comparative systematic quantification of attitudes or perceptions in sustained collaborative work, such as that pursued by Azuma and Hess (Azuma, Kashiwagi, & Hess, 1981; see also Chapter 13, this volume), occurs only in some few cases. In my own case, since my graduate school days at the University of Chicago, I have had the advantage of working in interdisciplinary contexts, both as a psychologist and as an anthropologist. I have recognized from the beginning that there is but one *social* science, but there are differing methodological approaches. To adequately understand humans we must take *multilevel* approaches to particular problems (De Vos, 1994b).

Any knowledge of human behavior starts with an ecological appreciation of *environmental forces;* it continues through a knowledge of *social organizational determinants;* then, there must be sufficient appreciation of the force of *conscious human thought* in shaping human history. One cannot neglect knowledge of frequently unconscious motivations arising from *internal structures* of psychological organization. And finally, *physiological characteristics* cause differences among humans or limit the possibilities of human behavior. Too often, particular disciplines assume some priority over other endeavors that permits ignorance or neglect of some levels of necessary analysis. For example, many Marxists see no need to examine the determinative influences of peculiar socialization practices, individual consciousness, or psychodynamic features of human belonging in specific cultures in understanding the direction and rapidity of social change in one society compared with another.

In my four decades of research with the Japanese, I have addressed a number of theoretical issues. I have always been interested as a psychologist in problems of mental health or human malaise (De Vos, 1965a, 1974, 1976; De Vos, Murakami, & Murase, 1964; Mizushima & De Vos, 1967), but as an anthropologist, I have been concerned equally with *normative thought and behavior.* I have published most on four topics:

1. The pervasive high level of achievement motivation in Japanese, related both to positive accomplishment and to patterns of personal alienation or delinquency. (Caudill & De Vos, 1956; De Vos, 1959, 1964, 1965a, 1967a, 1973, 1974, 1975, 1996).

2. Patterns of internalization and social identity related to socialization within the primary family (Connor & De Vos, 1989; De Vos, 1960, 1965c, 1961, 1968a, 1968b, 1975a, 1986a, 1992a, 1992b, 1993; De Vos & Sofue, 1986; De Vos & Suárez-Orozco, 1986; De Vos & Wagatsuma, 1959; Slote & De Vos, 1996; Wagatsuma & De Vos, 1962).

3. Problems of minority status in Japan as they relate to general social theory about the psychological adjustment and social adaptation of minorities (Connor & De Vos, 1989; De Vos, 1960, 1965, 1961, 1968b, 1975b, 1986a, 1992a, 1992b, 1995; De Vos & Kim, 1993a, 1993b; De Vos & Sofue, 1986; De Vos & Suárez-Orozco, 1986; De Vos & Wagatsuma, 1959, 1995; Wagatsuma & De Vos, 1962).

4. The general Japanese psychological preoccupation with purity and pollution, related to their myth of genealogical uniqueness. This preoccupation has resulted in caste-like attitudes directed toward their own minorities, and difficulties in relations with other societies (De Vos, 1967b, 1971, 1975a, 1985a, 1986a; De Vos & Wagatsuma, 1966).

I will now review for you some of my contributions to issues of achievement and alienation as continuities in Japanese, related to their normative socialization experiences. I shall refer most to my continuing work with psychological tests, incidentally relating my research results to comparative studies of school performance and delinquency in the United States and Japan.

Throughout, my studies have been focused rather specifically on the effects of minority status as they influence both individual and group behavior in a Japanese context. This research has also been directly related to the possibilities of a more general psychocultural theory of human behavior. In a recent volume, *Status Inequality: The Self in Culture* (1990), I brought out my unifying theory, attempting a more interrelated and consistent psychocultural approach than found in my individual writings, drawing upon anthropological, sociological, and psychoanalytic insights into human behavior. My theoretical orientation, detailed in *Status Inequality*, seeks directly to synthesize what to some are the seeming opposite priorities of social structure and personality structure.

In a second volume, *Social Cohesion and Alienation: Minorities in the U.S. and Japan* (1992b), I illustrated my theoretical contentions by drawing on my work on Japanese society and culture. Comparative studies in Japan help us understand the operation of general contemporary patterns of social cohesion or anomy within contemporary societies. In this volume I made a retrospective comparative overview of much of my specific work within Japanese culture as it reflected the continuing presence of several forms of status inequality, and the vicissitudes of social conformity and deviancy in Japan. Comparing hierarchically organized Japan with the segmented contemporary American multiethnic society, I pay special attention to the underlying psychocultural determinants of class, caste, age, gender, and ethnic identity in Japan compared to those operative in the American setting. Distinctive patterns start in early childhood socialization.

My abiding specific interest has been in the effects of minority status upon the *psychological* development of the individual in the primary family and social group. This interest began under sociologist–anthropologist Lloyd Warner at the University of Chicago in 1946. It remains manifest in the content and methods unifying my subsequent research in Japan and Europe. I have directed special research attention to understanding such deviant behavior as delinquency and suicide, as well as forms and processes of minority discrimination. I have attempted to understand the socially "adaptive" responses of individuals and groups of any given cultural background to the experience of minority status, and how on another level of analysis, these responses are interactively influenced by underlying "adjustive" psychological structures determined by what I call "differential socialization" (De Vos, 1974, 1976, 1983b.).

ACHIEVEMENT, CULTURE, AND PERSONALITY: THE CASE OF THE JAPANESE-AMERICANS

At the University of Chicago in 1947, I helped form a research team studying the Japanese-Americans who were being relocated after their forced internment during World War II. Our team included a doctoral candidate in anthropology, William Caudill; psychoanalyst Charlotte Babcock; and a doctoral candidate in sociology, Setsuko Nishi, among others. I had returned to Chicago in 1946 from $3\frac{1}{2}$ years of army service, during which I had been placed in army Japanese language schools. This experience of learning about Japanese language and culture changed the course of my university studies from sociology toward anthropology, and then, psychology.

The "personality and culture" approach had become an important part of anthropology under the influence of Mead, Benedict, Hallowell, Kardiner, and others. I was particularly influenced by an anthropological study of the Alorese by Dubois, which utilized in part the Rorschach test. At the same time, Benedict (1946) had published *The Chrysanthemum and the Sword,* her attempt, at a distance, to understand the Japanese and their culture. I determined to learn psychological tests as a means of understanding human motivation.

Japanese-Americans were settling in the Chicago area as they were released from internment. Many of us at the university were concerned with their unfair treatment by our our government. Caudill and Nishi had received a small research grant to study the newly forming Japanese community in Chicago. Babcock had also read Benedict (1946) and was interested in conducting some work at the Institute for Psychoanalysis with clinical cases. We were all distressed by the ordeal of Japanese-Americans, and anticipated problems of a personal or social nature that might have resulted from the traumas of dislocation. We therefore decided to work together as a team and recruited some others to join us. I decided to employ the Rorschach test and received special training in its use. Caudill had been instructed in the use of the Thematic Apperception Test (TAT) by Irving Hallowell in Wisconsin and by William Henry at Chicago. Setsuko Nishi conducted depth interviews about social attitudes and studied the organization of the community then forming in Chicago, which included her own family.

The Japanese-American were moving into the marginal high-crime and delinquency areas that ringed the inner city of Chicago. After their arrival they performed in a manner contrary to what was expected from a derogated minority. Here was a group of people who had been subject not only to the usual forms of racially directed prejudice, but also to the additional ordeal of being wrenched from their homes on the American West Coast and put into special camps for several years. Both the social and psychological findings were far different from initial expectations—whatever the inner psychological costs they paid, they were adapting well.

My use of the Rorschach tests on Japanese-Americans were compared with normative samples of 157 Chicago residents, and special samples of 60 neurotic and 60 schizophrenic records. Over a period of 15 months, by visiting people in their homes, I gathered samples of 60 immigrant Issei, 60 American-born Nisei, and 30 selected "Kibei" (Nisei who had been sent to Japan previously for at least 5 years of primary schooling). Both generations demon-

Mother bathes child outside impoverished fishing village home, Sakuno-shima (Aichi), 1953. Courtesy of George De Vos.

strated on the *structural level of personality* that a strong drive to accomplish was a characteristic trait of significant numbers of American-born Japanese as well as in their immigrant parents. The Kibei exhibited more psychological problems, related to their culturally marginal experiences (De Vos, 1952, 1954, 1966a; De Vos & Boyer, 1989).

Caudill found the same strong drive for accomplishment evident *on a conscious level*, as revealed in TAT materials. As a result of our collaborative work, Caudill and I published some psychocultural conclusions about their internalized achievement motivation (Caudill & De Vos, 1956). Even as recently as 1992, this report has been republished numerous times in reports in minority education as similar patterns of positive educational adaptation are discovered among other immigrant Asian groups. I have also published evidence of a similar pattern of high achievement motivation on the TAT in a recent generation of immigrant Korean-Americans in California (De Vos, 1983b).

Multidisciplinary collaborators of George De Vos out on the town in Nagoya, 1952. From left to right, Drs. Taniguchi (psychologist), Marui (psychiatrist), Muramatsu (psychiatrist), Hoshino (psychologist), and Yamane and Kawagoe (sociologists). Courtesy of George De Vos.

SOCIALIZATION FOR ACHIEVEMENT IN JAPAN

I have pursued this motivational theme in my subsequent work with normative samples in Japan starting in 1953 (De Vos, 1973; De Vos & Boyer, 1989). As a Fulbright scholar, in 1953, I helped organize a large-scale study on culture and personality at Nagoya University with Professor of Psychiatry Tsuneo Muramatsu. Achievement motivation was our central issue. The Chicago research team had made a presentation of our results at the Institute for Psychoanalysis, which Muramatsu attended when he visited in 1951. When the Fulbright research scholar program opened in 1952, he asked both Caudill and me to come to Japan. Caudill was doing research at Yale that he could not interrupt. I was a chief psychologist at Elgin State Hospital, doing research on schizophrenic thought, but I decided to accept. I moved to the city of Nagoya in Japan with my family for 2 years. Conditions were still poor in Japan, as economic recovery was just beginning. Nagoya had been 85% destroyed by American air raids in 1945 and the university department of psychiatry was housed in temporary barracks.

Dr. Muramatsu had assembled a research staff of over 30 researchers, including several with whom I have maintained long-term relations (psychologists Eiji Murakami, Mayumi Taniguchi, and Akira Hoshino, and sociologist Tsuneo Yamane). Some came to work collaboratively with me in the United States subsequently (Taniguchi, De Vos, & Murakami, 1958; De Vos & Murakami, 1974; De Vos et al., 1964). In 1953 we worked together for 6 months, planning our study and selecting the interview schedules to be presented to a basic sample of 2,400 individuals in two cities and three rural villages. We selected a farming village, a fishing village, and a mountain village involved in processing timber. Niiike, the farming village, had already been selected and studied intensively by an interdisciplinary team from the University of Michigan. We used census tracts for the cities of Nagoya and Okayama to select families, and then the individuals within the family.

Subsamples of 800 individuals each were given the Rorschach, the TAT, and a special "Problem Situation Test" I devised. Other subsamples were given opinion questionnaires concerning attitudes about childrearing, family traditions, or various aspects of modernization. We also used the F scale translated from the work on authoritarian personality that had been developed at Berkeley. This was the first time that any psychological level of research with projective techniques was to be attempted on a normative population with this intensity. Every aspect of the results confirmed our findings from Chicago about achievement motivation. The Rorschach material was strikingly similar to the records obtained from the immigrant generation in the United States.

Socialization toward a Sensitivity to Guilt

Based on these TAT data, I argued in favor of understanding "guilt" as an important characteristic of the Japanese educational performance and work ethic (De Vos, 1960). I argued against the prior writings of Benedict (1946), which suggested shame as a predominant motivator of Japanese behavior, and I disputed the theoretical positions of Piers and Singer (1953) and Lynd (1958) that considered guilt too much in Western cultural terms, as related to a sense of moral transgression. They believed any sense of social failure would be related to the experience of shame rather than guilt. I have argued instead that guilt in Japanese is less concerned with a sense of transgression, sexual or otherwise, than it traditionally has been among Christians. Rather, it *is* more related to a sense of failure and the improper actualization of one's expected social–vocational role, and experienced as destructive to one's family. The failure to repay *on* (deeply felt obligation) to one's parents or mentor is experienced as an inadvertent destructive act on one's part. Any unconscious destructive intention or hostility that may be related to failure is deeply repressed.

The Japanese find psychoanalysis a deeply disturbing process. By and large there is much less receptivity to this therapeutic approach in Japan than in Europe and North and South America (De Vos, 1980, 1984). It is extremely difficult for Japanese to bring to conscious thought for examination any negative feelings about a parent. Babcock, who worked with Caudill and myself in Chicago (Babock & Caudill, 1958), discussed with us the difficulty faced by a therapist who seeks to uncover the deeply repressed hostility of a Japanese toward a parent. In work with one Nisei social worker, it took Babcock over 2 years before there was the least awareness of any destructive feelings toward her mother and over 2 years more before increasing awareness relieved the somatic symptoms.

In fact, the potential for guilt over a failure to succeed is not unique to the Japanese, but characterizes a need to accomplish in some Westerners too. A "Jewish mother syndrome" can be stimulated in children whereby the mother "suffers" sacrificially for the sake of the child. I have contended that a frequent Japanese socialization pattern features such maternal dedication within the Japanese family and has been responsible for a characteristic proneness to guilt in many Japanese (De Vos, 1960, 1986b, 1992a). It is also related to lifelong patterns of dependency and the practice of what Takeo Doi (1973) has written about as *amae*—a form of what I term "instrumental dependency." In examining Japanese suicidal behavior I have further discussed the deeply unconscious destructive feelings that are stimulated by a sense of social failure, symbolized by the wounding of a beloved mother (De Vos 1968b, 1973, 1992a).

SOCIALIZATION TOWARD NONACHIEVEMENT: DELINQUENCY AND MINORITY STATUS

As described by Emile Durkheim, Robert Merton (1949), and other sociologists, opposites of positive achievement motivation in any society are either active criminality or alienated withdrawal and other forms of passivity. In my early studies at Chicago, while still in sociology, I became aware of the city of Chicago in respect to its deviant inner-city patterns of crime and delinquency, as well as its general movement of upwardly mobile individuals into the suburbs. Since I first began to study Japanese-Americans, I have become increasingly critical of both overarching psychological theories of positive achievement motivation or relativistic anthropological theories of negative subcultural adaptation.

In this regard, I (De Vos, 1965a; De Vos & Suárez-Orozco, 1990a) have been especially critical of McClelland's ethnocentric view of achievement as individualistic (e.g., McClelland, 1955, 1961). Particular forms of psychological adaptation cannot be seen independent of a total social pattern. In explaining achievement motivation, McClelland, Atkinson, Clark, and Lowelle (1953) and others overemphasize individualistic forms of achievement that are found in American society, and generally see competitive achievement as inversely related to affiliative concerns. Their theories do not explain the successful Japanese pattern in which there is emphasis on interdependency and nurture.

At the same time, examining patterns of minority adaptation both in the United States and Japan, I have decried sociological theories which consider delinquency or deviancy solely in terms of the situational economic or social factors operative in American city ghettos (De Vos, 1978b, 1982). These theories do not explain why different minority groups develop *different* patterns of adaptation in response to discrimination and economic hardship. I have also challenged relativistic anthropological theories that see adaptive differences in groups as due simply to cultural considerations, without considering the relative adequacy or inadequacy of such adaptations. Those espousing cultural relativism do not recognize that internal maladjustment may be related to inadequate socialization which hinders rather than facilitates psychosocial development (De Vos, 1976). On the contrary, the social behavior of some group members can be symptomatic of underlying psychological rigidities that make it difficult to adapt to change. There *are* psychological consequences that become evident in the behavior of members of some groups related to the deprivation, neglect, and abuse. Achieving adequate mental and emotional balance is *a common problem in all societies,* and there are panhuman criteria of psychological adjustment and maladjustment. Humans are psychopsysiologically alike despite different socialization experiences, but the *socialization of cognition and emotion* of particular ethnic minority youth can be negatively influenced by *disrupted family life* as well as by generationally continuous *derogated status,* as in the United States (De Vos, 1978c, 1982).

Looking at the relative adaptation of minority children of different minorities in both the United States and Japan, cultural, psychological, *and* sociological factors *all* play a role in the behavior of minorities. But this is not understood by many social scientists, who give the most causal weight to one or another favored determinant. Both the unexpectedly better adaptation in the face of discrimination by Japanese- and Korean-Americans, and the continuing problems manifest in other minorities in the United States and Japan, bear comparative examination and explanation.

Family and Delinquency in Japan

Working in California during the late 1950s and early 1960s as a consultant for prison research, I looked further at patterns of social deviancy in Japan and examined positive patterns of achievement. Suicides rates were relatively high, especially among the young, but Japanese statistics indicated that for measures of social anomy such as crime, delinquency, divorce, and family desertion, the rates were very low. The family was working relatively well as a social institution. But who becomes delinquent in Japan? Were there delinquents among Japanese minorities about whom very little was said in the press or in education studies? What selective features of early socialization related to social status lead to conformity or deviancy in Japanese children? I determined to initiate a study of delinquency formation in Japan to compare social, cultural, and psychological patterns between the United States and Japan.

Psychological anthropologist Hiroshi Wagatsuma had begun his continuing collaboration with me, first as a student at the University of Michigan, in 1955. Later, at the University of California, he became director of fieldwork on my 8-year research project (from 1959 to 1967) studying delinquency and deviancy in Japan, sponsored by The National Institute of Mental Health (De Vos & Wagatsuma, 1959, 1961, 1970; Wagatsuma & De Vos, 1962, 1978, 1980, 1984a, 1984b). During this period Wagatsuma and I also investigated the plight of the ex-pariah Burakumin, Japan's invisible minority of close to 3 million individuals (De Vos & Wagatsuma 1966, 1969; Wagatsuma & De Vos, 1967). A valuable collaborator with me on our work on delinquency from 1960 on was psychologist and criminologist Keiichi Mizushima (De Vos & Mizushima, 1962, 1967; Mizushima & De Vos, 1967; Gough, De Vos, & Mizushima, 1968). Since my early work at the University of Michigan, I also collaborated periodically with anthropologist Takao Sofue (De Vos & Sofue, 1986). Later, from 1976 through 1979, I worked with several Koreans, principally Changsoo Lee and Kwang-Kyu Lee, on a study of conformity and deviancy in the Korean minority in Japan (C. S. Lee & De Vos, 1981; De Vos & K. K. Lee, 1981). Before I pursue general issues of differential minority adaptation and deviant behavior, let me first reiterate some of my major contentions about the cultural psychology of the Japanese.

FAMILY COHESION AND URBANIZATION

Firsthand empirical evidence and experience that deepened my understanding of social cohesion and status inequality in Japan was obtained, first, by 2 years at Nagoya University from 1953 to 1955, which included interviews in both rural and urban settings, and later by Mizushima, Wagatsuma, and myself over several years in the 1960s among the the Burakumin of the Kansai area, and the merchants and artisans of Arakawa Ward in Tokyo. Subsequent repeated visits and the extensive reports and writings of others, as well as examination of the plots of films and literary works (De Vos, 1968b, 1973; De Vos & Bock, 1975; De Vos & Dahl, 1974; Wagatsuma & De Vos, 1978) strengthen the contentions I have made about urban Japan. (See also Abegglen, 1958; Cole, 1971; Dore, 1958; Nakane, 1970; and Vogel, 1963.)

Part of our work in Tokyo's Arakawa Ward was a historical analysis of patterns of immigration into the city (Wagatsuma & De Vos, 1984). More recently, I have examined historically the cohesive influence of Confucianism on the Japanese family (De Vos & Sofue, 1986; Conner & De Vos, 1989; De Vos, 1992a). Socialization experienced in childhood prepares individuals to live in an adult society that reflects an ethos, or emotional climate, that seems "natural" to its members. In some of my writings I have examined the Japanese social hierarchy from this perspective, and have traced out how forms of status inequality found in a society are in tune with expectations engendered from childhood on (De Vos & Suárez-Orozco, 1990b).

The Japanese are not as continually prone to protest or rebellion as Americans, according to our TAT protocols over the years. This is not to say that social and personal protest do not occur periodically in Japan, as elsewhere. Protest movements have appeared in Japanese society, both in the premodern and modern periods (De Vos, 1984b), but I would argue that Japanese are not as quickly restive about social inequality or acts of exploitation as are members of some other societies. In the social opinion scales we used in Nagoya, we found strong attitudes about gratitude toward superiors still very operative in age-graded situations, including positive attitudes toward undergoing an apprenticeship (Muramatsu, 1962).

Later, in the early 1960s, Wagatsuma and I found such attitudes still in force in Arakawa Ward (De Vos, 1973). Such thinking characterized the implicit attitudes of patrons and subordinates among the small entrepreneurs and artisans who lived there. Underlying feelings of deference and gratitude were still embedded in the roles of apprentice and patron, as in the urban and rural samples we interviewed in the 1950s. Such attitudes were generally relevant to economic–historical processes at work in the course of Japanese industrialization from the turn of the century on (De Vos, 1965c, 1975a). However, no one can predict how much longer these attitudes will persist in the face of present-day social forces. At least, such attitudes helped set the tone for contemporary Japanese organizational behavior and family life for the immediate post-World War II generation.

I have generalized that these Japanese attitudes toward authority differ from those operative in contemporary Western societies. Until recently, whatever negative feelings about authority appear, public authority has been generally respected and was seldom perceived as venal or distrusted (De Vos, 1984). Authority figures— external administrators, company executives, police, teachers, or older family members—have been granted, for the most part, a degree of respect increasingly rare in the United States. At present, however, there seems to be a progressive diminution of such respect for politicians running for public office. In his brilliant analysis of contemporary Japanese political processes, van Wolferen (1989) details many of the more recent misgivings expressed about political figures, rather than about administrative personnel. Recent political scandals, involving in some cases connections with organized crime, have spread a sense of disillusionment, especially among the young.

I have discussed (De Vos & Suárez-Orozco, 1990b), in more general terms, how secular organizations as well as the religious structure of a society must be considered in looking at awe and respect in superior–subordinate relationships. Traditionally, it has been emotionally feasible for Japanese to expect dependent gratifications for performing religiously toned, morally prescribed compliant behavior as part of a social or occupational role. For many traditional Japanese, attitudes toward civil authority or occupational mentors resembled the attitudes found only among believers in Western religion that consider that moral obedience gains God's reward of benevolent nurture. Traditional Christianity depicts God as both an awesome, fearful deity of justice as well as a merciful source of benevolence. In Japan in the past, such "religious" attitudes have appeared directed toward mentors as well as ancestors and parents.

Curiously enough, from the perspective of social cohesion, it is the Japanese, today espousing a Western capitalist ideology, who still seem to be capable of maintaining some worker morale that socialist theorists have suggested should occur only in a well-managed, socialist economic system (De Vos, 1975a). Japanese leftist or progressive theorists decry what they see as the effects of traditional cultural attitudes that have prevented, and still prevent, the realization of workers' gains (see Vogel, 1975). But these very traditional attitudes are at present still being utilized in Japan, to some extent at least, for collective national competitive economic efforts. We must consider the possibility that the Japanese have been successful economically in part because they have carried forward expressive, sometimes irrational, attitudes inherited from a premodern past. They still manifest the influence of a Confucian system of thought, no longer consciously considered (De Vos, 1992a, 1993). Mothers still foster a sense of hierarchy and a need to repay early nurture and later vocational mentoring. Social attitudes are first internalized through the methods and social attitudes expressed in child-rearing practices within the Japanese family. The forces affecting cultural continuity or change lie in the primary family.

Socialization toward Technological Mastery

In the course of Japanese industrialization, former merchants, artisans, and farmers have been recruited as industrial workers who have been either hired in modern, industrial plants or apprenticed in small, urban house-factories that remain part of Japan's dual economic structure. We studied three generations of petty merchants and artisans in Arakawa for 5 years, starting in 1960 (Wagatsuma & De Vos, 1984). We witnessed in Arakawa Tokyo the urban migration of relatively impoverished youth that was for most neither personally alienating nor socially disruptive. We found economic destitution but not *poverty*, and no evidence of any form of general disaffection or of anomic disorganization in the more newly forming urban communities. There was no evidence of the psychological stigma of poverty observable in some American urbanizing groups.

Rather, we found evidence of how newly constituted communities functioned to integrate the individual and his or her family into more or less encompassing, if not entirely satisfying, larger units of social organization. In Arakawa there was an urbanizing pattern by which the "downtown"(*shitamachi*) traditional, townsman culture of northwest Tokyo was taken on by those from rural areas who had moved steadily into the newly settled areas of northeast Tokyo. The *shitamachi* culture pattern was transmitted to them with considerable force. It incorporated new recruits from the country-side into familial-like patterns so as to counter any disruptive processes generated by the large-scale industrial movement of single people leaving their families of origin (Wagatsuma & De Vos, 1984).

If we compare Japan and the United States, the urbanization of Japan has been less traumatic. There is no evidence of the rate of psychological breakdown with urbanization that has been found among some groups coming into American cities (Malzberg & Lee, 1956; Malzberg, 1969). Japanese organizations take in youth and gradually fit them in as new members of an age-graded hierarchy. Rather than becoming part of a mass society, they become bound together in face-to-face groups, and subject to community sanction.

Even granting the integrative force of the community organizational features of Japanese local neighborhoods, one must still turn to the psychocultural influences within the work situation itself to explain the relative lack of alienation among Japanese workers, no matter their periodic economic distress. Reasons are to be found in the *expressive satisfactions* of Japanese paternalism—both in the way one plays the superordinate role as a boss, or the subordinate role as either apprentice or a long-term, factory employee. One has to examine more carefully, therefore, the *cultural forms of secondary socialization* into occupational roles, which follow upon the primary socialization occurring within the family.

In the traditional Japanese social system, a youth was usually introduced into a network of age-graded occupational expectations as an apprentice. The apprentice role was defined in quasi-familial terms and became part of a network of mutual expectation—both instrumental and expressive in nature. Since some of the apprentice's expectations could be actualized only in the distant future as part of his or her work role, the apprentice was also being trained to develop a future-time orientation. He or she was resigned to what an outsider might consider harsh, exploitative treatment for the sake of the future promise of continuing paternalistic support. This sense of age-graded reciprocity through time was reinforced generally by the social attitudes of the apprentice's own family and others. He or she had already been internalized to seek success.

By degrees, the Japanese individual is expected to gain a sense of pleasure from increasing competence, as he or she gradually internalizes the standards of excellence related to the craft. Ideally, the apprentice would also be increasingly rewarded with signs of appreciation for his or her growing skill. Hence, there is a gradual socialization of inner satisfactions to be gained by approximating the standards of skill set by the master or teacher within any given tradition. These attitudes were what I still found embedded in TAT stories (De Vos, 1973). The TAT reflected how expected attitudes of gratitude and repayment were turned from the parents onto occupational mentors or teachers in the quasi-familial master–apprentice situation. Ideally, the boss or master was not free to ignore the dependent expectations of the former apprentice. The master's own sense of actualizing this status derived from a capacity to meet some of these expectations and to do well for those who had been depending on him or her.

The relative success of the Japanese system of vocational socialization is quite apparent when we compare Japanese working-class youth with their counterparts in the United States. We have more signs of distress related not only to direct problems of employment opportunities, but also to alienating attitudes that predispose American youth to having difficulty in coping with job frustrations. One reliable sociological index of social alienation and low tolerance for frustration is delinquency among youth. The majority Japanese manifest a very low rate of delinquency when compared to other modern urban societies. After a 15-year postwar surge in youthful delinquency among lower-class youth in Japan, the overall rates declined during the 1960s, then remained stable rather than going up (De Vos, 1962, 1967b).

Instead of finding restive alienation among the lower-class youth in Japan, we found that it was the university youth from higher status backgrounds who expressed more social criticism and feelings of social alienation (De Vos, 1973). There has been increased malaise about the impersonal, albeit vastly expanded, system of higher formal education. College students exhibit more signs of personal social stress than youth who go to work in either large- or small-scale industries. The students from middle-class families lack direct integrating personal interaction with occupational mentors. The teacher's role has become not only distant but much more impersonal than in the past. In contrast, industrial workers, or employed college graduates quickly become part of an organization and take on a sense of belonging.

Central to a psychocultural analysis is a thorough consideration of the nature of the subjective experience of exploitation from an expressive and instrumental standpoint. One has to examine, for example, how emotionally satisfying or expressive features of a subordinate role can conflict, in the inner experience of Japanese employers with the instrumental advantages of uninhibited economic exploitation of subordinates. Conversely, one has to examine how culturally patterned dependent expectations on the part of subordinates can, in certain instances, distort perception of the actual situation, so that they hide from themselves the degree to which they are exploited. In their mutual internal perceptions, some young Japanese still see the work situation as a reciprocal payment of present labor for future-oriented training in a skill. In many occupational situations in Japan there is a lifelong perpetuation of *kobun* (child status), where the individuals remain subadult and maintain an emotional and financial dependency on an *oya-kata* (parent figure) who periodically rewards followers. Such ties remain highly emotional, internally reinforced by potential guilt should the subordinate not repay the benefactor.

How does this all relate to the continuing family atmosphere in Japan? I contend that there has been at least until very recently, a religious force maintaining sacred hierarchy within the family. This is the major topic to which I have turned recently in my attempt to understand the traditional sources of social cohesion in contemporary Japan (De Vos, 1992a).

"Self"- Development in Japanese Thought, Related to Childrearing Practices

One issue concerned with the effects of the childhood training within a Japanese family is whether childrearing leads to passivity and resignation, or conversely to a sense of initiative in achieving social expectations. Are Japanese brought up to be passively resigned to uncontrollable circumstance or to seek instrumental means to bend circumstances to their advantage? On a cognitive level of problem solving, Japanese childrearing has emphazied seeking a realistic solution to a problem rather than recourse to magic or prayer. As I have discussed (e.g., De Vos & Suárez-Orozco, 1990a), belief in magic can be related to forms of *mechanical* pre-causality found in children, in which the locus of power is sensed within and expressed through some manipulative instrumental activity. That failing, one finds a specialist (magician) who knows how to cause change in line with what is desired. This form of thinking is different from prayer, which acknowledges an expressively sensed inner helplessness and the need for the intercession of an outside *intentional* power to amend one's fate. Neither of these means of coping are fostered among the Japanese. Rather, usual maternal training emphasizes the development of self-discipline.

During World War II some psychoanalytically oriented anthropologists attempted to understand patterns of behavior, suggesting that psychological rigidity and self-righteousness were characteristic results of severe toilet training among Japanese (Gorer, 1943; La Barre, 1945). These efforts were ill-founded, as later evidence showed. Further, these earlier attempts to explain a "national character" by specific childrearing practices related to toilet training relied too heavily on Western psychoanalytic theory and clinical observations, and not observation of actual Japanese socialization. The general consensus resulting from later direct observational studies (e.g., Lanham, 1956, 1962; see also Chapter 6, this volume) is that toilet training in Japan was never imposed with any of the rigor characteristic of some groups observed in traditional Western childrearing. In Japan, what is controlled very early is proper bowing and other deference behavior directed toward important outsiders. There is a continued sensitivity aroused from early on about properly controlled motoric behavior.

I have related this part of early childhood experience in Japan to a moral sense located in the musculature (De Vos, 1992b, 1993). Early on, social relationships are symbolized in proper posture, which is as important as verbal deference. A Japanese mother's concern with social compliance, or with other consequences of a child's behavior, is most often centered on how a child may hurt the feelings of others (Stevenson, Azuma, & Hakuta, 1986). If children are too directly aggressive, they will receive threats of isolation (T. Lebra & W. Lebra, 1976). Maternal discipline in Japan avoids a test of wills, as Japanese mothers are more likely to appeal to a child's awareness of consequences (Azuma et al., 1981; Azuma, Chapter 13, this volume). The child is made aware of his potential to hurt objects and people. This is a form of moral inculcation, rather than a tempering of contentious wills, as characterizes parent–child interaction in the United States. Japanese children are quickly made sensitive to their capacity to arouse negative feelings in others. As compared in systematic studies by developmental psychologists, American mothers are more apt to make desired behavior, whether toilet training or other forms of compliance, a question of obedience to the will of the mother. The Japanese mother avoids any such confrontation, and uses her closeness to move the child toward compliance with her wishes without making them a direct issue.

Obedience per se is not the desired goal; rather, mothers seek to awaken in a child awareness of the potentially negative consequences of behavior (cf. Miyake, Chen, & Campos, 1986). The *potential* for hurting one's family, not only oneself, is learned fairly early. Present behavior can cause collective harm a long time distant. Vigilance becomes part of a future-time orientation, while the child's sense of "self" remains embedded within his or her family. As already discussed, Japanese socialization for achievement is defined collectively, not individualistically (De Vos, 1973), and social or occupational failure produces guilt because it hurts those deserving gratitude (De Vos, 1960). In fact, on a directly conscious level the mother (and sometimes the wife) may be idealized as a sacrificial figure in a fashion discussed in the West in respect to Christ as a savior (De Vos, 1984a, 1985a). In a past generation of American immigrants, one often found such idealization of Jewish mothers by their American-born sons.

In Japan one learns increasingly to put off immediate gratification, but with a defined collective future social purpose and an awareness of the satisfactions to be gained from future social and occupational mastery. Such a sense of future-oriented mastery means that Japanese self-development *is defined within one's prescribed social role.* One is not simply taught to remain passive to avoid conflict, but to sense internally an *active* potential to be exercised in the future. One seeks individually to enhance an active locus of control within, even while one's overt behavior may remain docile in appearance. For many Japanese all causality remains ultimately moral—a central feature of Confucian teaching, although such teaching is no longer consciously visible in Japanese modern thought (Bito, 1986).

Behavior is not submission to the rules set by a potentially wrathful deity (De Vos, 1992a). Morality is still related to inner will (once termed *Yamato damashi*, in a patriotic context). Emotional intensity is a part of one's *ki*, or spirit, or the essence of *kokoro*, heart. In Japanese child training reverence and gratitude can continue to be expressed religiously *within* the family system or toward a teacher, a *sensei* who guides one's efforts. Such a "benevolent" person is to be revered as are one's mother and father and more distant ancestors (Morioka, 1986). A supernatural image is not usually evoked. The sense of deep gratitude need not be attributed to a figure such as Jesus or a nurturing Virgin Mary. The figures of Amida and Kannon, derivative of popular Buddhism, have been used by some Japanese as objects of gratitude, but many others, with the same emotions seeking expression, do not transcend the actual family. The fact that the deepest gratitude need not be expressed toward a supernatural object can be related to the preempting of such emotional states by family teachings, in which such emotional focus remains turned back into the social world.

The Confucian heritage of the Japanese family fosters cohesiveness and the setting of internalized goals, and positive attitudes toward mentors and teachers (Slote & De Vos, 1996). Learning more about this tradition has increased my understanding of overall Japanese- and Korean-American social adaptation as relatively successful Asian minorities (De Vos, 1992). It has also helped me to understand more specifically why most children with this heritage, both in the United States and Japan, have persisted on into relatively successful vocational careers. For many women, their successful *vocation* has been the rearing of successful children.

But as a psychologist, I could not consider this level of inquiry into Japanese conscious thought the end of my investigation. The underlying *structural* level of personality also required further inquiry in comparative, cross-cultural studies. Granted the positive social attitudes toward education held by Japanese, is there not also some explanation of school performance to be understood on the level of how socialization influences cognitive development itself?

MINORITY STATUS AND CLASSROOM COMPETENCE

Considering Japanese patterns of achievement, I now turn to my structural level of psychological analysis that goes below the level of conscious, culturally inherited attitudes. In mentioning above the potential for guilt in Japanese, I have already touched upon unconscious processes. There are also *cognitive* developmental aspects of mental functions to be considered comparatively, as they, too, are aspects of personality structure. Japanese children in their cognitive development attain levels of "field independence" that indicate that they have reached a capacity for objective perception. On a *social level,* this is consonant with the internalization of moral directives that emphasize forms of social sensitivity and social compliance related to family responsibility. In Japanese, cognitive independence is coupled with compliant receptivity to teachers or other mentors, allowing for better adaptive learning.

The Use of Cross-Cultural Testing in School-Age Youth

There have been serious questions about the cross-cultural use of psychological tests. Such criticism of cross-cultural testing is a very complex issue on which I can comment only briefly. Whatever the problems of inference and interpretation, there are reported in the psychological literature produced in Asia systematic differences in IQ and other tests obtained from different groups, which are related quite directly to educational and vocational performance within given societies. Specific to Japan, differences in normative results among members of different subcultural groups on tests *are* relevant to an understanding of both social functioning and cognitive functioning in given contexts. Granted that such differences can be interpreted by the bigoted or prejudiced in a socially derogatory manner as related to hopeless inferiority rather than as indicators of debilitative or inhibitive social experiences, tests selectively show higher results when given to some groups compared with others.

It is a fact, however painful or disconcerting it may be, that early testing of American children from 6 years of age on does predict later school performance to a highly significant degree. In my personal opinion, this predictability does not argue simply for some biological or physiological constancy, but for the deeply formative effects of early preschool socialization experience on the facilitation or inhibition of given cognitive and affective patterns observable in effective social learning. I have written about related problems of self-esteem that appear very early, probably in the preschool period, in considering the documented poor school performance of minorities in Japan, namely the Burakumin (De Vos & Wagatsuma, 1966) and the Koreans (C. S. Lee & De Vos, 1981). Parallels are found in evidence from Native American Apache in tests with which I have worked (De Vos & Boyer, 1989).

Regardless of cultural biases or, if you will, characteristic modes of coping found in testing *between different groups,* the validity of assuming panhuman coping patterns is documented by the fact that *within-group* differentiations are highly predictive of the *relative performance* of specific individuals in whatever group is tested, whether on IQ tests, projective tests, or such seemingly culture-bound tests as the California Psychological Inventory (CPI). For example, using translations of the CPI test into Cantonese, Fukienese, Mandarin, and Japanese for our research on delinquents versus nondelinquents in Japan (Mizushima & De Vos, 1967; Gough et al., 1968) and Taiwan (Abbott, 1975), we found that the CPI (especially CPI scores low on the Socialization Scale) differentiated not only between delinquent and nondelinquent subjects, but also between the parents of delinquents and those of nondelinquents! Comparative analyses of test results demonstrate that the tests *are* valid predictors of *comparative* performance within the societies examined, whether they be the United States, Europe, Japan, or Taiwan.

In Japan, we (De Vos & Wagatsuma, 1966) have noted, citing the statistics then (but no longer) available, that there are quite apparent relationships between minority status, poor IQ scores, poor school performance, lack of family cohesion, and high rates of delinquency. These interrelationships are complex. For example, delinquency and IQ have no significant direct relationship, but in Japan, as in the United States, delinquency is significantly high in broken families. We also have demonstrated in both Japan (Wagatsuma & De Vos, 1984) and Italy (De Vos, 1980a) that male delinquency occurs in families with little internal cohesion, poor supervision, inconsistent discipline, and lack of affection afforded a *particular* son. Statistical evidence in the United States and Japan continues to emphasize that delinquency is significantly higher among truants and poor performers in school.

In no minority group we have dealt with intensively can we report any lack of respect for schooling or any devaluing of formal education. I would contend that social values are not that different between American or Japanese minority groups and the majority. What differ are the priorities of other social concerns, such negative experiences as neglect and maternal deprivation, absence of a father during *particular* childhood years, and the methods of discipline used by parents to encourage internalization of social expectations on the part of their children. In our volume *Heritage of Endurance* (1984), Wagatsuma and I discussed these determinants in detail, referring to intensively studied extended family histories.

TWO FORMS OF DEPENDENCE: COGNITIVE AND SOCIAL

The Need for Structural Psychological Comparisons of Social Groups

Within the field of cross-cultural psychology in the United States, there has been developing some partial response to the crisis occurring in the vocational training of minority youth. Not only is there a relatively poor showing of some ethnic minorities in the schools, but delinquency and other manifestations of personal alienation are appearing with greater frequency in youth, especially in the youth of some particularly disadvantaged American minorities. Basically, there are two levels on which poor school performance may be further investigated. On one level, exemplified by the work of Ogbu (1991), the conscious attitudes of minority youth are related to a sense of future opportunity or futility. He distinguishes carefully between the youth of voluntary immigrant minorities who seek new opportunities, and several forms of caste-like minorities who have historically been enslaved, colonized, and relegated to a derogated status position in a society. The evidence he cites is very forceful, and explains not only American groups, but what we have observed among the Burakumin and Koreans in Japan.

But we still must examine further on a structural level, by psychological testing devices, the coping methods related to internal psychological organization that exist below the level of conscious attitudes. Some of these coping problems are directly reflected in test results. What we shall illustrate here are the specific cognitive functions that progress developmentally from "field dependency" toward a progressively more mature level of cognitive "field independence."

Various other possible aspects of psychological coping on a structural level can be related to comparative school functioning. For instance, in addition to the continuing use and modification of standard intelligence or IQ tests, researchers have been conducting comparisons of social-class differences in verbal communication related to modes of childhood socialization in the United Kingdom (e.g., Bernstein, 1964, 1972, 1973; Cook-Gumperz, 1972) and elsewhere. Although Bernstein calls his approach "sociological," in that his line of investigation was inspired by Durkheim's (1947, 1951) discussion of socialization related to social structure, his level of analysis is *structurally* psychological. Among his findings were basic class differences in verbal–conceptual communication patterns. Middle-class children are socialized verbally by an "elaborated" communication pattern that facilities abstraction and analysis. It permits generalization and a flexible transfer of understanding to new situations. Lower-class children are more prone to socialization through a "restricted" verbal code, patterns in which the content of utilized speech is likely to be concrete, descriptive, and narrative. Continuing this line of investigation, Cook-Gumperz (1972) demonstrated in her research that the working class were prone to use more "affective" nonreasoning appeals within what she termed the personal communication code. Her findings about lower-class family socialization parallel the description of families with field-dependent children in the United States (e.g., Witkin et al., 1974). Behavior processed by these codes will develop different forms of self-regulation. I am not aware of how this research is examined in the context of a psychoanalytic understanding of the nature of internalization (De Vos & Suárez-Orozco, 1990). Rather, its inferences are characteristically related to a sociological form of interaction theory suggested by G. H. Mead (1936).

The Witkin Approach to Developing Perceptual Structures in Children: Its Relation to Internalization

What I shall illustrate here on a cognitive-perceptual level of functioning is how poor school performance is related to the continuation of "field dependency" in thought processes. As is now being substantiated in the research of Curtis A. Vaughn (Chapter 5, this volume), both poor performance and field dependency are psychodynamically related to difficulties in internalization or "identification" in the psychoanalytic sense. What is called a field-dependent cognitive pattern appears in individuals who have not yet sufficiently internalized and, therefore, are not yet as psychologically confident enough to make an independent judgment from *internally organized perceptual cues*. They remain dependent on outside judgments or cues.

Witkin (1967, 1969) and his associates have developed a series of "perception" experiments that are intriguing in their implications for a theory of panhuman cognitive development related to primary family patterns. They show a progression in human cognition in which younger children, earlier on, seek confirmation of their perceptions by looking for external cues for interpretation, rather than trusting cues arising out of their own bodies or experiences. Witkin and his associates have found that on various psychological tests there is an invariant progression in cognitive development generally, from a more field-dependent orientation toward a more field-independent one (e.g., Witkin, 1967; Witkin with Berry, 1975). One never goes from field independence back to a field-dependent form of judgment. These researchers have also studied American ethnic minorities with their measures and found that field dependence is related to (1) affiliative or cooperative social patterns, (2) more authoritarian, sometimes punishing, hierarchical-type primary family situations, or (3) families showing less internal companionate forms of social cohesion (Witkin & Goodenough, 1977; Goodenough & Witkin, 1977; Witkin et al., 1974; Madsen & Shapira, 1973.)

According to Witkin's assumptions, one would suppose that Japanese coming from a tradition of strong family hierarchy should be highly field dependent. Certainly, they manifest much of the conformist social behavior described for field-dependent youth in their compliance to peer group pressures. But our evidence about cognitive functioning suggests the contrary. As Vaughn (Chapter 5, this volume) demonstrates, the tests show Japanese scoring higher on field independence than American majority students from better-rated high schools. Our Japanese evidence indicates that there are thus two forms of dependence: one on a cognitive level, the second on an attitudinal level of social consciousness.

The first level of dependency, operating on a structural, cognitive level is characteristic of early childhood development. In psychosocial development, perceptual-emotional patterning first necessitates automatic use of external cues to ascertain a perception or its interpretation. In normal development, this adjustive coping mode can be gradually superseded by a growing capacity to trust internalized cues. Tests show that this latter pattern of internal cognitive development is attained in most Japanese children.

On a second, more conscious level, however, there remains another form of dependency, discussed by Doi (1973) and others, that is related to a persisting need to adhere to a social group. This need may, regressively, actually distort perceptions if group inclusion is threatened, so there may be lack of conscious recognition of an independent social self, or *jibun*. This does not mean that there is no internalized identification in personality formation. In the Japanese, the internalized family role remains basic to identity formation and asserts priority over the peer group as the ultimate reference group. At the same time, Japanese children are socialized into patterns of social dependency that continue to emphasize conscious conformity as well as positive regard for authority and hierarchy.

Viewed psychologically in respect to perceptual-developmental processes, Japanese, and Japanese-Americans in the United States, generally combine perceptual field independence with culturally emphasized conformity or behavioral submission to the group, including an emphasis on affiliative behavior. Instrumentally, they remain consciously constrained toward cooperative behavior. At the same time they demonstrate a highly internalized achievement motivation, and apply internalized standards for judgment that indicate a capacity for independent thought. They have also a highly internalized sense of social as well as family responsibility, and so remain internally preoccupied by worries over the development of their capacities for mastery. They can be very severe in their judgments, which leads to a continuing sense of dissatisfaction with oneself (higher in females than males), as is witnessed in some of the psychological measures obtained by Kashiwagi (1986).

The evidence to date suggests that Japanese and Japanese-Americans are cognitively field independent compared with some American minorities coming from other cultural backgrounds, such as Mexican-Americans and Hawaiians (Madsen, 1967; Kagan & Buriel, 1977; Howard, 1971, 1974; Gallimore, Boggs, & Jordan, 1974). Japanese-Americans remain much more concerned with internalized directives to achieve, inculcated by parents without the use of physical punishment, while at the same time they are socialized to remain subject to reference group pressures from their peers. They are successfully internalized to be capable of cognitive field independence, but are taught to *adapt socially* by remaining interdependent with others. And, as discussed above, they continue in adulthood to conform to the authority of elders because they expect nurture and care from superiors. Conversely, the authority role for a Japanese implies not only having high performance expectations in mentoring others, but the bestowing of care as well (De Vos, 1975a). All these patterns emphasize harmonious group cohesion as an overall ideal. Instrumental concerns with need achievement are interwoven with fantasies of aging into an authority position, not to be free of the influence of others, as is the aim of Americans, but to arrive at a mentoring role, in turn bestowing knowledge or care on younger individuals. Instrumental goals are conceptualized in a continuing paternalistic framework in which those in authority are supposed to gain expressive satisfaction from their nurturing as well as controlling roles. The young peer group, generally speaking, supports authority so conceived, rather than expressing conflict with the expectations of those in authority.

By contrast to both the American and the Japanese, in Mexican-American culture the concept of paternal authority can sometimes be idealized in the role of a "don," a detached fatherly gentleman, but seldom are ordinary government officials or other authorities conceptualized as benevolent donors. Sometimes the Catholic priest as "father" is allocated a type of mentoring or guiding role, but he has given up competitively defined, materially oriented ambition, and is also not perceived as a *macho* authority figure. More characteristically, officials and even family heads are distrusted. Authority is often perceived as exercised for personal benefit, not for benevolence. There is an impasse in contemporary Mexican-American minority culture between seeking socially disruptive, individualistically motivated material success and remaining a peer-oriented person, not seeking special economic advantage. Conceptually, instrumental self-interest is not harmoniously synthesized with expressive social needs. A person who pushes himself forward is quickly considered by the collectivity as self-seeking and socially without virtue. The socialization of children toward conformity and noncompetitive behavior is somewhat related to this felt impasse.

One can distinguish in the writings of Kagan and Madsen (1972a, 1972b) some careful differentiation between positively perceived "competition" as a means of self-fulfillment, and the negative attributes of "rivalry" as intended to maximize one's own gain at the expense of others. One notes in their writings, however, that there is no sufficient differentiation between positive "coopera- tion," which emphasizes joint effort and mutuality in the reaching of goals, and certain negative-adaptive concomitants by which chil- dren maintain a less differentiated, field-dependent cognitive style. That is to say, excessive emphasis on cooperation which is not ac- companied by internalized self-sustaining directives may inhibit cer- tain forms of intellectual development. Indeed, it may lead to social subordination and diffidence, which can incapacitate members of the group so that they cannot reach positively considered goals. In my judgment, some social scientists are influenced in their conclu- sions by their value judgments about what they perceive as excessive competition in American society. In some of this literature that I am citing, there is an implicit bias toward viewing too positively all forms of cooperation or rigidified cognitive patterning leading to cooperation, regardless of the less adaptable features of field de- pendence. These latter features *necessitate* more affiliative forms of dependency on others. Hence, one notes a present controversy over the implications of Witkin's theory. There is in effect an im- plicit confusion in some of these writers between *psychologically ad- justive* cognitive differentiation and *socially adaptive,* albeit subordi- nating, forms of cooperation.

Kagan and Kogan (1970), Kagan (1974), and Kagan and Bu- riel (1977), particularly, suggest that there is a dilemma of values represented in Witkin's research. They state that field indepen- dence is correlated with learning and achievement in American schools, and hence, necessarily linked to patters of social adapta- tion, emphasizing sometimes socially disruptive competition. In contrast, field-dependent individuals are considered by Kagan to remain adaptively more alert to social stimuli, capable of achieving consensus in less time than field-independent groups; they are probably more skilled at interpersonal accommodation maintaining social cohesion.

The Japanese case, however (De Vos, 1992a, 1992b), demon- strates that cognitively independent youngsters can also be trained to be equally sensitive and alert to social stimuli. Moreover, field- independent persons may achieve democratic forms of social cohe- sion more readily than field-dependent individuals. I contend that field-independent persons may be better able to resist influences of others in give-and-take democratic discussions, but at the same time may also be trained to be socially sensitive in their concern for the viewpoint of others. Field-dependent youngsters are less able to become objective or detached in assessing the merits of a decision.

One could, therefore, make a counterargument that field-dependent individuals are less capable of carrying any democratic discussions that demand individual integrity in working toward a satisfactory resolution.

Sequential Development in Adjustive Cognitive Patterns

The fact is, through methods such as those first used by Piaget (e.g., 1930) and others (Piaget & Inhelder, 1969), psychology as a science has affirmed the fact that psychophysiological maturation occurs in given sequences (Dasen, 1972). And despite the effects of culturally influenced retardation or facilitation influencing the timing of such sequences, they are not reversible, except in emotionally disruptive situations wherein one goes back to previous forms of cognition as part of a psychopathological defensive maneuver. Despite continuous attempts to demonstrate the contrary, no research to date can document any reversal of a Piagetian sequence as either positively adaptive or adjustive. Considered in respect to adjustive structures, an earlier emotional rigidified form of cognition is never as adaptive as more progressive, flexible later forms. This is observably true in considering the sequential development from field dependence toward field independence.

Cross-cultural cognitive relativism is too quickly espoused by individuals attempting to take a supposedly nonevaluative anthropological approach. The fact of the matter is that there *are* necessarily progressive maturational sequences in panhuman psychology toward greater adaptive flexibility. Different cultures, ethnic subcultures, or social class strata, in their socialization practices, may influence individuals to take a shorter or longer time to achieve certain points of maturation, depending upon cultural facilitation or inhibition. Nowhere has there been discovered or demonstrated a different progressive sequence in regard to maturation in the cognitive or emotional realm. Ultimately, greater cognitive differentiation is more adaptive in more varied circumstances; it is related, in most instances, to less rigidified forms of personality orientation.

This is not to deny that in some cultures certain features of cognitive differentiation can be accompanied by some form of emotional rigidification. It is sometimes too quickly assumed that it is only in a cognitive pattern that rigidity is an issue, whereas rigidification can and does appear in the emotional realm without impairing cognitive functions. Finding individuals in some cultures emotionally rigidified, but with highly differentiated cognitive abilities (as sometimes occurs in individuals with so-called obsessive-compulsive personalities) does not argue against the greater instrumental occupational adaptability of cognitive differentiation itself. A cultural emphasis on analytic thought as part of personality structure may also be more "adaptive" in an American classroom organized to maximize a competitive form of social adaptability. This is independent of the fact that considered *adjustively,* on a structural psychological level, analytic thought is more differentiated, regardless of other personality problems found in individuals with more abstract analytic capacities. That is, analytic thought is part of a progressive maturational development beyond a global field-dependent cognitive pattern, which appears at an earlier stage. Given a particular culture pattern, analytic thought can be part of an imbalanced personality pattern that selectively emphasizes defensive cognitive coping at the expense of a concomitant progressive maturation of social rapport. But social sensitivity per se is *not necessarily an equal positive alternative pattern to cognitive differentiation.*

Emotionally progressive social maturation and cognitive maturation can become adequately balanced if underlying coping mechanisms do not become selectively rigidified in socially emphasized defensive maneuvers. On the one hand, rigidified coping may inhibit cognitive maturation or, on the other hand, inhibit sensitivity to the feelings of others. This seems to be the case in the undue emphasis on independent behavior at the expense of social harmony in some American youth compared with Mexican-American or Japanese children.

It is interesting to note that contrary to the easy supposition that field-dependent teachers would do better with field-dependent pupils, research evidence (Kagan & Buriel, 1977) points to the fact that teachers rated high on field independence actually do better both with field-dependent and field-independent pupils. Again, the social sensitivity of some teachers and their field-independent cognitive capacities are not necessarily psychological alternatives. What is more generally lacking in "Anglo" culture, in comparison with the Mexican minority subculture or the Japanese, is socialization that emphasizes empathic concern with the feelings of others. It follows that there is a need in contemporary psychological research to distinguish between the *cognitive* and the *social* in interpreting dependent and independent behavior patterns. The internalization of social directives and emphasis on self-control do not preclude a parallel maturation of other coping mechanisms related to social sensitivity, as shown by Vaughn's (1988) work with the Japanese. In the traditional Japanese cultural context, cognitive independence is characteristically coupled with compliant receptivity to teachers or other mentors, allowing for better adaptive learning. In the

American pattern, cognitive independence is more frequently coupled with social and psychological competitiveness and more individualistically oriented internalization of achievement motivation. As discussed by Vaughn (Chapter 5, this volume), lower-class American children often are less internalized with respect to a need for achievement, and so are often not interested in formal class learning. They feel more psychologically free to defy the teacher, more or less openly.

Studies show different forms of group involvement and group compliance between American and Japanese class rooms, in both primary and secondary schools. American teachers generally decry the difficulties in maintaining order, and in inner city schools time spent on disciplinary problems often exceeds that devoted to instruction. The amount of defiance and disrespect displayed toward teachers has produced crises in many school districts. A good number of teachers are leaving the profession, not due solely to the relatively low salaries (itself a symptom of social disrespect), but due to the direct physical as well as status violence directed toward them in the classroom. One rarely observes such irreverent behavior toward a teacher among Asian-American children, who treat teachers with respect. Asian children may occasionally wish to express some rebelliousness, but such errant thoughts very rarely receive collective reinforcement.

My impression is that the more hierarchically organized Japanese society still bridges the generation gap induced by rapid social change. The family is changing from one concerned with generational continuity toward an emphasis on the immediate primary family, but the primary family itself remains relatively cohesive. The youth period among workers is not a period of protest or alienation for most. It is the Japanese upper-middle-class youth, during their transitional liminality as noncommitted students, who experience crises related to occupational choice. In brief, overall, there are still forces operative that maintain age-graded social cohesion in modern Japanese society.

Although in Japan at present there are some increasing signs of unrest in the primary and secondary schools (Lock, 1991), by and large Japanese internalization still emphasizes socialization that stresses an anticipation of the consequences of behavior to family as well as self. Compliance is not simply on the basis of obedience to a frightening authority. Compared with Americans generally, Japanese children show more immediate social sensitivity and concern with the opinions of others, but they also manifest an awareness of behavioral consequences in a future-time orientation.

In other words, Japanese children are still socialized toward present social sensitivities to a degree inordinately conformist from an American point of view, but their conformity is to be understood in the context of a future-time orientation. Early on, they are socialized toward group compliance, not by a fear of authority, but rather though a form of maternal guidance that instills a reverence for authority reinforced ritualistically by verbal and physical gestures of deference. Later, majority children remain socially compliant to peer pressure, but the majority peer group itself is consonant with school expectations and is not a negative force, as happens frequently among some minorities both in the United States and Japan.

I have written extensively about the cognitive constriction of educative intake related to what I term the "selective permeability," or psychological repression, that characterizes the cognitive coping patterns in defense of minority identity used by some minority youth in both Japan or the United States (De Vos, 1978c, 1982, 1983b). On a cognitive, psychodynamic level of coping in majority Japanese, one finds less repression of consciousness, but more behavioral restraint. Constraint in behavioral expression demands the *suppression* of thought and affect rather than severe *repression* of either. Majority Japanese are not blocked by possible earlier problems over proper internalization of parental figures, which characterize some ethnic minorities in the United States or in Japan. Most Japanese children do not become cognitively blocked, although some do. More characteristically, there is no retardation of an internalized, potential for self-guided cognition that can continue to be used from an inner locus of control. Japanese intake of learning is evidenced by their relatively high scores on math and science tests compared with their American counterparts. This may occur because from childhood on majority Japanese learn severe behavioral constraints, maintained for social purpose. There is a compliant intake of knowledge imparted by hierarchical figures acting in the status of parent.

A FINAL RETROSPECTIVE GLANCE

Looking back at my 48 years of work in the area of Japanese culture and personality, I have been requested by the editors of this volume to consider changes in my thought related to childhood socialization or to work in the field generally. I can honestly say that my theoretical orientation has not changed, nor has my view that a multidisciplinary approach is inherent in true comparative social science investigation. I have always believed in the necessity for empirical research on and between the analytic levels, involving the physiological, the psychological, the level of conscious cultural experience embodied in daily thought (as well as in art, religion, philosophy, and history), the social-role level, the social organizational level, and the geographic environment.

I have illustrated in this chapter a point of view that has not changed, although my work in the field and continuous background reading of the works of others have deepened and enriched my understanding of Japanese culture and the thinking and emotional experiences of the Japanese, individually and collectively (De Vos, 1994b).

As to contemporary work in the social sciences generally, I have been disappointed by the continuing relative reluctance of academic psychologists to extend their research activities beyond the limits of middle-class American subjects. Despite lip service to the influence of culture patterns on childhood socialization, relatively little has been done to encourage graduate students in psychology departments to commit themselves to cross-cultural projects in testing their theories or their instruments. In fact, attention to a comparative approach to socialization within psychology has been more notable in Japan than elsewhere. But even in Japan more needs to be done. I find that psychologists generally are timid in really exploring cross-cultural evidence, especially when it demonstrates any possible psychological problems related to minority status. There is easy agreement on the negative social effects of status discrimination wherever found. There is less readiness to examine the not easily remedied negative, possibly permanent, psychological effects of early socialization experiences related to minority family problems.

In anthropology I have been disappointed in the retreat from the systematic use of psychological testing devices as part of anthropology. Academic department of anthropology have never insisted on adequate training in psychological anthropology, and the earlier American interest in culture and personality, from the 1940s into the 1960s, has not been pursued with the same level of interest. The lack of any development of disciplined instruction in graduate training is related to this diminution. The early works of M. Mead and Benedict are still recited as representing the field, with insufficient attention given to recent developments in cognitive psychology that cry for cross-cultural verification. Interest, at best, has remained casual. To be considered scientifically useful as part of anthropology, training in psychological measures must become subject to the same higher standards we now see instituted in biological applications to physical and physiological, anthropology and primatology, or in the dating techniques used in archaeology, but such has not been the case. Quantitative psychological approaches have also been resisted in anthropology. There is, instead, recourse to French-style global theorizing, or to so-called "postmodern" subjective ruminations based on ad hoc forms of psychologizing about human nature.

There is even to be found in some recent writings a new emphasis on an ultimate incapacity to understand or to communicate with those of another culture or ethnic group. This shows a lack of appreciation of the fact that humans share a common psychology that makes it possible to approach the subjective experiences of others, although they have been socialized in another culture. There is also a prolongation of the British-derived social anthropological approach to behavior that continues to ignore the psychological dimension. Rather than additional discussion about the failure of paradigms, what is needed in anthropological training in some vigorous insistence on more disciplined training, and less permission or encouragement of free theorizing based on diminishing requirements of field experience.

Despite such discouraging thoughts, I do believe in the slow accumulation of valid knowledge that the documentation found in this book represents. As evident in the various chapters of this book, a newer generation of scholars *are* progressing forward with an appreciation of the genuine contributions of those preceding. Questioning what has been done before is part of science, but global rejection or disregard of past efforts simply changes voices without sequential progression. Our fields of inquiry are moving forward through both collaborative and individual efforts based on respect for objectivity, even when imperfectly attained. We are continuing a scientific tradition.

REFERENCES

Abegglen, J. G. (1958). *The Japanese factory: Aspects of its social organization.* Glencoe, IL: Free Press.

Abbott, K. (1975). Culture change and the persistence of Chinese personality. In G. De Vos (Ed.), *Responses to change.* New York: Van Nostrand.

Adorno, T. W. (1950). *The authoritarian personality.* New York: Harper's.

Azuma, H., Kashiwagi, H., & Hess, R. (1981). *The influence of maternal teaching style upon the cognitive development of children.* Tokyo: University of Tokyo Press.

Babcock, C., & Caudill, W. (1958). Personal and cultural factors in treating a Nisei man. In G. Seward (Ed.), *Clinical studies in culture conflict* (pp. 408–448). New York: Roland Press.

Benedict, R. (1946). *The chrysanthemum and the sword: Patterns of Japanese culture.* Boston: Houghton Mifflin.

Bernstein, B. (1964). Elaborated and restricted codes: Their social origins and some consequences. In J. Gumperz & D. Hymes (Eds.), The ethnography of communication [Special issue]. *American Anthropologist, 66* (2).

Bernstein, B. (1972). A socio-linguistic approach to socialization: With some references to educability. In J. Gumperz & D. Hymes (Eds.), *Directions in sociolinguistics* (pp. 69–96). New York: Holt, Rinehart & Winston.

Bernstein, B. (1973). *Class, codes and control.* London: Paladin.

Bito, M. (1986). Confucian thought during the Tokugawa period. In G. A. De Vos & T. Sofue (Eds.), *Religion and the family in east Asia* (pp. 127–138). Berkeley: University of California Press.

Caudill, W., & De Vos, G. (1956). Achievement, culture and personality: The case of the Japanese Americans. *American Anthropologist, 58*(6), 1102–1126.

Cole, R. E. (1971). *Japanese blue collar: The changing tradition.* Berkeley: University of California Press.

Conner, J. W., & De Vos, G. (1989). Cultural influences on achievement motivation and orientation toward work in Japanese and American youth. In D. Stern & D. Eichorn (Eds.), *Adolescence and work: Influence of social structure, labor markets, and culture* (pp. 291–326). Hillsdale, NJ: Erlbaum.

Cook-Gumperz, J. (1972). *Social control and socialization: A study of class differences in the language of maternal control.* London: Routledge & Kegan Paul.

Dasen, P. (1972). Cross-cultural Piagetian research: A summary. *Journal of Cross-Cultural Psychology, 3,* 23–29.

De Vos, G. A. (1952). A quantitative approach to affective symbolism in Rorschach responses. *Journal of Projective Techniques, 16*(2),133–150.

De Vos, G. A. (1954). A comparison of the personality differences in two generations of Japanese Americans by means of the Rorschach Test. *Nagoya Journal of Medical Science, 17*(3), 153–265.

De Vos, G. A. (1955). A quantitative Rorschach assessment of maladjustment and rigidity in acculturating Japanese Americans. *Genetic Psychology Monographs, 52,* 51–87.

De Vos, G. A. (1959). Psycho-cultural attitudes toward primary relationships in Japanese delinquents—a study in progress. *International Mental Health Research Newsletter, 2*(1,2), 10–12.

De Vos, G. A. (1960). The relation of guilt toward parents to achievement and arranged marriage among the Japanese. *Psychiatry, 23*(3), 287–301.

De Vos, G. A. (1961). Symbolic analysis in the cross-cultural study of personality. In B. Kaplan (Ed.), *Studying personality cross-culturally* (pp. 391–405). Evanston, IL: Row-Peterson.

De Vos, G. A. (1962). Deviancy and social change: A psychocultural evaluation of trends in Japanese delinquency and suicide. In R. Smith &

R. Beardsley (Eds.), *Japanese culture: Its development and characteristics* (pp. 153–170). Chicago: Aldine.

De Vos, G. A. (1964). The legendary yakuza. *California Monthly, 74*(5), 8–11.

De Vos, G. A. (1965a). Achievement orientation, social self-identity, and Japanese economic growth. *Asian Survey, 5*(12), 575–589.

De Vos, G. A. (1965b). Assimilation and social self identity in the Japanese former outcaste group. In M. Kantor (Ed.), *Mobility and mental health* (pp. 48–75). Springfield, IL: Charles C Thomas.

De Vos, G. A. (1965c). Social values and personal attitudes in primary human relationships in Niiike. *Occasional Papers,* No. 9, 53–91. Ann Arbor: University of Michigan, Center for Japanese Studies.

De Vos, G. A. (1965d). Transcultural diagnosis of mental health by means of psychological tests. In A. V. S., de Reuck & R. Porter (Eds.), *Ciba Foundation Symposium on Transcultural Psychiatry* (pp. 328–354). London: Churchill.

De Vos, G. A. (1966a). *A comparison of the personality differences in two generations of Japanese Americans by means of the Rorschach test.* University of Hawaii Social Science Research Institute. (Reprint of 1952 monograph).

De Vos, G. A. (1966b). Conflict, dominance and exploitation in human systems of social segregation: Some theoretical perspectives from the study of personality in culture. In A. V. S. de Reuck & J. Knight (Eds.), *Ciba Foundation Symposium on Conflict in Society* (pp. 60–81). London: Churchill.

De Vos, G. A. (1967a). The Japanese adolescent delinquent in a period of social change. *East West Center Review, 4*(2), 35–53.

De Vos, G. A. (1967b). Psychology of purity and pollution as related to social self-identity and caste. In A. V. S. de Reuck & J. Knight (Eds.), *Caste and race: Comparative approaches* (pp. 292–315). London: Churchill.

De Vos, G. A. (1968a). Achievement and innovation in culture and personality. In E. Norbeck, D. Price-Williams, & W. McCord (Eds.), *The study of personality: An interdisciplinary appraisal* (pp. 348–370). New York: Holt, Rinehart & Winston.

De Vos, G. A. (1968b). Suicide in cross-cultural perspective. In H. L. P. Resnick (Ed.), *Suicidal behaviors: Diagnosis and management* (pp. 105–134). Boston: Little, Brown.

De Vos, G. A. (1969a). Minority group identity. In J. Finney (Ed.), *Culture change, mental health, and poverty* (pp. 81–96). Lexington: University of Kentucky Press.

De Vos, G. A. (1969b). Parental interaction and delinquency formation . . . some perspectives from Japan. *The Young Adult, 37,* 47–72. Des Plaines, IL: Forest Hospital Guest Lecture Series.

De Vos, G. A. (1971, March). *Japan's outcastes: The problem of the Burakumin.* London: Minority Rights Group, Report No. 3.

De Vos, G. A. (1973). *Socialization for achievement: Essays on the cultural psychology of the Japanese.* Berkeley: University of California Press.

De Vos, G. A. (1974). Cross-cultural studies of mental disorder: An anthropological perspective. In G. Caplan (Ed.), *American handbook of psychiatry* (Vol. 3, pp. 551–567). New York: Basic Books.

De Vos, G. A. (1975a). Apprenticeship and paternalism: Psychocultural continuities underlying Japanese social organization. In E. Vogel (Ed.), *Modern Japanese organization and decision making* (pp. 20–227). Berkeley: University of California Press.

De Vos, G. A. (1975b). Japan's international future: Cultural dilemmas in citizenship and social belonging. In *Proceedings of the 2nd Tsukuba International Symposium on the Role of Japan in the Future World of Technology, Economy and Culture* (pp. 45–64). University of Tsukuba, Japan.

De Vos, G. A. (1976). The interrelationship of social and psychological structures in trans-cultural psychiatry. In W. Lebra (Ed.), *Culture-bound syndromes, ethnopsychiatry, and alternate therapies* (pp. 278–298). Honolulu: University of Hawaii Press.

De Vos, G. A. (1978a). Adaptation and adjustment: Cross-cultural perspective on mental health. *Colloquia in anthropology* (Vol. 2, pp. 21–45). Taos, NM: Fort Burgwin Research Center, Southern Methodist University.

De Vos, G. A. (1978b). The Japanese adapt to change. In G. Spindler (Ed.), *The making of psychological anthropology* (pp. 217–257). Berkeley: University of California Press.

De Vos, G. A. (1978c). Selective permeability and reference groups' sanctioning: Psychocultural continuities in role degradation. In M. Yinger (Ed.), *Major social issues: A multi-community view* (pp. 9–24). Glencoe, IL: Free Press.

De Vos, G. A. (1980a). Afterword. In D. Reynolds, *The quiet therapies* (pp. 113–132). Honolulu: University of Hawaii Press.

De Vos, G. A. (1980b). Delinquency and minority status: A psychocultural perspective. In G. Newman (Ed.), *Crime and deviancy: A comparative perspective* (pp. 130–180). Beverly Hills, CA: Sage.

De Vos, G. A. (1980c). L'Identité ethnique et le statut de minorité. In P. Tap (Ed.), *Identitiés collectives et changements sociaux* (pp. 27–38). Toulouse, France: Privat.

De Vos, G. A. (1982). Adaptive strategies in American minorities. In E. E. Jones & S. Korchin (Eds.), *Minority mental health* (pp. 74–117). New York: Praeger.

De Vos, G. A. (1983a). Achievement motivation and intra-family attitudes in immigrant Koreans. *Journal of Psychoanalytic Anthropology, 6*(2), 125–162.

De Vos, G. A. (1983b). Adaptive conflict and adjustive coping: Psychocultural approaches to ethnic identity. In T. Sarbin & K. E. Scheibe (Eds.), *Studies in social identity* (pp. 204–230). New York: Praeger.

De Vos, G. A. (1984a). Ethnic identity and minority status: Some psychocultural considerations. In A. Jacobson-Widding (Ed.), *Identity: Personal and socio-cultural.* Stockholm, Sweden: Almquist & Wiksell International.

De Vos, G. A. (1984b). *The incredibility of Western prophets*. Amsterdam: University of Amsterdam Press.

De Vos, G. A. (1984c). *Institutions for change in Japanese society* (Research Papers and Policy Studies, No. 9). Berkeley: University of California, Berkeley, Institute of East Asian Studies.

De Vos, G. A. (1985a). Dimensions of self in Japanese culture. In A. Marsella, G. De Vos, & F. Hsu (Eds.), *Culture and self: Asian and Western perspectives* (pp. 141–184). London: Metheun.

De Vos, G. A. (1985b). Japanese citizenship and Korean ethnic identity: Can they be reconciled? A psychocultural dilemma. In *Korean residents in Japan and Korea–Japan relations* (pp. 107–134). Seoul, Korea: International Cultural Society of Korea.

De Vos, G. A. (1986a). Confucian family socialization: The religion, morality and aesthetics of propriety. In W. Slote (Ed.), *The psycho-cultural dynamics of the Confucian family: Past and present* (Forum Series No. 8, pp. 327–412). Seoul, Korea: International Cultural Society of Korea.

De Vos, G. A. (1986b). Japanese citizenship and Korean ethnic identity: Can they be reconciled? A psychocultural dilemma. *Seoul Law Journal, 27*(1), 75–100.

De Vos, G. A. (1992a). A cross cultural perspective: The Japanese family as a unit in moral socialization. In P. Cowan, J. Filed, D. Hansen, M. Scolnick, & G. Swanson (Eds.), *Family, self, and society: Towards a new agenda for family research* (pp. 115–142). Hillsdale NJ: Erlbaum.

De Vos, G. A. (1992b). *Social cohesion and alienation: Minorities in the United States and Japan*. Boulder, CO: Westview Press.

De Vos, G. A. (1993). The rites of pleasure: The religion, morality and aesthetics of bodily propriety. In I. Dosamantes (Ed.), *Body image in cultural context: Interdisciplinary essays* (pp. 35–63). Los Angeles: DMT Publications.

De Vos, G. A. (1994a). Japanese sense of self: A review. *Journal of Japanese Studies, 20*(2), 187–194.

De Vos, G. A. (1994b). Psychological anthropology: A professional odyssey. In B. Boyer, R. Boyer, & H. F. Stein (Eds.), *The psychoanalytic study of society* (Vol. 19, pp. 23–88). Hillsdale, NJ: Analytic Press.

De Vos, G. A. (1995). Ethnic pluralism: Conflict and accommodation. In L. Romanucci-Ross & G. De Vos (Eds.), *Ethnic identity: Creation, conflict, and accommodation* (pp. 15–48). London: Altamira Press.

De Vos, G. A. (1996). Internalized achievement or external authority: Some cultural comparisons of responses to TAT Card 1. In I. B. Weiner (Ed.), *Rorschachiana XXI yearbook of the International Rorschach Society*. Göttingen: Hogrefe & Huber.

De Vos, G., & Bock, A. (1975). *Themes in Japanese society as seen through the Japanese film*. Berkeley: University of California, Pacific Film Archive.

De Vos, G., & Borders, O. (1979). A Rorschach comparison of delinquent and non-delinquent Japanese family members. *Journal of Psychological Anthropology, 2*(4), 425–442.

De Vos, G., & Boyer, L. B. (1989). *Symbolic analysis cross-culturally: The Rorschach Test*. Berkeley: University of California Press.

De Vos, G., & Dahl, W. (1974). *Japanese culture through the camera's eye.* Berkeley: University of California Extension.

De Vos, G., Hauswald, L., & Borders, O. (1979). Cultural differences in family socialization: A psychocultural comparison of Chinese and Japanese. In A. Craig (Ed.), *Japan: A comparative view* (pp. 214–269). Princeton, NJ: Princeton University Press.

De Vos, G. A., & Kim, E. Y. (1993a). Koreans in Japan: Problems with achievement, alienation, and authority. In I. Light & P. Bhachu (Eds.), *California immigrants in world perspective.* New Brunswick, NJ: Transaction Books.

De Vos, G. A., & Kim, E. Y. (1993b). Problems with achievement, alienation, and authority in Korean minorities in the United States and Japan. In K. K. Lee & W. Slote (Eds.), *Overseas Koreans in the global context* (pp. 145–180). Seoul, Korea: Association for the Study of Koreans Abroad.

De Vos, G., & Mizushima, K. (1962). The school and delinquency: Perspectives from Japan. *Teachers College Record, 63*(8), 626–638.

De Vos, G., & Mizushima, K. (1967). Organization and social function of Japanese gangs. In R. P. Dore (Ed.), *Aspects of social change in modern Japan* (pp. 289–325). Princeton, NJ: Princeton University Press.

De Vos, G., & Murakami, E. (1974). Violence and aggression in fantasy: A comparison of American and Japanese lower-class youth. In W. Lebra (Ed.), *Youth, socialization and mental health* (pp. 153–177). Honolulu: University of Hawaii Press.

De Vos, G., Murakami, E., & Murase, T. (1964). Recent research, psychodiagnosis, and therapy in Japan. In L. Abt & B. F. Reiss, (Eds.), *Progress in clinical psychology* (pp. 226–234). New York: Grune & Stratton.

De Vos, G. A., & Sofue, T. (Eds.). (1986). *Religion and the family in east Asia* (Rev. ed.). Berkeley: University of California Press.

De Vos, G., & Suárez-Orozco, M. (1986). Child development in Japan and the United States: Prospectives of cross-cultural comparison. In H. Stevenson, H. Azuma, & K. Hakuta (Eds.), *Child development and education in Japan* (pp. 289–298). New York: Freeman.

De Vos, G., & Suárez-Orozco, M. (1990a). *Social cohesion and alienation: Minorities in the United States and Japan.* Boulder, CO: Westview Press.

De Vos, G. A., & Suárez-Orozco, M. (1990b). *Status inequality: The self in culture.* Newbury Park, CA: Sage.

De Vos, G. A., & Tsuda, T. (1996). Socialization and social validity: A psychocultural perspective. In A. Clesse (Ed.), *The vitality of Japan.* Luxembourg: Institute of Economic and Industrial Studies.

De Vos, G. A., & Wagatsuma, H. (1959). Psycho-cultural significance of concern over death and illness among rural Japanese. *International Journal of Social Psychiatry, 5*(1), 6–19.

De Vos, G., & Wagatsuma, H. (1961). Value attitudes toward role behavior of women in two Japanese villages. *American Anthropologist, 63*(6), 1204–1230.

De Vos, G., & Wagatsuma, H. (1966). *Japan's invisible race: Caste in culture and personality.* Berkeley: University of California Press.

De Vos, G., & Wagatsuma, H. (1969). Minority status and delinquency in Japan. In W. Caudill & Tsung-yi-Lin (Eds.), *Mental health research in Asia and the Pacific* (pp. 342–357). Honolulu: University of Hawaii Press.

De Vos, G., & Wagatsuma, H. (1970). Status and role behavior in changing Japan: Psycho-cultural continuities. In G. Seward & R. C. Williams (Eds.), *Sex roles in changing society* (pp. 334–370). New York: Random House.

De Vos, G. A., & Wagatsuma, H. (1996). Cultural identity and minority status in Japan. In L. Romanucci-Ross & G. A. De Vos (Eds.), *Ethnic identity: Creation, conflict, and accommodation.* London: Altamira Press.

De Vos, G., & Wetherall, W. (1974). *Japan's minorities.* London: Minority Rights Group.

Doi, T. (1973). *Anatomy of dependence.* Tokyo: Kodansha International.

Dore, R. (1958). *City life in Japan.* Berkeley: University of California Press.

Dore, R. P. (Ed.). (1967). *Aspects of social change in modern Japan.* Princeton, NJ: Princeton University Press.

Durkheim, E. (1947). *The elementary forms of the religious life.* Glencoe, IL: Free Press.

Gallimore, R., Boggs, J., & Jordan, C. (1974). *Culture, behavior and education: A study of Hawaiian-Americans.* Beverly Hills, CA: Sage.

Gorer, G. (1943). Themes in Japanese culture. *New York Academy of Science, 5,* 106–124.

Gough, H., De Vos, G., & Mizushima, K. (1968). A Japanese validation of the CPI Social Maturity Index. *Psychological Reports, 22,* 143–146.

Howard, A. (1971). *Households, families and friends in a Hawaiian-American community* (Working paper 19). Honolulu: East-West Population Institute.

Howard, A. (1974). *Ain't no big thing.* Honolulu: University of Hawaii Press.

Kagan, S. (1974). Field independence and conformity of rural Mexican and Urban Anglo-American children. *Child Development, 45,* 765–771.

Kagan, S., & Buriel, R. (1977). Field dependence-independence and Mexican-American culture and education. In J. Martinez, (Ed.), *Chicano psychology.* New York: Academic Press.

Kashiwagi, K. (1986). Personality development of adolescents. In H. Stevenson, H. Azuma, & K. Hakuta (Eds.), *Child development and education in Japan* (167–185). New York: Freeman.

La Barre, W. (1945). Some observations on character structure in the Orient. *Psychiatry, 8,* 319–342.

Lanham, B. (1956). Aspects of child care in Japan: Preliminary report. In D. G. Haring (Ed.), *Personal character and cultural Milieu* (pp. 69–89). Syracuse, NY: Syracuse University Press.

Lanham, B. (1962). *Aspects of child-rearing in Kainan, Japan.* Unpublished doctoral dissertation, Syracuse University.

Lebra, T., & Lebra, W. (1976). *Japanese patterns of behavior.* Honolulu: University of Hawaii Press.

Lee, C. S., & De Vos, G. (1981). *Koreans in Japan: Ethnic conflict and accommodation.* Berkeley: University of California Press.

Lock, M. (1991). Flawed jewels and national disorder: Narratives on adolescent dissent in Japan. *Journal of Psychohistory, 18*(4), 443–456.

Lynd, H. (1958). *On shame and the search for identity.* New York: Wiley.

Madsen, M. (1967). Cooperative and competitive motivation of children in three Mexican subcultures. *Psychological Reports, 20,* 1307–1320.

Malzberg, B. (1969). Are immigrants psychologically disturbed? In S. Plog & R. Edgerton (Eds.), *Changing perspectives in mental illness* (pp. 395–421). New York: Holt, Rinehart & Winston.

Malzburg, B., & Lee, E. E. (1956). *Migration and mental disease: A study of first admissions to hospitals for mental disease.* New York: Social Science Research Council.

McClelland, D. (Ed.). (1955). *Studies in motivation.* New York: Appleton.

McClelland, D. (1961). *The achieving society.* Princeton, NJ: Van Nostrand.

McClelland, D., Atkinson, J. W., Clark, R. H., & Lowelle, E. L. (1953). *The achievement motive.* New York: Appleton-Century-Crofts.

Mead, G. H. (1936). *Mind, self and society.* Chicago: University of Chicago Press.

Merton, R. (1949). *Social theory and social structure.* Glencoe, IL: Free Press.

Miyake, K., Chen, S., & Campos, J. (1986). Infant temperament, mother's mode of interaction, and attachment in Japan: An interim report. In I. Bretherton & E. Waters (Eds.), Growing points of attachment theory and research. *Monographs of the Society for Research in Child Development, 50*(Serial No. 209), 276–297.

Mizushima, K., & De Vos, G. (1967). An application of the California Psychological Inventory in a study of Japanese delinquency. *Journal of Social Psychology, 71,* 45–51.

Morioka, K. (1986). Ancestor worship in contemporary Japan: Continuity and change. In G. A. De Vos & T. Sofue (Eds.), *Religion and the family in east Asia* (Rev. ed., pp. 201–216). Berkeley: University of California Press.

Muramatsu, T. (1962). *Nihonjin bunka to pasonaritei no jissho-teki kenkyu [An empirical study in culture and personality].* Tokyo: Reimei Shobo.

Nakane, C. (1970). *Japanese society.* Berkeley: University of California Press.

Ogbu, J. (1978). *Minority education and caste: The American system in cross-cultural perspective.* New York: Academic Press.

Ogbu, J. (1991). Minority coping responses and school experience. *Journal of Psychohistory, 18*(4), 443–456.

Piers, G., & Singer, M. B. (1953). *Shame and guilt: A psychoanalytic and cultural study.* Springfield IL: Charles C Thomas.

Slote, W., & De Vos, G. A. (Eds.). (1996). *Confucianism and the family in an interdisciplinary, comparative context.* Albany: State University of New York Press.

Stevenson, H., Azuma, H., & Hakuta, K. (Eds.). (1986). *Child development and education in Japan.* New York: Freeman.

Suárez-Orozco, M. (Ed.). (1991). Belonging and alienation: Essays in honor of George De Vos. *Journal of Psychohistory, 18*(4), 443–456.

Taniguchi, M., De Vos, G., & Murakami, E. (1958). Identification of mother and father cards on the Rorschach by Japanese normal and delinquent adolescents. *Journal of Projective Techniques, 22*(4), 453–460.

Vaughn, C. (1988). *Cognitive independence, social independence, and achievement orientation: A comparison of Japanese and U.S. students.* Unpublished doctoral dissertation, University of California, Berkeley.

Vogel, E. (1962). Entrance examinations and emotional disturbances in Japan's "new middle class." In J. Smith & R. Beardsley (Eds.), *Japanese culture: Its development and characteristics* (pp. 140–152). Chicago: Aldine.

Vogel, E. (1963). *Japan's new middle class.* Berkeley: University of California Press.

Vogel, E. (Ed.). (1975). *Modern Japanese organization and decision making.* Berkeley: University of California Press.

Wagatsuma, H., & De Vos, G. (1962). Attitudes toward arranged marriage in rural Japan. *Human Organization, 21*(3), 187–200.

Wagatsuma, H., & De Vos, G. (1967). The outcaste tradition in modern Japan: A problem in social self-identity. In R. P. Dore (Ed.), *Aspects of social change in modern Japan* (pp. 373–407). Princeton, NJ: Princeton University Press.

Wagatsuma, H., & De Vos, G. (1978). A koan of sincerity: Osama Dazai. *Hartford Studies in Literature, 10*(2), 156–181.

Wagatsuma, H., & De Vos, G. (1980). Arakawa Ward: Urban growth and modernization. *Rice University Studies: The cultural context: Essays in honor of Edward Norbeck, 66*(1), 201–224.

Wagatsuma, H., & De Vos, G. (1984). *Heritage of endurance: Family patterns and delinquency formation in urban Japan.* Berkeley: University of California Press.

Witkin, H. A. (1967). Cognitive styles across cultures. *International Journal of Psychology, 2,* 233–250.

Witkin, H. A. (1969). Social influences in the development of cognitive style. In D. A. Goslin (Ed.), *Handbook of socialization theory and research.* New York: Rand Mc Nally.

Witkin, H. A., Price-Williams, D., Bertini, M., Christiansen, B., Oltman, P. K., Ramirez, M., & Van Meel, J. (1974). Social conformity and psychological differentiation. *International Journal of Psychology, 9,* 11–29.

Witkin, H. A., with Berry, J. W. (1975). Psychological differentiation in cross-cultural perspective. *Journal of Cross-Cultural Psychology, 6,* 4–87.

Socialization and School Adaptation
On the Lifework of George De Vos

Curtis A. Vaughn

George De Vos has excavated deep and broad channels through the infrastructure of various social science theories. His work, while contributing to our understanding of Japanese personality development, achievement, and ethnicity, raises numerous significant questions to be asked in future comparative research.

De Vos's collaborative research on Japanese-American minority adaptation and achievement motivation, begun in the late 1940s at the University of Chicago, continues to be instructive in understanding the complexity of adaptation to social change. One lesson I learned from his earliest research with Japanese-Americans is that a given set of adverse economic and sociological forces may have a variety of consequences, depending on the minority group (De Vos, 1982, 1980). For example, children of Japanese immigrants since the 1930s on have achieved well in American schools, despite their parents' deficiencies in English and their own difficulty with English on achievement tests. In light of this example, De Vos has noted the misapplication of linguistic theories to explain ethnic differences in successful school adaptation (De Vos, 1992). With respect to the Japanese, he has brought to our attention a broader set of psychocultural considerations in looking at successful school adaptation, such as how the peer group and the Confucian-based family tradition facilitate learning at school.

In his work on ethnic minority adaptation to social degradation, he has stressed the importance of a sense of cultural history and shown how self-perceptions strongly influence adjustive reactions (De Vos, 1978). The interface between Japanese culture and the adjustment of Japanese-Americans to the harsh circumstances of forced relocation during World War II was a topic in his early work (Caudill & De Vos, 1956), while correlates of social cohesion and alienation in minorities in Japan and the United States is a more recent theme (De Vos, 1992). He has avoided the pitfall of explaining complex social behavior as solely a function of a single set of constructs, for example, those related only to individual psychology, sociology, or culture. As noted in an article entitled "The Japanese Adapt to Change" (De Vos, 1978), he has been "forever critical of any formal social science generalization that leaves out concern with the intense reality of subjective personal experience" (p. 219).

In reconciling his psychological orientation with a structural view of society, and within the multidisciplinary culture and personality approach, he has been influenced by the works of Kardiner, Mead, Bateson, Hallowell, and Du Bois. Also noticeable are the influences of Henry Murray's (1938, 1943) work with the Thematic Apperception Test (TAT) and the work of Parsons and Bales (1955), who analyzed primary family role behavior in terms of "instrumental" and "expressive" categories. As a psychological anthropologist, he includes insights and observations from philosophical and historical perspectives. His methods range from quantitative psychological tests to the analysis of literature and biography.

Another scholar once described De Vos's contributions to me as those of an architect, in contrast to the brick-laying activities in which many of us engage as we test other people's theoretical assumptions. Another colleague referred to De Vos's blending of observations and theoretical assumptions from different pools of knowledge as that of an "interpretive anthropologist."

De Vos has been criticized for his emphasis on the total cultural context, and a lack of specificity regarding the distributive locus of culture in his conceptualization of achievement motivation. In a review of *Socialization for Achievement: Essays on the Cultural Psychology of the Japanese* (De Vos, 1973), Bennett (1974) noted that more uniformity in the process of socialization has been assumed than is justified. If culture is distributed unequally and unevenly, cultural patterns of socialization and child training will not be uniform.

Such criticism is less applicable to De Vos's description of family patterns and delinquency formation in Japan. In *Heritage of En-*

durance, Wagatsuma and De Vos's (1984) analysis of a cross-section of youth confirms a number of previously held notions about the influences of family life on delinquency. Similar psychological and social factors were shown to be at work in Japan and the United States. In both cultures, social deviancy in youth was described as more likely to occur among those experiencing neglect or deprivation in their formative years. They described features of Japanese adaptation to problems of delinquency that now deserve reexamination. Are the Japanese community-based voluntary associations and social networks involved with problems of delinquency and its prevention presently functioning as they were during the 1960s, when De Vos and Wagatsuma conducted their fieldwork? How have parental relationships, delinquency, and attitudes toward responsibility and authority changed?

When these issues are examined in the future, the approach will likely be different. Unless developmental psychologists are trained to integrate several levels of analysis (e.g., psychological, social, historical), we will not benefit from the holistic focus of research characteristic of studies like *Heritage of Endurance.* Longitudinal research combining intensive interviews with observations and psychological testing is expensive, but will financial constraints lessen our ability to replicate earlier research?

MY OWN RESEARCH

The ultimate test of one's doubts regarding methodological and theoretical concerns is systematic confirmatory data collection. Before I first conducted my own research in Japan, I believed that the TAT was "outdated" and of little value. I was also critical of the small samples in some of the earlier research cited by De Vos (1973). My skepticism diminished after I collected large samples of thematic concerns from Japanese adolescents, and discovered for myself the validity of the projective hypothesis.

During the summer of 1986, accompanied by my Japanese wife and two young children, I went to Japan and gathered psychological test data from 969 students at six different high schools. Several months later I returned to California and collected similar data on stratified samples of economically and ethnically diverse American high school students. Since then I have returned to Japan twice and collected follow-up data at one of the schools and new materials at another high school.

Boys from a high school not known for academics preen their hair, sitting casually on the subway floor, Nagoya, 1996. Courtesy of Davy Shwalb.

One goal of my trips subsequent to the 1986 visit has been to review with Japanese researchers and students the results of previously collected data, particularly projective materials. This allowed me to check whether responses and my interpretations reflected the reality of Japanese self-perceptions. By presenting such data to members of the various ethnic groups in one's sample, I can see if there is any "empathetic identification" with the subject responses through what I call "process consultation." This is important for projective materials collected for the purpose of sampling value orientations. One needs to know if the feelings and attitudes expressed in written stories reflect the generalized concerns of a social group.

One area in which both De Vos and I have been interested is the development of self-sufficiency and actual competence among schoolage children. Trained at Berkeley in educational and school psychology, and having spent 9 years working professionally as a psychologist with multiethnic school populations in California, I have been interested in influences on school adaptation and in the reasons why so many children cannot learn at school.

In the remainder of this reaction to De Vos's chapter I will focus on the interrelated areas of socialization and cognition in successful school adaptation. In comparative research, using the California Psychological Inventory (CPI), TAT, and Group Embedded Figures Test, I have attempted to test several of De Vos's contentions related to Japanese social motivation.

In his chapter De Vos offers a compelling statement supporting the value of psychological testing in cross-cultural research, based upon his training in both clinical psychology and anthropology. Nevertheless, because of his extensive experience in using a wide range of assessment techniques, De Vos is quite aware of the limitations of psychological testing.

Research has in fact shown that the psychometric properties of several test instruments, particularly regarding construct validity, are consistent across cultures and are relatively free of bias when used appropriately. Various measures of intellectual functioning have been found to differentiate adequately both intellectually gifted and disadvantaged individuals across Asian, African-American, Hispanic, and Caucasian-American populations (Miele, 1979; Sandoval, 1979).

A number of psychological instruments have been specifically designed for cross-cultural research. A clear and definitive goal of the CPI has been to provide measures that retain their validity in cross-cultural application. With concepts chosen to reflect attributes of interpersonal behavior found in all cultures and societies, the test has been used in hundreds of studies. It has been used successfully with Chinese subjects (e.g., Abbott, 1970) and in Japan (e.g., Mizushima & De Vos, 1967). Several of the scales on the CPI, such as the Socialization scale and measures of intellectual efficiency and achievement potential, have correlated consistently with academic achievement in cross-national comparisons.

Socialization for Achievement Revisited

In order to succeed in formal educational settings, a child must develop an adequate respect for rules, responsiveness to what others feel and think, and a sense of interpersonal obligation. Such are the attributes measured on the Socialization scale (So) of the CPI. This scale classifies individuals along a continuum of socialization, proceeding from highly asocial at one end to highly socialized and respectful of rules at the other. Low socialization scores tend to reflect a lack of or unperceptive concern for the inner needs and feelings of others, or for the nuances of interpersonal relations (Megargee, 1972). While the scale is not a measure of "social dependence," it taps into aspects of social orientation that reflect social sensitivity and empathy, and contains items about warmth, satisfaction, family stability, resentment, and alienation. Higher So scores indicate a more "interdependent social orientation," a sense of self-identity that is more open to external guidance, and a tendency to pay more attention to social cues.

Attributes associated with high So scores are similar to those frequently used to describe a "Japanese" social orientation. De Vos has noted that the Japanese develop a self that is very sensitive to the opinions of significant others. As a Japanese, one's internal frame of reference includes a strong awareness of the continuity between self and nonself (De Vos, personal communication, 1983). The developing Japanese child is sensitized to interpersonal consequences of his or her actions, and the Japanese mother emphasizes an inherent capacity for empathy within the child, who then learns that behavior has consequences for injury to others (De Vos & Suárez-Orozco, 1986). These early interactions are a precursor to the mentor–student relationship in school, and serve as a foundation for socially interdependent behavior. Sensitivity and responsiveness to the expectations of others is necessary for a child to be receptive to instruction.

In my comparative research on Japanese and American adolescents, the Socialization variable accounts for the most explained variance among the several factors correlated with academic achievement. Given a certain minimum level of cognitive ability, an appropriately socialized attitude and behavioral disposition are necessary to accomplish goals that fall within the average range of difficulty. This is painfully evident to psychologists and teachers who work with socially maladjusted or delinquent children, whose academic achievement is frequently below the expected level based on their intellectual functioning and age.

Socialization also emerged as a meaningfully significant between-country variable. The mean score for the Japanese high school students (32.34) was significantly higher than their U.S. counterparts (28.81), although variance was equal between the two cultural groups.

The Self in Achievement Motivation Theory

Achievement motivation has been a central theme in much of De Vos's work on the Japanese. He has noted a sharp contrast between the social orientation typically found in Japanese achievement-related attitudes, and descriptions of achievement motivation in the United States (De Vos, 1973). Theories of achievement motivation representative of attitudes and behavior in the United States emphasize concepts of self-reliance and independence (Heckhausen,

1967; McClelland, Atkinson, Clark, & Lowell, 1976). According to such theorists, achievement-oriented persons are highly concerned with a sense of separate identity. Japanese self-concerns more typically involve the development of strong affiliative and dependency needs.

In examining the projective stories written in response to the TAT, both De Vos, in his earlier studies, and I, more recently, have found notable differences between the categories of Japanese and American motivational concerns. What is most interesting is the continuity between the interpersonal concerns first observed in projective stories collected by De Vos 4 decades ago with the motivational concerns of youth in the 1990s. Moreover, psychocultural continuities in Japanese social motivation are paralleled by continuity in different motivational concerns in sets of data collected in the United States. From a comparative perspective, one sees evidence of intergenerational continuation in Japanese and American value orientations. Among Japanese adolescents there continues to be a strong emphasis on self-initiated achievement, concerns over adequacy, and the perception of interdependence with significant others in the achievement context.

According to my research, Japanese adolescents perceive the usefulness of effort and hard work to a far greater degree than do the adolescents in the United States. In addition, competence (concerns over adequacy in meeting achievement-related goals) is a more pressing issue for Japanese adolescents. In a society where entrance to public schools is based upon achieved status, Japanese pupils know that they must study hard. The association between hard work, self-sacrifice, and educational rewards are clearly visible to Japanese students. One would be hard-pressed to imagine in any American city, groups of junior high students regularly attending afterschool evening classes in order to pass an entrance exam for public high school. Such activities are for many high-achieving Japanese students normative behavior patterns.

In projective materials, particularly those of students from the more competitive Japanese high schools, self-initiated achievement and concerns over adequacy in completing a task frequently emerge as salient themes in TAT Card 1 (a boy looking at a violin) responses. Card 1 is perhaps the single most valuable picture in the TAT, and is most useful to make statements about the total personality or achievement-related value orientations.

In contrast, the salient interpersonal concerns of American adolescents, in data collected from ethnically and economically diverse samples, revolve around ambivalence toward authority and the assertion of individual decision making. In Japanese projective stories, personal feelings and concerns of the characters are usually subordinated to an internalized achievement orientation that mirrors externally defined obligations.

The following extracts illustrate Card 1 stories, one from a high-achieving Japanese adolescent and a contrasting one from an American adolescent. The stories reflect motivational concerns that are representative of more Japanese versus American social orientations. Both illustrative responses are from students at relatively high-achieving schools (Vaughn, 1992).

> #599 (Japanese): He is worrying. He is feeling some discouragement about playing the violin because he has been practicing but can't see a big improvement. He is thinking about quitting his lessons, but the instructor is encouraging him to continue. After this state of worrying he will get strong encouragement/inspiration (*satori o hiraku*). Then he will practice very hard and splendidly became a great violinist.

In U.S. samples themes are frequently related to conflict between autonomy and authority, as represented in the following story from an American adolescent. Self-concerns are viewed as more independent of the wishes of others. In American adolescent fantasies, achievement-related pursuits are often viewed as a "negotiable issue," and parents are seen as acquiescing to the child's wishes. In the American context, peer-related motivational concerns are frequently depicted as opposed to the goals sanctioned by parents.

> #1038 (American): The boy is looking at the violin. His mom and teacher want him to play and practice for his big recital which is coming up next week. He doesn't like playing and just got in a fight with his mom about it. He's gonna talk to his dad about whether or not he still has to play it. He wants to join a baseball team with all his friends. If he joins the team his parents know he'll never have time to play the violin, but they know he doesn't like playing it and they want him to be happy.

Employing a system for coding interpersonal concerns in materials from cross-culturally diverse subject populations, it is possible to examine statistical differences in qualitative data. Analyses of coded projective stories from students at relatively high-achieving Japanese and American schools shows that American adolescent stories emphasize opposition to parental authority and a separation of self from others. Although some Japanese Card 1 responses fall into such a "parental pressure" category, the stories are typically resolved in congruence with parental expectations, with little separation of self-oriented concerns from the motivational concerns of others.

There are also between-school differences within each country comparing low- and high-achieving schools, which suggest qualitatively different levels of adjustment in adolescence. For instance, negatively toned expressive concerns are noted more often in the projective stories of the lower-achieving Japanese adolescents (Vaughn, 1992).

Cognitive Independence and the Japanese

Japanese adolescents are less openly oppositional toward authority than American adolescents and have a more socially dependent achievement orientation, yet they are cognitively more field-independent than American adolescents (Vaughn, 1988). Contrary to Witkin's psychological differentiation theory (Witkin, Dyk, Faterson, Goodenough, & Karp, 1974), as noted by De Vos (Chapter 4, this volume), the Japanese are not consistent across psychological domains in terms of independence (i.e., social vs. cognitive). De Vos was one of the first investigators to hypothesize that the Japanese might be higher on the cognitive-style dimension of field independence than Americans.

Successful school adaptation, as well as success at many vocational and professional activities, involves the ability to break down or analyze a problem as a step toward its solution. In cross-cultural research it can be useful to present "work samples" to see how differently individuals perform on tasks, especially with tasks that predict educational–vocational pursuits. Studies that have examined the relationship of educational and vocational interests show that responses of people who are more field-independent are similar to those of people in the math and science domains (e.g., Witkin & Goodenough, 1977), areas of performance in which the Japanese have excelled.

The stimulus properties of the Group Embedded Figures Test are relatively free of content that might be more familiar to Japanese or American students. Based upon samples from six Japanese high schools and three high schools in California, the Japanese students performed significantly better (means: Japan = 16.16; United States = 10.26). There is considerable variation within the U.S. school population in terms of ethnic diversity and school achievement, which one must take into account when looking at

the aggregate scores. A within-country comparison of pupils between the three U.S. schools reveals that not only is there a main
effect for ethnicity in cognitive field independence, but that significant differences between schools correspond with relative ranking on achievement test criteria. Within the Japanese sample there
is a similar ranking with overall scores for pupils at the more competitive schools significantly higher than those at less competitive
schools (Vaughn, 1988). Yet even students at the lowest ranked Japanese school, where teachers described their students as "less capable" or less able to keep up with the prescribed curriculum, had
higher cognitive independence scores than students at a California
school that is among the top 10 in the state.

SOCIAL CHANGE: ACCULTURATION
AND ETHNIC IDENTITY

During a recent stay in Japan I was told by members of the older
generation that Japanese youth today have fewer opportunities
than did their fathers and grandfathers. A grandson working for a
large corporation may have less chance of becoming a section chief
than did his grandfather, because of the large number of individuals competing for the same position in today's economy. Mothers
describe their school-age children growing up in the large cities as
sacrificing their free time for an overcompetitive school system. As
one parent told me, "Our children cannot dream big dreams; they
have fewer alternatives."

In order to achieve instrumental goals or satisfy expressive concerns, some Japanese adolescents are seeking educational opportunities abroad. They have become agents of change, and a growing
number of Japanese high schools are having to adapt to these students with international experience. While teaching at a high
school in Yokohama, I was told by Japanese teachers how difficult
it is to instruct students who have lived abroad, particularly return-
ees who express individuality by deviating from the order of the
group. My observations suggest one problem these students face is
their lack of opportunity to integrate experiences abroad into the
educational experiences they receive upon returning to Japan.

In closing, I pose the following questions for future research,
which reflect some of the ongoing concerns in George De Vos's
work. How is the identity of returnee students maintained as a result of continual contact between members of different cultures?
What adjustments have they made in regard to reference group

allegiances and social-role expectations? To what extent are returning students like members of a minority group within Japanese culture?

One goal of developmental psychology is to identify adaptive and adjustive patterns of both students and teachers in the acculturative process and to translate these insights into learning. Since acculturation implies that the borrowing groups' members are conscious of what is taking place and that they are conscious of the advisability of change (De Vos, 1976), our research should be sensitive to how adolescents view their own cross-cultural experiences. Focus groups (e.g., Krueger, 1988), which have high face validity and facilitate sharing of insights not available from individual interviews, questionnaires, or other data sources, can be useful in promoting self-disclosure among adolescents. Focus groups can be used as both research and educational tools.

As we look to the future, De Vos's concepts of "selective permeability" and "affective dissonance" will continue to be instructive, by directing attention to interpersonal influences on receptivity to learning. He has taught us that contact between cultures produces a potential for conflict as well as opportunities for learning and occupational specialization. If we keep this thought in mind, perhaps we can help our children to dream big dreams.

REFERENCES

Abbott, K. A. (1970). Harmony and individualism: Changing Chinese psychosocial functioning in Taipei and San Francisco. *Asian Folklore and Social Life Monographs, 12.*

Bennett, J. W. (1974). The Japanese character. *Reviews in Anthropology, 1,* 469–484.

Caudill, W., & De Vos, G. (1956). Achievement, culture and personality: The case of the Japanese Americans. *American Anthropologist, 58*(6), 1102–1126.

De Vos, G. A. (Ed.). (1973). *Socialization for achievement: Essays on the cultural psychology of the Japanese.* Berkeley: University of California Press.

De Vos, G. A. (Ed.). (1976). *Responses to change: Society, culture, and personality.* New York: Van Nostrand.

De Vos, G. A. (1978). The Japanese adapt to change. In G. D. Spindler (Ed.), *The making of psychological anthropology* (pp. 217–257). Berkeley: University of California Press.

De Vos, G. A. (1980). Ethnic adaptation and minority status. *Journal of Cross-Cultural Psychology, 11,* 101–125.

De Vos, G. A. (1982). Adaptive strategies in U.S. minorities. In E. E. Jones & S. Korchin (Eds.), *Minority mental health* (pp. 74–117). New York: Praeger.

De Vos, G. A. (1992). *Social cohesion and alienation: Minorities in the United States and Japan.* San Francisco: Westview Press.

De Vos, G. A., & Romanucci-Ross, L. (Eds.). (1982). *Ethnic identity: Cultural continuities and change.* Chicago: University of Chicago Press.

De Vos, G. A., & Suárez-Orozco, M. M. (1986). Child development in Japan and the United States: Prospective of cross-cultural comparisons. In H. Stevenson, H. Azuma, & K. Hakuta (Eds.), *Child development and education in Japan* (pp. 289–298). New York: Freeman.

Heckhausen, H. (1967). *The anatomy of achievement motivation.* New York: Academic Press.

Krueger, R. A. (1988). *Focus groups: A practical guide for applied research.* London: Sage.

McClelland, D. C., Atkinson, J. W., Clark, R. A., & Lowell, E. L. (1976). *The achievement motive.* New York: Irvington.

Megargee, E. I. (1972). *The California Psychological Inventory handbook.* San Francisco: Jossey-Bass.

Miele, F. (1979). Cultural bias in the WISC-R. *Intelligence, 3,* 149–164.

Mizushima, K., & De Vos, G. (1967). An application of the California Psychological Inventory in a study of Japanese delinquency. *Journal of Social Psychology, 71,* 45–71.

Murray, H. A. (1938). *Explorations in personality.* New York: Oxford University Press.

Murray, H. A. (1943). *Thematic Apperception Test manual.* Cambridge, MA: Harvard University Printing Office.

Parsons, T., & Bales, R. (1955). *Family socialization and interaction process.* Glencoe, IL: Free Press.

Sandoval, J. (1979). The WISC-R and internal evidence of test bias with minority groups. *Journal of Consulting and Clinical Psychology, 47,* 919–927.

Vaughn, C. (1988). *Cognitive independence, social independence, and achievement orientation: A comparison of Japanese and U.S. students.* Unpublished doctoral dissertation, University of California, Berkeley.

Vaughn, C. (1992). *The reflected self in adolescent fantasy: A comparison of American and Japanese motivational concerns.* Unpublished manuscript.

Wagatsuma, H., & De Vos, G. A. (1984). *Heritage of endurance: Family patterns and delinquency formation in urban Japan.* Berkeley: University of California Press.

Witkin, H. A., Dyk, R. B., Faterson, H. F., Goodenough, D. R., & Karp, S. A. (1974). *Psychological differentiation.* New York: Halstead. (Original work published 1964)

Witkin, H. A., & Goodenough, D. R. (1977). Field dependence and interpersonal behavior. *Psychological Bulletin, 84,* 661–689.

CHAPTER 6

Adult to Child in Japan
Interaction and Relations

Betty B. Lanham
Regina J. Garrick

The first section of this chapter, Part I, is Betty Lanham's first-person account of her research from 1952 through 1986. Part II, written by Lanham and Garrick, draws upon both authors' research and experience in providing an analysis of relevant studies in the past and present.

PART I: LANHAM'S RESEARCH (1952–1986)

Background

Before World War II, the United States' ties in the Far East were mostly with China, and those of England were with Japan. There were few scholars with expertise on Japan in the United States, and those few were either former missionaries or their offspring. One important social scientist of this generation was my mentor, Douglas G. Haring, who was a missionary for 9 years before moving to Syracuse University in 1927. In Japan, he had acquired a fluency in the language, an affection for the people, an appreciation for the culture, and an understanding of life under a regimented authoritarian state. When I arrived at Syracuse University in 1950 for studies in sociology and anthropology with a concentration on Japan, I was fortunate to study under an esteemed scholar who had a reputation for giving extensively of his time to graduate students. Dr. Haring also had a genteel, generous, and kindly manner that closely resembled traits common to the people of Japan.

In 1951, Haring was invited to make a study for the U.S. government in Amami Oshima (an island of the Ryukyu chain, which

97

includes Okinawa). This study, accompanied by Haring's recommendation, contributed to the return of the Ryukyu Islands to Japan. Also in 1951–1952, I received a grant from the Wenner–Gren Foundation for Anthropological Research to study social change in Japan. While the Occupation of Japan was still in force, permission to go there was not easily obtained. Fortunately, a special position for a foreigner to teach English at one of the national universities, Wakayama, made possible my presence in the country. The smaller city of Kainan, 6 miles away, proved the most satisfactory location for my research. Quickly, I discovered that it would be exceedingly difficult to study social change. In addition to my own lack of a prior firsthand knowledge of the culture, there was another more important reason. For people who are in the midst of change, the process is both continuous and gradual. In addition, it is difficult for an individual to recall a culture from 30 years back. Within anthropology, community studies were popular, and this seemed a good substitute project for becoming acquainted with the culture and locale. But it was not a particularly appropriate subject for a dissertation. A population of 35,000 was too large for the breadth required of a community study. Instead, a side project that started out as a short questionnaire on childcare and childrearing grew in length. As a novice I did not know to cut it back in scope, and the volume of this material became overwhelming. I decided to restrict the subject of my dissertation and subsequent work to the study of children and to adult–child relations.

Wakayama University assumed the responsibility of finding lodging. Provision was made with a house intended both for guests and as a *chashitsu*—a special structure for performing the tea ceremony. Although full of mosquitoes and cold in the winter, the house and garden were truly beautiful. The nostalgia of the abode lived in my dreams both literally and figuratively for many years after returning to the United States. In those days cooking was accomplished with a charcoal fire that had to be lit from scratch for each meal because no one was at home during my absence. The Japanese in the larger house nearby, within the same enclosure, were very kind. During the time of the Occupation (which ended while I was in Japan), and for a while afterwards, the Japanese were more cordial to Americans than might be considered normal. They expressed gratitude for newly found freedoms and liberties, for political and economic reforms, and for chemicals that rid their homes of insects that accumulated in the straw *tatami* flooring. The Japanese were apologetic for the war—an expected reaction within their culture under the circumstances of defeat. The reciprocal reaction of forgiveness on the part of the United States was also in keeping with expectations within their cultural milieu. Under these circumstances, the United States took on the status of "big brother." During my second visit to Japan in 1959, student riots against the United States over the nature of the peace treaty were so intense that Eisenhower's planned trip to Japan was cancelled. Yet antagonism was directed against the U.S. government and not against American citizens, who moved about freely even in Tokyo, the site of the demonstrations.

In 1951–1952, the teaching position at Wakayama University established my identity and ensured that people were receptive to my research. Faculty colleagues at Wakayama assisted with contacts in Kainan. In an early visit to the mayor I explained the nature of the study, and the local newspaper editor kindly published accounts of my research activities and news of subsequent publications after I returned to the U.S. In the early days, I was the only American in Kainan, and as such was a source of cordial curiosity to the children in schoolyards and elsewhere. After returning to the United States, reversion to the status of ordinary citizen was a letdown.

Sources of Data

The discussion that follows is based primarily on my fieldwork of 1951–1952, 1960, and 1965. During the first period, I circulated a lengthy questionnaire on childrearing and followed up with the interview of nine families of varying income levels. This work was supplemented by general information from interviews with city officials, public health officials, and others. In 1960 I circulated a number of additional questionnaires through the schools. The earlier study had been deficient in a programed observation of adult–child relations. This deficiency was remedied in 1960 by observation of a preschool *(yochien)* class of 4-year-old children, for an hour on each of 20 days. At that time there was a tuition charge, even though this was a public school; hence, it could be assumed that the children were from families of higher than average income. One of the 1960 questionnaires asked the reasons for punishing, forms of punishment, and forms of threat that parents employed. Another concerned mother–child and father–child conversations used in the training of children. In 1965, incidents of specified forms of behavior were recorded in three preschools representing varying income levels in the Osaka area; comparable data were obtained in the same manner for the United States. I also conducted observations of 4-year-old preschool children in the United States from 1954 to the present in several locations. Subsequent visits to Japan in 1972 and 1980 involved research of a different nature. In 1986, I collected information on the extent of liberty and restraint respondents felt appropriate in the rearing of children. It is important to note that at no time in Japan did I replicate identical surveys on childrearing, which prevents an analysis of change based on my own data. All of the research was conducted in Kainan except for the student observations in Osaka, and the 1985 interviews in the Kanto area. Other sources of my data also include an examination of pre- and postwar texts used in the teaching of ethics to children in Japan and the United States and a comparative analysis of the 10 folktales most commonly told to children in Japan and in the United States.

Writings on Childrearing Prior to 1951

When in 1868, after some 250 years, Japan was open for contact with the outside world, there were no U.S. researchers of child development. Some accounts are available from foreigners who remained in Japan for a considerable period of time. Alice Mable Bacon (1902) commented that children received gentle and courteous treatment from those about them and that they received verbal teachings of self-reliance and thoughtfulness toward others. Etsu Sugimoto (1925) wrote in detail of her childhood as the daughter of a *samurai,* but her experiences were confined to those of the upper social class. Embree (1939), in his ethnographic study of a village in Japan, wrote: "Anything a child asks for or cries for long enough he gets. He learns the ways of society not through discipline but through example and instruction patiently and endlessly repeated by his mother" (p. 185).

At the time of World War II, as anthropological research expanded and became well known, the value of the discipline as a means for interpreting an enemy nation was recognized. A number of anthropologists embarked on the study of "culture at a distance" (Barnouw, 1973). The interviewed subjects were emigrants from Japan and their American offspring who were interned in what were euphemistically called "relocation" camps. A large number had not been in Japan for many years. Benedict's (1946) well-known book, *The Chrysanthemum and the Sword,* derived from this source. She included a chapter titled "The Child Learns." Some of her descriptions probably were a correct portrayal of an earlier period that had changed by the time of my arrival in 1951, such as her statement that "girls of 19 bear more children than women of any other age" (p. 256). Benedict's comment that young girls frequently carried babies on their backs when at play was still true in 1952, although this practice on the part of mothers today has all but disappeared. Other practices Benedict described were present at the time of my study and, indeed, still occur today, such as the use of distraction rather than confrontation to remove a child from an undesired activity.

During World War II, a number of writings were affected by the political events of the era in accompaniment with then-current psychoanalytic theories, and inaccuracies occurred. Benedict, along with LaBarre (1945), Gorer (1943), and Spitzer (1947) had contended that Japanese toilet training was early and severe. Gorer went further to say that the structure of houses was fragile and dangerous to the extent that small children needed to exercise caution. These statements did not jive with the experiences, reports, and observations of long-term Western residents in the country. LaBarre (1945) contended that severe toilet training produced a com-

Ten-month-old baby stays with mother as she works in Kainan City (Wakayama), 1952. From Haring (1956), *Personal Character and Cultural Milieu.* Reprinted with permission from Syracuse University Press. Courtesy of Betty Lanham.

pulsive personality that was responsible for a long list of traits which he considered negative, including hypochondria, arrogance, persistence, and excessive cleanliness. Japanese political events also were attributed to a compulsive national personality. Known practices that from a psychoanalytic point of view would have portrayed the Japanese in a favorable light rarely were mentioned, such as the physical closeness of the mother and child when bathing and sleeping, and when the child was being carried on the back.

A perspective on early writings about childrearing in Japan is gained by contrasts with the radical swings in advice to parents that have occurred in the United States over the last 80 years. Wolfenstein (1955) wrote that in 1914 a U.S. government publication, reflecting the ideas of specialists of the time, advocated that fathers not play with their infants after work, lest the children become nervous. The pajamas of a male infant were to be pinned to the bed so that he would not inadvertently stimulate himself, and sleeves of garments were to be purposely long to prevent thumb-sucking. During the more permissive 1940s, parents were advised to delay toilet training to avoid the adverse effects of an anal complex, although subsequent research did not confirm this assumption. Later, in the 1960s, parents were encouraged to allow near-complete freedom so children could pursue their desires. Young children were not to be coerced in any way. In the 1980s parents were again advised to be "firm," a term that could mean consistent setting of behavioral standards but which also could mean restraint. In short, the extent of required adherence to rules and the extent of punishment for defiance is not defined. An identical practice may be described by one observer as positive in that it accords a child freedom and affection or by another as negative in that it is overly permissive, indulgent, lenient, or submissive (Lanham, 1970). Over the years, therefore, misleading assumptions have been common, and advice to parents has shifted based on inadequate research, not only in Japan but in the West.

Results of Questionnaires, 1952–1960

In 1952, it seemed important to obtain reliable data on the actual practices regarding toilet training and other forms of childrearing and childcare in Japan. I embarked upon this task, and did not make analytic interpretations. My initial study did not inquire into psychological relationships, although my subsequent interests have been more psychological. The 1952 questionnaires asked about the respondents' children and the childhoods of the father and mother of the same family. Teachers checked the names of students as the forms were returned. Of the 500 that were sent out, 449 were returned. The form asked when toilet training was begun, when the child was first punished, and when a lapse in training was not supposed to occur. On this particular question, there were over 300 responses (Lanham, 1962). The results were quite similar to common practice in the United States at the time and these findings were later obtained by other researchers as well.

Spitzer (1947) had contended that since nursing was continued for an extended period, abrupt weaning accompanying the birth of a second child would be traumatic. This was supposed to be the time at which weaning took place. My 1952 data showed that 79 of 190 children were weaned at least a year before the next child was born. In addition, the range for the beginning and termination of both toilet training and weaning was considerable, particularly for weaning (Lanham, 1956, 1962, 1970). After publication of these results, psychological theories about the Japanese personality which had been based on the assumption of severe toilet training and upon shock engendered by weaning at the birth of the next child were discarded.

Other items surveyed included parental teasing, fulfillment of promises, and physical punishment. Bateson and Mead (1942), working in Bali, had found excessive teasing and theorized that the result was sufficiently traumatic to be retained into adulthood, and displayed on an unconscious level in a ceremonial dance. Research conducted in Japan did reveal that parents tease their children, but as a form of jest rather than in a destructive manner.

Parents' acknowledged failure to fulfill promises appeared to cause their offspring little disturbance since children's expectations of fulfillment were based on past experience. Parents acknowledged that their own parents had in turn been delinquent in this respect.

An unexpected finding was the use of physical punishment by 72% of the respondents. This primarily involved a slap on the buttocks. Finally, the 1952 questionnaire sought through use of the categories "income" and "occupation" to determine if status influenced the nature of childcare and childrearing, but there was no evidence of such variation.

On a second trip to Japan in 1959–1960, supported by a predoctoral fellowship from the American Association of University Women, I obtained further information on childrearing. In a questionnaire survey 255 parents indicated which forms of threat they used. Two hundred fifty-five questionnaires were returned. The threat "people will laugh at you" was marked by 64% of respondents, while "people will laugh at your family" was marked by 19%. Some 16% of the girls were threatened that "no one will want you for a bride" and 16% of the boys were told "you will be locked out of the house at night." Forty-five percent of the parents reported threatening children that sickness would result from misbehavior. If LaBarre (1945) was correct in assuming that hypochondria was common among the Japanese, the explanation could lie in the use of this form of threat.

A later (1960) questionnaire asked 221 mothers and 106 fathers (from different households) to record a conversation used in training their youngest child of at least 3 years of age. The results tended to represent the ideal rather than actual behavior. It is to be noted, however, that a Japanese colleague who looked at the data was surprised at the frankness of respondents who were critical of themselves as well as of their children. This questionnaire provided new insights and for the first time, a comprehension of basic differences between childrearing in Japan and the United States was in the offering (Lanham, 1966).

Japanese responses continued to stress the importance of *wa-karaseru* (having the child understand), implying that compliance without a willing desire on the part of the child was of little or no value. Mutual respect was evident in the recorded parent–child conversations. Demands and belittling comments by parents, such as "You do . . . because I tell you to" or "You are to obey because I'm your mother," were seldom observed. Rather, the reason for obedience was that the undesirable behavior would cause others trouble. In each case, when the mother could not talk the child out of something either she or the father fulfilled the request. On the streets, parents did not force their children by pulling an arm or punishing a refusal to leave because of a desired purchase. Reports indicated that children criticized fathers and mothers when they failed to measure up to requirements made of themselves and the typical parental response was an apology. Children evidenced maturity and objectivity in the handling of their own emotional reactions. Parents encouraged their children to be mentally alert and were critical of carelessness.

Preschool observations I made of 4-year-olds in the United States and Japan in 1960 revealed striking differences in the teacher's manner of relating to the children. In Japan the teacher did not intervene in the interactions between children, nor did she criticize individuals. Other children went to assist a child in need. In the United States the child was much more often oriented toward the teacher, from whom praise, approval, acceptance, or permission were sought.

Contrasts of the practices in Japan with those common to the United States, in 1960 and today, may be explained by the desire of American adults (1) to increase independence and individualism by means of permitting challenges to authority and/or (2) to interfere in the children's activities for the purpose of enjoyed personal involvement and attention.

The accepted frequency in the United States with which 2- and 3-year-old children are permitted to challenge parental instructions would seem to suggest that a nonintentional game is being played that is enjoyed by both participants. Close observation reveals that when out-of-doors, a young child of 2 or 3 is likely to start to run away from the mother many times to attract attention; that is, the child waits until the mother turns around to see him or her in the process. The mother could be definite in curbing this behavior, as when the child touches a hot stove or runs into the street, but this is not done.

Folktales

The possibility of discerning values to which children are early exposed was in the offering with an itemized analysis of 10 folktales commonly told to children in Japan. We examined ten others frequently told in the United States for comparative purposes (Lanham & Shimura, 1967). The content of the stories of the two cultures diverged considerably. The hero figure in Japan is typically a male youth or adult—older than individuals portrayed in the Western tales. Heroes evidenced the character traits of bravery, robust strength, and perseverance. In the United States, by contrast, stories usually involved young women who are described as happy, gentle, kind, loving, wise, and/or virtuous. Romanticism is important. Since folktales were initially intended for adults, ethical themes apparently were a later addition, when the stories were told to a young audience. The morals that do appear reflect the considered importance of the inhabitants of the culture where the folktales are told. In Japan, admonishments are against envy, greed, and jealousy. An emphasis on kindliness to animals appears in half of the stories that were examined. A request for forgiveness is common in the Japanese stories, for instance in one version of "Little Red Riding Hood," where the wolf is portrayed with tears flowing from his eyes while asking forgiveness. The infrequent ethical themes emphasized in the Western stories were related to vanity and envy.

Readers on Ethics

Values for children and adults were explicitly changed with a movement toward democracy in the postwar period of Japan. A clear differentiation from the prewar era could be discerned with the examination of texts used during the two periods for teaching ethics. Fortunately, books with much the same intent were available for comparative purposes in the United States (Lanham, 1979). These books included (1) *Shushin: The Ethics of a Defeated Nation* (Hall, 1949), (2) the *Shogaku Dotoku* readers by Kumura, Amano, and Uchimi (1965) and the accompanying teachers' manuals (Uchimi & Amano, n.d.), (3) *McGuffey's Eclectic Readers* (McGuffey, 1879), and (4) the *Golden Rule Series* by Laevell and Friebele (1961) and Laevell, Friebele, and Cushman (1964) along with the *Teacher's Guide Book* (Laevell, 1961).

The prewar *Shushin* books were a product of an imperialistic Japan in which nationalism, militarism, and emperor worship were important. Stories were included of war heroes who sometimes commited suicide to insure victory. The Occupational Forces as well as the teachers in Japan were anxious to prevent any suggestion of a return to this earlier era. Still, there was a desire on the part of parents and others to incorporate ethics in the school curriculum. The postwar *Dotoku* books deleted the objectional references to the extent that soldiers, war, and Shintoism (the native religion which had enhanced worship of the Emperor) were not mentioned. The postwar American books did however, acclaim war heroes, and in some instances clearly evidenced ethnocentrism. In Japan, ethical traits that had been long present, such as diligence, patience, and the importance of hard work, were incorporated in the books of both the pre- and postwar periods. In addition, the more recent books reflected newly established democratic principles. They encouraged group discussions about classroom incidents and insisted that all students participate.

The prewar *McGuffey* readers, used for an extended period in the American schools, were not primarily intended for the teaching of ethics, although admonishments of the sort were common—phrased largely in terms of "good," "do," or "don't" and "should" and "shouldn't." The close resemblance of the revised method of teaching ethical precepts presented in the postwar *Dotoku* books of Japan and the *Golden Rule* books (specifically designed for teaching ethics in the United States) was striking. During the more modern era, stories were of the personal problems a child is likely to face in everyday life. Rather than providing a conclusion to a story, the reader was left free to ponder and think through a solution for him or herself or arrive at a decision through group discussion. There was an attempt to establish empathy for the emotional problems of others, especially those who are ill treated. Stories in the separate books of the postwar period did resemble the cultures from which they were derived. In Japan, perseverance in the face of adversity was strongly emphasized beginning in the first grade. Difficulties were often enhanced by the ridicule and laughter of others when the main character undertook a seemingly impossible task. The Japanese teacher's manuals instruct teachers to discourage impulsive thoughts, emotional opinions, and flippant ideas. Instead, mental concentration was to be focused on the task at hand. The American books emphasized benevolence, selflessness, justice, and fairness. The special problems that commonly arise in each culture were addressed. A number of stories read by Japanese children suggested a need to stand up against and oppose the group when the group is in the wrong—an innovative approach for Japan. The American books included more stories demonstrating a need to be friendly with persons of diverse racial or national origins.

Change

The comments that follow derive from (1) parents' reports obtained in 1952 of the childrearing practices they experienced as children compared with the methods they used with their own children, (2) data obtained in 1952 in which parents compared education in Japan during the pre- and early postwar periods, (3) texts on ethics used during the pre- and postwar periods (published in 1935–1939 and 1965), and (4) my own personal contacts during intermittent trips to Japan since 1952.

There was little differentiation between parents' reports in 1952 of punishment administered to their children and their own experiences before the war about 35 years earlier (around 1917). The data suggests that physical punishment had not decreased during this generation.

In 1952, most respondents were pleased with the modified postwar educational system. They reported less awe and fear of the teacher—more affection and respect—and were pleased that the children who were encouraged to think for themselves manifested a spirit of inquiry and were less dependent on rote memory. A few parents complained that the change had reduced perseverance and made children too carefree in their attitudes and behavior (Lanham, 1970).

In the immediate postwar era, the birthrate was high as a result of demobilization, as in the United States. Women's clothes were designed to easily, facilitate nursing which then was acceptable in public. There was a hesitancy and an awkward feeling about purchasing contraceptives, and abortions became an alternative solution. Today, with an ever-increasing standard of living and costs that have kept pace, the voluntary limit on number of children per family has caused some to worry about maintaining the population replacement level.

A child's world today differs markedly from what it was in the early 1950s when candy vendors, storytellers, and entertainers clad in historical attire performed in the narrow lanes between homes. At that time, a variety of small stores of about 100 square feet in size were within close walking distance of homes. Artisans frequently worked in front of their houses, a source of entertainment for children.

As the offspring of a high birthrate reached adulthood, the pressure for dwellings became intense and farmland disappeared. Apartment living is now common and frequently the only abode a young couple can afford. The advent of supermarkets means that mothers now travel a farther distance to purchase groceries, often by bicycle. Two children, one in front and another on a special seat in back are all that can be managed without considerable difficulty. In 1952, with stores close by, a baby carriage would seat two, and a third child could walk beside the mother.

Housework has also become easier. A table of standard U.S. height used for serving meals means that the mother need no longer stoop down each time she carries food to a low table. Modern conveniences include gas ranges, gas-heated baths, electric refrigerators, electric rice cookers, vacuum cleaners, and prepared foods. Activities still take place mostly on the floor, which has the advantage of providing special heating arrangements in winter and of being constantly at the height of a young child. Today, affluence has increased consumption and conceptions of need, such as obtaining a college education. I wish to emphasize, nonetheless, that while material consumption has changed extensively in Japan, the nature of social relations has remained rather stable.

Research in Japan: Methods in Retrospect

Although my first 1952 survey attained a sample of 449 returns, not every parent answered all questions. Still, Japan was an ideal country for the use of anonymous questionnaires in that respondents would rather leave a displeasing item blank than develop hostility toward the total inquiry. When on a multiple-choice question parents did not find an appropriate response, they wrote the correct answer in the margin, which enhanced the accuracy of my interpretations. In one 1960 survey parents did not hesitate to answer an open-ended question about conversations they held with their children that were designed for training purposes. Respondents occasionally referred to an event that took place in the past, and, in some cases, they created conversations for the benefit of the investigation. The return was good and many answers were lengthy. By contrast, American respondents put to the same task worried about the intent of the research, how their answers might be evaluated, and presumably about the exactitude of their recorded conversations. As a result, the Japanese materials were richly rewarding, but the American data were sparse and of little use. On the other hand, parents in the United States readily answered multiple-choice questionnaires where only a simple mark was requested.

I used a variety of methods in Japan: both open-ended and multiple-choice questionnaires, interviews, and an analysis of documentary materials. Each method had both advantages and disadvantages for obtaining quantity and variety of data, and for validity and reliability.

Since 1952, the research process has become easier in many ways. For instance, earlier questionnaires had to be written by hand. The wax stencils I initially used melted when placed under a bright lamp and had to be replaced. Tabulations and correlations derived from the first of my questionnaires required a year of work on an IBM sorter. Today, the use of a Japanese typewriter and computer enables printing, tabulation, and presentation of the data in a relatively short period of time; however, in spite of the more modern equipment available today, there still remain methodological cautions that deserve special attention. Quite apart from formulating a questionnaire in such a way as to assure easy tabulation, adequate space should be provided for the addition of written comments—a practice commonly resorted to in Japan (not in the United States) when a short answer is not sufficiently exact or clear. A researcher can also take advantage of the cathartic effect present when a respondent desires to vent rather strong feelings on a subject, as was the case when one respondent wrote extensively about his displeasure over the freedoms accorded children during the postwar era.

The importance of an accurate translation is obvious. My initial questionnaires involved six translators working independently of each other. Despite these efforts, errors did occur, as with a previous report on the use of *moxa*. Moxa is a dried herb placed on the skin and burned. It is used both for medicinal purposes and to drive out evil spirits, thought to cause misbehavior. Confusion arose from the use of "yes" in the Japanese language to affirm a question phrased in the negative. Also, questions needed to be more explicit then I had realized earlier. For instance, when using the hand to punish, does this mean the flat of a hand, a fist, pinching, or flipping fingernails on the face? Is the strike once or many times, as in the difference between a slap and spanking? Apparently, in 1952, the Japanese seldom, if ever, employed the latter method. An excellent illustration of translation difficulties is found in White and LeVine's (1986) list of variant meanings for commonly used Japanese terms relevant to childrearing, for example, use of the term *sunao,* which is loosely translated as "obedience."

Questions of validity occur in the use of terms pertaining to the present as well as the past when making cross-cultural comparisons—more specifically with the use of categories indicating the frequency of a given practice such as "rarely, seldom, often." A respondent's comparisons are necessarily with individuals known to him or her only in their own culture. Responses of this nature are useful as an indication of the extent to which a given practice is considered acceptable, but questionable when applied to cross-cultural analysis. Another term that causes confusion is the word "spoiled" when applied in comparisons of Japan to the United States. Certainly considerable indulgence and permissiveness characterizes early childrearing in Japan. The mother, at the same time, however, carefully instructs the child in proper expressions, bodily movements, and acceptable behavior. When I was interviewing parents in 1952, neighborhood children of varying ages frequently gathered, sat, and listened quietly without ever causing a disturbance. A mother's own child of 2, 3, or 4 years of age never interrupted. By contrast, in the United States I have found interviewing unpleasant in the presence of a small child, who typically seeks to distract the mother in order to direct attention to him- or herself. Once when I was dining at a home in Japan, a child of 3 was present. In an adult-like manner, she appropriately took her turn in the conversation. However, on another occasion when the same child was very demanding, it was considered appropriate to acquiesce. The tradition in Japan has long been for restraints to be imposed as the child matures in age. Certainly by the age of 10, a Japanese who has been indulged as a child will have become "proper," sedate, demure, and of cheerful disposition. Typically in the United States, if a mother is very acquiescent when a child is young, it is considered to have lifetime ramifications.

If I were to start my research from the beginning, I might have concentrated on single projects of less ambitious magnitude. The sheer quantity of returned questionnaires that consisted of small print on large sheets of paper stacked several feet high was overwhelming. Still, this quantity was valuable, given the parents tended to leave a considerable number of questions blank. Also, administering surveys in smaller segments would have required a greater number of trips to Japan—not easily accomplished—and would have unnecessarily impinged upon the goodwill of participants.

PART II: THEORETICAL PRECEPTS—
LANHAM AND GARRICK

The following section of this chapter examines concepts previously set forth in light of more recent writings that have confirmed, elaborated upon, and added to materials that appeared shortly after World War II. Rarely have there been contradictions. Three topics deserve special attention because of distinctive features that characterize the socialization of children in Japan: (1) the nature of respect accorded a child, (2) mechanisms of control, and (3) devices that provide emotional security. Initially, it should be mentioned that as with any research, a measuring tool is needed to define and describe the nature of findings. The home culture of the investigators (in our case, the U.S.) must necessarily serve this purpose.

Respect Accorded a Child

In Japan, coercion and punishment are seldom used with smaller children. Norbeck and Norbeck (1956) commented that these two forms of control are reserved until a child is considered to "have sense" (p. 660), that is, until he or she can talk and understand. Even at a later age requests are generally granted if the parent cannot talk the child out of a desired item. Parental control is maintained primarily through internal means, that is, getting the child to comply voluntarily for self-motivated reasons (Lanham, 1970). By comparison, American parents more often rely on external control. In a sense, the child is free to think as he or she pleases as long as he or she is compliant. There is also the assumption that through coercion the child will gradually acquire "self-discipline", that is, learn to control voluntarily his or her own actions.

A complex of theoretical precepts accompanies chidrearing methods commonly employed in Japan. Children are thought to be basically virtuous at and from birth. When they misbehave, it is because they have not yet learned to distinguish right from wrong. This interpretation is not recent. Kojima (1986) writes that these same assumptions about children appear early in Chinese sources, having been mentioned by Mencius in the 3rd century B.C. Similarly, early Japanese writers wrote that although evil could be learned, every individual also had the potential for virtue. According to an ancient Japanese belief, four souls inhabit the body: a gentle spirit, a rough spirit, a luck spirit, and a wonder spirit. Any of these can be dominant at a particular time, and all may be manifest in a person's behavior at different times during his life (Kato, 1926, pp. 32–47). In this context, forgiveness takes on a different meaning than in the West. In the United States, the Biblical precept associated with baptism implies a need to be purified. In the past more than at present, the American child was conceived to be self-willed and in need of restraint to mold him or her into an acceptable human being. The phrase "spare the rod and spoil the child" reflects this sentiment.

In Japan, parents extend verbal courtesies to children, while in the United States, hostile parental expressions are common. The following conversations recorded in American preschools in 1966 and 1989 contrast with the gentler Japanese way of handling young children:

> "Let me see your arm. Did you hurt it? Get off that box before you hurt yourself." (Lanham, 1966, p. 330)

> "Kerry, listen to me. Look at me while I am talking to you. I want you to go over there and clean up the Legos. . . . Look at me. . . . You have nothing to say? Then you can sit over there on the time-out chair and think about it until you are ready to clean up." (Tobin, Wu, & Davidson, 1989, p. 134)

The above conversations are recognizably appropriate when speaking to children in an American setting but would not be acceptable in adult-to-adult dialogue. However, I have observed American school settings in which the preceding conversations would not have occurred.

The Japanese language itself discourages conflict. A mother's explanation that "We don't do . . . because . . ." typically is suffixed with *ne*, which in effect adds to her statement the question "Isn't that right? Don't you agree?" The assumption is that the child wishes to be informed and concurs with the propriety of the mother's instruction, suggesting a mutuality of the relationship. The grammatical structure of a Japanese sentence allows deletion of a subject. In this case there is no necessary differentiation between "you" and "me." Also, the word *chigaimasu* ("different") enables a contradiction without offense to or involvement of the ego. The implication is that a factual error is involved, for which the speaker claims neither credit nor blame.

Restraint and Control

The nature of restraint and control varies with each culture. In the United States, the expression "show respect," when applied in child-to-adult situations, refers to obedience, that is, the extent to which a child complies with the requests and wishes of the parent. A statistical study by Conroy, Hess, Azuma, and Kashiwagi (1980) confirmed that American mothers are considerably more authoritarian with their children than are the Japanese.

Our comparative observations indicate that, in general, American adults restrain a young child who embarks upon or engages in any new or unusual exploratory activities. In other words, the behavior is prohibited unless it is explicitly permitted. By contrast, the Japanese come closer to permitting behavior unless it is explicitly prohibited. A parent who sees a child embarking upon unacceptable behavior is likely to quietly and gently say why one should not do thus and such. White (1987) comments that "it sometimes seems that American classrooms, and American parents as well, . . . teach that goodness results from inhibition rather than joy, and that the demands on a child to be good cannot be consonant with whatever produces happiness" (p. 122). De Vos (De Vos with Suárez-Orozco, 1986) effectively describes the parent–child relationship:

> A Japanese mother sensitizes her children to the interpersonal consequences of action; an American mother makes behavior a resultant of a prevailing will. The Japanese mother supports but deemphasizes the authority role. She neutralizes the interpersonal confrontational possibilities of constraint, whereas the American mother's battle with her child over proper behavior often results in a contest of wills. (p. 297)

Several anecdotes that occurred during Lanham's early research demonstrate differences in how adults do or do not intervene to control children's behavior. One occurred on a train, when a child who was alone suddenly looked up at the straps above his head and had an inspiration. Proceeding to stand on the seat, he reached up and began to swing as if on a school playground. There was no response from a car full of adults. On another occasion, a

Japanese principal paid no attention to a young student of about 10 years of age who was sprawled on a chair in his office and refused to move even in the presence of a visitor. Other students, on their own, took the situation in hand by moving him bodily to another room. By contrast, in an American school, I (Lanham) observed a principal interrupting a conversation with a visitor to reprimand a young boy who had run down the steps, which at the time were empty.

Twenty hours of observation of Japanese 4-year-olds at a school in 1960 revealed that the teacher did not intervene in the interaction between children. A child's unusual behavior received no comment (Lanham, 1966). Lewis (1984), who has engaged in far more extensive observations of teacher–pupil relationships, reports that compared with American teachers, the Japanese teacher "keeps a low profile" and avoids relating on an individual basis. By maintaining a watchful eye, through indirect or subtle means, he or she corrects behavior and boosts the self-esteem of the child. Tobin et al. (1989) report that Japanese viewers of a videotape of an American kindergarten were not pleased with the way disputes among children were handled. Americans sought to judge who was in the wrong and then act accordingly, while in Japan primary emphasis was upon establishing harmony.

Emotional Security

A number of mechanisms assuring emotional security characterize childrearing in Japan. Doi (1973) has elaborated upon one important aspect of this process. He describes an intimate parent–child relationship that encourages the offspring's extensive reliance on the mother, who in turn rewards and accepts dependent behavior as an indication of her enhanced affection. The frequent use in Japan of the descriptive term *amae* indicates a recognized and favored relationship (Peak, 1991). Probably this form of dependency is present in all societies to some extent, but what may be special in Japan is a recognition and approbation of the *amae* relationship, which in turn may emphasize the behavior. By contrast, the American approach to the phenomenon is a denial that the practice exists even when present, because "dependence" is negatively connoted.

In Japan, security is strengthened by group support in the school situation. The building of self-esteem and academic accomplishment has been set forth by Lewis (1984, 1988, 1989). American educators have made a noble effort to move toward cooperation but the limitations of their accomplishment are clearly evident when comparisons are made with the results of research in Japan.

Perhaps one of the most significant differences between the two countries that has had immeasurable impact upon self-esteem and early mental development is the teacher's concept of his or her pupils' mental ability. Tobin et al. (1989) comment that children in Japan are treated as if all are equal, whereas in the United States there is continual reference to the different potentials of individual children. Japanese teachers expressed dismay over the possibility that a young child who was the product of labeling might have less of a chance than would others.

The characterizing of a child as "hyperactive" can have disastrous repercussions. The Japanese teachers say they have no children who fit into this category (Peak, 1989). Children who are more high spirited than normal are commended for their liveliness. In the United States, a child who fits into this category may be put on medication, may be subject to behavior modification, or might actually be failed a grade—regardless of his or her academic achievements or potential. It is to be noted that in Japan classes are larger, not smaller. All children pass from one grade to another. None are failed. Lanham's observation in 1960 revealed that a single child who was functionally different from others was not recognized or treated as such either by the teacher or other children if he or she acted in an odd manner or differently from the group. The teacher said nothing if the child stood on a chair when others were seated or if it took more time for this child to catch a ball. It was simply thrown more often.

In the United States, lack of support from peers coupled with competition and an emphasis upon success means that some children will achieve, but at the expense of others, whose confidence may be impaired. The overall effect is likely to be a concern about self rather than about academic matters. Failure to achieve may result in a child's rejection of the whole educational process. As early as 1942, Margaret Mead called attention to this problem, which has remained unsolved through the years.

SUGGESTIONS FOR FURTHER RESEARCH

Adolescence

In recent years, little attention has been given to Benedict's (1938) concept of "continuities and discontinuities." A comparative analysis of the socialization processes in the United States and Japan might shed light on the problems relating to adolescence that occur in both countries. Relevant is the question of whether the considerable indulgence and permissiveness that characterize childrearing in Japan act to strengthen affectional ties with the mother and as a consequence strengthen her impact later in life.

Differences occur in the focal interests of adolescents in Japan and the United States. White (1987) has pointed out that Japanese high school students say that the most important activity in their lives is their studies, whereas the Americans say either sex or romantic attachments. Could romance provide an escape from unsuccessful academic endeavors? If so, success in this endeavor would provide temporary security, prestige, and affection, as well as an escape from other activities.

Group Activities

Research by Lewis (1984) has emphasized the importance of group activities among younger students in Japanese schools. Studies of a more specific nature are needed: For instance, to what extent do groups enable (1) enhanced creativity, (2) the talents of each member to be effectively expressed, (3) the reduction of frustration through free expression without fear of repercussion, or (4) the furtherance of democratic principles? In a negative sense, under what circumstances may group activities lead to (1) a fear of acting on one's own, (2) forced conformity, (3) dominance and hierarchical relationships, or (4) an intensifying of antagonisms toward outsiders.

Childrearing

Previously reported studies of childrearing in Japan by Lanham and others have been quite favorable. In the interest of objectivity and accuracy, it seems desirable to comment on some less favorable forms of behavior. For instance, some hidden aspects of the close mother–child relationship in Japan deserve special attention. Mothers have esteemed the bold, assertive behavior of their small sons, but might this behavior, when coupled with frequent praise and gratification of demands, interfere with the development of mechanisms for adjustment? Iga (1961) once suggested the possible creation of a vulnerable male ego that is incapable of handling stress. Research by Bennett, Passin, and McKnight (1958) on Japanese youth studying in the United States found that women adjusted more satisfactorily with fewer problems than did men.

Bullying

In recent years a number of problems indicating dysfunction have come to the attention of educators in Japan, including school avoidance, bullying, and violent behavior in school and at home. Since the early 1980s, the Japanese have noted a surge in violent behavior committed by increasingly younger children (Saisho, 1982). In Japan, bullying, or *ijime*, has been linked to school avoidance, school violence, family violence, and juvenile delinquency, and has led to severe physical injury, retaliatory behavior resulting in murder, grievous psychological harm, and suicide (Ishikawa, Ito, Shimomura, & Sekine, 1991; Morita, 1991) among children and adolescents.

Japanese authorities define bullying as follows: to inflict pain by physical attacks against one or sometimes several specially selected people; to intimidate another by speech or action; to harass; to inflict repeated or intermittent psychological pressures by excluding or ignoring a person(s) in a group setting *(Keisatsu Hakusho,* 1986).

In addition to verbal and physical abuse, social ostracism is a component of bullying. In Japan, where self-identity is inextricably connected with group membership and group identity, social exclusion can be psychologically devastating. With roots in agrarian Japan, ostracism *(mura hachibu)* has been used consciously and effectively as a legitimized means to control nonconformist and uncooperative people in Japanese society (Smith, 1961). Among children, exclusion from the group is called *nakama hazure* (Duke, 1986; Hiyama, 1986), meaning that one is an "outsider" even within one's own group.

Most victims of bullying are smaller, weaker, younger than, or "different" from the bullies. Perceived physical, racial, linguistic, ethnic, and other differences are thought to target children for bullying and social exclusion (Sugeno, 1986; Yamamoto, 1985). The victims may be students who transfer from other schools *(tenkosei)* or Japanese students who return to Japan after having lived abroad for several years *(kikokushijo)* (Sugeno, 1986; Miyachi, 1990; Noda, 1991; Duke, 1986).

Bullying often occurs when children are going to or from school and are not supervised by adults. Many teachers are aware of bullying among their students but ignore or tolerate the behavior, believing that children should resolve their own interpersonal problems. Some teachers hesitate to interfere, fearing that their intervention may exacerbate the behavior. Teachers thus often tacitly allow serious bullying to develop and persist among children.

Certain Japanese cultural values (Lanham, 1979) also may contribute to children's hesitance to report bullying: for example, silent endurance of pain and adversity, emphasis on harmonious relationships, and reluctance to oppose one's group for fear of possible exclusion. In Japan it is also true that in the case of quarrels the victim often is considered at fault for provoking his antagonist. These values may preclude children's seeking help from authorities and admitting their situation.

Bullying has been attributed to competitive examinations (Schoolland, 1986), rigid administrative control in the schools, and a social system in which members of the majority group use membership to enhance their identity at the expense of others (Mihashi, 1987). Psychological studies indicate that children who have experienced bullying from parents, siblings, or friends displace their own painful experiences onto even weaker children (Sakagami, 1983). Victims' responses may provide bullies with tangible rewards (Olweus, 1978; Perry, Williard, & Perry, 1990). O'Moore (1987) identified "provocative victims" and "passive victims"; the latter appear to be smaller, passive, vulnerable, or lacking in social skills. Children's response to aggression may be related to their relative peer status and extent of social isolation (Dodge, Coie, Pettit, & Price, 1990).

Future Research

Most recent Western research on Japanese children has been conducted in the context of the classroom rather than in the family. It is important for contemporary research to document the changes that are occurring in Japanese society, family life, and values. Interdisciplinary studies are necessary to learn how and what contemporary Japanese parents teach their children about human relationships, ethical issues, personal responsibility, and conflict resolution. Comparative studies may provide insights and solutions to similar questions in American culture.

Conclusions

A few comments on methodology are in order. First, cultural relativism is relevant to all of the preceding issues, since values differ from one society to another. Also, the contextual significance of any given form of behavior varies as well. People who are native to a culture make their own choices. Still, behavioral forms that produce stress, tension, and unhappiness are seldom desired, regardless of the people among whom they occur. It is this subject area that deserves increased emphasis.

All ethnographic investigations are affected by both the researcher's culture and his or her personality. In addition, the anthropologist differentiates behaviors that conform to or differ from expected cultural values and those that grant culturally specific emotional rewards. The wearing of a wedding ring or shoes inside a house fit into the former category. On the other hand, behavior may instead fulfill an emotional need that is tied in with experiences of the past and present. An example is provided in the United States by the opposition of parents to the teaching of sex education in the schools when they themselves do not assume the responsibility. From whence the strong emotional reaction?

Within a single culture, childhood experiences, in general, will be similar, particularly with respect to restraints, needs, and emotional reactions. It is entirely possible that prescribed childrearing practices will have an effect on later adult behavior, with respect to desires and sources of emotional comfort and discomfort. Within all societies humans need affection, a sense of well-being, security as a means for alleviating emotional stress, and sources of excitement. Obviously, there are cultural differences in the extent to which each is fulfilled within a society. This chapter has concentrated primarily on the methods used in training to assure compliance with cultural expectations, a process that describes the nature of communication between parent and child—that is, the extent of chastisement, mechanisms for building self-esteem, degree of warmth and cordiality, and mutual respect. These traits can best be illustrated for Japan by quotes from five conversations recorded by Lanham in 1961.

MOTHER *(age 39):* [One day I found that her pocketbook was heavy with money.] Sachiko-chan, what did you do? . . . this money? [Then I was horrified when thinking back. She did not spend money so often. I had assumed that she was saving it somewhere for herself. Now I realized that she had begun to carry money with her recently.] Children should not carry lots of money like grown-up. If they do, they will grow to be a wicked person. [She muttered something, looking down. Then she wept alone and went to school. Since then, she never takes money out of her father's pocket.]

MOTHER *(age 42):* Your teacher told me not to let you be friendly with Taro *(a boy's name).*

SON *(in junior high school):* I don't think you are right, Mother. If he is without friends, no one will treat him right; he will become worse than now. We should help him to be good.

MOTHER: [I had to think again myself.]

MOTHER *(age 33)*: [He was weeping one morning and would not get up.]

SON *(age 4)*: [while strenuously beating me] Don't say anything.

MOTHER: [I almost mentioned his having wet the bed but didn't.] Now let's change your night clothes and get dressed [while helping him change his clothes].

SON: I'm sorry, Mom. I was asleep when this happened.

MOTHER: [I could not scold him when hearing this but held him tight.]

OLDEST DAUGHTER: Bring me a handkerchief and tissue, Mom.

MOTHER *(age 36)*: Can't you get them for yourself?

CHILD *(age 4)*: Well, you are severe today, aren't you? You scolded Sister for such a little thing. What if she is run over by a street-car?

MOTHER: [being surprised] From whom did you learn those words?

CHILD *(age 4)*: You say that to Sister when she goes out.

MOTHER: Oh yes. That's right. How foolish I am. I'm sorry. [Everyone laughed merrily, and I felt happy all of a sudden.]

DAUGHTER *(age 8)*: I'll go to get Kimitoshi at the nursery school and bring him home today.

MOTHER *(age 34)*: He will fight and make you cry again when he returns home. Can you be so kind as to bring him home?

DAUGHTER: But other mothers go to get their children. Kimitoshi will be too miserable having no one come for him.

MOTHER: [They return home hand in hand, singing merrily.]

Another occasion, same family:

MOTHER: Kimitoshi, why do you make your big sister cry so much?

SON: It's fun to see her cry.

DAUGHTER: That's because you, Mom, listen to him and grant him everything he wants; so he has become selfish and naughty.

MOTHER: [I felt rather ashamed.]

As illustrated above, the Japanese are not prone to use harsh words, but rather are sensitive to the feelings of their children. By means of a running dialogue, parents continuously communicate in a positive manner the nature of unacceptable behavior, so that children come to want to do what is right; thus, a confrontation is not necessary. The societal emphasis upon cooperation rather than competition enhances emotional security. An acceptance and encouragement of curiosity and enthusiasm facilitate learning and self-expression. Finally, the presence of mutual respect allows the child freedom to express his or her feelings.

The traits just described have been maintained through the years. They are, moreover, supported by a stable economic and political system, so that deferred gratification has been obtainable through an egalitarian educational system, stability of the family, and maintenance of an insular identity. Disruptions in these areas could bring about change. A continued emphasis upon materialism and acquired social status accompanied by a movement from a more community-like (*gemeinschaft*) to a mass (*gesellshaft*) society also may have an impact on the future.

REFERENCES

Bacon, A. (1902). *Japanese girls and women.* New York: Houghton Mifflin.

Barnouw, V. (1973). *Culture and personality.* Homewood, IL: Dorsey Press.

Bateson, G., & Mead, M. (1942). *Balinese character: A photographic analysis.* New York: New York Academy of Sciences.

Benedict, R. (1938). Continuities and discontinuities in cultural conditioning. *Psychiatry, 1,* 161–167.

Benedict, R. (1946). *The chrysanthemum and the sword.* Boston: Houghton Mifflin.

Bennett, J., Passin, H., & McKnight, R. (1958). *In search of identity: The Japanese overseas scholar in America and Japan.* Minneapolis: University of Minnesota Press.

Conroy, M., Hess, R., Azuma, H., & Kashiwagi, K. (1980). Maternal strategies for regulating children's behavior. *Journal of Cross-Cultural Psychology, 11*(2), 153–172.

De Vos, G., with Suárez-Orozco, M. (1986). Child development in Japan and the United States: Prospectives of cross-cultural comparisons. In H. Stevenson, H. Azuma, & K. Hakuta (Eds.), *Child development and education in Japan* (pp. 289–298). New York: Freeman.

Dodge, K., Coie, J., Pettit, G., & Price, J. (1990). Peer status and aggression in boys' groups: Developmental and contextual analyses. *Child Development, 61*(5), 1289–1309.

Doi, T. (1973). *The anatomy of dependence.* New York: Kodansha International.

Duke, B. (1986). *The Japanese school.* New York: Praeger.

Embree, J. (1939). *Suye Mura: A Japanese village.* Chicago: University of Chicago Press.

Gorer, G. (1943). Themes in Japanese culture. *Transactions of the New York Academy of Sciences* (Series II), *5,* 106–124.

Hall, R. (1949). *Shushin: The ethics of a defeated nation.* New York: Columbia University.

Haring, D. (Ed.). (1956). *Personal character and cultural milieu.* Syracuse, NY: Syracuse University Press.

Hiyama, S. (1986). *Gakko to hiko: Ijime o chushin to shite [Schools and delinquence: Focus on bullying].* Tokyo: Shin Nippon Horitsu Shuppan Kabushiki Gaisha.

Iga, M. (1961). Cultural factors in suicide of Japanese youth with focus on personality. *Sociology and Social Research, 46,* 75–90.

Ishikawa, E., Ito, S., Shimomura, T., & Sekine, M. (1991). Ijime no hoteki mondai to gakko, katei [Legal problems of bullying and schools and family]. *Jurisuto [Jurist], 976*(April), 15–41.

Kato, G. (1926). *A study of Shinto: The religion of the Japanese nation.* Tokyo: Meiji Japan Society.

Keisatsu hakusho [The police white paper]. (1986). Tokyo: Japan Police Agency, National Institute of Police Science.

Kojima, H. (1986). Japanese concepts of child development from the mid-17th to mid-19th century. *International Journal of Behavioral Development, 9,* 315–329.

Kumura, T., Amano, T., & Uchimi, I. (Eds.). (1965). *Shogaku dotoku* (Vols. 1–6). Osaka: Osaka Shoseki Kabushiki Gaisha.

LaBarre, W. (1945). Some observations on character structures in the Orient: The Japanese. *Psychiatry, 8,* 319–342.

Laevell, U. (1961). *Teacher's guide book.* New York: American Book Company.

Laevell, U., & Friebele, M. (1961). *Golden rule series: Vol. 1. Open windows; Vol. 2. Open doors; Vol. 3. Open roads.* New York: American Book Company.

Laevell, U., Friebele, M., & Cushman, T. (1964). *Golden rule series: Vol. 4. Paths to follow; Vol. 5. Frontiers to explore; Vol. 6. Widening horizons.* New York: American Book Company.

Lanham, B. (1956). Aspects of child care in Japan: Preliminary report. In D. Haring (Ed.), *Personal character and cultural milieu* (pp. 565–583). Syracuse, NY: Syracuse University Press.

Lanham, B. (1962). *Aspects of child rearing in Kainan, Japan.* Unpublished doctoral dissertation, University of Michigan, Ann Arbor, MI.

Lanham, B. (1966). The psychological orientation of the mother–child relationship in Japan. *Monumenta Nipponica, 21*(3–4), 322–333.

Lanham, B. (1970). Early socialization: Stability and change. *Rice University Studies, 56*(4), 219–230.

Lanham, B. (1979). Ethics and moral precepts taught in schools of Japan and the United States. *Ethos, 7*(1), 1–18.

Lanham, B., & Shimura, M. (1967). Folktales commonly told American and Japanese children: Ethical themes of omission and commission. *Journal of American Folklore, 80*(315), 33–48.

Lewis, C. (1984). Cooperation and control in Japanese nursery schools. *Comparative Education Review, 28*(1), 69–84.

Lewis, C. (1988). Japanese first-grade classrooms: Implications for U.S. theory and research. *Comparative Education Review, 32*(2), 159–172.

Lewis, C. (1989). From indulgence to internalization: Social control in the early school years. *Journal of Japanese Studies, 15*(1), 139–159.

McGuffey, W. (1879). *McGuffey's eclectic readers.* New York: American Book Company.

Mead, M. (1942). *And keep your powder dry: An anthropologist looks at America.* New York: Morrow.

Mihashi, O. (1987). The symbolism of social discrimination. *Current Anthropology, 28*(4), S19–S29.

Miyachi, S. (1990). *Kikokushijo [Returnee students].* Tokyo: Chuo Koron-sha.

Morita, Y. (1991). Ijime sosho to gakko kyoiku [Bullying litigation and school education]. *Horitsu no Hiroba [Forum for Law], 44*(4), 31–37.

Noda, I. (1991). *Kikokushijo kyoiku no gendai to tenbo: Shoto, chuto kyoiku o chushin to shite, toku-shu [Focus on primary and middle school education: Contemporary education and prospects for returnee children, special edition].* Tokyo: Monbusho.

Norbeck, E., & Norbeck, M. (1956). Child training in a Japanese fishing community. In D. Haring (Ed.), *Personal character and cultural milieu* (pp. 651–673). Syracuse, NY: Syracuse University Press.

Olweus, D. (1978). *Aggression in the schools: Bullies and whipping boys.* Washington, DC: Hemisphere.

O'Moore, M. (1987, August). *Bullying in the schools.* Paper presented at European teachers' seminar, Stavanger, Norway.

Peak, L. (1989). Learning to become part of the group: The Japanese child's transition to preschool life. *Journal of Japanese Studies, 15*(1), 93–123.

Peak, L. (1991). *Learning to go to school in Japan: The transition from home to preschool life.* Berkeley: University of California Press.

Perry, D., Williard, J., & Perry, L. (1990). Peers' perceptions of the consequences that victimized children provide aggressors. *Child Development, 61*(5), 1310–1325.

Saisho, A. (1982). Boryoku-teki hiko [Violent behavior]. In R. Hirano (Ed.), *Koza: Shonen hogo [Symposium: Protecting youth]* (Vol. 1, pp. 83–96). Tokyo: Taisei Shuppan-sha.

Sakagami, Y. (1983). *Shin seishin-eisei-gaku [New mental health].* Tokyo: Aikawa Shobo.

Schoolland, K. (1986). The bullying of Japanese youth. *International Education, 15*(2), 5–28.

Smith, R. (1961). The Japanese rural community: Norms, sanctions, and ostracism. *American Anthropologist, 63*(3), 522–533.

Spitzer, H. (1947). Psychoanalytic approaches to the Japanese character. *Psychoanalysis and the Social Sciences, 1,* 131–156.

Sugeno, T. (1986). *Ijime ikoru gakkyu no ningen-gaku [Bullying: Humanistic studies of classrooms].* Tokyo: Shinyo-sha.

Sugimoto, E. (1925). *A daughter of the samurai.* Garden City, NY: Doubleday.

Tobin, J., Wu, D., & Davidson, D. (1989). *Preschool in three cultures: Japan, China, and the United States.* New Haven: Yale University Press.

Uchimi, I., & Amano, T. (Eds.). (n.d.). *Shogaku dotoku shidosho* (Vols. 1–6). Osaka: Osaka Shoseki Kabushiki Gaisha.

White, M. (1987). *The Japanese educational challenge: A commitment to children.* New York: Free Press.

White, M., & LeVine, R. (1986). What is an *ii ko* [good child]? In H. Stevenson, H. Azuma, & K. Hakuta (Eds.), *Child development and education in Japan* (pp. 55–62). New York: Freeman.

Wolfenstein, M. (1955). Fun morality: An analysis of recent American child-training literature. In M. Mead & M. Wolfenstein (Eds.), *Childhood in contemporary cultures* (pp. 168–175). Chicago: University of Chicago Press.

Yamamoto, K. (1985). Ijime seishin [The psychology of bullying]. *Oya to Ko [Parent and Child], 32*(6), 27.

The Contributions of Betty Lanham
A Neglected Legacy

Catherine Lewis

I first encountered Betty Lanham's work—and the work of most of the other senior scholars in this book—in 1971, in an undergraduate course on Japanese society taught by Ezra Vogel at Harvard University (see Chapter 11, this volume). Twenty-five years later I still have my full lecture notes, a stack of yellowing reprints that includes several heavily dog-eared articles by Betty Lanham, and vivid memories of the course. Ezra Vogel's remarkable fount of information about human development in Japan, his quick wit, and his willingness to cross disciplinary boundaries and pull together research by economists, sociologists, psychologists, and anthropologists astonished me. Even more remarkable was the fact that, each Monday, he made himself available to undergraduates for a brown bag lunch, an informal time for students to raise questions and discuss issues of interest. Such opportunities for informal, small-group discussions with professors had been rare in my undergraduate experience. One of the issues we discussed was Lanham's data suggesting frequent use of *moxa* (see Chapter 6, this volume), a surprising finding in light of the generally nonpunitive, harmonious picture of Japanese childrearing she portrayed. Twenty-three years later this volume solves the mystery; Lanham and Garrick document the mistranslation of that questionnaire item. Dr. Lanham wrote to me of her delight in finally having the opportunity to correct that error. How many scholars—from that era or any other—have shown such eagerness to correct errors in their earlier work?

In the years since I attended those brown bag lunches, much

has been written about the importance of "caring community" in schools, and about the critical role of mentorship in students' learning and motivation (Solomon, Schaps, Watson, & Battistich, 1992; Bryk & Driscoll, 1988). Some of my own research has focused on the ways that elementary school teachers create a sense of safety in the classroom—safety that allows students to ask questions, reveal their ignorance, and test out their new ideas (Lewis, 1994). That security is what I remember best about Ezra Vogel's brown bag lunches, which made them a striking departure from most of my academic experiences up to that date. I remember telling my friends, in awe, that Ezra Vogel ate peanut butter sandwiches that he made himself, but only now do I understand why this impressed me so. Seeing the author of *Japan's New Middle Class* eat his home-made peanut butter sandwich, I discovered that research was conceived and created by real people. Suddenly the works of Betty Lanham, Takeo Doi, William Caudill, and others went beyond intellectual interest. I realized that I, too, could pursue the issues they raised.

I was originally drawn to the study of Japanese childrearing because of my own experiences in Japan. My introduction to Japan differed in many ways from Betty Lanham's, yet our interests evolved in remarkably parallel directions. At age 16, knowing only a few words of Japanese, I arrived on the doorstep of a host family in Tokyo, to spend a year (the 1967–1968 Japanese school year) as a foreign exchange student at Japan Women's University Attached High School. This year challenged my deepest assumptions about human behavior. On the first day of school, as the 53 girls in my class hurried to find hockey sticks and other hockey equipment, they scurried to equip *each other.* Before taking shinguards or pads for themselves, students tried to make sure classmates were properly outfitted, resulting in a number of comical exchanges of the "You first . . . No, you first . . . No, *you* first" variety. At age 16, I found this very puzzling. We had played field hockey in my American gym class, too, and I was used to grabbing shinguards and pads, intent on getting my own before my 22 classmates exhausted the supply.

As I learned more Japanese, things became not clearer but "curiouser and curiouser." The more Japanese I comprehended, the more perplexed I became. My Japanese high school classmates cleaned the school, maintained the landscape, and ran class and school meetings, all with little or no assistance from adults. They also took turns leading discussions, conducting the band, and supervising athletic workouts, without teachers present. My peers took seriously, and enforced on themselves, a number of regulations that seemed unduly restrictive to me—such as not stopping off to eat on the long commute home (for many students as much as 2 hours). In many ways, my research over the past 15 years has been an attempt to make sense of that high school year, and of the considerable challenge it presented to my beliefs about human nature. And I doubt I could have made much sense of those experiences if not for the work of Betty Lanham, Ezra Vogel, Takeo Doi, and virtually every other senior author represented in this volume. They gave me a view of Japanese socialization "from the shoulders of giants" (Kabayama, 1990).

Betty Lanham and I first came to know Japan under completely different circumstances. She lived in rural Wakayama during the poor, grim years following World War II, whereas I visited Tokyo during the post-Olympic prosperity of 1967–1968. She was an advanced graduate student with a methodology and framework for studying human behavior, while I was a naive high school student who had reflected little on human behavior until the cooperation and self-management of Japanese school life collided with my expectations. Yet despite these disparities of time, place, and disciplinary training, it is remarkable how Betty Lanham asked the same research questions that have caught my attention and that of my contemporaries (Lois Peak, Merry White, Joseph Tobin, and David and Barbara Shwalb, among others.) At the close of this reaction chapter, I would like to ask why our interests came to resemble Lanham's, and whether it is desirable that research questions transcend the generations.

Betty Lanham pioneered the use of quantitative, replicable measures to study Japanese childrearing, and broke out of the Freudian model that dominated childrearing studies in the early 1950s—a considerable feat in light of the sparse literature available on Japanese childrearing then (e.g., Benedict, 1946; Embree, 1939), her relatively isolated location (both geographically and professionally), and her limited command of Japanese. Reading the account of her rustic teahouse abode, where meal preparation began by lighting charcoal, I am even more impressed by her accomplishments, and feel almost guilty about the ease of doing research in contemporary Japan. Whether one studies infancy, moral development, or science education, nowadays one can easily find Japanese counterparts and appropriate professional organizations. We are spoiled by a mind-boggling array of convenience products, from handheld video monitors to instant meals, so that the time devoted to the substance of research can be much greater. I had never even heard of wax stencils (thank heaven!) until I read Betty Lanham's account.

Betty Lanham uncovered four issues that have continued to fascinate both Western and Japanese researchers: the (1) respectful treatment of young children by adults, (2) strategies used to control children's behavior, (3) emphasis on helping children feel emotionally secure, and (4) contents of moral education. Related by Lanham during the 1960's mainly to the context of the parent–child relationship, these issues have been resurrected in the 1980s and 1990s and examined in institutional settings: preschools *(yochien),* day nurseries *(hoikuen),* and elementary schools *(shogakko).* I would like to mention just a few examples of research that show remarkable similarity to the themes raised by Betty Lanham, citing mainly works not discussed in Chapter 6 by Lanham and Garrick.

RECENT STUDIES OF JAPANESE INSTITUTIONS

The Day Nursery

The husband–wife team of Mariko Fujita and Toshiyuki Sano has conducted ethnographic research in American and Japanese childcare centers (Sano, 1989; Fujita & Sano, 1988). In these institutional settings, they have gravitated toward many of the same themes that interested Betty Lanham—that is, how adults establish discipline, exercise control, and build relationships with children. Their observations of childcare workers are remarkably similar to those by Lanham, nearly 40 years earlier, of parent–child relationships, including an emphasis on harmony and avoidance of confrontation in the Japanese setting, and on rules and consequences in the American setting. They also document many strategies used by Japanese caregivers to maintain harmony while building social order. These include, for example, (1) *kibuntenkan* (literally, "mood change"), in which caregivers use music, humor, or voice signals to induce a change in mood and shift group attention to a new activity without making a direct request, and (2) relaxed acceptance of a degree of noise and activity that many American caregivers would term "chaotic" (Sano, 1989). Studying Japanese parents and children 3 decades earlier, Lanham noted the preferred use of distraction over confrontation when a problem arises in the parent–child relationship, and the importance of having the child understand (*wakaru*—that is, understand and *want* to do that which is correct: Lanham, 1966, 1988; Lanham & Garrick, Chapter 6, this volume).

Japanese Preschools

In addition to research in Japanese day nurseries, research in Japanese preschools also shows remarkable continuity with Lanham's earlier observations. My own work (Lewis, 1984, 1989, 1995) and that of Peak (1991) is reviewed by Lanham and Garrick (Chapter 6, this volume). Continuities between Lanham's research and studies of Japanese preschools conducted two decades later include the the subtle role of adult authority, the emphasis on harmony in the adult–child relationship, the focus on building a sense of belonging, and the explicit highlighting of moral values. In addition, Kotloff's (1993, 1996) ethnography of a Japanese preschool with Christian, progressive origins richly details the methods used by Japanese preschool teachers to foster a sense of belonging and shared purpose, and to maintain harmony in the case of conflicting needs. For example, in the preschool studied by Kotloff, all students rotated through all roles of a class play, in order to develop an understanding and sense of responsibility for the whole play. Each child had the opportunity to play every part, and the preschoolers were expected to work out among themselves who would play what part in the final performance before the parents. Kotloff notes that once

Cooperation and group spirit in elementary school are seen on Sports Day. The teachers (not shown) stand facing their pupils, performing calisthenics with them, Nagoya, 1993. Courtesy of David Shwalb.

Individual effort is also seen on Sports Day, as every child runs a sprint race, Nagoya, 1993. Courtesy of David Shwalb.

when two students could not work out who would play the lead in the Christmas Pageant, two Virgin Marys performed in unison, side by side! In the school studied by Kotloff, daily class meetings were another means to build friendships and a sense of belonging among children. Teachers asked children to introduce their free-play projects to one another, encouraging children to elaborate upon one another's ideas and to create shared projects. For instance, a song written and set to music by a particularly talented class member became "the song Tomoko wrote for us" and eventually, "our" song for the class play (Kotloff, 1993, 1996). Kotloff's rich ethnographic work thus focuses on many of the same issues that intrigued Betty Lanham both in her surveys of parents and studies of moral education: the emphasis on cooperation, concern for others, and responsibility.

Japanese Elementary Schools

Recent research on Japanese elementary schools also shows remarkable continuity with Lanham's research. Lanham and Garrick argue (Chapter 6, this volume), based on Lanham's data from the 1950s and 1960s, (1) that American adults often use a language of commands toward children that would not be appropriately directed at other adults (e.g., "Look at me while I am talking to you" and "Get off that box before you hurt yourself"), and (2) that Japanese adults by contrast show considerable respect for even very young children. Ethnographers Jack and Elizabeth Easley (1983), who spent 4 months conducting ethnographic research in a Japanese elementary school, made a remarkably similar observation about a Tokyo elementary school in the 1980s:

> We noted in Kitamaeno School, as compared with U.S. schools we know, that children are, from the outset, given greater responsibility and treated with greater respect for their own person and their own learning. This is true during and between classes, where, for periods of up to 30 minutes, all the children in the school will be unattended by a teacher or anyone else who is legally responsible for them. . . . When a teacher is absent, other teachers, the assistant principal, or the principal, drop in from time to time to assign work to the class, as there are no substitute teachers. . . . A child who disrupts a lesson is rarely singled out for special treatment by the teacher, who usually waits for the disruption to cease or goes on in spite of it. In short, the children are treated more the way we treat adults. (pp. 40–41)

In 1966, Lanham wrote: "A [Japanese] child reacts and is treated much as is an adult in the United States. He early develops a maturity, a sense of responsibility, and sensitivity to the attitudes and feelings of others. A mother is careful not to insult the personality that she is gingerly developing" (p. 324). In both of these passages, we see the same theme: respectful treatment of children.

ACROSS THE GENERATIONS:
GAPS AND CONTINUITIES

Despite the growing body of research on Japanese preschool, elementary, and secondary education, few Westerners have chosen to study Japanese childrearing in recent decades. The effort to study the Japanese parent–child relationship using replicable tools, pioneered by Betty Lanham, has found few heirs. Robert Hess, Mary Conroy, Hiroshi Azuma, Keiko Kashiwagi, and their colleagues, who studied maternal socialization strategies mainly as they affect children's academic achievement, perhaps come the closest (Azuma, Chapter 13, this volume; Conroy, Hess, Azuma, & Kashiwagi, 1980). Large-sample quantitative studies of American and Japanese parents *residing in the United States* are another continuation of Lanham's work (Power & Kobayashi-Winata, 1992).

In recent decades, why has the balance shifted from studies of family settings to studies of preschool and elementary settings? Perhaps my own experience provides a clue. As a graduate student, I had intended to do comparative research on Japanese and American childrearing, but was overwhelmed by the time and resources required to select comparable samples of Japanese and American parents and study them systematically. And so I chose to forgo that study on childrearing. Preschools, on the other hand, lent themselves to ethnographic research: one did not necessarily need to select a large, cross-national sample. As a postdoctoral researcher, I began to notice the discrepancy between accounts of "indulgent" Japanese early childrearing and the considerable discipline of Japanese elementary school life. Preschools were an important "missing link" in the research on Japanese socialization, particularly given the lack of English-language writings on Japanese preschools as of 1979. Methodologically, I felt comfortable writing about a small sample of preschools, whereas I would not have felt comfortable writing about an equally small sample of families. The "culture" consciously created by schools for public consumption makes preschools more accessible than are families, whose "cultures" are likely to be much more private and resistant to scrutiny. For example, in a preschool, the systems of chores, fixed small groups, rotating student leadership, and the like are carefully nurtured over many months, and could hardly be marshalled just for the visit of a foreign researcher. School values are transmitted through a variety of school festivals, ceremonies, and regulations. In contrast, the cultures created by families are likely to be inaccessible to outsiders (except through long, intimate acquaintance) and can be quite idiosyncratic. In other words, I studied educational institutions because socialization in these institutions is more straightforward and readily observable.

A second factor that led me to shy away from studying Japanese childrearing was the compelling portrait already provided by the Vogels (Chapters 10 and 11, this volume). It was hard for me to imagine how I could improve on *Japan's New Middle Class* (Vogel, 1963). In recent years, I have recommended to several graduate students searching for a dissertation topic that it is time to write the 1990s version of the Vogels' classic study of families. But nobody has taken on this challenge. Broad, "big picture" studies of childrearing are rare these days. In between detailed ethnography in which authors carefully refrain from generalizing about broad cultural patterns and large-scale survey studies in which the cultural meaning of items is hard to ascertain, lies fallow the territory so thoughtfully worked by the Vogels many years ago: ethnographically grounded investigation of "big" questions about cultural differences in patterns of childrearing and family life. Among my generation of Western specialists on Japan, I am not alone in abandoning the family to study school life. For instance, Peak went to Japan a few years later than I did, with the intention of studying techniques used by Japanese parents to prepare children for school. She was quickly convinced by the Japanese parents she interviewed that socialization for school happens at the preschool (Peak, 1991).

The generational shift from childrearing to preschool studies has produced some unfortunate gaps. Very little is written in English about contemporary Japanese childrearing. Japanese scholars are gravely concerned about young women who reject the role of mother (Hara & Minagawa, Chapter 2, this volume), and about overbearing mothers and absent fathers (Doi, 1973). Yet we know little about these topics or about how Japanese childrearing has changed, as we must assume it has, over the past 4 decades. This is a troubling gap, not just for our understanding of human development, but also for our understanding of Japanese schooling, which cannot be understood in a vacuum. As David Shwalb (1993) points out, "home and preschool are experienced in the same mind of the same child, so that their influences cannot be separated except on paper" (p. 27). That is, the distinction between contexts may be meaningful only to scholars. For example, Japanese preschool discipline, which emphasizes the bond of trust between child and teacher, may work only because of the early and continuing experiences of trust and harmony between parents and child.

We also know little about changes in Japanese preschools and elementary school education in the 20th century. Although Uno (1984) and Wollens (1993) have written fascinating accounts of some of the earliest Japanese day nurseries and preschools, most studies of preschool and elementary education have been conducted since 1980. Some commentators suggest that Japanese preschool and early elementary education was more authoritarian and regimented prior to World War II. Yet for nearly 100 years, Western observers have also been impressed by the responsibility and opportunities for self-management afforded to Japanese children. For example, in 1904, Lafcadio Hearn (1904/1974) wrote of Japanese elementary education that "the teacher does not act as master, but as elder brother. . . . Whatever restraint exists is chiefly exerted on the child by the common opinion of his class" (p. 422). In 1919, John Dewey, a founder of the American progressive education movement, wrote about his visits to Japanese preschools and elementary schools: "They have a great deal of freedom there. . . . The children were under no visible discipline, but were good as well as happy" (quoted in Kobayashi, 1964).

While Lanham lacks heirs, we who study institutional socialization lack predecessors. On both counts the gaps are unfortunate. In neither area can we say much about historical change or continuity or find many clues about how socialization may change or be changed by other forces such as the economy, demography, or organization of work. Nor do we know how childrearing and education influence one another—for example, how the early parent–child *amae* (dependence) may influence the child's relationships at school, or how the pressures of school may shape the parent–child relationship.

At the outset of this chapter I noted the remarkable continuity between Lanham's findings and those of a number of contemporary scholars. To be sure, some of them read Lanham's work, but others did not. And as the quotes from Lafcadio Hearn and John Dewey demonstrate, the continuity goes back well beyond Betty Lanham. In fact, in 1645, European sojourner Francoys Caron (1645/1967) wrote of his travels in Japan:

> They raise their children attentively and gently. Even if a child fusses or cries all night, physical punishment would not be used. Using patience and gentleness, the child would be helped to understand; punishment or criticism would not be thought appropriate. They believe that children have not yet developed understanding, that understanding comes with age and experience, that children must be guided with patience and nurturance. (p. 166)

For decades and perhaps centuries, Westerners including Betty Lanham have repeatedly been drawn to the same aspects of Japanese childrearing and school socialization—the harmony and empathy between parent and child, the downplaying of adult authority, and the considerable responsibility given children. No doubt these issues are striking because they challenge Western assumptions regarding the proper role of adult authority, the importance of "firm control" in children's upbringing, and the capacity of young children to exercise self-management. Maybe it is inevitable that Westerners focus on these issues. But this selective focus underscores the need for Americans to collaborate with Japanese scientists, who are likely to focus on a somewhat different set of issues.

For example, most American research on children's self-regulation focuses on children who are aggressive or who act out. In contrast, the Japanese psychologist Keiko Kashiwagi (1989) has focused on the opposite end of the self-regulation spectrum: children who have trouble asserting themselves.

FUTURE RESEARCH

The research of Betty Lanham represents to me a great legacy, and also reminds me how much remains to be studied. I believe that the most pressing research needs include the following.

1. We must explore diversity within Japan, in childrearing and in education. In many countries, socioeconomic differences in childrearing and in education are profound (Lambert, Hamers, & Frasure-Smith, 1979). Lanham's 1952 survey of parental disciplinary practices detected no class differences in Japanese childrearing. Yet much more investigation of socioeconomic, regional, and ethnic differences in Japanese childrearing and education needs to take place, building on the work of researchers like George De Vos (Chapter 4, this volume) and Nancy Sato (1991). A better understanding of Japan's diversity has obvious ramifications for the Japanese, as they seek to build "international citizenship" and to Embrace an increasingly large and diverse minority population. It may also have ramifications for Americans, if, as some accounts suggest, Japanese elementary schools succeed in helping most children, whatever their talents and backgrounds, feel a sense of belonging and commitment to schooling (Lewis, 1995).

2. Research is needed on how Japanese preschool and elementary teachers learn about discipline. American educators often ask me how Japanese teachers learn to use their disciplinary techniques: to emphasize empathy rather than reward or punishment as the basis for obedience; to have children solve problems rather than rely on adult authority; to involve children in daily management of the classroom; to build a sense of belonging and unity within the classroom. To what extent are these techniques explicitly taught in teacher education programs, and to what extent are they "folkways" known to most Japanese?

3. We need large-sample, multimethod studies of Japanese childrearing and education. Lanham's effort to provide quantitative, cross-national comparisons of Japanese and American child-

rearing has not been followed up sufficiently in my generation, although two major studies of Japanese educational achievement have studied parenting as it relates to academic achievement (Stevenson & Stigler, 1992; Hess & Azuma, 1991). Small-scale and ethnographic studies of Japanese preschool and elementary education have provided a rich understanding of the particular settings studied, but one must question how widely their findings may be applied (Lewis, 1994; Peak, 1991; Tobin, Wu, & Davidson, 1989; Hendry, 1986). Clearly, it is time for the two methods to be merged.

The work of Lanham in the 1950s and 1960s established central themes to be studied concerning Japanese childrearing. Much remains to be learned about these themes. As we pursue the preceding three lines of research, we can begin to fulfill the promise of her legacy.

REFERENCES

Benedict, R. (1946). *The chrysanthemum and the sword.* Boston: Houghton Mifflin.

Bryk, A. S., & Driscoll, M. E. (1988). *The school as community: Theoretical foundations, contextual influences, and consequences for students and teachers.* Madison, WI: National Center on Effective Secondary Schools.

Caron, F. (1967). *Beschrijvinghe van het machtigh Coninckrijck Japan [Nihon taiokokushi].* Tokyo: Heibonsha. (Original work published 1645)

Conroy, M., Hess, R., Azuma, H., & Kashiwagi, K. (1980). Maternal strategies for regulating children's behavior: Japanese and American families. *Journal of Cross-Cultural Psychology, 11,* 153–172.

Doi, T. (1973). *The anatomy of dependence.* Tokyo: Kodansha International.

Easley, J., & Easley, E. (1983). Kitamaeno school as an environment in which children study mathematics themselves. *Japanese Journal of Science Education, 7,* 39–48.

Embree, J. (1939). *Suye Mura: A Japanese village.* Chicago: University of Chicago Press.

Fujita, M., & Sano, T. (1988). Children in American and Japanese day care centers: Ethnography and reflective cross-cultural interviewing. In H. T. Trueba & C. Delgado-Gaitan (Eds.), *School and society: Learning content through culture* (pp. 73–97). New York: Praeger.

Hearn, L. (1974). *Japan: An interpretation.* Rutland, VT: Tuttle. (Original work published 1904)

Hendry, J. (1986). *Becoming Japanese: The world of the Japanese preschool child.* Honolulu: University of Hawaii Press.

Hess, R. D., & Azuma, H. (1991). Cultural support for schooling: Contrasts between Japan and the United States. *Educational Researcher, 20,* 2–8, 12.

Kabayama, K. (1990). Transformation of the European system of learning: A case study of France in the seventeenth century. *Senri Ethnological Studies, 28,* 99–110.

Kashiwagi, K. (1989). *Development of self-regulation in Japanese children.* Paper presented at 10th Meeting of the International Society for the Study of Behavioral Development, Jyvaskyla, Finland.

Kobayashi, V. (1964). *John Dewey in Japanese educational thought.* Ann Arbor: University of Michigan School of Education.

Kotloff, L. J. (1993). Fostering cooperative group spirit and individuality: Examples from a Japanese preschool. *Young Children, 48*(3), 17–23.

Kotloff, L. J. (1966). ". . . and Tomoko wrote this song for us." In T. P. Rohlen & G. K. LeTendre (Eds.), *Teaching and learning in Japan* (pp. 129–161). New York: Cambridge University Press.

Lambert, W. E., Hamers, J. F., & Frasure-Smith, N. (1979). *Child-rearing values: A cross-national study.* New York: Praeger.

Lanham, B. (1966). The psychological orientation of the mother–child relationship in Japan. *Monumenta Nipponica, 21*(3–4), 322–333.

Lanham, B. (1988). Freedom, restraint, and security: Japan and the United States. *Ethos, 16*(3), 273–284.

Lewis, C. C. (1984). Cooperation and control in Japanese nursery schools. *Comparative Education Review, 32,* 69–84.

Lewis, C. (1989). From indulgence to internalization: Social control in the early school years. *Journal of Japanese Studies, 15,* 139–157.

Lewis, C. (1995). *Educating hearts and minds: Reflections on Japanese preschool and early elementary education.* New York: Cambridge University Press.

Peak, L. (1991). *Learning to go to school in Japan.* Berkeley: University of California Press.

Power, T. G., & Kobayashi-Winata, H. (1992). Childrearing patterns in Japan and the United States: A cluster analytic study. *International Journal of Behavioral Development, 15,* 185–205.

Sano, T. (1989). Methods of social control and socialization in Japanese day-care centers. *Journal of Japanese Studies, 15,* 125–138.

Sato, N. (1991). *Ethnography of Japanese elementary schools: Quest for equality. DAI, 52*(09A), 3171.

Shwalb, D. (1993). The source of Japanese school readiness: Preschool or family? *Cross-Cultural Psychology Bulletin, 27,* 25–29.

Solomon, D., Schaps, E., Watson, M., & Battistich, V. (1992). Creating caring school and classroom communities for all students. In R. Villa, J. Thousand, W. Stainback, & C. Stainback (Eds.), *Restructuring for caring and effective education: An administrative guide to creating heterogeneous schools* (pp. 41–60). Baltimore: Brookes.

Stevenson, H., & Stigler, J. (1992). *The learning gap: Why our schools are failing and what we can learn from Japanese and Chinese education.* New York: Summit.

Tobin, J., Wu, D. Y., & Davidson, D. H. (1989). *Preschool in three cultures.* New Haven: Yale University Press.

Uno, K. S. (1984). Day-care and family life in late-Meiji/Taisho Japan. *Transactions of the Asiatic Society of Japan, 19,* 17–31.

Vogel, E. (1963). *Japan's new middle class.* Berkeley: University of California Press.

Wollens, R. (1993). The black forest in a bamboo garden: Missionary kindergartens in Japan, 1868–1912. *History of Education Quarterly, 33,* 1–35.

CHAPTER 8

William Caudill and the Reproduction of Culture
Infant, Child, and Maternal Behavior in Japan and the United States

Carmi Schooler

In 1960, William Caudill conceived a longitudinal comparative study of how culture is transmitted from mother to child in Japan and the United States. Although he died in 1972, before all of the analyses were completed, Caudill essentially achieved his goal. Despite a variety of limitations, he found meaningful cross-cultural differences in parent and child behavior at ages 3 months, at $2\frac{1}{2}$ years, and again at 6 years. Compared to the Japanese, Americans— both mothers and children—were found to be more active, more vocally and physically emotional, more independent, and more likely to functionally manipulate both their social and physical environments.

The strength and complementariness of these relationships, and the ways in which the differences in both parent and child behavior in the two countries mirror differences in the cultural values of the two societies, make a strong case that dissimilarities in behavior of children in the two cultures result from culturally determined differences in their mothers' parenting behavior. We shall see that although Caudill himself raised possible alternative explanations of his findings, and although other explanations have been raised by later studies, Caudill's data as a whole provide strong evidence for his hypotheses about cultural transmission.

Caudill's research design was original and advanced in several important ways. His was the first study of children and childrearing to combine a longitudinal cross-cultural design with (1) culturally knowledgeable participant observation, (2) extensive semistructured family interviews, and (3) detailed time-sampled categorically structured observations. In addition, once gathered, the data were analyzed with the most advanced statistical procedures then available. The study thus represented, as of the early 1960s, a unique combination of the most sophisticated techniques of anthropology, developmental psychology, and statistical analysis.

BIOGRAPHICAL BACKGROUND

Both Caudill's decision to compare mother and child behavior in Japan and the United States, and the specific ways in which he conducted the study, appear to have been natural developments of his personal and intellectual history. His first introduction to Japanese culture was as a graduate student after service in the U.S. Navy in World War II. At the University of Chicago he was involved with, among others, George De Vos and the psychoanalyst Charlotte Babcock (see De Vos, Chapter 4, this volume), in the study of the characteristics of the personality and community life of that city's Japanese-Americans. For a full discussion of Caudill's early intellectual background one should read De Vos and Vogel (1973), which is the editorial introduction to two special issues of the *Journal of Nervous and Mental Disease* memorializing Caudill (Vogel & Schooler, 1973).

Caudill's involvement in psychoanalytically oriented research reflected a deep personal and professional commitment. This commitment continued in his next major research project, his pioneering and controversial study of the social organization and interpersonal relationships of patients in the neuropsychiatric wards of Yale University Hospital. For this study, Caudill entered the hospital posing as a patient; except for the top officials at the hospital, no one knew his real status. His inner turmoil was not apparent in the compelling and insightful book he wrote on the topic (Caudill, 1958). But as described later by De Vos and Vogel (1973), "The strain on Bill between his role as an objective observer and his human sensitivity to people who were deceived by his dissembling developed into a very severe personal and career crisis" (p. 234).

Caudill's interest in both medical sociology and psychoanalysis continued when he became an assistant professor in the Department of Social Relations at Harvard, in 1952. During his stay in

Boston, he even completed a training analysis at the orthodox Freudian Boston Psychoanalytic School. In 1954–1955, he had the opportunity, funded by the U.S. government, to go to Japan to study the problematic relationships between the American military and their Japanese hosts. Although Caudill had been clearly excited by the earlier contact with Japanese culture during his Chicago research, on this, his first trip to Japan, he was enthralled. He had an immediate sympathy for the culture, and Japan met his personal, social, professional, and aesthetic needs. He was intrigued by what he saw as its guilt-free sensuousness and emotional connection among people. He not only met his future wife, but made lifelong friendships with many of his Japanese contemporaries who would become leaders in Japanese psychiatry and social science, including Takeo Doi (1973), and Shoshiru Kuromaru (1973). He clearly had found the site for his lifework. Caudill's enthusiasm for Japan had some immediate effects with important long-term consequences for America's understanding of Japan. When he returned to Harvard, his enthusiasm for Japan rubbed off on Ezra Vogel, then a graduate student in the Department of Social Relations. As Vogel later put it, "I had come to him as a student of the sociology of health, and following his footsteps, ended as an East Asian specialist" (De Vos & Vogel, 1973, p. 235).

By the late 1950s it became clear that Harvard, with its usual lack of perspicacity in dealing with junior faculty, did not appreciate Caudill, and he was obviously not at peace with his surroundings. It was then that he left university life and joined the Laboratory of Socio-environmental Studies of the Intramural Program of the National Institute of Mental Health.

The Laboratory, to which I had recently come as a new Ph.D. in social psychology, was a multidisciplinary, full-time research group whose goal was to examine how social processes affect normal and abnormal psychological functioning. Besides being a non-academic setting that did not require teaching, it differed from Harvard in several ways that directly affected Caudill's research. One of these was that it could command the resources necessary to support the plans he developed for his Japanese research. The second was that the Laboratory was methodologically a hard-nosed, quantitatively oriented place, whose other members were not particularly sympathetic to psychoanalysis, which had remained part of the core of Caudill's thinking.

Although both my statistical orientation and my distaste for psychoanalytic thought were at least as strong as those of anybody else in the Laboratory, Bill's arrival and plans excited me. I had by then been strongly interested in Japan for several years. The sources of my interest were primarily philosophical: I had been strongly influenced by Alan Watts (1950) and D. T. Suzuki's (1949) writings on Zen Buddhism, and I also was attracted by traditional Japanese aesthetics, which often seemed to parallel my own. In addition, besides finding myself greatly attracted to Japanese art, pottery, and philosophy, I had, since, my college days at Hamilton College, been intrigued by the question of why Japan had modernized so readily.

As a consequence of our mutual interest in Japan, Bill, who was about a dozen years older, and I developed a relationship in which he was my mentor in things Japanese and I his consultant in quantifying and analyzing his behavioral observations. We also collaborated in comparisons of Japan and the United States in other areas of mutual interest, such as birth-order effects and schizophrenic symptomatology. Through all of this, Caudill was more likely to see the differences between the two countries and I the similarities. This divergence was possibly due to differences in our professional orientations. As an anthropologist, Bill was intrigued by cultural differences; as a psychologist and sociologist, I was more inclined to look for underlying psychological and social-structural similarities.

At least in part as a result of Caudill's sponsorship, in 1971 I received a Japanese Government Research Award for Foreign Specialists, which permitted me to actually visit Japan for the first time and to spend 7 months there. This opportunity proved ominously fortunate. When Caudill died in early 1972, shortly after my return to the United States, my firsthand experience with Japan gave me the confidence to finish the analyses and interpretation of the data he had collected.

RESEARCH RESULTS

The results of Caudill's comparative study of mother and child behavior in Japan and the United States appeared in four core papers: (1) "Maternal Care and Infant Behavior in Japan and America" (Caudill & Weinstein, 1969), (2) "Tiny Dramas: Vocal Communication between Mother and Infant in Japanese and American Families" (Caudill, 1972), (3) "A Comparison of Maternal Care and Infant Behavior in Japanese-American, American and Japanese Families" (Caudill & Frost, 1974), and (4) "Child Behavior and Child Rearing in Japan and the United States: An Interim Report" (Caudill & Schooler, 1973). For a full summary of Caudill and Weinstein (1969), Caudill (1972), and Caudill and Frost (1974), one should see Caudill and Schooler (1973). That posthumous summary, which used Caudill's words as much as possible, provided the basis for the present review of those papers.

The Caudill and Weinstein paper describes the procedures and basic results of the initial infant study. Helen Weinstein, who was in her late 40s at the time, and who unfortunately died before Caudill, received her M.A. in Anthropology from American University in 1962. She did the American observations and helped in all stages of data analysis. The Japanese observations were made by a Japanese psychologist, Mrs. Seiko Notsuki. Both Mrs. Weinstein and Mrs. Notsuki were extensively trained by Caudill. Interobserver reliability was checked in seven Japanese cases and three American ones. Caudill was the "constant" in the reliability check, being paired with Notsuki in Japan and Weinstein in the United States. The levels of reliability across the different ratings were very high. In addition, a weight for each variable was constructed that standardized Notsuki's and Weinstein's scores to those of the constant observer— Caudill (cf. Caudill & Weinstein, 1969, pp. 23–25). An examination of the nature of these weights indicates that, if anything, using them was a conservative measure that decreased the likelihood of confirming Caudill's hypotheses.

As Caudill and Weinstein reported, 30 first-born, urban, middle-class infants, equally divided by sex, were selected in Japan and then matched for age, sex, social class, and size of the business in which the father was employed with 30 Caucasian, American infants and their families. Subjects were all first-borns recruited by pediatricians. Twenty of the Japanese cases came from Tokyo, and 10 from Kyoto. Kyoto might have been expected to have a somewhat more traditional form of childrearing than Tokyo; family living quarters were definitely larger in Kyoto. Nevertheless, there were no significant differences between the two cities in infant or caretaker behavior, and the data from the two cities were combined.

The initial study was carried out during 1962–1964. Observations were made in the homes of the 3- to 4-month-old infants on the morning of one day and the afternoon of the next day. Using a predetermined set of categories and time sampling, one observation of infant and parent behavior was recorded every 15th second over a 10-minute period. There was a 5-minute break between each

William Caudill records observations of mother–infant interactions, in the living room of a Tokyo family. Courtesy of Carmi Schooler.

of these observation periods, and 10 such observation periods were carried out each day, giving a total of 400 pairs of observations for each child.

Analyses of these observations revealed a basic similarity in biologically rooted behavior, for example, in the total time the child spent eating and sleeping and the mother in feeding and diapering. There were, however, distinct cultural differences. American infants showed greater amounts of gross bodily activity, play, and happy vocalization; Japanese infants seemed passive, showing only a greater amount of unhappy vocalization. American mothers were more likely to look at, position, and chat to their infants; Japanese mothers did more carrying, rocking, and lulling.

Caudill regarded the general findings as indicating that mothers in the two cultures engage in different styles of caretaking. He saw the American mother as encouraging her baby to be active and vocally responsive, while the Japanese mother acts to soothe and quiet her baby. He believed that by 3 or 4 months, infants in both cultures become habituated to respond appropriately to these different styles of caretaking in ways that are strikingly in line with the general expectations of behavior in the two cultures. In the United States the individual should be physically and verbally assertive; in Japan one should be physically and verbally restrained (Caudill & Schooler, 1973).

Noting that the greater happy vocalization of the American infant is significantly correlated with the mother's looking at and chatting with her baby, while the Japanese infant's lesser amount of happier vocalization does not show any relationship with the mother's behavior, Caudill hypothesized that vocal communication between mother and infant in the two cultures serves different purposes. He tested this hypothesis in his "Tiny Dramas" paper (Caudill, 1972). In this paper, a pioneering example of the now popular microsequential mode of analysis, Caudill examined the behavioral sequences that occurred in all of the instances in which the infant was awake and alone to discover what happened when the infant began a string of happy, unhappy, or mixed vocalizations. He found first that not only did American mothers respond more quickly to their baby's vocalizations, regardless of whether they were happy or unhappy, but, more importantly, the American mothers differentiated more sharply between kinds of vocalization than did the Japanese mothers, by responding more quickly to unhappy sounds than they did to happy sounds. Caudill saw this faster responsiveness of American mothers to their children's unhappy vocalizations as one means through which the American mothers taught their infants to make discriminating use of their voices. In the same vein, American mothers had more vocal interactions with their babies, especially chatting with them at the times they were happily vocal.

The Japanese mothers seemed to be more entangled than the American ones in the process of their baby's going to sleep. They seemed to often show a pattern in which they carried, rocked, and lulled their babies to sleep, with the result that when the sleeping baby was put down, it would awaken and cry and the process would begin all over again. In addition, the Japanese mother was more likely than the American mother to adjust the covers, wipe the sweat off the sleeping baby's forehead, or carry out other actions that seemed to interfere with the baby's normal rhythm of sleep. Caudill saw the Japanese mother's style of parenting as pointing to a lesser reliance on and refinement of vocal communication between mother and infant, while, at the same time, emphasizing the importance of physical contact.

Comparing the overall patterns of behavior in the two cultures,

Caudill concluded that the American mother views her baby as a separate, autonomous being with its own needs and desires that she learns to recognize and care for, but who should learn to do and think for itself. In Japan, on the other hand, the mother views her baby more as an extension of herself, so that psychologically the boundaries between her and her child are blurred. Thus, the mother is likely to feel that she knows what is best for her baby, and there is no particular need for verbal communication. Caudill saw these results as making it likely that a considerable amount of culturally patterned behavior has come into being by 3 or 4 months of age. In the United States, the infant is encouraged to be independent and to care for its own needs, while in Japan the infant comes to expect that its needs will be taken care of by others, particularly if it complains hard enough.

It should also be noted that Caudill, particularly in the "Tiny Dramas" paper, went to great lengths to show that the temporal sequences of the mother–child interaction strongly suggest that the causal direction is from the mother's behavior to the child's. Such a causal direction would argue strongly against the contention that the differences between the United States and Japan in mother–infant interactions are in large part a function of innate biological differences between the Japanese and American infants and of the resulting differences in the way their mothers deal with them.

An even stronger argument against the possibility that the differences between the two cultures are genetic in origin is provided by Caudill and Frost (1974). In 1969–1970, Lois Frost, for her master's thesis at Sacramento State College, studied a sample of 21 fourth-generation Japanese-American infants—infants who were genetically Japanese, but whose parents had become culturally much more American than Japanese. She designed her study after she read Caudill and Weinstein (1969) and used the same methods.

When Frost wrote Caudill about her research, he rushed to take advantage of the opportunity. In January of 1971, Caudill and Frost carried out observations together in the homes of four infants in order to obtain data for testing interobserver reliability and for standardizing the scores on the dependent variables. After establishing the reliability of Frost's observations, Caudill and Frost compared the infant and mother behavior of the Japanese-Americans to that of Caudill's own Caucasian-American and Japanese samples. If group genetic factors underlie the differences Caudill found between his American and Japanese subjects, then the Japanese-American infants should be more like the Japanese. On the other hand, if learned differences are predominant, then the Japanese-

American infants should be more like the Caucasian-Americans. The latter turned out to be the case. The Japanese-American and the Caucasian-American infants were alike in that they both responded to the high level of stimulation from their mothers, with high levels of happy vocalization and physical activity.

The Caudill and Schooler (1973) paper reports on the observations of the original infants when they were $2\frac{1}{2}$ and 6 years old. Caudill planned the longitudinal part of the study to determine whether the cross-cultural differences found in infancy led to parallel differences in later ages. The sample for the two time periods consisted of the 20 oldest children from each culture. At each age, the mother was interviewed with an extensive semistructured interview schedule that centered on the child's family life and psychological and physical functioning. William Caudill carried out the United States interviews, and his wife Mieko (Mie) Imagi Caudill, who had a M.A. in Anthropology, carried out the Japanese ones.

It should also be noted that, for whatever reason, Mie Caudill's contribution to the overall research program has not always been fully acknowledged. Her contributions went substantially beyond interviewing the Japanese mothers. She was a valuable collaborator at each stage of the research. During its planning and implementation she was a source of advice, support, and practical help. She brought to these tasks both the viewpoint of a trained social scientist and a real personal knowledge of both cultures.

The observations in Japan were made by William Caudill and those in the United States by Helen Weinstein. Observations were made for 4 hours one afternoon and 4 hours the next evening. During these periods the observer wrote a running account of the child's overt behavior, following the general approach of Barker and Wright (1951), in notebooks that had been previously divided to permit recordings on the basis of 2-minute segments.

The recorded observations were coded according to an elaborate scheme in which each 2-minute observation was classified according to (1) location and number of people present, (2) who was the principal caretaker, (3) level and nature of the activity of caretaker and child, (4) physical contact between caretaker and child, (5) emotional tone of the caretaker and child, (6) characteristics of verbal interaction, using among other measures the Bales Interaction Protocol (Bales, 1951), and (7) behaviors related to self-indulgence, possessiveness, and independence on the part of the caretaker and child. The percentage of absolute agreement on independent coding of the different variables was generally between 85 and 95, and never below 80.

The basic method of statistical analysis was multivariate analysis of variance. Analyses were carried out for six sets of dependent variables: (1) activity, (2) affect, (3) dependence-related behavior, (4) independence-related behavior, (5) caretaker attempts to mold or discipline child, and (6) child performing adult tasks.

The general tenor of the findings was that the essential cross-cultural differences found when the children were infants were repeated at ages $2\frac{1}{2}$ and 6. Compared to the Japanese, the Americans were more active, more vocally and physically emotional, more independent, and more likely to functionally manipulate their social and physical environments. At each of the age periods the cross-cultural differences in the behavior of the parents mirrored those of the children.

These findings provide strong support for Caudill's hypothesis that culturally patterned differences in parental behavior lead to the transmission of culturally patterned differences in the behavior of the next generation. This would seem to be especially the case if these findings about differences in the behavior of Japanese and American $2\frac{1}{2}$- and 6-year-old children and their mothers are taken together with (1) Caudill and Weinstein's demonstration of parallel cross-cultural differences during infancy, (2) the strong evidence of the causal importance of the mother's behavior that Caudill derived from his analyses of the temporal sequences in the tiny dramas of mother–infant interaction, and (3) Caudill and Frost's finding that Japanese-American infants and mothers are much more similar to Caucasian-American infants and mothers than they are to Japanese ones.

METHODOLOGICAL CONCERNS AND PROBLEMS

Although I believe that Caudill's longitudinal findings make a strong case for his hypotheses about the transmission of cultural behavior patterns through parenting behavior, methodological questions casting doubt on the validity and generality of these conclusions were raised both in the original articles and by later critics.

Some of these doubts relate to the nature of the samples. In both countries, the samples were ones of convenience and far from representative. At a minimum, individuals who volunteer to take part in a study in which strangers come into their homes to assess the way they raise their children are different from those who do not. In both countries, the samples, although matched on age and education, were heavily skewed toward the urban middle class. We know that in both countries there are sharp social stratification differences in childrearing values and behavior. Lower socioeconomic status parents are likely to value conformity in their children; higher socioeconomic status parents are more likely to value self-directedness (Kohn, 1969; Kohn & Schooler, 1969, 1983; Smith & Schooler, 1978; Schooler & Smith, 1978; Kohn, A. Naoi, Schoenbach, Schooler, & Slomczynski, 1990). Urban–rural differences have also been shown to exist in both countries, with urban parents being more likely to value self-direction, and rural parents, conformity (Schooler, 1972; Smith & Schooler, 1978; Schooler & Smith, 1978). More generally, social-structural variables related to environmental complexity result in an emphasis on individuality (Schooler, 1972; Schooler & Smith, 1978; Schooler, 1984; Schooler, 1990a, 1990b). Although these social-structural effects may well be independent of cross-cultural differences (Caudill, 1972; A. Naoi & Schooler, 1985; Schooler & A. Naoi, 1988; M. Naoi & Schooler, 1990), we cannot be certain that the same cross-national differences would be found if representative samples from both countries were compared. My personal guess, however, given the degree to which the differences in parents' and children's behaviors reflected the cultural norms of the two countries, is that at the time of the original studies the cross-cultural differences Caudill found would have held up even if representative samples had been used.

Other potential criticisms of Caudill's research more directly concern the nature of the observations. One question that has been raised (Lewis, 1976; Chen & Miyake, 1986) is that of possible effects on mother and child behavior of differences in the size and layout of American and Japanese houses. Although such possible effects cannot be completely discounted, it should be noted that no differences were found in mother and infant behaviors between the Japanese families living in Tokyo and those living in Kyoto, even though the family accommodations of those living in Kyoto were considerably more spacious than those living in Tokyo.

A second concern is about the possible effects in Japan of the presence of a foreign observer. Except for those seven Japanese cases in which Caudill was present to gather reliability cases, all of the infant observations were carried out by researchers of the same nationality as those being observed. It is true that Caudill himself gathered the Japanese data when the children were $2\frac{1}{2}$ and 6 years of age, but it should be borne in mind that he was reasonably fluent in Japanese and quite experienced in both participant-observation techniques and the nuances of a wide variety of Japanese social settings.

A more general concern has also been raised about the possibility that "the very presence of an observer in mother–infant context could have created significant behavioral differences between the two nationalities" (Chen & Miyake, 1986, p. 138). This possibility cannot of course be ruled out. However, similar questions could be raised about any overt method of cross-cultural comparison (e.g., videotaping, experiments, surveys, ethnographic observation) in which the subjects, in this case mothers and children, know they are being studied.

I feel less secure about another limitation of generalization— that of time. Thirty years have gone by since the original data were collected, and both countries have clearly changed. Whether they have necessarily gotten more similar is a matter of much dispute. Although there is a whole body of *Nihonjinron* literature devoted to Japanese uniqueness, the various hypotheses predicting increasing levels of cultural and behavioral convergence among industrial and postindustrial societies are still very much alive.

Leaving aside for the moment more profound and scientific approaches to the issue of change in Japan and granting that, as I have noted above, I am more inclined to see cross-cultural similarities than differences, my views about possible shifts in Japanese childrearing practices have been affected by my informal personal observations. For example, in the more than 20 years that I have been taking public transportation fairly regularly in Japan, I believe that I have seen a substantial diminution in the frequency with which Japanese mothers fondle, change the posture, or otherwise physically intrude on their sleeping children. In part because of such informal personal observations, I would not be surprised if some of the differences between Caudill's findings and those of some of the later studies I will be discussing shortly are not attributable to the historical and cultural changes that have taken place over the years.

A quite different type of sampling problem underlies another reservation about Caudill's conclusions. In Caudill and Schooler (1973), we tried to prove that the differences in behavior between children in the two cultures result from differences in the behavior of their parents by showing that the behavioral differences we found between mothers from the two cultures had similar effects among the individuals within each culture, as we postulated they had across cultures. For example, if the higher level of verbal communication of American children is caused by the higher level of verbal communication of their mothers, then Japanese mothers who are relatively more verbal should have children who are relatively more verbal, and American mothers who are relatively less verbal should have children who are relatively less verbal. Finding that the presumed cause definitely preceded the effect would greatly strengthen such a line of reasoning. Thus, the most convincing test of a causal link between mother's and child's behavior would have been within-culture correlations between the mother's behavior toward her infant and the child's behavior at $2\frac{1}{2}$ and 6 years of age, or between the mother's behavior at $2\frac{1}{2}$ and the child's behavior at 6. However, when we examined the relevant correlations, although we found some significant ones, no pattern of correlations emerged that could have been readily predicted from the general hypotheses of the study. In fact, given the large number of correlations we examined, the number of significant correlations we found were not too different from what we would have expected by chance.

I concluded that these attempts at causal analysis were unsuccessful because they were based on the inappropriate sampling assumption that it would be possible to demonstrate longitudinal causal relationships with data based on only one afternoon's and one evening's observation at each time period for each subject. A basic tenet of sampling theory is that the reliability of the generalization from a sample of a population to that population is much more a function of the absolute size of the sample than of its size relative to the population. We have a sample of 20 with which to characterize the behavior of mothers and children in Japan or the United States at three age levels, but only one morning and one afternoon's behavior at each age level to characterize the behavior of each child and caretaker. The cross-cultural differences that are based on a sample of 20 in each culture are both significant and meaningfully patterned. On the other hand, our causal explanations based on correlations of individuals' behaviors within cultures require that we have reliable estimates of each individual's behavior so that we can compare each one's behavior with that of others in our sample from that culture. Sampling data from one afternoon and one evening just does not provide the requisite reliability to characterize the individual. Even without being a statistician, it is not hard to imagine how the child's having a cold or stomachache at the particular time that the observations were carried out might effect the way the child was characterized at that age. If Caudill had followed a somewhat different time-sampling strategy and sampled behavior over a greater number of occasions, his characterizations of each individual subject's behavior would have been more reliable. Since the subject would have become more accustomed to the observer's presence, carrying out the observations over several occasions would probably also have reduced any effects the observer might have had on the subject's behavior.

Unfortunately, when I attempted further analyses of Caudill's data, this inability to reliably characterize individuals proved an insurmountable stumbling block. This well might have been the case even if Caudill had lived to carry out his plans for linking each child's behavior to its family's dynamics and cultural milieu. My misplaced optimism about being able to overcome this sampling problem is reflected in my subtitling our paper, "An Interim Report." Caudill and Schooler (1973) was, in fact, the last paper deriving directly from Caudill's own work.

THE STURDINESS OF CAUDILL'S FINDINGS IN LIGHT OF LATER REPLICATIONS AND EXTENSIONS

Quite a few studies have more or less followed Caudill's pioneering program. In 1989, Bornstein reviewed 10 major studies comparing motoric activity and development in Japanese and American infants. Subsequently, there have been several more. The first major attempt to test Caudill's findings was carried out by Shand and Kosawa (Shand & Kosawa, 1985a, 1985b; Shand, Chapter 15, this volume). They used video cameras to record the behavior of 49 Japanese and 93 Caucasian-American mothers at their child's birth, and at 1 month and 3 months of age. As was the case with the Caudill observations, the behavioral sample was gathered in only two consecutive day sessions. Their findings are also comparable to Caudill's in many important respects: For example, they found that American infants are more likely to explore their environments and American mothers more likely to chat with their infants than are their Japanese counterparts. Nevertheless, the general tenor of their conclusions appears to be quite opposite of Caudill's. Finding the Japanese infants more active than the American ones, Shand and Kosawa trace this greater activity to genetically caused differences visible at birth and see the cross-cultural differences in parenting style as in some possibly large part a function of the mothers' reactions to the biological differences in their babies.

A closer examination of both their reasoning and the pattern of their findings throws some doubt on these conclusions. First of all, there is no necessary reason to believe that activity level immediately after birth represents a reliable measure of temperament and activity level. The nature of even "normal" birth processes varies according to difficulty, anesthesia, and other factors. Second, as Shand and Kosawa note, the neonate is far from fully developed. Postbirth neurological development may not be universally consistent in nature or timing. Third, stability in infant activity level "is not altogether common (e.g., Bornstein & Tamis-LeMonda, 1988; Moss, 1967)" (Bornstein, 1989, p. 182).

Even within Shand and Kosawa's own data, the correlation of overall activity between birth and 3 months was not significant, and there were some complex sex interactions for particular behaviors (e.g., among males those less active at birth later spent more time feeding and awake later than those more active; among females, neonatally active females later made fewer noncrying vocalizations than did neonatally less active ones). Furthermore, not only did both maternal and infant overall behavior change significantly over time, but maternal behavior was more stable and infant behavior more malleable. This relative malleability of infant behavior would seem to argue against the predominant importance of stable genetically determined biological factors in explaining the behavioral differences among the infants.

All in all, the pattern of Shand and Kosawa's findings would not seem to strongly support their argument that the cross-cultural mother and infant behavioral differences they found are substantially a function of national differences in the mothers' differential reactions to stable differences in activity levels of their children. Babies' characteristics may well influence their mother's behaviors; "the characteristics of infant group members . . . may possibly influence the behavior of the primary culture transmitter, its mother, and thus modify culture itself" (Shand & Kosawa, 1985a, p. 870). Shand and Kosawa are, however, I believe, stretching their data to support these sociobiological hypotheses.

Bornstein (1989) reviewed the papers appearing to the mid-1980s that compared Japanese and American infant and mother behavior. He found that when studies compared Japanese data on various standardized tests of motoric activity with American norms, the Japanese babies tended to appear more active. In terms of more exact replications, Bornstein located two studies—Sengoku, Davitz, and Davitz (1982) and Otaki, Durrett, Richards, Nyquist, and Pennebaker (1986)—that were deliberate attempts to repeat Caudill and Weinstein's procedures. Taken together, these two studies generally support Caudill and Weinstein's findings. Both studies agree with Caudill and Weinstein (as well as with Shand) that American and Japanese babies behave equivalently in the biological sphere. Sengoku et al. agree with Caudill and Weinstein that Japanese babies are more motorically active; Otaki et al. replicate Caudill and Weinstein's finding that United States mothers stimulated their babies more than Japanese ones.

Bornstein's and his collaborators' own studies also tend to support Caudill's conclusions. Coding videotapes of single observation sessions of comparable dyads of 5-month-old Japanese and American mothers and children (24 in each culture), Bornstein (1988) found that American babies explored and vocalized positively more than Japanese babies, while Japanese babies tended toward more negative vocalization than American ones. Examining maternal responsiveness, Bornstein, Azuma, Tamis-LeMonda, and Ogino (1990) found that while American mothers responded more to their infants vocalizing in a nondistressed way while looking at objects, Japanese mothers responded more to their infants' nondistressed vocalizing while looking at them. These national differences are consonant with the more general values in the two cultures.

In attempting to link mother and infant behaviors, Bornstein, Azuma, et al. (1990) found that Japanese mothers who socially engaged their babies more often had babies who positively vocalized more often, while mothers who tended to encourage their infants didactically had infants who vocalized less often. Among Americans, on the other hand, infants' positive vocalization tended to relate to their environmental exploration. The authors see this pattern as pointing to the possibility that by 5 months infant vocalization is beginning to function according to the demands thought to typify each society.

In evaluating the relationship between the behavior of individual mothers and individual children, as well as in evaluating the relatively low levels of covariation of activities among both the children and the mothers that Bornstein, Azuma, et al. (1990) remark on, we must bear in mind that the behaviors of the mothers and children in the Bornstein et al. studies (Bornstein, Azuma, et al., 1990; Bornstein, Tamis-LeMonda, et al., 1990), as, indeed, in apparently all of the studies we have considered, were gathered during only one or two observation periods. As noted above in the discussion of the relative absence of significant correlations between mothers' and children's behavior in the Caudill and Schooler

(1973) article, the unreliability of the behavior estimates sampled from one or two periods of observation probably results in an underestimate of how closely the behaviors of a given mother and child are likely to be related.

Bornstein, Azuma, et al. (1990) also raise the possibility that they did not find some expected differences between the behaviors of their Japanese and American mothers (e.g., in ways of engaging their infants socially) because cultural differences are waning with the modernization and urbanization of Japan. They note that in a previous study (Bornstein, Miyake, & Tamis-LeMonda, 1985–1986) conducted in the far north of Japan, mothers stimulated their infants to the environment significantly less than did New York City mothers. They hypothesize that "a developmentally earlier and stronger orientation to the environment characterizes the more modern, urban and Western mother, and that mothers in Tokyo are becoming more like those in the West" (p. 282).

Summarizing their findings on mothers' behaviors in the United States, Japan, and France (which they also studied), Bornstein, Tamis-LeMonda, et al. (1992) conclude that their "results give evidence of culture universals as well as culturally-specific differences in responsiveness in American, French and Japanese mothers" (p. 817). Expanded to include the behavior of babies, the same general conclusions can, after all of these years, still be drawn from Caudill's research. Despite all of the caveats raised by Caudill, me, and others, the central core of Caudill's hypotheses still holds. Japanese and American infants and children differ in their behavior because of culturally determined differences in their mothers' behaviors that serve to reproduce culturally valued patterns of behavior in their children. The continued essential validity of Caudill's findings after all these years provides a strong challenge to all of the now fashionable biological and genetic reductionists who would ascribe most of the psychological and behavioral differences between individuals, even those coming from divergent cultures, to differences in biological functioning.

MY LATER WORK ON JAPAN

One major way in which Caudill influenced my own research on Japan was by serving as my mentor in acquainting me with the country. This not only involved sharing his knowledge about the relative strengths of the Japanese academics in the different disciplines in which I was interested, but also his generously providing me with introductions to his many Japanese friends, some of whom became my own friends and collaborators. This mentorship also took a more directly intellectual form. His viewpoint on Japanese culture and character informed my initial view of the country and served as a foil against which my own research and theorizing on Japanese culture, social structure, and psychological functioning developed.

My own work on Japan has involved several different approaches and areas. One set of studies, begun with the help of Caudill's close friend Shoshiru Kuromaru during my first stay in Japan in 1972, concerns the social-structural antecedents of Japanese women's values and behaviors in their roles as wives (Schooler & Smith, 1978) and mothers (Smith & Schooler, 1978). The general impetus for this research was my personal discomfort at the apparent place of women in Japanese society. Although, as I have mentioned, I found much of traditional Japanese culture congenial to my aesthetic and philosophical orientation, after several months in Japan, I came to the conclusion, only semifacetiously, that being an intelligent woman was probably reason enough to emigrate. I also could not help being struck by the social and emotional relationships that seemed to exist in Japanese marriages. As Caudill had noted, even within the Japanese nuclear family, the relationship between mother and child seemed central; the conjugal couple relationship appeared distinctly secondary.

Consequently, in collaboration with Karen Smith, a Japanese-speaking American sociologist to whom I had been introduced by Professor Kuromaru, I designed a study to examine the cultural and social-structural determinants of Japanese women's conjugal and maternal role values and behavior. We developed a questionnaire that was administered in 1972 to a sample of 145 mothers of first- or fourth-grade children in four elementary schools representative of the Kobe area. Overall, the general tenor of our findings supported Caudill's conclusions and my informal observations (Schooler & Smith, 1978; Smith & Schooler, 1978). Although our respondents' uncomplaining acceptance of household chores and responsibilities appears to make them fit the stereotype of the selfless domestic desirous of fulfilling her husband's every wish, the women seem to have been more disinterested than willing servants, their husbands being nowhere as important a factor in their social and psychological existence as were their children.

Our findings, however, also suggested the possibility that these values and attitudes were not unchangeable. They supported the hypothesis that social-structural variables related to environmental complexity (e.g., being young, well educated, urban, and having fathers and husbands with high-status occupations; cf. Schooler, 1972, 1984) result in an increase in individuality and in the importance placed on the couple relationship and decrease in such signs of complete absorption in the maternal role as the belief that good mothers always place their children's welfare ahead of their own. We (Smith & Schooler, 1978) concluded that with

> further urbanization and higher educational levels Japanese women may increasingly emphasize individualism even in their most traditional role, that of mother. However, if such an increased emphasis on individualism does occur, it will certainly be marked by the cultural and stylistic continuity which seems so distinctive of Japan. (p. 619)

In another aspect of my Japanese research I have focused on the psychological effects of working conditions. Japan has been used in these studies, in part, to serve as a test of the replicability of a series of findings in the United States (Kohn & Schooler, 1973, 1978, 1983) indicating that job conditions that facilitate occupational self-direction increase intellectual flexibility and promote a self-directed orientation to self and society. Japan represents a particularly appropriate place to test the generalizability of these conclusions because self-directedness is not seen as being culturally valued there. As Caudill (1972) notes, one of the most consistent themes running through impressionistic social descriptions of Japan is the "sense of the group or community as being of central importance. . . . An individual in Japan, in a profound sense, exists only in terms of the group to which he belongs, and there is little separate identity apart from such contexts" (p. 730). Yet despite this, the results of our survey of a representative sample of 629 men (A. Naoi & Schooler, 1985; Schooler & A. Naoi, 1988) indicate that in Japan occupational self-direction also leads not only to ideational flexibility, but to a self-directed orientation to self and society. Other results center on the more extensive relationship in Japan between position in the work organization and psychological functioning. The pervasiveness of this relationship provides evidence for those who emphasize the importance of the organization for the Japanese worker. The organizational effects that were found (e.g., the increase in self-esteem and authoritarian conservatism resulting from ownership, high bureaucratic level, and bureaucratization) reflect patterns of Japanese culture and organizational functioning.

Even stronger evidence of the generalizability of the Kohn–Schooler hypothesis about the psychological effects of occupational self-direction was found among Japanese women, the wives of the men in our sample, whom we also interviewed (M. Naoi & Schooler, 1990). Even in a culture where self-directedness for women is apparently particularly disvalued, among the employed wives of the men in our sample, as with their husbands, self-directed work increases intellectual flexibility and self-directed orientations while also leading to less traditional attitudes (M. Naoi & Schooler, 1990). Our evidence also shows that Japanese women are substantially less likely than their husbands to do self-directed work on the job. The resultant occupationally induced lessening of self-directed orientation may contribute to women's accepting cultural norms that keep them in subservient positions. Thus, the culturally and social-structurally determined occupational experiences of Japanese women clearly affect how they confront major social problems and view their roles as wives and mothers.

Since we interviewed not only our sample of men and their wives, but also one of their children, we also hope to be able eventually to examine how occupational and other social-structurally determined environmental conditions affect the intergenerational transmission of various values and aspects of psychological functioning. Our preliminary analyses of the children's data, however, have focused on replicating American findings (Miller, Kohn, & Schooler, 1985, 1986) that self-directed complex schoolwork increases children's intellectual flexibility and self-directed orientations, just as self-directed complex work affects their parents. At present, our analyses remain preliminary and problematical, both because of the relatively small size ($n = 86$) of our sample of children in school and because the generally uniform nature of the centralized Japanese educational system makes it difficult to get measures of the self-directedness and complexity of the educational experience that are substantially independent of the process of selecting the children into the schools. Nevertheless, regression analyses conducted by my Japanese collaborator Toru Kikkawa and me at least partially replicate the earlier American findings by showing that close supervision in school predicts low intellectual flexibility, high authoritarianism, and ideational conformity, independent of all other social background characteristics and parents' psychological functioning. Another set of findings that has emerged, which is especially interesting in light of the culturally prescribed sex roles in Japan, is that boys are more authoritarian, more self-confident, less self-deprecating, less anxious, and less alienated than girls.

Some of my work on Japan uses a quite different approach than the statistically oriented survey research I have been describing. This research (Schooler, 1990a, 1990b), which is essentially historical in nature, starts with a general question in which Caudill was very interested—what is the relative contribution of cultural as opposed to social-structural factors in determining the behavior and psychological functioning of the Japanese (cf. Caudill, 1972)? It expands to the broader questions of how historical/cultural, social-structural/institutional, and economic/production factors may interact with environmental complexity to explain the comparative levels of individualism and group orientation in the course of Japanese history and how these levels may relate to economic development. Using a variety of historical sources, I describe how Japan underwent a sequence of historical periods during which the level of environmental complexity, technical development, and individualism paralleled that of similar periods in Europe. Thus, 16th-century Japan was remarkably similar to the European Renaissance in its individualism, socioeconomic and cultural vitality and levels of environmental complexity. In both Japan and Western Europe, this renaissance followed the breakdown of an imperium and its replacement by a feudal system. The historical parallel continues in those parts of Europe in which absolutist governments were successfully imposed; Japan went through a similar phenomenon, accompanied by a similar decline in individualism and economic development. In interpreting the implications of this historical pattern, I speculate on the nature of the causal interconnections among culture, socioeconomic development and environmental complexity, bringing to bear the evidence from present-day research on the effects of complex environments. I try to show how each of the historical stages may play some part in the development of technology and individualism and suggest ways in which technology and individualism may reciprocally effect each other. Clearly, in taking such an approach and suggesting such conclusions, I have diverged drastically from Caudill. At a minimum, my hypothesis that Japan is distinctive among non-Western countries because of its historical and psychological similarities to the West is not only controversial, but quite different from anything Caudill is likely to have believed.

But others do not have to take my path. Bill Caudill's pioneering research does not necessarily lead to my conclusions, or to any particular conclusions about how Japan came to be the way it is or what it will become. What Caudill's work does do is provide us with a still-believable picture of how the behaviors of Japanese and American mothers differed several decades ago. Taken together with the evidence that the general direction of causality is from mother's to child's behavior and that these differences in behavior are not primarily genetic in origin, Caudill's findings continue to strongly suggest that culturally determined differences in mothers' behaviors play a meaningful part in the development of children's behavior patterns. Given the striking way in which these behavioral dissimilarities between the two samples reflect differences in their cultural values, the implications of Caudill's findings generalize beyond the particular instances of Japan and the United States to tell us something about how cultures reproduce themselves. All is not biology.

REFERENCES

Bales, R. F. (1951). *Interaction process analysis.* Cambridge, MA: Addison-Wesley.

Barker, R. G., & Wright, H. F. (1951). *One boy's day: A specimen of behavior.* New York: Harper.

Bornstein, M. H. (1988). Mothers, infants, and the development of cognitive competence. In H. E. Fitzgerald, B. M. Lester, & M. W. Yogman (Eds.), *Theory and research in behavioral pediatrics* (pp. 67–99). New York: Plenum.

Bornstein, M. H. (1989). Cross-cultural developmental comparisons: The case of Japanese-American infant and mother activities and interactions. What we know, what we need to know, and why we need to know. *Developmental Review, 9,* 171–204.

Bornstein, M. H., Azuma, H., Tamis-LeMonda, C., & Ogino, M. (1990). Mother and infant activity and interaction in Japan and the United States: I. A comparative macroanalysis of naturalistic exchanges. *International Journal of Behavioral Development, 13,* 267–287.

Bornstein, M. H., Miyake, K., & Tamis-LeMonda, C. (1985–1986). A cross-national study of mother and infant activities and interactions: Some preliminary comparisons between Japan and the United States. In *Annual report of the Research and Clinical Center for Child Development* (pp. 1–12). Sapporo, Japan: University of Hokkaido.

Bornstein, M. H., & Tamis-LeMonda, C. (1988). *Activities and interactions of mothers and their firstborn infants in the first six months of life: Reliability, stability, continuity, covariation, correspondence, and prediction.* Unpublished manuscript, National Institute on Child Health and Human Development.

Bornstein, M. H., Tamis-LeMonda, C., Ludemann, P., Rahn, C. W., Tal, J., Toda, S., Pecheux, M.-G., Azuma, H., & Vardi, D. (1992). Maternal responsiveness to infants in three societies: The United States, France, and Japan. *Child Development, 63,* 807–821.

Caudill, W. (1958). *The psychiatric hospital as a small society.* Boston: Harvard University Press.

Caudill, W. (1972). Tiny dramas: Vocal communication between mother and infant in Japanese and American families. In W. Lebra (Ed.), *Mental health research in Asia and the Pacific* (Vol. 2, pp. 25–48). Honolulu: East–West Center Press.

Caudill, W. (1973). The influence of social structure and culture on humans in modern Japan. *Journal of Nervous and Mental Disease, 157,* 240–257.

Caudill, W., & Frost, L. (1974). A comparison of maternal care and infant behavior in Japanese-American, American, and Japanese families. In W. Lebra (Ed.), *Mental health research in Asia and the Pacific* (Vol. 3, pp. 4–15). Honolulu: East–West Center Press.

Caudill, W., & Schooler, C. (1973). Child behavior and child rearing in Japan and the United States: An interim report. *Journal of Nervous and Mental Disease, 157,* 323–338.

Caudill, W., & Weinstein, H. (1969). Maternal care and infant behavior in Japan and America. *Psychiatry, 32,* 12–43.

Chen, S., & Miyake, K. (1986). Japanese studies of infant development. In H. Stevenson, H. Azuma, & K. Hakuta (Eds.), *Child development and education in Japan* (pp. 135–146). New York: Freeman.

De Vos, G., & Vogel, E. F. (1973). Achievement, culture and personality: The case of William Caudill. *Journal of Nervous and Mental Disease, 157,* 232–236.

Doi, L. T. (1973). Omote and ura: Concepts derived from the Japanese 2-fold structure of consciousness. *Journal of Nervous and Mental Disease, 157,* 258–261.

Kohn, M. L. (1969). *Class and conformity: A study in values.* Homewood, IL: Dorsey Press.

Kohn, M. L., Naoi, A., Schoenbach, C., Schooler, C., & Slomczynski, K. M. (1990). Position in the class structure and psychological functioning: A comparative analysis of the United States, Japan, and Poland. *American Journal of Sociology, 95,* 964–1008.

Kohn, M., & Schooler, C. (1969). Class, occupation, and orientation. *American Sociological Review, 34,* 659–678.

Kohn, M. L., & Schooler, C. (1973). Occupational experience and psychological functioning: An assessment of reciprocal effects. *American Sociological Review, 38,* 97–118.

Kohn, M. L., & Schooler, C. (1978). The reciprocal effects of the substantive complexity of work and intellectual flexibility: A longitudinal assessment. *American Journal of Sociology, 84,* 24–52.

Kohn, M. L., & Schooler, C. (1983). *Work and personality: An inquiry into the impact of social stratification.* Norwood, NJ: Ablex.

Kuromaru, S. (1973). Changes in Japanese mother–child separation anxiety in Japan (1963–1972). *Journal of Nervous and Mental Disease, 157,* 339–345.

Lewis, C. (1976). *A case study of two Japanese mothers in the U.S.: Speculations on the determinants of childrearing.* Unpublished manuscript.

Miller, K. A., Kohn, M. L., & Schooler, C. (1985). Educational self-direction and cognitive functioning of students. *Social Forces, 63*(4), 923–944.

Miller, K. A., Kohn, M. L., & Schooler, C. (1986). Educational self-direction and personality. *American Sociological Review, 51,* 372–390.

Moss, H. (1967). Sex, age, and state as determinants of mother–infant interaction. *Merrill-Palmer Quarterly, 13,* 19–26.

Naoi, A., & Schooler, C. (1985). Occupational conditions and psychological functioning in Japan. *American Journal of Sociology, 90,* 729–752.

Naoi, M., & Schooler, C. (1990). Psychological consequences of occupational conditions among Japanese wives. *Social Psychology Quarterly, 58,* 100–116.

Otaki, M., Durrett, M. E., Richards, P., Nyquist, L., & Pennebaker, J. W. (1986). Maternal and infant behavior in Japan and America: A partial replication. *Journal of Cross-Cultural Psychology, 17,* 251–268.

Schooler, C. (1972). Social antecedents of adult psychological functioning. *American Journal of Sociology, 78,* 299–322.

Schooler, C. (1984). Psychological effects of complex environments during the life span: A review and theory. *Intelligence, 8,* 259–281.

Schooler, C. (1990a). The individual in Japanese history: Parallels to and divergences from the European experience. *Sociological Forum, 5,* 569–594.

Schooler, C. (1990b). Individualism and the historical and social-structural determinants of people's concern over self-directedness and efficacy. In J. Rodin, C. Schooler, & K. W. Schaie (Eds.), *Self directedness and efficacy: Causes and effects throughout the life course* (pp. 19–49). Hillsdale, NJ: Erlbaum.

Schooler, C., & Naoi, A. (1988). The psychological effects of traditional and of economically peripheral job settings in Japan. *American Journal of Sociology, 94*(2), 335–355.

Schooler, C., & Smith, K. C. (1978). . . . and a Japanese wife: Social antecedents of women's role values in Japan. *Sex Roles, 4,* 23–41.

Sengoku, T., Davitz, L., & Davitz, J. (1982). *Mother–infant interaction: A cross-cultural study of behavior in Japan and the United States.* Unpublished manuscript, Japan Youth Research Institute.

Shand, N., & Kosawa, Y. (1985a). Culture transmission: Caudill's model and alternative hypotheses. *American Anthropologist, 87,* 862–871.

Shand, N., & Kosawa, Y. (1985b). Japanese and American behavior types at three months: Infants and infant–mother dyads. *Infant Behavior and Development, 8,* 225–240.

Smith, K., & Schooler, C. (1978). Women as mothers in Japan: The effects of social structure and culture on values and behavior. *Journal of Marriage and the Family, 40,* 613–620.

Suzuki, D. T. (1949). *Introduction to Zen Buddhism.* New York: Harper.
Vogel, E. F., & Schooler, C. (1973). In memory of William A. Caudill (Parts I and II). *Journal of Nervous and Mental Disease, 157,* 231–312, 313–395.
Watts, A. (1950). *The supreme identity.* New York: Pantheon.

CHAPTER 9

Production and Reproduction of Culture
The Dynamic Role of Mothers and Children in Early Socialization

Susan D. Holloway
Masahiko Minami

Over the last 36 years, William Caudill's work has challenged scholars to question the status quo regarding models of human development. While many of his contemporaries focused exclusively on the parent–child dyad or the individual, Caudill investigated dyadic interaction within the larger contexts of class and culture. His insistence on capturing the multiple layers of socialization prefigured current sociocultural theories. Additionally, his work is still very relevant to the ongoing debate concerning the relative importance of infants' temperament and physiological characteristics.

In this chapter, we contrast Caudill's theory of cultural transmission with current sociocultural models that conceptualize parent and child as interactive partners in the joint creation of cultural meanings. Next, expanding upon Caudill's interest in the views of parents from different occupational strata, we highlight recent work describing how individuals, in collaboration with others, make sense of the barriers and opportunities afforded by the social structure of their environments. The concluding section contains some observations concerning recent trends in the nature of collaborative research between Americans and Japanese investigators.

THE CULTURAL TRANSMISSION MODEL
OF SOCIALIZATION

Caudill's view of human socialization is an example of a *cultural transmission* model. Such models tend to assume that cultural norms affect parent behavior, which in turn exert an influence, primarily unidirectional, upon the child. Caudill's starting assumption was that parents in a particular culture maintain a certain model of what a child's development should be like. Parents' goals and plans are then implemented in a wide variety of ways. Caudill and his colleagues focused their research primarily on the role of maternal language toward children. His assumption was that U.S. norms favoring individualism encouraged mothers to stimulate verbalizations by their children.

Caudill tended to appraise the Japanese data in terms of the dependency relationship between mother and child, referred to as *amae*. The term *amae,* brought to the attention of English-speaking audiences by Doi (1973), refers to the state of dependency on the indulgence or benevolence of another person. It can be used to describe a child's feelings and behavior toward a parent (Lebra, 1976). Japanese mothers' language to their infants and toddlers can be seen as consistent with an *amae* relationship, characterized by mothers' acceptance and enjoyment of the child's immaturity rather than a desire to coax the child into acting in a different or more mature fashion. While the *amae* relationship implies distinct roles for both members of the dyad, the way it is operationalized in Caudill's data puts the emphasis on how mothers express their feelings and not on how the child independently affects the interchange.

Contrast with Biological Model

Caudill's team illustrated the greater utility of the cultural transmission model in comparison to a biological model. They provided a variety of data to show that maternal behavior was a function of culture rather than a response to racially based genetic characteristics of their infants. In the central study, they controlled the variables of infant age, birth conditions, and birth order; they also assessed activity levels both when the infant was alone and in the presence of the mother.

In a related study, Caudill and Frost (1973) compared Caucasian-American infants with fourth-generation Japanese-American infants living in the United States, who were genetically similar to

Japanese infants but whose mothers had presumably adopted American childrearing patterns. They reflected carefully on factors that had not been assessed, but which might have affected the results, including the size and layout of Japanese and American homes and differences in climate and infants' clothing. Their thorough discussion of alternative explanations is an outstanding feature of the original work; Caudill preempted his later critics by identifying the potential weaknesses of his quasinaturalistic design.

Studies of mother–infant communication continue to be a major focus of infancy researchers. Advances in theory and assessment techniques have resulted in increasing acceptance of the role of infants' biological makeup in their interactions with adults. However, debate continues regarding the nature and extent of such influence.

Increasingly, the field observations favored by Caudill have been replaced by observations in laboratory settings as the method of choice. For example, Fogel, Toda, and Kawai (1988) chose to study face-to-face play in a laboratory setting because it allowed them to standardize the postures and distances between mother and infant, as well as lighting and camera angles. Use of laboratory-based assessments will continue as long as they rely on equipment that cannot be transported to the field, such as elaborate cameras and devices for recording physiological responses (e.g., Calkins & Fox, 1992).

NEW DIRECTIONS: SOCIAL INTERACTIONAL MODELS OF SOCIALIZATION

Biological models are not the only sources of challenge to theories of cultural transmission. In the time since Caudill collected his data, competing conceptions have been developed regarding the role of cultural processes in socialization. Examples of these theories are present in work by Lave (1991), Ochs (1986), and Rogoff (Rogoff, Mistry, Goncu, & Mosier, 1993). Current sociocultural approaches to children's socialization, while varied in some ways, have at least two characteristics in common. First, they reject the unidirectional notion that parents pass along cultural formulas to their children. Instead, these theories try to depict how children's active processing of information results in both the reproduction of culture and the production of new elements (e.g., Gaskins, Miller, & Corsaro, 1992). Language functions not solely as a medium for conveying known information, but rather is "the primary tool by which human beings negotiate divergent points of view and construct shared realities and the primary tool by which children gain entry into the interpretive frameworks of their culture" (Gaskins et al., 1992, p. 13).

Second, they attempt to discover the cultural meanings held by particular parents and children rather than assuming common understandings. To understand the individual's own creation of meanings, researchers working within this framework conduct close analyses of conversations between parents and children, and attempt to show at a very fine-grained level what particular words and actions signify to the participants (e.g., Schieffelin & Ochs, 1986).

Sociocultural Studies Emphasizing Linguistic Interaction

Several recent studies comparing American and Japanese socialization processes within the sociocultural perspective have focused on mother–child linguistic interaction. Analyzing conversations between five mother–child pairs, Clancy (1986) shows how Japanese mothers use *omoiyari*, or empathy for others, to understand their children's needs and desires. At the same time, these mothers are reproducing the cultural norm of *omoiyari* in their own children by modeling it as well as directly instructing children in when to use empathy, how to express it, and whom to express it to. Her findings are particularly relevant to a discussion of Caudill's work because she reveals how *omoiyari* is compatible with the terse linguistic style observed in mothers' language to infants and young children. She argues that a Japanese person who is truly empathic does not rely on explicit verbal cues to understand someone's wishes because these should be intuited through more subtle cues of gesture and tone. The elliptical style favored by Japanese mothers demonstrates that they are sensitive to their children, and it also helps their children to learn this communicative style (Azuma, 1986; Shigaki, 1987).

A salient characteristic of sociocultural approaches that analyze language interaction is their avoidance of general categories that may convey a positive or negative value orientation (e.g., "happy" vs. "unhappy" vocalizations). Recent work by Minami and McCabe (1993, 1995) on mother–child discourse in Japan and the United States employs categories of meaning that emerge from the data. They found that English-speaking mothers allowed their children to take long monologic turns, asked their children many questions about the content of the monologue, and offered positive evaluation of the narrative. And while Japanese mothers also paid close attention to their children's narratives, they more often facilitated frequent turn exchanges and offered fewer evaluative comments. This type of fine-grained analysis may produce fewer statements that imply a deficit on the part of one culture or another.

Sociocultural Studies Emphasizing Parental Beliefs as Social Representations

The cultural transmission model has tended to view parental goals and beliefs about childrearing as static entities that are passed down from one generation to the next. While Caudill and his colleagues draw upon important cultural concepts such as *amae,* their work does not show the dynamic process by which certain concepts are integrated with other concepts and experiences, and essentially reworked by each generation. Recent reformulations have paid more attention to the active role of the individual in shaping beliefs, and it is to this work that we now turn our attention.

Moscovici (1984) has characterized the dynamic process by which people "concoct spontaneous unofficial 'philosophies' which have a decisive impact on their social relations, their choices, the way they bring up their children, plan ahead, and so forth" (p. 16). He contributes the important notion that parental views are not inherited wholesale from previous generations, but rather are the product of active cognition, using as its object the experiences gained from daily interaction within the immediate context. Moscovici makes it clear that a parent's behavior toward a child is the product of the social representations that have been created over time.

Recent work by Holloway and colleagues on low-income mothers' choice of childcare illustrates the active construction of childrearing beliefs by low-income mothers from different ethnic groups within the United States (Holloway, Rambaud, Fuller, & Eggers-Piérola, 1995). While these mothers' views about appropriate socialization practices were clearly affected by cultural values, the dynamic process by which the beliefs were constructed emerged clearly in the data. They incorporated current experiences into the beliefs about childrearing, along with reflections on past events and advice from caregivers, social service workers, friends, and family members.

In the case of Japan, little is known about the "meaning-making" process that individual parents go through as they construct beliefs about childrearing. One of the few examples is a recent study (B. Shwalb, D. Shwalb, & Shoji, 1994) that elicits Japanese mothers' perceptions of their infants' behavioral styles. Results suggested that Japanese mothers' descriptions of their infants depart in some ways from the standard dimensions contained in Western temperament questionnaires. Shwalb and her colleagues conclude that mothers' perceptions are both pancultural and culture specific. Further research on the various influences on Japanese parents' beliefs and the ways these sources are integrated would be particularly interesting in light of the rapid societal changes Japan has experienced over the last half-century.

Application of Sociocultural Models to the Study of Social Structure

The notion of social structure constitutes a important theme running throughout Caudill's work. At a micro level, the work provokes interesting questions about the relationship of modernization to Westernization. Schooler (Chapter 8, this volume) questions whether results obtained in Japan 3 decades ago still apply if Japanese parents have been adopting Western views of childrearing. A thorough treatment of the issue of modernization and its relation to Westernization is far beyond the scope of this chapter; here we can only emphasize the value of studying how Westernization may affect family values and practices in Japan. Kagitçibasi (1989) has argued that urban non-Western families often evolve a hybrid structure in which certain values and practices consonant with Western views (e.g., importance of formal education) coexist with traditional non-Western values (e.g., importance of extended family). While this hybrid structure represents a move away from rural non-Western values, it is not, she contends, a midpoint in an inevitable progression toward the Western nuclear family. Research in Japan can further test the inevitability of a "world system" characterized by values inherent in Western democratic capitalism (e.g., Meyer & Hannan, 1979).

A second point concerns more micro-level considerations about the role of social structure in socialization processes. In the United States, social-class differences in parental childrearing beliefs and expectations have been amply documented, along with resultant differences in discourse style (e.g., Heath, 1983; Miller, 1982). Many scholars familiar with the literature on Japanese schools and families have called for more attention to variation among social classes as well as between rural and urban families. We feel, along with Schooler, that sources of diversity within Japan have to be recognized. If, for example, the presence of Korean and

Chinese minorities in Japan is considered, it becomes evident that the portrayal of monolithic collectivism is too simplistic a view of Japanese society.

Caudill's work illuminates the role of an important social structural variable: paternal occupation. Following Vogel (1963), Caudill compared mothers whose families were involved in small businesses with those whose husbands were salaried employees of larger firms. Unlike many who have studied social stratification in developing nations, Caudill did not rely upon indicators used in American research, notably education level and occupational prestige. The analysis of employment category revealed that

> the mother in the salaried Japanese family seems more like the American mother, who, in the general cross-cultural analysis, looks at her infant more often. But the American mother also chats with her infant frequently, whereas the Japanese salaried mother is more silent than the Japanese independent business mother. (Caudill & Weinstein, 1969, pp. 41–42)

This example illustrates nicely how the meaning of social-structural categories can vary from one society to the next.

Caudill's analysis of social structure did not formally include more micro-level elements, although he and others commenting on his work speculate about the effects of housing type, presence of extended family or neighbors within earshot, and other factors that might affect mother–infant interaction. The interconnection between socialization beliefs and micro-level elements of the social structure is also illustrated in Holloway's (1988) analysis of the contextual determinants of Japanese and American concepts of ability and effort. Many observers have suggested that Japanese children's educational achievements may stem from a cultural emphasis on commitment and perseverance. Holloway identifies the social-structural arrangements that contribute to the formulation and maintenance of an effort orientation. Abundant evidence from the United States suggests that children are more likely to attribute successful performance to their own effort under cooperative reward structures, when overt performance evaluation is avoided, and when caregivers use democratic rather than authoritarian control strategies. It is possible that Japanese schools and homes evidence these characteristics to a greater degree, on average, than do those in the United States, and thus encourage children to view effort as the primary cause of achievement.

While close examination of social-structural determinants of parental beliefs may yield much of interest, previous investigations of social structure have tended to view individuals as "passive role players shaped exclusively by structural forces beyond their control" (Mehan, 1992). Currently, scholars interested in the effects of social structure are beginning to challenge the deterministic notion that social structure inevitably affects individuals in a uniform manner. In other words, emphasis on social structure must always be tempered with a consideration of the role played by the individual, who selectively perceives, interprets, and acts upon those elements of the social structure. A recent variation on the social-interactional paradigm, sometimes known as resistance theory, rejects the notion of culture as a "pale reflection of structural forces"; rather, individuals are seen as active sense makers, who view alternatives and exercise choice, thus participating in the creation of their social circumstances (Mehan, 1992).

Japan can provide fascinating examples of the ingenious ways people find to subvert established rules and regulations. It is not surprising that, like in the United States, it is adolescents who provide us with the most salient examples of active production—rather than the rote reproduction—of social circumstances. For instance, several writers have described the highly elaborated regulations governing dress and behavior in Japanese middle schools (Feiler, 1991; White, 1993). Yet, operating nominally within this circumscribed set of rules, youngsters still manage to subvert the authority structure through subtle indicators. For example, students may signal their peer group affiliation by leaving certain buttons undone on their uniform jacket.

COMMENTS ON THE POLITICS AND PROCESS OF COMPARATIVE RESEARCH

In the 40 years since Caudill began his work in Japan, notable changes have occurred in the nature of collaboration among researchers from Japan and America. To the extent that research itself is a process of explicitly constructing and exploring social representations, the actors involved and the process of interaction among them is crucial in determining the final product. Our sense is that the field has moved in the direction of more equal collaboration among researchers in both countries. Some of the past barriers to extensive collaboration may be falling. Certainly, the increasingly proficient use of English by Japanese has helped tremendously. Travel may be somewhat faster and easier, and alternative modes of communication like E-mail facilitate collaboration in the absence of face-to-face communication. While Japanese universities still give relatively few doctorates in the social sciences relative to other fields, the number of research-oriented academics has increased in Japan (Araki, 1990). These and other changes may have imbued Americans with a greater sense of what can be learned from the Japanese, and the Japanese with a greater sense of confidence about challenging and modifying theories and constructs developed in the West.

FUTURE THEMES FOR COLLABORATIVE WORK

Within the context of collaborative work, we foresee the emergence of studies investigating the social-interaction paradigm. Throughout the chapter we have tried to suggest fruitful avenues for future research on mother–child interaction. In addition to further studies of mothers and children, more comparative studies are needed on the role of fathers. Popular accounts in Japan and the United States have focused overwhelmingly on the purportedly negligible presence of Japanese fathers. Within Japan, a number of surveys have begun to sketch out a more fine-tuned depiction of the role of fathers (see Shwalb, Imaizumi, & Nakazawa, 1987, for a review). But few if any studies capture father–child interaction in the depth sought by sociocultural perspectives on socialization. Similarly, few studies have attempted to connect elements of the social structure to fathers' beliefs or childrearing practices. Recent evidence suggests that Japanese corporations are reacting to the strain experienced by families by reexamining expectations concerning employee job transfers and implicit requirements for after-hours socializing. At the same time, increasing numbers of women with children are entering the labor force (Fujita, 1989). It will be interesting to watch the changes in family dynamics that result from these shifts in world of work.

As socialization theories more explicitly characterize the active role of the child, correspondingly more attention is paid to the importance of all the child's social relationships, including those with siblings and peers. Corsaro's (1988; Corsaro & Eder, 1990; Corsaro & Rosier, 1992) studies illustrate the important role of peer interaction in reproducing as well as extending elements of family and community life. The press has focused on the problem of *ijime*, or bullying, and some attempt to analyze this dynamic has been made by Japanese and American researchers (e.g., Murakami,

Father escorts child to the preschool bus, Nagoya, 1996. The 3-year-old wears a uniform and a backpack like the one she will use in primary school. The teacher bows to the child. Courtesy of David Shwalb.

1991). However, little is known about more common forms of interaction, including the development of friendships and gender differences in social interaction with peers.

CONCLUDING COMMENTS

Caudill was preoccupied with elaborating the contribution of culture in determining childrearing practices. He downplayed the possible contribution of biologically based differences between Japanese and Caucasian-American infants. In the $3\frac{1}{2}$ decades since he conducted his seminal study, the pendulum of research has continued to swing between these two alternative theories, with significant advances made on both sides. We have tried here to articulate a third set of explanatory principles. Like cultural transmission theory, sociocultural theories give weight to culture but try to define it more precisely at the level of discourse between people. Like biological studies they focus on the role of child but look more at children's actions and perceptions than at their physiological makeup. This reconceptualization of socialization, building upon the significant contributions of Caudill and his team, urges us to look not just at how culture is "reproduced" but to consider more clearly how it is "produced" by children in interaction with those around them.

DEDICATION

We would like to dedicate this chapter to the memory of Robert D. Hess. His warm friendships with Japanese colleagues and generous guidance of new generations of American scholars have been truly inspirational.

REFERENCES

Araki, T. (1990). *Hakase sama wa "riko buntei"* [A distribution of doctorates indicates that more are given to sciences and less to liberal arts]. *Asahi Shimbun Extra Report and Analysis, 3*(4), 38–39.

Azuma, H. (1986). Why study child development in Japan? In H. Stevenson, H. Azuma, & K. Hakuta (Eds.), *Child development and education in Japan* (pp. 3–12). New York: Freeman.

Calkins, S. D., & Fox, N. (1992). The relations among infant temperament, security of attachment, and behavioral inhibition at twenty-four months. *Child Development, 63*, 1456–1472.

Caudill, W., & Frost, L. (1973). A comparison of maternal care and infant behavior in Japanese-American, American, and Japanese families. In W. Lebra (Ed.), *Mental health research in Asia and the Pacific* (Vol. 3, pp. 3–15). Honolulu: East–West Press.

Caudill, W., & Weinstein, H. (1969). Maternal care and infant behavior in Japan and America. *Psychiatry, 32*, 12–43.

Clancy, P. M. (1986). The acquisition of communicative style in Japanese. In B. B. Schieffelin & E. Ochs (Eds.), *Language socialization across cultures* (pp. 373–524). New York: Cambridge University Press.

Corsaro, W. A. (1988). Routines in the peer culture of American and Italian nursery school children. *Sociology of Education, 61*, 1–14.

Corsaro, W. A., & Eder, D. (1990). Children's peer cultures. *Annual Review of Sociology, 16*, 197–220.

Corsaro, W. A., & Rosier, K. B. (1992). Documenting productive–reproductive processes in children's lives: Transition narratives of a black family living in poverty. In W. A. Corsaro & P. J. Miller (Eds.), *Interpretive approaches to children's socialization* (pp. 67–97). San Francisco: Jossey-Bass.

Doi, T. (1973). *The anatomy of dependence.* Tokyo: Kodansha International.

Feiler, B. S. (1991). *Learning to bow: Inside the heart of Japan.* New York: Ticknor & Fields.

Fogel, A., Toda, S., & Kawai, M. (1988). Mother–infant face-to-face interaction in Japan and the United States; A laboratory comparison using 3-month-old infants. *Developmental Psychology, 24,* 398–406.

Fujita, M. (1989). "It's all the mother's fault": Child care and the socialization of working mothers in Japan. *Journal of Japanese Studies, 15,* 67–91.

Gaskins, S., Miller, P. J., & Corsaro, W. A. (1992). Theoretical and methodological perspectives in the interpretive study of children. In W. A. Corsaro & P. J. Miller (Eds.), *Interpretive approaches to children's socialization* (pp. 5–24). San Francisco: Jossey-Bass.

Heath, S. B. (1983). *Ways with words: Language, life and work in communities and classrooms.* New York: Cambridge University Press.

Holloway, S. D. (1988). Concepts of ability and effort in Japan and the United States. *Review of Educational Research, 58,* 327–345.

Holloway, S. D., Rambaud, M. F., Fuller, B., & Eggers-Pierola, C. (1995). What is "appropriate practice" at home and in child care?: Low-income mothers' views on preparing their children for school. *Early Childhood Research Quarterly, 10,* 451–473.

Kagitçibasi, Ç. (1989). Family and socialization in cross-cultural perspective: A model of change. In J. Berman (Ed.), *Nebraska Symposium on Motivation* (Vol. 37, pp. 135–200). Lincoln: University of Nebraska Press.

Lave, J. (1991). Situating learning in communities of practice. In L. B. Resnick, J. M. Levine, & S. D. Teasley (Eds.), *Perspectives on socially shared cognition* (pp. 63–82). Washington DC: American Psychological Association.

Lebra, T. S. (1976). *Japanese patterns of behavior.* Honolulu: University of Hawaii Press.

Mehan, H. (1992). Understanding inequality in schools: The contribution of interpretive studies. *Sociology of Education, 65,* 1–20.

Meyer, J. W., & Hannan, M. (Eds.). (1979). *National development and the world system: Educational, economic, and political change, 1950–1970.* Chicago: University of Chicago Press.

Miller, P. (1982). *Amy, Wendy, and Beth: Language acquisition in South Baltimore.* Austin: University of Texas Press.

Minami, M., & McCabe, A. (1993, July). *Social interaction and discourse style: Culture-specific parental styles of interviewing and children's narrative structure.* Paper presented at the 4th International Pragmatics Conference, Kobe, Japan.

Minami, M., & McCabe, A. (1995). Rice balls and bear hunts: Japanese and North American family narrative patterns. *Journal of Child Language, 22,* 423–445.

Moscovici, S. (1984). The phenomenon of social representations. In R. M. Farr & S. Moscovici (Eds.), *Social representations* (pp. 3–69). New York: Cambridge University Press.

Murakami, Y. (1991). Bullies in the classroom. In B. Finkelstein, A. E. Imamura, & J. J. Tobin (Eds.), *Transcending stereotypes* (pp. 190–196). Yarmouth, ME: Intercultural Press.

Ochs, E. (1986). Introduction. In B. B. Schieffelin & E. Ochs (Eds.), *Language socialization across cultures* (pp. 1–13). New York: Cambridge University Press.

Rogoff, B., Mistry, J., Goncu, A., & Mosier, C. (1993). Guided participation in cultural activity by toddlers and caregivers. *Monographs of the Society for Research in Child Development, 58*(8, Serial No. 236).

Schieffelin, B. B., & Ochs, E. (Eds.). (1986). *Language socialization across cultures.* New York: Cambridge University Press.

Shigaki, I. S. (1987). Language and the transmission of values: Implications from Japanese day care. In B. Fillion, C. N. Hedley, & E. C. DiMartino (Eds.), *Home and school: Early language and reading* (pp. 111–121). Norwood, NJ: Ablex.

Shwalb, B. J., Shwalb, D. W., & Shoji, J. (1994). Structure and dimensions of maternal perceptions of Japanese infant temperament. *Developmental Psychology, 30,* 131–141.

Shwalb, D. W., Imaizumi, N., & Nakazawa, J. (1987). The modern Japanese father: Roles and problems in a changing society. In M. E. Lamb (Ed.), *The father's role: Cross-cultural perspectives.* (pp. 247–269). Hillsdale, NJ: Erlbaum.

Vogel, E. A. (1963). *Japan's new middle class.* Berkeley: University of California Press.

White, M. (1993). *The material child: Coming of age in Japan and America.* New York: Free Press.

Urban Middle-Class Japanese Family Life, 1958–1996
A Personal and Evolving Perspective

Suzanne Hall Vogel

To look back at a 38-year relationship with Japan is to view not only the objective changes that have taken place in Japanese society but also to recognize the life changes of this viewer. While Japanese family life has been changing, so, too, has the eye of the observer. What I see, then and now, is determined not only by developments within Japan, but also by my personal viewpoint as influenced by my own changing life situation and social context.

The eyes with which I initially viewed Japanese families were the eyes of an American wife. From 1958 to 1960, for the purpose of studying Japanese family life, Ezra Vogel and I and our toddler son lived first in Tokyo and then in a suburban community that Ezra called Mamachi when he wrote *Japan's New Middle Class* (E. F. Vogel, 1963). Today, however, I am single, a full-time clinical social worker/psychotherapist at Harvard University Health Services and in private practice. I also spend 6 weeks each year teaching casework and psychotherapy at a Tokyo psychiatric hospital. So my perspective today, as I pursue my continuing interest in Japanese families, is that of a mental health professional. In the years between I discern two other aspects of my evolution: that of a women's studies enthusiast and that of a college counselor. As my life has evolved, I have studied a changing Japan through my own changing personal and professional perspective.

FROM THE PERSPECTIVE OF WIFE:
THE INITIAL STUDY, 1958–1960

It is true when I went to Japan in 1958, I was equipped with graduate degrees in both sociology and psychiatric social work, and had
experience as a psychiatric research interviewer. I went, however,
not in any official academic or professional capacity, but as a scholar's wife. This was well before the time of the women's movement
in the United States. It never occurred to Ezra or to me that I
should have an official position or any salary of my own as part of
his research grant. We thought that I might participate in his research project, but I had no clear idea of whether or how that possibility would materialize. I already had a 1-year-old child in tow, was
hoping to have another during our 2 years in Tokyo, and had had
no training in Japanese language or culture.

Even Ezra at that time had only rudimentary knowledge of Japanese language and culture. He was not a Japanologist. Rather, he
was a new Ph.D. sociologist who had been told by his advisor Florence Kluckhohn (of Harvard's Social Relations Department) that
he, as a small-town American boy, needed the perspective of a cross-
cultural experience. Neither he nor I had any particular prior interest in Japan. We chose Japan as the site for this experience partly
due to the influence of Ezra's friend and mentor William Caudill
(at that time also of Harvard's Social Relations Department) and
partly due to Japan's being the non-Western country with the clean-
est water and safest food for our 1-year-old.

Japanese hospitality greeted us at Haneda Airport in the form
of Bill Caudill and his wife, Mie, who gave us our first instruction
on tatami sleeping and on the use of Japanese-style toilets (at that
time with no flush!). Mie showed me the wonders of Tokyo department stores, complete with rooftop playgrounds for children and
the only available supply of Western foodstuffs to supplement our
rapidly developing Japanese diet. The Caudills also introduced us
to Takeo Doi, who told us of a simple but pleasant Japanese house
for rent next door to him in Ikejiri, Setagaya-ku. As soon as we
moved in, we hired a live-in maid, another bit of good luck that
would have been much more difficult just a few years later, as industrial development during the 1960s absorbed most domestic help.
Without Mitsuko-san I would have been completely overwhelmed
by housekeeping tasks, both because of my total ignorance of Japanese houses and kitchens, and because of the lack of any electric
appliances except a refrigerator and a television. But with her as a
babysitter, I soon enrolled in the daily beginners classes at the Na-

ganuma School of the Japanese Language. I knew that I wanted to talk with Japanese people as soon and as much as possible!

I had an intellectual interest in this trip as well, since Ezra's research was close to my own background and interests. Not only had my own graduate work involved sociology and family studies, but Ezra's topic had a mental health focus. His research grant was from the Foundations' Fund for Research in Psychiatry, as his plan was to compare families of "neurotic" children with families of "well" children, modeled after the Kluckhohn–Spiegel project in Boston that Ezra had worked on during his graduate student years at Harvard. In Japan, he and I were affiliated with the Japan National Institute of Mental Health (JNIMH) in Chiba Prefecture, and our research was done in collaboration with their staff. The "neurotic" children and their families were in treatment there, and the "well" families were introduced to us by the principal of the local grade school, via a JNIMH staff member. Although we asked to be introduced to six *ordinary* middle-class families, my impression is that only the more socially and academically secure families had the courage to take on these young American researchers!

As it turned out, Ezra left the field of mental health in 1961 when he began the study of Chinese society. When he wrote up our 1958–1960 research in *Japan's New Middle Class,* he did not directly deal with the mental health questions in his original research design but rather focused on the newly developing patterns among all our Mamachi families, particularly the "well" ones whom we came to know best. Since that time, I have been the one who has continued an interest in the relation of sociology and mental health in Japan, adding an enriching dimension to my major career path as a clinical social worker/psychotherapist in the United States.

My first 9 months in Japan consisted of language study and learning to manage a household and child in the Tokyo environment. Toward the end of that time, however, three circumstances converged to propel me into an active role in the research project during our second year in Japan, 1959–1960: Ezra's Japanese interpreter and cointerviewer resigned her position in order to marry, I lost a 6-month pregnancy via miscarriage, and we moved to "Mamachi" to be in the same community with our interview subjects. Subsequently, Ezra never hired another interpreter and I assumed major interviewing responsibility. I visited the homes of our six "well" families every week, talking for 1 or more hours with the wives and whomever else was there—children, grandparents, friends, neighbors, or relatives—and taught English conversation to some of their high school-age children. I undertook the weekly

At a kindergarten family picnic outing, with the Vogels and son David (wearing preschool apron and backpack), Mamachi, 1960. Courtesy of Suzanne Vogel.

casework treatment of the mother of one of the six "neurotic" families. In addition, I conducted a survey of childrearing practices among mothers at the neighborhood nursery school that our son attended. My daily life became completely embedded in our Mamachi relationships, perhaps more as participant than observer. I saw Americans so infrequently that, when I did, I was shocked at how large, angular, and gaudily dressed they were.

I took on this interviewing with hesitation. It seemed presumptuous, if not impossible, for me to think I could interview in Japanese after only 9 months' language study. However, subsequent experiences taught me thoroughly what graduate school had only began to impart: the central importance of relationship and the power of nonverbal communication. Since I talked with these families on a weekly basis, we got to know each other as people rather than just as researcher and subjects. Wife-to-wife and family-to-family friendships began to develop. My limited Japanese, although extremely awkward, was less of a handicap than I could ever have imagined. Of course, I tape recorded all my interviews and listened to them afterwards with a language instructor. The tapes became my source of language study as well as an accurate record of the interview. Most illustrative of the power of relationship were the times that my language instructor could not understand my incorrect Japanese, as all too accurately recorded on the tape, but my interviewee understood what I *intended* to say and, without hesitation, responded accordingly. How grateful I still am to them for understanding *me*!

As our family-to-family friendships developed, I, as an American wife and mother, was in for a number of culture shocks as I got to know the Japanese women. At first, I tended to believe my new friends when they expressed their envy of our socializing together as a couple. Although I had some knowledge of the Japanese family system, with its separate worlds for husbands and wives, it seemed natural to me that any wife would want shared companionship and recreation with her husband. Several events, however, jolted me into a realization that our Mamachi wives had little or no wish to socialize with their husbands.

The first jolt was perhaps the biggest one. Soon after our getting settled in Mamachi, we decided to hold an open house party for all our six "well" families and invited mothers, fathers, children, and grandparents. Much to our surprise, the six wives met and decided to disinvite their husbands! Consequently, our guests at the open house were mothers, children of all ages, and a few grandparents. The women explained to us later that if the men had come, they would have dominated the scene and no one else would have

PTA mothers visit the home of Ezra and Suzanne Vogel, seated in their living room, Mamachi (Chiba), 1959. Courtesy of Suzanne Vogel.

felt free to enjoy themselves! Whatever notions we had of "weak and submissive" Japanese women were erased that day!

The second jolt came a few weeks later. While I was talking with two of the wives, one of them talked of her plans for a weekend trip to Hong Kong with her husband, an unusual occurrence. The other wife expressed envy at the upcoming trip, but then became concerned, asking, "After you finish talking about the children, what will you and your husband talk about?" The two women agreed they had more fun traveling with women friends or with their children than with their husbands.

In subsequent months another wife helped me to comprehend the primacy in Japan of the mother–child bond over the marital relationship. Curious as to how I related to my husband in comparison to my child, she was pleased when I brought my son with me for a visit or when she learned of my policy of being home when he returned from nursery school. She clearly felt that the mother–child bond was by nature the strongest one, and was eager to find evidence that this applied to American families as well. What mattered most to her were her children. She was not interested in emancipation from family burdens. What she strived for, and largely achieved, was control over her children's upbringing and over the household. She served her husband as if he were a guest in the house and preferred that his involvement be peripheral. This woman came to epitomize for me a basic equation in Mamachi: Woman equals *mother*. Schooler and Smith (1978) later documented the primacy of the role of mother over that of wife.

A different kind of jolt occurred one evening when the usual quiet of our neighborhood was broken by the sound of a child's crying and pounding on the entrance gate next door. Ezra and I quizzically turned to our Japanese maid. She readily explained that the grade school child, crying for forgiveness, had obviously been shut out of the house for punishment. My immediate mischievous thought was that any American child so punished would probably run off down the street gleefully. The more usual method of punishment in the United States would be to send a child to his or her room or "ground" the child for the weekend. Next, we began to notice that mothers walking down the street with unruly toddlers did not hold their hands tightly and command them to stay close and not run off, as we had often seen American mothers do. Rather, the Mamachi mother would run a bit ahead of the straying child, who would then become anxious, run after his mother, and thereafter stay close to her. I mused that our American assumption was that a child wanted to be free and independent, and hence we punished him with confinement or enforced dependence. In contrast, the Japanese assumed a child most wanted dependence and punished him by evoking fear of abandonment.

Takeo Doi's concept of *amae* helped us understand this basic dependent need. Although *The Anatomy of Dependence* (Doi, 1973) was not published in Japan as *Amae no Kozo* until 1971, Doi was already in 1958 writing and talking about *amae* as a key to understanding Japanese psychology. *Amae* can perhaps best be defined as the feeling of dependence or the desire to be loved and cared for. Ezra and I, during the early months in Tokyo living next door to the Doi family, had not only heard the concept but had ourselves experienced the feeling as we had depended on him and his wife Yachiyo for everything from broad cultural orientation to specific daily information about where to put the garbage.

Doi, a Tokyo psychiatrist trained in psychoanalysis in the United States during the 1950s, was by 1958 already the major bridge between Japanese psychiatry and Western psychiatry/psychology. Noting that the English language had no word for such a commonly used Japanese phrase as *amae,* he had explored the meaning of *amae* within the Japanese psyche. Discussions with him taught me about American as well as Japanese psychology. I pondered that this common human experience did not even have an English word and that the closest word, *dependent,* had a pejorative connotation! I realized for the first time just how uncomfortable we Americans are with our dependent feelings and how often we try to deny their existence, preferring to see them as sexual longings or to justify them as our "rights." Conversely, Japanese often seem similarly uncomfortable with and denying of anger, expressing it via passive dependence or excessive politeness.

Amae helped explain the role of the close mother–child relationship in the training and discipline of small children. We had been puzzled by the sparsity of commands or rebukes from mothers, and impressed by the relative lack of rebelliousness from children of any age. We observed the continual physical contact between mother and child and the mother's anticipation of her child's every need. We thus came to hypothesize that it was this close emotional bonding that shaped the child's behavior and maintained discipline without resorting to authoritarian methods that often provoke rebellion.

At the time of the original study, then, my eyes were those of a young American wife and mother, assisting my husband with his research. I looked at the housewives of Mamachi and saw their roles as being narrowly but deeply focused on motherhood, very much in contrast to the role diversity characteristic of myself and the women I knew in America. Although much more confined to the house than American housewives, even those of the 1950s, Japanese mothers were also more in control of the house and more skillfully in control of their children. While their marital relationships, from my point of view, looked distant and shallow, I was impressed that these Mamachi wives were much less emotionally dependent on their husbands than were most American wives. They seldom looked to their husbands for attention, companionship, or even affection.

FROM THE PERSPECTIVE OF WOMEN'S STUDIES: A TRANSITION, PERSONAL AND PROFESSIONAL

Between 1960 and 1975 we made three trips to Japan and kept in touch with the Mamachi families. But Ezra's interests by then were mainly focused on China and mine on our growing family of three children and my part-time job as a psychotherapist in an outpatient clinic. In 1975 the two younger children and I accompanied Ezra to Tokyo for a sabbatical year of research. This time Ezra was studying economic and political aspects of the social system rather than family life, so I planned my own separate study, unpaid but sponsored by the Radcliffe Institute of Harvard University. Since I knew that Japanese men were often uncomfortable with American women, I decided to do what was easiest, namely, interview women. I focused on three types of Japanese women: housewives, unmarried career women, and mothers with careers. Prior to this trip, I had not been involved in the American women's movement, nor particularly interested in women's studies. I went to Japan as before, as a wife accompanying my husband, although this time I knew I needed something of my own to do there. It was the nature of my research topic that took me into the field of women's studies, and from that standpoint I looked anew at the changes in Japanese women's lives.

Such were the objective circumstances. However, in retrospect, I realize that this choice of topic was influenced by undercurrents in my own life and in the world around me. Women in Boston for some time had been raising questions about women's roles, and I was struggling privately with my own questions about my role in an increasingly unsettled marriage. The developments in myself, my world, and my research during that year in Tokyo led to separation from Ezra in 1978 and to a new focus on women's studies and women's roles, in Japan and in America.

This new focus brought me new friends, colleagues, and teachers, in the United States and Japan. During 1975–1976, I was challenged and inspired by the monthly Tokyo meetings of the newly organized International Women's Studies Group *(Kokusai Joseigakkai)*, which went on to hold its first international women's symposium in 1978 in Tokyo, at which I presented a paper on Japanese housewives (S. H. Vogel, 1978a). Through this women's network, from 1975 on, I have greatly benefited from conversations with and the writings of many women, including Merry (Corky) White (1987, 1992), Wakako Hironaka (1979), Sachiko Ide (Ide & McGloin, 1991), Sumiko Iwao (1992), Orie Endō (1987), Hiroko Hara (Iwao & Hara, 1979), Reiko Ishida, Yayohi Aoki (1978), Chizuko Ueno (1988), Barbara Molony (1978) and Kathleen Molony (1978). During the late 1970s, I also met Kiyomi Kawano, who had just graduated from Simmons College School of Social Work in Boston and has since pioneered feminist therapy in Japan, as described in her recent book (Kawano, 1991). In the United States, the new psychology of women associated with Jean Baker Miller and her colleagues at the Stone Center at Wellesley College (Jordan, Kaplan, Miller, Stiver, & Surrey, 1991) gave me new self-understanding as well as deeper empathy with my women clients. Their relational theory of women's development shed more light on women's psychology and our struggles with the important people in our lives than any other theory I had ever encountered.

During the mid-1970s, Tokyo women were clearly on the move, becoming more active outside the home, whether through education, recreation, employment, the consumers' movement, or the newly arisen women's movements. For the first time, I talked extensively with career women, both married and unmarried. Their issues taught me much about the housewives of Mamachi as well as about themselves. The housewives, although more confined than the career women, were also less conflicted than the career women. The housewives accepted what they saw as the natural role for women and had no need to think too deeply about it. I was thankful that my long and continuing acquaintance with them had given me a feel for their lives. Most of them would not have been able to explain themselves to me in an interview or two, as most of them were not that self-conscious. In contrast, most of the career women were quite articulate about their choices, their satisfactions, their conflicts, their disappointments. This fact alone showed me that having a career was suspect in Japanese society and that these women felt strongly the need to explain and justify their lifestyle to themselves as much as to others.

The unmarried career women had to explain to themselves, if not to others, why they were unmarried in a society that considered motherhood synonomous with womanhood. However, they were usually respected for their dedication to their work. The married career women, although they passed the test for womanhood, faced the moral conflict of divided loyalties in a society that expected total dedication to one person or to one cause. These women tended to be seen as deficient in dedication, both at home and at work. Problems at home tended to be blamed on the fact that the mother was working, and problems at work tended to be blamed on the woman's divided attention. In the society at large I could find very little notion of valuing a well-rounded life or a woman's ability to balance the various demands on her time. The women tended to criticize themselves for being *yokubari*—too greedy for "wanting it all." Their husbands typically felt no obligation to help with the house or children since their wives were seen as working for their own pleasure. The samurai ethic of total loyalty to one lord, every day and all day, clearly applied to women as well as men!

Although young housewives in 1975 were more educated, more independent from mothers-in-law, and more free to pursue outside interests that did not compromise their home responsibilities than were housewives in 1958, the basic role and underlying value system impressed me as essentially the same. But in 1975, from my new viewpoint of women's issues, I found myself asking new questions, most particularly, where did Japanese women turn for nurturance, for *amae*? In contrast to American women who were often considered more feminine if they were "dependent" and looked to others, especially men, for sympathy and affection, Japanese femininity seemed to consist solely of caregiving, with very little dependence, except financial. The stereotype of Japanese women as weak and dependent was clearly preposterous, when Japanese wives were on duty 24 hours a day, every day, providing food, relaxation, emotional support, and housekeeping to husbands, children, and other relatives. They were even responsible for banking, house repairs, gardening, often for making reservations and carrying bags on family trips! And they very seldom turned to their husbands for emotional support. Where did they turn? It was not easy finding a satisfactory answer. To a large extent, it seemed that their *amae* was vicarious, that in caring for others they felt fulfilled. Many mothers, however, turned to their children as they grew up, either looking to a daughter for mutual aid and understanding, or looking to a son for the closeness that was not expected in the marital relationship. Others turned to sisters or female friends, although often

these were not close by. Others told me of feeling solace in their gardens or with nature. For many women, however, vicarious care-giving was clearly not enough. A buildup of resentment over the years was evident with some middle-aged wives who developed psychosomatic symptoms or suddenly became angry with their husbands. Underlying resentment that their caretaking had been insufficiently appreciated or not reciprocated seemed all too understandable to this American woman.

During the discussion following my paper on Japanese housewives at the 1978 Tokyo Symposium on Women (S. H. Vogel, 1978a), one Japanese woman challenged me by asking if I would like to be a Japanese housewife. She clearly implied that I was praising Japanese housewives too much. Although I do not remember my reply nearly as well as I recall the question, I knew in my heart, as she probably knew too, that I, with my American needs and expectations, would find the Japanese role both confining and depriving. I had written my original paper on Japanese housewives in the *Japan Interpreter* (S. H. Vogel, 1978b) for an American audience, hoping to dislodge American ethnocentricity, telling of the strengths of Japanese women and of a value system different from our own.

My efforts to provoke Americans into looking at themselves from a different angle continued at home. Some time later I presented a paper to my mental health colleagues at the Harvard University Health Services entitled "The *Advantages* of Being a Japanese Housewife." I explained, for instance, that, traditionally, Japanese women looked upon marriage as a *job,* a social responsibility to be fulfilled. As Takie Lebra (Lebra, 1984) had so well described, while Japanese women were constrained by their role commitment, their self-actualization and self-fulfillment were found in it too. Since, as of the 1970s, they had no unrealistic expectations for romantic love or for understanding from husbands, they were not as disappointed as their American counterparts often were. Furthermore, Japanese wives felt secure in their roles, since maintaining family structure was of crucial importance and the divorce rate was low. Japanese wives felt less pressure than Americans for continually re-creating sex appeal and emotional intimacy. Marriage did not depend on the ability to maintain intimacy or sexual attraction. Japanese wives felt sorry for American wives who had to dress up and make up for their husbands. A couple that could together produce and raise children was successful. Emotional intimacy and mutual gratification were not mandatory, as they were for American couples. Japanese mothers and fathers could find emotional support, companionship, and intimacy elsewhere, with children, with friends, with work groups, with lovers.

So what did my years of focus on women's roles teach me about myself as an American woman and about the Japanese housewife role? I have realized how thoroughly I am an American, that I would not trade the relative freedom and versatility of American housewives nor the companionship and emotional sharing of American marriages for the greater security and status of Japanese motherhood—even though during my own process of divorce, their greater stability looked especially good to me. On the other hand, I have increasingly realized that Japanese women surpass us Americans in the possession and skillful use of one kind of power, what might be called emotional power or the power of relationship; they wield enormous influence by virtue of their children's and their husbands' total dependence on them for daily care and emotional support. This has made me stop and think that there are many different kinds of power, that women in different cultures and in difficult circumstances have been flexible and creative in developing ways to take care of themselves and their families, and that American women have much to learn from other countries. As the years have passed, I have more and more admired how Japanese women, from their power base within the home, and most often without direct confrontation with either their husbands or the political authorities, have greatly expanded the scope of their activities and their influence over the whole society. As Iwao (1992) points out, Japanese women today have more freedom and more opportunities for personal fulfillment than do men, most of whom still have little life outside their jobs. Japanese housewives, by enriching their own lives and working together to improve the home environment, have become leaders in a quiet revolution that is reorganizing relationships within the home and between the home and the workplace.

THE PERSPECTIVE OF A COLLEGE SOCIAL WORKER: JAPANESE FAMILIES CONFRONT LIFE IN THE UNITED STATES

As the 1970s rolled into the 1980s, I was preoccupied with stabilizing my life as a newly divorced woman and, as part of that, with developing my career as a psychotherapist at the Harvard University Health Services and in private practice. I did not know if I would ever again pursue work in Japan, although I had kept in touch, thanks to occasional invitations to give a workshop in Kyoto or a speech in Tokyo. In 1983 it occurred to me that the growing numbers of Japanese scholars and families who came to Harvard University for a year or two offered me an excellent way to keep in touch with Japanese families while providing a service. I did not have to leave home in order to do meaningful work with Japanese! Under the auspices of Harvard University Health Services, and with the cooperation of Harvard's International Office, I organized for the newly arrived wives of Japanese students and scholars at Harvard a discussion and support group entitled "The Pleasures and Problems of Living Overseas." I knew that Japanese families in the United States suffered culture shock as surely as did American families in Japan, and found that my experience of family life in Japan helped me understand their stresses here. An article about this group, aimed at increasing the cross-cultural awareness of college health professionals, was published in the *Journal of American College Health* (S. H. Vogel, 1986).

One finding from these meetings was that the Japanese wives in Boston who did not know how to drive and whose conversational English was not as proficient as their husband's suffered the greatest stress. These women, who in Japan had independently managed all family matters and taken care of husbands who often could not make a cup of tea or negotiate family banking, suddenly found themselves in a dependent position. In Boston, they had to turn to their husbands for many things—dealing with banks or landlords, translating at doctors' appointments, even driving to the supermarket. This unaccustomed dependence often undermined their self-confidence and was felt as a burden by the husbands, who were filled with their own anxieties about work and were used to thinking of family as a source of support, not as needing support. Of course, things usually improved as the husbands gained confidence with their work and the wives became more proficient in English usage, in driving, and in managing other matters on their own. But in the meanwhile, this reversal in the patterning of who was dependent on whom was a strain for both husband and wife.

Another finding was that the increased intimacy and interdependence that typically comes with life in Boston was a source of stress for many Japanese couples. Husbands who in Japan were used to spending only sleeping hours and Sundays with their families found themselves having dinner every night at home in Boston with wife and children, cooperating with family chores on the weekends, and taking vacations with their families. One such husband was aghast at the prospect of spending every day of a 2-week traveling vacation cooped up in a car with his wife and children! While some families enjoyed the opportunity for increased togetherness, others found that close cooperation and sharing of responsibilities brought friction and conflict.

Observing the reaction of these Japanese families to their American surroundings provoked further thinking about how Americans and Japanese deal with dependent feelings. Increased dependent need is a given when one is living outside one's own society, since one is without the usual supports of family, friends, and known signposts for social interaction. Since Japanese readily recognize *amae*, they instinctively extend help, support, and hospitality to foreigners. Americans, in contrast, value independence and equality and are wary of intruding on an individual's self-determination. Japanese in Boston are doubly deprived—of their own cultural supports and of the supports proffered to visitors in Japan. Instead of having everything planned and arranged for them (called *zendate*, or "setting the table"), as for guests in Japan, they are treated in America as equals, which means they are left to fend for themselves! At best they are offered choices, since Americans place high value on choice, but find themselves, in this unknown territory, only more confused. Instead of having someone sense and anticipate their needs as a Japanese host would do, Japanese find that Americans respond only to wishes expressed clearly and assertively, something their socialization has taught them not to do.

THE PERSPECTIVE OF A MENTAL HEALTH PROFESSIONAL: SOME PRESENT-DAY SOCIAL AND PSYCHOLOGICAL PROBLEM AREAS

By the mid-1980s after some years of stability on the home front, personally and professionally, I began to feel the urge to involve myself fully with Japan again, to spend at least a year there. Our Mamachi families, now three generations strong and with three decades of contact, seemed a rare resource, too rich to ignore. Besides, I had long wished that I could do my own professional work in Japan, that is, work as a social worker or psychotherapist, but had generally thought that my language ability was just not good enough for conducting therapy in Japanese. Psychiatric patients, after all, could not be expected to struggle with understanding *me*, as our research families had done so generously. Still, by the mid-1980s it began to dawn on me that I did not have to be an East

Asian scholar (nor married to one) in order to do research in Japan, that perhaps I could apply independently for a research grant. I wanted to do a 30-year follow-up of our Mamachi families and at the same time use my clinical experience to look into what psychiatric patients might teach me sociologically. I was interested in the social and psychological strains associated with the rapid changes in Japanese society. I began studying the language anew, this time focusing on professionally useful vocabulary and on reading that I had previously neglected in my eagerness to converse. I arranged to take a leave of absence from Harvard, and applied for a Fulbright research grant. In September 1988 I found myself settling into a Tokyo *hanare* (a small house originally designed for a young couple, next to the elder couple's larger house), planning my year of doing psychotherapy and consultation at St. Luke's International Hospital (the well-known general hospital in downtown Tokyo), and looking forward to reunions with the Mamachi families.

At St. Luke's, my work in collaboration with the social work and psychiatry staffs (especially social workers Satoko Fukazawa, Chikako Nishida, Mayumi Nakano and psychiatrists Takeo Doi, Junichi Suzuki, Kanzō Nakano, and Ken Ōhira) fulfilled my wish to do psychosocial assessments and ongoing psychotherapy with psychiatric outpatients and to learn something of the experiences and thinking of Japanese mental health professionals. Subsequently, I have continued my work in the field of Japanese mental health through my association with Hasegawa Hospital, a private psychiatric hospital in the Tokyo suburbs, thanks to my introduction to Dr. Mikiko Hasegawa by Dr. Takashi Yamaguchi, a Nihon University psychiatrist who had done his residency during the 1960s at Massachusetts Mental Health Center. Weekly supervision–consultation sessions with the social work staff began in April and continued through August 1989. In subsequent years, I have continued this staff development program by spending 6 weeks each year in consultation at the hospital.

Any social system has its strengths and strains, and the study of social change has convinced me that as society solves one problem, a new one arises. Listening to a multitude of case presentations over the last several years has given me much food for thought about stresses characteristic of the Japanese society of 1989 and later in contrast to that of 1959. In 1959, many child psychiatry cases seemed to involve children being caught in the conflicts of multigenerational households, and the most striking women's problem was that of young brides who were overworked and dominated by their mothers-in-law. By 1989, with urbanization and the postindustrial society, these problems had subsided. The nuclear family had largely replaced the extended family, and young wives had been liberated from their mothers-in-law. But, of course, new problems had arisen. Among children there had developed a symptom complex called school refusal *(tokōkyohi),* which was often accompanied by family violence *(kateinaibōryoku).* And the now autonomous mothers seemed much more unsure of their childrearing methods than their mothers had been.

School refusal is indeed a widespread concern in Japan in recent years. Chiland and Young (1990), in their book about school refusal internationally, give greatest attention to the situation in Japan. Professionals in many different settings in Japan are trying to understand its causes and discover cures. Extensive research is being done, for instance by Ishikawa (Ishikawa & Aoki, 1986) and his colleagues at the Psychiatric Research Institute of Tokyo. I myself had the opportunity to work with a few such families and have heard presentations of many such cases.

School refusal in Japan is different from school phobia or truancy problems in the United States. School refusal, rather than being a separation-from-mother problem of first graders or a delinquency problem of adolescents, is typically a junior high student's inability to make himself or herself go to school any longer, apparently due to anxiety, depression, and/or psychosomatic symptoms. Family violence, as the Japanese discuss it, is not child abuse but parent abuse. The onset of school refusal is related to the increasing pressures of the examination system, which are most severe from fifth grade through tenth grade (first year of high school). The typical pattern is that the youngster quits going to school, withdraws to his or her room at home, avoids social contact, sleeps during the day, and watches videos at night, communicating almost exclusively with his or her mother. Severe cases often involve violence on the part of the youngster, breaking things around the house and hitting his or her parents, most particularly the mother. School refusal in Japan means more than dropping out of school. It means giving up one's place in the ongoing social process, an acceptance of failure or at least a severe drop in one's expected level of success, as it is quite impossible to just pick up where one left off at a later date. It often means withdrawal from society. Female school refusers are almost as frequent as males and also may be violent, with similar social consequences. The psychiatric diagnosis given school refusers varies. For instance, a diagnosis of neurosis, psychosis, or borderline personality disorder may be applied.

Several present-day social strains stand out for me when I hear cases of school refusal: (1) the pressures of the examination system, which now reaches into every segment of society and has become the one universal standard for defining merit or achievement, (2) the absence and/or emotional detachment of the salary-man father, now more the rule than the exception, (3) parental indulgence as related to economic affluence and a softening of the prewar morality, (4) the increased intensity of the mother–child bond, as the number of children has decreased to one or two and as mothers have become more autonomous but often more socially isolated.

Of course, I was particularly interested in these modern-day mothers, in the difference in their lives compared to that of their mothers and grandmothers, and in the source of their current anxieties. I wrote about the changes in the lives of the Mamachi women in the second edition of *Japan's New Middle Class* (S. H. Vogel, 1991), and about some of the stresses I observed among psychiatric outpatients at St. Luke's Hospital in an article entitled "Some Reflections on Changing Strains in the Housewife/Mother Role" (S. H. Vogel, 1989).

Paradoxically, the autonomy of the present-day housewife is the source of her expanded independence and strength but also the source of her anxieties. For instance, autonomy often means social isolation. A mother is no longer surrounded by a network of female relatives. In the urban nuclear family, extended family members no longer live together and often not even close by. Husbands, away at work during most waking hours, are unavailable either for help with childcare or for companionship. And although most urban housewives live in large apartment complexes or in neighborhoods full of families, their typical way of getting along with their neighbors is to be polite and distant, revealing little personal information and seldom consulting about problems. The women's network that has grown up in some places does not extend far enough. Many mothers make friends with other mothers when their children start nursery school, but the mothers of preschool children who most need the support of other mothers are often without adult companionship all day and evening long. The use of babysitters is still not widely accepted. As mentioned in my article on the strains in the housewife–mother role (S. H. Vogel, 1989), a monthlong rain that kept one mother and her 2-year-old indoors alone day after day precipitated anxiety attacks that necessitated psychiatric care for the mother.

Today's autonomous mothers, in control of their households

and of childrearing, may have no place to turn for guidance. Young mothers, no longer having to conform to their husbands' families' methods of childrearing, may lack relatives nearby to consult with. Their husbands are often unavailable or unknowledgeable about children. Paternal authority has weakened and husbands typically leave childrearing totally to their wives. Fathers, when present, are more likely to be playmates than disciplinarians. Many young mothers have had no training or experience with children or even housework before marriage. Growing up female in Japan no longer means bride training nor even helping mother with the house. Mothers take care of all housework so that daughters as well as sons can study.

The role of today's mothers has therefore expanded to include that of disciplinarian as well as that of nurturer. Their very autonomy means that they have to be father *and* mother to their children. The traditional maternal role has not prepared them for this new responsibility. The traditional mothering I admired in 1958 was not characterized by discipline nor limit setting, but by the strong nurturing mother–child bond of the mother sensing and meeting the child's needs and shaping his or her behavior, all from a low-key, nonauthoritarian position. Successful mothers allied with their children and helped them meet the rigorous demands of the outside world, as represented by father, relatives, neighbors, and the school system. Present-day mothers still rely on this basic nurturing approach. When it is insufficient, as when the child is older, many have no other methods at hand. Today's mothers, much like those in 1958, continue to look to others to take the disciplinarian role, but today the school system is often the only remaining source of discipline (S. H. Vogel, 1991). It is no wonder that such mothers often lack confidence in their ability to manage their teenage children.

Today's mothers, then, carry enormous responsibility, often alone, often with little support from others. They are given the credit—or the blame—for the success or failure of their children in school and in society. This sole responsibility is awesome and anxiety-provoking.

Looking at Japanese mothers from the viewpoint of the "self in relation" theories of Jean Baker Miller and others at the Stone Center (Jordan et al., 1991), one notes that the role definition of motherhood in Japan is giving and taking care of others, all day, every day. There is no legitimation for taking care of oneself or taking time for oneself or even for expressing oneself. There is no ideal of a well-rounded or balanced lifestyle. Silence is golden, and self-sacrifice is virtuous.

Of course, many mothers today, at least of school-age or older children, are spending much time on their own interests or recreation. However, one often senses a conflict between this new wish for self-fulfillment and the older ideal of total devotion to family. As Imamura (1987) has well documented, the conflict is typically resolved by the women going out for work or recreation only at times when childcare and household responsibilities will not be interfered with. Mothers, for instance, accept part-time jobs in the neighborhood that enable them to be home when children return from school and to manage all housework without troubling their husbands. Furthermore, most women's activities are justified not as promoting individual interests, but as improving family life. Activities that are not in some way for the sake of the family are more difficult to rationalize and leave a woman vulnerable to criticism (from herself as well as others) for being selfish *(wagamama)*. I have been surprised to find that apparently very self-confident women, successful with career and family, often harbor feelings of guilt or feminine inadequacy because they are doing *what they want to do.*

Most Japanese mothers today handle these conflicts and heavy responsibilities without excessive anxiety and with considerable creativity in locating activities suitable for their interests while also doing their best with their family responsibilities. Stress, however, does take the form of psychiatric symptoms in some women, or may show up in family or children's problems, such as school refusal. One mother, for instance, became anorexic when a move to a distant city meant the loss of her mother's and sister's support. Successful, although lengthy, therapy included helping her to educate her husband on why and how she needed his cooperation with family care—an idea that had never occurred to him before.

In hearing about the mothers of children suffering from school refusal, I have been impressed that they are extreme examples of women who feel totally responsible for their children, expecting themselves to be all-giving and feel guilty for any lack thereof. These overprotective, overindulgent mothers tend to blame themselves for a possible lack of *amae* for not being loving or giving enough, rather than criticizing themselves for not being firm or not being consistent. They try to cure all problems by being more giving, more indulgent. They may spend great sums of money in an effort to satisfy all the youngster's demands, even outrageous ones. They tolerate his or her sleeping days and watching TV all night. They bring the youngster whatever he or she wants to eat. They ask nothing of the child. Many parents will not even insist that a school-refusing child see a counselor or doctor, but will let him follow his or her own wishes, which most often means avoidance of any discomfort. Some mothers feel they must accept even physical abuse from their children if that is how the children need to express their feelings. A few mothers even masturbate their teenage sons in order to soothe them.

The efforts of such mothers more often escalate than alleviate the problem. The mother feels a failure when her indulged child is unable to cope with the demands of school and feels enormously guilty when he or she angrily blames her. The child, also feeling guilty, retreats to his or her room, but again strikes out at the one he or she is closest to. It seems that neither mother nor child has any other outlet for feelings. I have called this "acting-in" (S. H. Vogel, 1991). Whereas disturbed American teenagers are more likely to get in trouble outside the house (acting-out), these Japanese teenagers confine their behavioral expressions to inside the home.

The concept of limit setting seems to be missing with these mothers. In fact, there is not a commonly used Japanese phrase for it. In Hasegawa Hospital, the staff have "Japanized" the English word, demonstrating that the concept is imported. Many mothers of school refusers seem quite unable to say no. Refusing a sick child is felt to be either selfish or mean or both. Furthermore, the mothers greatly fear the anger, and the violence, of these adolescent children. In contrast to the mothers of 1959, these mothers are much more afraid of their children than of their husbands!

Incidentally, some fathers are equally afraid of their children and equally unable to say no. I was particularly astonished to hear of a case where both parents ran away from home to protect themselves from abusive, demanding children, leaving the house to the two teenagers. In the United States, I have heard of children running away from home or of being sent away from home, but never of parents running away!

Is it possible that these children do suffer from insufficient *amae,* even with such permissive, indulgent mothers? Psychoanalysts like Doi say some mothers who seem attentive and caring lack real empathy for a child's feelings and may instead project their own needs onto the child. The school refuser's mother or the much-criticized *kyoiku mama* (education mother) may be examples of mothers who project their own needs for success onto the child.

Japanese society does seem to be slowly moving in directions that will alleviate these present-day stresses of mothers. Mothers' groups and women's networks are growing. Counseling centers are expanding. Women, less defensive of their control of the home, are finding ways to involve their husbands in family activities, and gradually shortening work hours are allowing men time at home. Even the educational system is becoming a bit more flexible, opening more diverse roads to success for children and their mothers.

CONCLUSION

My career has been the career of a woman. Like that of many women of my generation, it has not been unilinear or goal-oriented, but has had twists and turns as it has had to fit into my first priorities of family and personal life. My work on Japan, in particular, has never had any long-range goal, but has arisen out of my interests and my circumstances at the time. I have no regrets about this. In fact, I see many advantages. Since what I have depended on has been my family and/or my employment as a clinical social worker, my Japanese work has been enjoyable and relatively free of anxiety. I can see now that those early interviews with the Mamachi families were more free, relaxed, and probably perceptive because I did not carry the overall responsibility for the success of the research. Furthermore, my being there primarily as wife and mother probably contributed to my being accepted into the lives and confidences of those Mamachi mothers.

Nevertheless, the retrospective look shows continuity. While my original focus, as a wife, was family and childrearing, and my more recent focus, as a single professional, is on mental health, I have always been interested in all the above topics. The single most unifying topic has been women within the family: social roles and psychology. Since I have looked at Japan with the eyes of a woman, a woman whose career is secondary to family, what I have naturally focused on most has been women, particularly housewives and mothers.

In terms of theoretical approach, I can see in retrospect that Takeo Doi's concept of *amae* at some point became basic to all my clinical thinking, in the United States as well as in Japan. In fact, I see *amae* as the universal basic instinct, more universal and more basic than Freud's two instincts, sex and aggression. These latter seem secondary to and derivative of *amae*. The profound theoretical challenge implicit in Doi's thinking has never been recognized by American psychoanalysts, who have been perhaps all too inclined to see *amae* as peculiarly Japanese. Or perhaps the challenge has been obscured by Doi's very low-key, modest manner. He does not assert and prove the logic of his thesis as a Western essayist would. His more Oriental style is evocative: metaphorical, suggestive, almost poetic. His work has not stirred up confrontative theoretical debate, but rather has built bridges of international understanding between Western and Eastern psychiatry.

A Westerner did not discover *amae*, I think, because Westerners are reluctant to recognize their dependent needs and prefer to label them sexual instincts.

The Stone Center theories about empathy and relationship in human development, however, are needed to make explicit and to further develop what is implicit in Doi's theory of *amae*. *Amae* is about what the child needs and receives from his or her mother. Implied in Doi's discussion is that what children need is caretaking that is truly empathic, that is in tune with the child's true needs and feelings and not just a projection of the parent's needs. Also implied is that *amae* (or empathy) becomes reciprocal. A child bonded to his or her mother becomes perceptive of her feelings and wants to give to her. The Stone Center theory makes explicit that healthy development involves *empathic interaction* between growing child and parent. The Japanese theory, perhaps because it comes from a vertically organized culture, emphasizes what the child receives and has to receive first, while the American theory, coming from a horizontal, peer culture, emphasizes the active participation of the child. In my own thinking, these two theories, one created to explain Japanese psychology and the other to explain American female psychology, come together to lay down the basis for healthy human development universally.

What has been my methodology? Participant-observation and clinical-type interviewing, yes, but more importantly, and for better or worse, my major research tool has been my *self*. I have made no attempt to keep my research "scientifically objective," nor do I think it is humanly possible for anyone to be purely objective. Rather I use my whole self—feelings, thoughts, struggles, perceptions, questions—when I relate to another person or group, whether in a therapy context or a research context. It is through such an empathic connection, I think, that one can best understand the experiences of other people, all the while being aware of how we are different as well as how we are similar, and being aware of how we are changing even as they are changing.

REFERENCES

Aoki, Y. (Ed.). (1976). *Dare no tame ni kodomo o umu ka? [For whom are children born?].* Tokyo: Futosha.

Chiland, C., & Young, J. G. (Eds.). (1990). *Why children reject school: Views from seven countries.* New Haven, CT: Yale University Press.

Doi, T. (1973). *The anatomy of dependence [Amae no kozo]* (J. Bestor, Trans.). Tokyo: Kodansha International.

Endō, O. (1987). *Ki ni naru kotoba [Words that bother me].* Tokyo: Nan Un Do.

Hironaka, W. (1979). *Futatsu no bunka no aida de [Essay on women].* Tokyo: Bunka Shuppankyoku.

Ide, S., & McGloin, N. H. (Eds.). (1991). *Aspects of Japanese women's language.* Tokyo: Kuroshio.

Imamura, A. E. (1987). *Urban Japanese housewives.* Honolulu: University of Hawaii Press.

Ishikawa, H., & Aoki, S. (1986). *Shishunki—kiki to kazoku: Tōkō kyohi, kateinai bōryoku no chiryō chimu [Adolescence—Crisis and family: School refusal and family violence treatment teams].* Tokyo: Iwasaki Gakujitsu Shuppansha.

Iwao, S. (1992). *The Japanese woman: Traditional image and changing reality.* New York: Free Press.

Iwao, S., & Hara, H. (1979). *Joseigaku kotohajime [The beginnings of women's studies].* Tokyo: Kodansha.

Jordan, J. V., Kaplan, A. G., Miller, J. B., Stiver, I. P., & Surrey, J. L., (1991). *Women's growth in connection: Writings from the Stone Center.* New York: Guilford Press.

Kawano, K. (1991). *Feminist counseling.* Tokyo: Shinsuisha.

Lebra, T. S. (1984). *Japanese women: Constraint and fulfillment.* Honolulu: University of Hawaii Press.

Molony, B. (1978). Women and social and political change. *Proceedings of the Tokyo Symposium on Women* (pp. 10–12). Tokyo: International Group for the Study of Women.

Molony, K. (1978). Feminist ideology in prewar Japan. In M. T. White & B. Molony (Eds.), *Proceedings of the Tokyo Symposium on Women* (Vol. 1, pp. 13–22). Tokyo: International Group for the Study of Women.

Schooler, C., & Smith, K. C. (1978). . . . and a Japanese wife. Social structural antecedents of women's role values in Japan. *Sex Roles, 4*(1), 23–41.

Ueno, C. (1988). *"Jo en" ga yononaka o kaeru [Women's networking changes the world].* Tokyo: Nihon Keizai Shimbunsha.

Vogel, E. F. (1963). *Japan's new middle class.* Berkeley: University of California Press.

Vogel, S. H. (1978a). The professional housewife. In M. T. White & B. Molony (Eds.), *Proceedings of the Tokyo Symposium on Women* (Vol. 1, pp. 150–155). Tokyo: International Group for the Study of Women.

Vogel, S. H. (1978b). Professional housewife: The career of urban middle class Japanese women. *Japan Interpreter, 12*(1), 16–43.

Vogel, S. H. (1986). Toward understanding the adjustment problems of foreign families in the college community: The case of Japanese wives at the Harvard University Health Services. *Journal of American College Health, 34*(6), 274–279.

Vogel, S. H. (1989). Some reflections on changing strains in the house-wife/mother role. *Kokoro to Shakai.* Tokyo: Nihon Seishin Eisei Kai [Japanese Mental Health Association], *57,* 137–149.

Vogel, S. H. (1991). Beyond success: Mamachi thirty years later. In E. F. Vogel, *Japan's new middle class* (2nd ed., pp. 282–311). Berkeley: University of California Press.

White, M. (1987). The virtue of Japanese mothers: Cultural definition of women's lives. *Daedalus, 116*(3), 149–61.

White, M. (1992). Immobile democracy? *Daedalus, 121* (4), 61–81.

CHAPTER 11

Japan's Old-Time New Middle Class

Ezra F. Vogel

WHY I FIRST STUDIED JAPANESE FAMILIES

When my Japanese friends ask me why I started studying Japan, I tell them it was a *miai* (arranged marriage) first and then evolved into *renai* (love), which is how Japanese explain successful arranged marriages. When I went to Japan in 1958 for a 2-year period of research, I had never been to Japan before, had no close Japanese friends, and indeed had no particular fascination with Japanese culture. I went at the suggestion of Florence Kluckhohn, for whom I worked as a research assistant for 3 years as part of the Kluckhohn–Spiegel project on cultural aspects of normal and emotionally disturbed families. She took me aside one day and said, "Ezra, you are terribly provincial. You have never lived in another culture. How could you understand American society without living in another culture? Before you settle down to teaching, you ought to go abroad to a very different culture and live in and soak up the culture."

I chose Japan among other cultures because of the influence of William Caudill. I entered Harvard's Social Relations Department as a graduate student in the fall of 1953 after serving 2 years in the U.S. Army. There I had been trained as a psychiatric social work technician, assigned for 18 months to interview mental patients at an army psychiatric hospital. I began working with Bill Caudill because he had been interested in the sociocultural aspects of mental health (Caudill, 1958). He had just returned from a year of field work in Japan and was full of Japanese culture. When I told him, following Kluckhohn's advice, that I was planning to spend a year or two studying another culture, he suggested that I apply for

Japan and that he would help me make contacts. While I formally had no courses on Asia before I received my Ph.D., I prepared for going to Japan by taking a reading course with John Peizel on Japanese society and culture. I also started Japanese conversation practice at Harvard with two students: Tatsuo Arima, who is now Japan's ambassador to Germany, and Yoshi Shimizu, who is now a professor of art history at Princeton University.

I had begun working for Florence Kluckhohn (an anthropologist) and John Spiegel (a psychoanalyst) because their project centered on social aspects of mental illness, a topic in which I wanted to specialize because of my army experience. I was able to use material gathered during my 3 years in that project for my doctoral thesis (see Vogel, 1990). In retrospect, I feel that I learned a great deal from that project, from Florence Kluckhohn about cultural values and the role of a participant-observer, and from John Spiegel about how to conduct interviews and observe the second- and third-order meanings from the interviews.

Another major influence in my graduate training was Talcott Parsons. I took part in his seminar for 3 years and in informal theory work-groups as well. I was therefore interested from the beginning in looking at the broad social system of an entire society. Indeed, this was a central organizing principle and was a part of the theoretical introduction which Norm Bell and I wrote for the book we edited, *A Modern Introduction to the Family* (Vogel & Bell, 1960).

My other mentor was Ronald Dore, who has remained a good friend, an intellectual big brother. In the spring of 1958, a few weeks before I was to leave for my 2 years of fieldwork in Japan, Ron had been invited to Tufts University to take part in a special research project, and I had an opportunity to meet him. He was kind enough to show me the page proofs for *City Life in Japan* (Dore, 1958). I was exhilarated to find such an informative, detailed picture of the Japanese family on the eve of departure. I was also depressed, worried that I had nothing left to write about. It took a great deal of thought and fieldwork to come up with an approach that would not simply repeat what he had done.

THE 1958–1960 RESEARCH

I received a 2-year postdoctoral research grant to Japan to begin in 1958. One year was for full-time language study, and 1 year for fieldwork among families, parallel to the work of the Kluckhohn–Spiegel project. In that research project, women psychiatric social workers had interviewed the wives of the families, and I and fellow graduate student Norman Bell had interviewed the husbands each week. We interviewed families with emotionally disturbed children as well as control families with normal children, from the same cultural background.

My wife, Suzanne, a psychiatric social worker, was very responsive when I first began discussing the possibility of the research in Japan, and early on she made it clear she was interested in taking part in the research. She had an M.A. in Sociology as well as an M.S. in Social Work, and was interested in research as well as interviewing. The research on Japanese families therefore was a partnership. She interviewed the wives, I interviewed the husbands, and each week we typed up our own interviews, discussed what we had learned with each other and jointly decided what kind of issues we would try to raise in the following week. When we returned to the United States, the plan was that we would coauthor a book on the research. I wrote the first draft, and she had agreed to work on the next draft. When she began to work on the revision of my origi-

Family picnic of parents and three grade school children, Mamachi, 1959. Courtesy of Suzanne Vogel.

nal draft, however, Suzanne felt less confident than I of making broader social interpretations, since she had not read as widely on Japan nor talked with as many Japanese social scientists. She therefore asked that I revise the book myself. As a result, it came out as my book, but all the field research was a partnership.

As I began to analyze our data I felt it was more interesting to describe the general Japanese pattern than the difference between "sick" (families with emotionally disturbed children) and "well" families. The most interesting pattern I discovered in Japanese families at the time was the major difference between the families of salaried employees (new middle class) and those of independent business people. The book was therefore called *Japan's New Middle Class* (Vogel, 1963/1991).

SUBSEQUENT WORK

When I returned from Japan, my first job was as an Assistant Professor in the Psychiatry Department at Yale. I was taking part in research on social aspects of schizophrenia, on a project led by Theodore Lidz and Steve Fleck. I enjoyed the work and could have continued, but during the year (1960–1961) I decided I was more interested in specializing in East Asia. During Thanksgiving break in the fall of 1960, I returned to Cambridge for a visit. During that visit, I stopped in to see John Pelzel. I told him that I was considering specializing in Japan rather than in mental health, and out of the blue he asked me how I would like to study China. I had not thought about it, but his advice at the time (which by now I think has proved to be wrong) was that there were probably no careers for anyone working only on Japanese society. Both he and Bob Bellah, a friend 2 years my senior in sociology at Harvard, had studied China as well. Pelzel suggested that if I wanted to specialize in Japan, I ought to also study Chinese society. Harvard had just received a grant to train people to work on Chinese society. They had difficulty finding well-trained sociologists to work on China, and since I had studied Japanese language, I obviously had the patience to endure Oriental language studies. Thus, I spent 3 years studying Chinese language and history before beginning to teach a course in Chinese Society at Harvard in 1964. As a good Parsonian, I also first tried to get a very good overview of the basic social structure before choosing a specific research problem. The opportunities for research were extremely restricted, and the question was how to find some topic on which there could be reasonably good information. It was for that reason that I focused on Guangdong, where the best data were available.

Suzanne, I, and our two children (our third was born later) spent a year, from 1963 to 1964, in Hong Kong, where I was interviewing former residents of China (since we could not yet enter China for fieldwork) about Chinese society. There she found a job as a psychiatric social work supervisor at Chung Chi College. When I first returned to Harvard I worked and taught primarily on Chinese society.

Bob Bellah had taught the Japanese Society course at Harvard in the 1960s, but when he went to Berkeley in 1969, I took over this course. Since I had been studying primarily the Japanese family, I arranged to spend the summer of 1969 in Japan getting a broader picture of Japanese political and economic structure, so that I could teach an overall course on Japan. The responsibility for teaching a course forced me to spell out in more detail an overview of the major subsectors of society. My model was the course by Talcott Parsons on American Society which I audited as a graduate student, and the outline of the topics covered for my courses in Chinese as well as Japanese Society still bear the influence of Talcott Parsons (1951).

LOOKING BACK

By the time we had finished our work in Mamachi (true name: Mama-cho, in Ichikawa City, Chiba Prefecture) in 1960, the six normal families we had been studying had become our friends, and we have kept up with them in the 32 years since. One of the families left Mamachi in 1990, but the other five still live in the same residences. Mamachi became our *furusato* (old home) in Japan. I have been to Mamachi almost every year since 1960, and even after Suzanne and I separated in 1978 both of us have kept in touch with the Mamachi families. Our children have gotten to know their children, and in some cases their grandchildren and even one great-grandchild. It was on the basis of continuing contacts that I was able to update *Japan's New Middle Class* with a new chapter on Mamachi 10 years later, and Suzanne was able to write a chapter on Mamachi 30 years later.

Although significant changes have taken place, I am not aware of new research by others or new perspectives that would cause me to revise fundamentally my description of Mamachi life as of the time of our study. Now that I handle the Japanese language much better than when we left Mamachi, I am amazed how much we learned at early stages of our research when our Japanese language was so limited. I guess that one-on-one relationships over a long period of time enable people to get to know each other very well even if their vocabulary is limited. I also believe that the training Suzanne and I had in psychology and interviewing techniques helped us penetrate to deeper levels than we could have without such training.

I have had students studying the new middle-class family in Korea and Taiwan, and I believe that many of the developments we noticed in Japan also applied to developments in their countries, as their societies went through similar social transformation. Such developments include the role of education and entrance examinations, and the nuclearization of the family with the growth of salaried employment.

Although my own intellectual interest in the last 20 years has centered more on overall societal developments than on family and childrearing, I consider myself fortunate that I began by studying the family and psychology. I believe this has given me a grounding in how Japanese look at the world that has been very useful in trying to understand how Japanese individuals respond to broader issues of economics, politics, and even world affairs.

If I had it to do over again, I would have done only one thing differently. I would have taken time off early to consolidate my Japanese language study rather than continuing to study with tutors and using tapes for the next 25 years at a slower pace. I probably would not have tried to do both Chinese and Japanese studies, as it has been very heavy pressure trying to keep up on both societies while doing teaching, research, and administration at the same time. And even if I had done both Chinese and Japanese studies, I would have taken more time off to consolidate the languages earlier, and I would not have taken on administrative responsibilities so early in my career. On balance I consider myself fortunate that I was able to first visit East Asia as economic development took off in Japan, in the four little dragons (Vogel, 1991), and in Guangdong, the part of China in which I concentrated my own research. I was also fortunate that Florence Kluckhohn, Bill Caudill, John Spiegel, John Pelzel, and Talcott Parsons prepared me for the work. Finally, I have enjoyed the close friendship of so many Japanese in so many different walks of life outside work relations. None of these relationships has been closer than those with some of the Mamachi families we came to know in 1959.

REFERENCES

Caudill, W. (1958). *The psychiatric hospital as a small society.* Cambridge, MA: Harvard University Press.

Dore, R. P. (1958). *City life in Japan.* Berkeley: University of California Press.

Parsons, T. (1951). *The social system.* Glencoe, IL: Free Press.

Vogel, E. A. (1991). *Japan's new middle class* (2nd ed.). Berkeley: University of California Press. (Original work published 1963)

Vogel, E. A. (1990). *The marital relationship of parents and the emotionally disturbed child.* New York: Garland.

Vogel, E.A. (1991). *The four little dragons: The spread of industrialization in East Asia.* Cambridge, MA: Harvard University Press.

Vogel, E. A., & Bell, N. W. (Eds.). (1960). *A modern introduction to the family.* New York: Free Press.

CHAPTER 12

Renewing the New Middle Class
Japan's Next Families

Merry White

It is very unusual that a book written three decades ago, even with the word "new" in its title, still serves as a pertinent, penetrative, and even predictive analysis of social conditions. While the families it describes are no longer "new," and the middle-class culture that was said to "homogenize" Japan seems now to be diversifying under the combined pressures of recession and the recognition of different subcultures and classes, *Japan's New Middle Class* (E. Vogel, 1963) remains much more than a memento of a historical epoch.

Ezra and Suzanne Vogel's research, as described in Ezra Vogel's book, was part of the basic training of my generation of social scientists studying Japan, and as such shaped a field and its future. Indeed, they established a template for the study of the family and society in Japan that has weathered well the 33 years since the book's first publication.

The transition from the family model constructed in the Meiji Civil Code of 1898 based on the samurai *ie* model to the *nyu famiri* of today is the story of changing relationships within households and new influences from outside the family. The enduring significance of the book lies in its capacity to chronicle a historical change and describe a moment in the process in such detail that lasting truths about the Japanese family and socialization processes emerge as well. Emphasizing change itself is one key to the book's capacity to survive decades of change. While the emphasis on hierarchy and Confucian codes of behavior in the Meiji Period may appear to have been a means for resisting Western influences sweeping Japan, in fact the agenda of national leadership was quite different. The goals of modernization and development demanded the creation of a consensus in Japanese society, and part of the invention of a national identity was the creation of a single norm for family behavior. While the hierarchical model chosen resembled only a small percentage of existing families, drawn from samurai stock, it represented an ideal that could stand for "the" Japanese family.

Similarly, a post-World War II model for the family emerged that could stand for a "modern family." Its features, as the Vogels describe it, include a nuclear household, strongly separated workplace and home environments, mothers in service to the children's educational needs, and fathers "married" to their companies. The demanding institutions of school and workplace ate up the time and attention of the children and father, and the home (mother) became a back-up support system.

But the family also became a source of change, not simply a reflection or recipient of external pressures. I would like to describe here the Japanese family as a context for the nurturance of identities, a socializer of the young and motivator of productivity, but more recently, and since the publication of *Japan's New Middle Class,* a locus where change is generated.

First, as the Vogels (Chapters 10 and 11, this volume) have done, I will chart my entry into the field, and with the advantages of hindsight I will try to demonstrate the heritage *Japan's New Middle Class* represents and the new directions it forecasts even now.

I first encountered Japan in 1963, a few years after the Vogels' first landing, and the year of publication of the book about their research. I had chosen to study Japanese society in anthropology at Harvard in the late 1950s. As an area study, the field of Japanese studies was then more commonly undertaken in the humanities: literature, religion, and art dominated the field. Anthropology then tended to emphasize the study of premodern, exotic societies, which after the devastation of war was indeed what Japan appeared to be. My reason for choosing to study Japan was at first an act of rebellion: I rejected the genteel college course of study my high school teachers had chosen for me in European art history, and instead wanted to get as far away as possible—geographically at least.

In the late 1950s, Japanese language classes at Harvard seemed to be frequented by the children of diplomats and missionaries, people who had lived in Japan and whose abilities were intimidating to a neophyte like me. We did have the advantages of small classes, for in the late 1950s there might be eight people in a class, while 35 years later Harvard's Japanese language program is bursting at the seams with over 100 students in introductory classes.

But I was hooked. After 3 years, my investment in study demanded testing in the field, and after graduation I immediately went to Japan, a year before the watershed Tokyo Olympics. The Olympics of 1964 provided a symbolic marker for the start of the economic boom: As in the opening of Japan in the Meiji era (1868–1912), the postwar opening also created an impetus for social and material change well beyond the mushrooming streetcorner English academies and imported Coca-Cola.

My introduction to postwar society was through Ronald Dore's (1958) *City Life in Japan.* I witnessed some of the same scenes Dore described of traditional community life; the sense of neighborhood as "village" was only occasionally made obsolete by less personal, "international style" urban architecture. Most buildings still were under eight stories, in conformity with earthquake codes; most neighborhood streets were not yet dangerous with traffic, but were still places where people convened to hang out laundry on bamboo poles, to clean bedding, or to talk and kibbitz. There were still dirt roads in Tokyo, in contrast with the splendid new National Stadium and Pool designed by Kenzo Tange, and the bootstrapping postwar mood was invigorating.

The two urban cultures Dore described, the Yamanote elite and the *Shitamachi* shopkeepers, were relatively intact. The Vogels took on the task of making a similarly rich description of the emerging new middle class in "Mamachi," a bedroom suburb of Tokyo of the late 1950s and early 1960s. Images of the three societies of postwar Japan—the *shibui* (restrained and understated) elegance of the elites on the hill; the straightforward ebullience of the downtowners; the bourgeois organization of family, school, and work among the "new middle class"—are not out of date today. Dore and the Vogels allow us to smell the *nabe* (casserole) cooking and feel the warmth of the *kotatsu* (hearth), which, in spite of busy lives and take-out meals, are still powerful evocations of family.

The books by Dore and Ezra Vogel still represent the bookends of my personal library, and I still use both in my sociology course on modern Japanese society. This demonstrates that the deeper you go into the lives of people as they themselves experience them, the more lasting the truth of the description. Not only does *Japan's New Middle Class* still pertinently frame the psychological relations of people within the family, but it shows how the relationships between family, school, and workplace form the triangular heart of Japanese society. There have been, of course, dramatic changes in Japan affecting families, but the Vogels' insights on the psychosocial settings and dynamics of family life are still useful, both because of the depth they achieved and because the lessons they drew were very forward looking.

Let me give some examples of such enduring messages, which I believe will continue to help us understand Japanese families, childrearing, and socialization even into the next generation.

THE USE OF LOCAL UNDERSTANDING: ETHNOPSYCHOLOGY BEFORE ITS TIME

The Vogels' long association with Takeo Doi and the strong influence of his work were fortunate and inevitable. Doi's (1973) work is a pioneering synthesis of Western psychotherapeutic methods and Japanese beliefs about the self and childhood socialization. In effect, it gave the Vogels intellectual permission to treat Japanese child development and psychology of the self in *Japanese* terms, rather than as filtered through ethnocentric or universalistic Western perspectives.

The concept of *amae* (dependence) was pivotal in the Vogels' understanding of the details of childrearing and the concerns of the parents they worked with. Centering ethnographic treatments in local perspective of course is a tenet of anthropological method, but the application of Doi's work allowed them to reveal the Japanese middle-class family as distinctly modern but not Western, and not on a trajectory converging with American models.

The Vogels gave credit to the idea of dependence as a valid element in childrearing rather than as a necessary evil. This led them to a key point in the mother–child relationship: that what we would call indulgence is a clear strategy for achieving a "good," *sunao,* (wholehearted, cooperative) child. To see a Japanese mother in the time-consuming task of *wakaraseru,* or "getting the child to understand" (E. Vogel, 1963, p. 245), avoiding opposition and confrontation, is to open a window on a principle underlying much Japanese educational pedagogy as well. The work of Lois Peak (1991) and Catherine Lewis (Chapter 7, this volume) has further elucidated these principles and practices in the home and school.

Doi established that the American notion of individualism (which denies the validity of almost *all* social embeddedness, at odds with the idea of society itself, as Rohlen [1983, p. 319] has said) need not be invoked as necessary for the creation of a "modern personality." Building on this insight, the Vogels then proceeded to develop a complex critique of Western ethnocentrism as they built a coherent picture of family life in Japan.

CHANGING IMAGES AND CHANGING ROLES IN THE FAMILY

Central to the lives of Japanese families is the *mother,* synonymous with home, childcare, and community. The primacy of the mother–child bond as the key to family structure, as well as to the reproduction of cultural norms and the success of children in school and workplace, created a "professional housewife" (S. Vogel, 1978) model that emphasized the functional aspects of the separation of spheres. The Japanese housewife might well appear "cabinn'd, cribbed and confined" like the suburban American housewife of the 1950s, but as others have observed (Iwao, 1992), the American woman could have something to learn from her Japanese counterparts of autonomy and decision making.

Over the years, as the Vogels have watched them, there have been changes in the lives of the six families they studied—most particularly in the lives of women. Indeed, as Suzanne Vogel has described them, women appear to have changed—in values, behavior, and self-expression—more than have men, although perhaps her attending more to women than to men produced this perception.

Suzanne Vogel's fascinating description of the trajectory of her own life in parallel with her perceptions of changes, or her unfolding awareness of different conditions in the lives of Japanese women is illuminating as a minihistory of women generically and of personal life histories, in both Japan and the United States.

One observation that might surprise American readers (especially contemporary women) is that Japanese women feel that they receive social value for their tasks as women and feel satisfaction in their identities. Some might say that Japanese housewives are victims of cultural oppression and of a false consciousness, or that they are manipulated by institutional and ideological demands (Lock, 1992). After all, how could they be satisfied by the "professionalization" of standards and practices, such as the high value given to packing a perfect school lunch box, related to the role of housewife, especially if housewife is their only option?

Western feminists have assumed that a woman defined as wife

and mother is an oppressed person, being defined by biology and culture rather than by her "free will" and other qualities inherent in her as an individual. Besides ignoring other definitions of satisfaction and value, even other definitions among women, this view also ignores intervening issues raised by history, class, and social structure. The unexpected fact that women in Japan would *choose* to be housewives and found satisfaction and identity in this role needed some explanation, and Suzanne Vogel presented evidence that women found their *ikigai* (motivation, life goal) in raising children.

We have such evidence from the women who served as the Vogels' primary informants for this study. Because of the separation of spheres, and because their viewpoint was from within the household, it naturally fell to women to explain the family to the researchers. Division of labor was not news to readers, but the home as a source of women's authority and decision-making power was, in 1963. More than the *hesokuri-gane* sneaking of savings for their own purposes (Vogel, 1963, p. 197), and more than indirect manipulations of male egos, these women had resources of their own and explicit power in the household. In 19th-century America the "cult of true womanhood" (Welter, 1966) apportioned nurturant tasks to the lower status "expressive" category, while those "instrumental" tasks involved with the outside world, and the economy—as in wage labor—were given higher social value. For a society such as Japan, where indulgence and even dependency have positive valence, we must rethink role and value and, even more than Vogel documents, allow for "separate but equal" spheres of authority.

But having accomplished this decentering, we must adjust further for social change, for now more and more young middle-class Japanese women say that their goals include a professional career. And although most wish still to be mothers (Iwao, 1992), their choices of spouse, timing of childbearing, desired family size, and even the decision to divorce are increasingly based on priorities other than a housewife identity. And, of course, assuming that all preferred to "stay home," even in the early 1960s, missed the views of many women who either had to work outside the home, or were doing so without noting it as significant because they were still privileging the definition of housewife as they spent much of their time earning a wage. While this change might appear to contradict the durability of the Vogels' description of "satisfied housewives," underlying psychosocial principles have endured, as women continue to value responsible mothering and emotional autonomy.

While the emotional independence of the new middle-class

woman of the late 1950s may have presaged the structural independence of the new woman of the 1990s, the men of both eras are
harder to characterize and track, in part because we have only a
limited view of them in contrast to the thorough treatment Suzanne Vogel and others have continued to provide of women.
While we see the company man of the 1950s (now called the *kyujin-
rui,* "old race," by his *shinjinrui,* "new race," children) as a product
of history and institutions, it is more difficult to name his 1990s
counterpart. He is neither a family man (hence the concern over
the absent father syndrome; see Shwalb, Imaizumi, & Nakazawa,
1987) nor a corporate warrior, choosing more free time over more
work loyalty. New institutional and economic factors are affecting
the direction of men's careers, including the increase in midcareer
job changes and other intimations that the permanent employment and seniority-driven employment pattern have changed.
Workplace conditions, too, are changing: A drive to reduce work
hours, promote leisure activities, create more individuated tasks,
and support family-care leave for men and women is producing
discussion of adjustments for better quality of life. These changes
affecting men and women both are the result of the new leverage
women employees have had recently to force workplaces to meet
their needs. Young men are also more engaged in childrearing and
domestic chores than were their fathers, though the responsibility
for households still rests with women. So, it may be the new *woman*
who is establishing the priorities for the new *man.*

THE ROLE OF SCHOOLING:
VOGEL'S "GATEWAY TO SALARY"

Japan's New Middle Class examined the meritocratic premise of the
advancement system based on educational credentials *(gakureki),*
and noted the once-and-for-all (or, considering the *ronin* [repeat-
ers], the "twice-and-for-all") nature of the examination system and
the intense pressure this places on middle-class families. The reproduction of social status through individual effort is outlined in its
purest and most optimistic form in the Vogels' depiction of middle-
class families' mobilization for their children's studies. An emphasis
on educational success producing high-status credentials was seen
to guarantee success. This also occurred during the Meiji era
(1868–1912), when a combination of educational and industrial
bootstrapping transformed Japanese society. What the Vogels describe was the beginning of a social phenomenon that was to flour-

ish in the mid-1960s, and which established familial priorities for the ensuing decades.

What followed, however, ultimately distorted the educational process. The pressure from the examination system on families to both nurture and motivate their children as students was high. Pressure grew on teachers to complete prescribed curricula devoted to fine-tuned preparation for examinations, and young people at high school level were placed into tracks that determined their occupational and marital futures. All of these trends led to the distortions we can now observe in the middle-class educational experience.

What had not yet emerged as a clear pattern in the late 1950s and early 1960s was the influence of social class on a child's educational opportunities. First, the population involved in "examination hell" tends to be middle class. Observations of Japanese educational systems and experiences tend to emphasize the middle class, but it should be noted that about 60% of the age cohort do *not* go on to institutions of higher learning, and most of these students do not even attempt to continue their education, having been discouraged by teachers or hampered by the economic need to earn a wage or work in a family trade. Among those who do engage in the battle for college entrance, the prizes of entry to prestigious universities increasingly go to those whose parents can afford to invest money in *juku* (afterschool classes), tutors, and other enhancements. Rohlen (1977) has illustrated the nonegalitarian tendencies of the system by looking at Kyoto University students and their family backgrounds, and found that there has been a steady rise in the percentage of wealthy families sending their children to elite universities.

LOOKING AHEAD: BEYOND SALARY, BEYOND SUCCESS, TO THE NEW NEW FAMILY AND A NEW SOCIETY?

The contexts in which families operated—neighborhood communities like those Dore (1958) described in the 1950s, schools and workplaces the Vogels described—have now changed. Families are much more influenced by the demands of outside institutions. Today's nuclear families, constrained by the time schedules of the companies, schools, and other activities in which both parents and children participate, may now appear limited in function other than acting as a support base for schooling and work. However,

A large percentage of junior high school students attend an after-school academic *juku*, Kasugai City, 1994. Photo courtesy of Atsushi Itoh.

families have done more than simply adjust to conditions, and are today more a source of salient identity than today's reduced family size and functions suggest.

Members of middle-class families, receiving increased institutional and ideological support for individuation, also seek opportunities to spend time together and to make their home expressive of their joint personality. *Maihoomushugi* ("my-home-ism"), as described by the Vogels, was a marketing ploy aimed at selling goods and houses. The miniature putting green for Dad, the automatic breadmaker for Mom, the computer and video games for the children, were advertised with images of people enjoying themselves together as a family. These "togetherness" goods were first promoted when shared time at home was the scarce commodity, but families now feel the effects of both recessionary decreases in money to spend on leisure, and increases in actual leisure time. In marketing surveys, the most common answer to the question "What do you do with your spare time?" is "relax at home"—even among adolescents (White, 1993). These children, said by marketers to have "six pockets," filled with money by four grandparents and two parents, are indeed out there being entertained and purchasing, but they still spend most of their nonschool hours at home (White, 1993).

Children and men, relatively more tied than women to institutions outside the home, may also be more tied to conservative values and practices. Even though educational reform is under discussion, the ties of credential-driven education and employment remain strong. Education is still perceived as the surest road to success, and schools usually continue to feed and satisfy parental anxieties over exam preparation, rather than taking experimental risks with their students. Educational reformers, however, looking at the larger picture of employment patterns and workforce needs, now are talking of new tracks, the diversification of options, and a wider range of talents and learning trajectories. No one is willing, however, to rock the boat and unseat the examination system from its central position. Recent reforms eliminating one, and now two Saturday school days a month, have led many parents simply to up their children's attendance at afterschool cram classes, and teachers say they will just cram more into the 5-day weeks. The *kyoiku mama* (education-obsessed mother) may continue into the future as a necessary evil.

Some workplaces, however, may be more sensitive to new influences and faster to introduce change than others. Government bureaucracies, for example, have led the way in giving more responsibility and rewards to women, and the private sector has been following. Women in management positions have demanded accommodation to family needs, and further change seems to depend on a critical mass of female workers at relatively high-status levels.

Marginal segments of the middle-class population, such as women and the elderly, have increased their leverage and influence in the shrinking Japanese workforce. So women are wooed and exhorted in two directions: by companies needing reliable labor and by government officials recommending they have more children and care for the sick or elderly at home (Lock, 1992). The elderly are encouraged to retire early to save their companies the cost of seniority-based wages and to let ambitious younger workers move up the hierarchy. But they are also solicited to fill lower-level positions after retirement.

Future changes in the Japanese life cycle will depend on women, in particular on their work/career tracks and on their reproductive choices. If predicted labor shortages materialize, and women become more attractive as regular line employees, I expect that laws like the 1986 Equal Employment Opportunity Act will be given teeth and that workplace conditions will improve for everyone. On a personal level, relationships for these women have changed, too. Young women now, much more circumspect about marriage, are much less dependent and wait to find an appropriate spouse. Some are even quite "cool" in their appraisal of men who are said now to be quite anxious to find a woman who will say "yes" to marriage. Women now look for more emotional fulfillment in love and marriage, more sexual self-expression before and in marriage, and the maintenance of their close relationships with friends after their children are born.

In a recent interview, one young Japanese woman told me, "Japanese women may sometimes be financially dependent on men, but not emotionally dependent. We never sit waiting for a man to call; American women sometimes are so weak." One can see a direct connection between the competent, autonomous housewife described by the Vogels in 1963 and this independent young woman of the 1990s.

If I were to look to the future of family studies in Japan, I would hope for new research on the relationship between families and other agencies, particularly with the increase in the population of the elderly, and the increasing need for women to serve more than family roles. I would expect that the current choice for fewer children will continue, and that the *hitori-ko* (the "one-child" family) problem, now cited by psychologists as a key issue in the future socialization of children, will be a key focus for research. Father absence, once a subject of gloomy rhetoric, may be diminishing as families protest job transfers and companies themselves sometimes even force employees to take more time off from work. How will families, thrown together again with more leisure time, cope with togetherness? Though there are many such questions for the future, I would also emphasize research agenda connecting pressures for change coming from without Japan, as well as within. New roles for Japan in the international community also force new domestic questions, within Japan and within the family. Will participation in a global economy, for example, change jobs and lives in Japan? Will "internationalization" affect children's educational and occupational prospects, the process of schooling, and, ultimately, the focus of family energies with regard to the upbringing of children?

The core of the family, the mother–child relationship, has changed less drastically than have Japanese women. And while relative to the 1950s, the Japanese middle-class family seems different in its connections with other sectors of society, such as school and workplace, the emotional tone and centrality of the family in people's lives has changed very little. Since the first publication of *Japan's New Middle Class,* Ezra Vogel's treatment of Japan has moved to a broader sociopolitical frame, while Suzanne Vogel has taken a more individualized psychosocial and gender perspective. The ground-level experiential view of Japanese society they created in their first research in Japan has served them both well since, because family relationships are key to understanding Japanese individuals, groups, and society. As such, the Vogels earlier research provided them with a baseline for their lifetimes of scholarship on a wide range of issues. The generous framing, attention to detail, the clear-minded intuitive sensitivity to the lives of the people they described makes *Japan's New Middle Class* authoritative and compelling even after 33 years.

REFERENCES

Doi, T. (1973). *The anatomy of dependence.* Tokyo: Kodansha International.

Dore, R. (1958). *City life in Japan.* Berkeley: University of California Press.

Iwao, S. (1992). *The Japanese woman.* New York: Free Press.

Lock, M. (1992). Ideology, female midlife and the greying of Japan. *Journal of Japanese Studies, 19*(1), 43–78.

Peak, L. (1991). *Learning to go to school in Japan.* Berkeley: University of California Press.

Rohlen, T. (1977). Is Japanese education becoming less egalitarian? Notes on high school stratification and reform. *Journal of Japanese Studies, 3*(Winter), 37–70.

Rohlen, T. (1984). *Japan's high schools.* Stanford: Stanford University Press.

Shwalb, D. W., Imaizumi, N., & Nakazawa, J. (1987). The modern Japanese father: Roles and problems in a changing society. In M. Lamb (Ed.), *The father's role.* Hillsdale, NJ: Erlbaum.

Vogel, E. F. (1963). *Japan's new middle class.* Berkeley: University of California Press.

Vogel, S. (1978). The professional housewife. *Japan Interpreter, 12*(1), 16–43.

Welter, B. (1966). The cult of true womanhood: 1820–1860. *American Quarterly, 18,* 151–174.

White, M. I. (1993). *The material child: Coming of age in Japan and America.* New York: Free Press.

Cross-National Research on Child Development
The Hess–Azuma Collaboration in Retrospect

Hiroshi Azuma

This chapter will assess what I learned from experiences in a cross-national study of American and Japanese family influences on school readiness and achievement, codirected by the late Robert D. Hess and myself. Dr. Hess and I agreed to write this chapter jointly, but Hess knew that he would soon be unable to write, due to the progress of amyotrophic lateral sclerosis (ALS), from which he suffered. So he invited me to spend the summer of 1993 in Stanford to work together. The first thing I learned after arriving in Stanford was that he was in critical condition, and the end of his life came a few days later. Since we had discussed over E-mail what we would like to say, while he was still able to communicate, a good portion of this chapter reflects our discussions. Robert Hess is indeed a virtual coauthor. After having debated the issue with myself, however, I decided to write this chapter under a single authorship. This was because I knew that while Hess would have agreed with most of what I write here, he would have given the ideas more careful and sophisticated expression had he been a coauthor.

We learned a great deal about the merits, inherent pleasures, problems, and intellectual challenges of cross-national research through our cross-national collaboration, which extended over more than a decade, beginning in 1971. We have reported the results of the study on other occasions (Azuma, 1984; Azuma, Kashiwagi, & Hess, 1982; Hess et al., 1986; Hess, Kashiwagi, Azuma, Price, & Dickson, 1980; Kashiwagi, 1984), and I will not report any new findings here. I believe this chapter will benefit future researchers mainly as a personal account of my experiences studying development across cultures.

RESEARCHERS ARE CULTURAL PRODUCTS

The comparison of behavior in different cultural settings has long been an important approach within psychology. In developmental psychology, where it is difficult to introduce experimental control over sociocultural variables that undoubtedly influence lifespan human development, cross-cultural comparisons have served as natural experiments. It is not possible here to list the many contributions of cross-cultural studies to our understanding of cognitive, affective, and social development. Yet without such investigations, it would have been much more difficult to separate genetic and experiential determinants of development, or to understand the interactions of heredity and environment.

Cross-cultural studies also have an important potential value that has escaped our attention until recently: the possibility that a deeper understanding of human psychology will develop when the same or parallel phenomena are observed and interpreted by researchers from different cultures. We have modeled scientific psychology too often after the physical and classical sciences, implicitly assuming that appropriately trained psychological researchers are culturally neutral observers. In fact, however, every researcher perceives phenomena through a looking glass uniquely tinted by her or his personal theory, which incorporates not only scientific training but also the naive psychology prevalent in his or her culture.

While it is well known that behavioral manifestations of psychological processes reflect cultural differences, it is ironic that observations of psychological phenomena and the theories of psychologists are probably more vulnerable to cultural influences than even the human psyche itself. We may idealize that the basic processes of the human psyche are more or less universal. But we understand only a little about these processes, and what we do know has been selected from a vast pool of potential knowledge. This selection process is heavily culture-bound, because the same culture that forms our meaning systems also determines which psychic processes become salient to our attention as researchers.

Psychology as a science was born and has progressed inside Western culture, that is, the United States and Europe. Every culture has its own intuitive psychology and has developed concepts suited to this intuitive psychology. Because scientific psychology has been conceived in the Western world, attention has been directed to aspects of human functioning that were important in Western culture, and observations have tended to be processed in terms of concepts prevalent in Western cultures. This has been true also in the natural sciences. Such cultural bias, however, is more limiting in the case of psychology because the phenomena that psychologists study is human behavior, which is be definition culture-bound. Thus, monoculturally developed psychology was destined to be parochial in terms of the population of events to be observed, the selection of problems to be tackled, and, most importantly, the concepts and logic for dealing with those problems.

For example, consider the dichotomy of individualistic versus collectivist cultures, which is frequently referred to as a conceptual tool in cross-cultural psychology (Triandis, Botempo, Villareal, Asai, & Lucca, 1988). While this dichotomy is useful and convenient, it is too presumptuous to group nonindividualistic cultures together under the category of "collectivist." Individualism is usually defined as a positive concept while collectivism is not. Perhaps almost everywhere human communities were once more or less relationistic. But as a historical coincidence, early capitalism and the Industrial Revolution developed in the contexts of Protestantism and rationalism, in Northwestern Europe and the United States, and prepared a niche for individualism. Other cultures including Japan, remained more or less relationistic, but what is mistakenly taken as common among the relationistic cultures is a negative definition—that is, they are not as individualistic as are so-called Western countries. Defined in more positive terms, relationistic cultures are as different among themselves as they are from the individualistic cultures. Yet they seem to be alike from a Western perspective, in terms of the weaker presence of the Western-style individualism. From a Japanese perspective, for instance, the verbal self-assertiveness of the Indian or the major Chinese subcultures appears to be somewhat similar to the individualism of American culture. Nevertheless, some may lump Asian cultures including Japan, China, and India into the same collectivist category.

This culture-boundness does not, of course, diminish the achievements and value of scientific psychology. When we have only a tinted looking glass, it is better to see through it than to keep our eyes shut to knowledge, and through it we can still obtain a great amount of genuine understanding. Nevertheless, if we would attempt to use looking glasses of various tints, we might achieve new and greater discoveries. For example, Japanese *amae* is defined as a feeling or act of dependency, accompanied by the expectation that this dependency will be readily accepted. We now know that this *amae* is universally observable. But until Doi (1973) elaborated the concept, as a psychiatrist in Japan where *amae* relationships have a pervasive influence on social adjustment, *amae* did not have a place in psychology.

During my collaboration with Robert Hess on preschool education and child development, I naively mentioned that Japanese teachers often use the strategy of enhancing *amae* to secure good instructional relationships. This point, however, provoked a puzzled reaction from Hess. He said it seemed contradictory to him to increase teachability by encouraging dependency, because one prerequisite for teachability was the independence of the learner. After a lengthy discussion that resulted in a joint paper (Hess & Azuma, 1991), Hess not only came to see the rationale for dependency, but also discovered that the same strategy was used by American teachers without specific awareness. In American culture, where the attainment of independence prevails over other virtues, the positive use of dependency to attain educational goals had therefore gone unnoticed. Of course, there are likewise many aspects of human psychology that Japanese would not have known in explicit terms had they not been exposed to Western culture, including the value placed on independence in teaching–learning relationships. Traditional Japanese thinking previously had denounced self-assertiveness, which was closely related to independence, leading to the assumption that assertiveness had little value in education.

MY BACKGROUND AS A JAPAN–UNITED STATES COMPARATIVE RESEARCHER

The foregoing argument leads to the conclusion that it is important to have an open-minded team of researchers to fully realize the potential of cross-cultural psychology. I admit that many cross-cultural studies have already been conducted by groups of researchers from different cultural backgrounds. These teams have included many good psychologists of non-Western origin, to be sure. But as they had to be trained in the psychology of the West, these scholars have tended to internalize a Western bias, unless they have made conscious efforts to accentuate within themselves non-Western aspects of their thinking. This was often difficult when the living standards and educational levels of their native cultures were lower than those in the West, and their collaborators were cutting-edge elites with the mission of exporting Western science.

Moreover, most cross-cultural studies have been and still are, funded by Western sources. Of necessity, Western members of the team have been instrumental in obtaining funds, making them accountable to the funding agencies. The final decisions over plans, analyses, and conclusions therefore were their responsibility. Members from non-Western cultures often took the roles of adviser, native informant, and/or data collector. But the work of design, instrumentation, analyses, and interpretations has been dominated by Western team members. This was the consequence of the financial structure, which took precedence over issues such as intellectual fairness.

To overcome the above problems, or at least to test whether they were genuine problems, it was necessary to put together researchers from a Western culture and counterparts from a drastically different society, and to fund each group from its respective culture. In such an arrangement both cultures would have equal voices on decisions at all phases of the study. This was the ideal that guided the organizational structure of our project. In the early 1970s, it seemed that the only non-Western psychologists who could obtain their own funds on par with American funds were the Japanese. Japan then had about 4,000 psychologists, most of whom were trained in Japanese universities in the Japanese language. Our living standards did not quite match those of the United States then, but were not inferior to that of other Western cultures, and Japanese education ranked among the best in the world.

Among industrialized nations, as of the early 1970s, America and Japan had the most sharply differing traditions. In addition to the contrast between East and West, there were strong contrasts between the United States and Japan in religious and philosophical traditions, and in the social, political, and economic practices of the two countries, through the premodern mid-19th century. In brief, America from the 16th through the 19th centuries was an expanding land, abundant with potential wealth and opportunities. Ambitious people could exploit resources for their own good, and also contribute to the wealth of the community. Independent, aggressive, and innovative individuals were on the cutting edge of this thriving culture. During these same centuries, Japan was a tightly closed society, a zero-sum state in which any gain made by one person was coupled with a loss by someone else. In this context, aggressive exploitation was almost immoral, so that any action had to be accompanied by consideration of the potential threat to others. Japanese people were very cautious in expressing pleasure when they were successful in business, because it meant that they had taken a larger portion of the limited resources. An aggressive and self-assertive personality was anathema to the delicate balance upon which the zero-sum society sustained itself. As a result, competition existed as it does everywhere, but competition was to do one's work better rather than to claim more rewards.

Different belief systems thus formed in the premodern era, and I believe the influence of such differences is still strong in the two countries. They may underlie even the present economic and trade conflicts between our two nations. Arguments between Americans and Japanese about business practices often are made as if they were ethical accusations, as the claim of each party seems ethically objectionable to the other. Perhaps Japanese ethical beliefs based on a zero-sum state are unrealistic in the contemporary open world market, but naive American individualism is also vulnerable in a world approaching the zero-sum state in physical resources. It was a great challenge for me to conduct empirical comparisons of behavior across cultures, even without the confounds of living standards and educational levels.

Honestly, however, my deeper motivation for working on the United States–Japan project was strongly rooted in the development of my personal history and interests. My youthful days were clouded by World War II, as I lived in a nationalistic and military state. The imposition of obviously irrational dogmas by our rulers made me and my classmates feel intellectually suffocated, a condition that still exists in the 1990s for youth in many countries around the world. In spite of our government's nationalistic propaganda, the United States still seemed to us a land of promise, with its sophisticated thinking and political freedom. In addition to that, my family was termed "American addicts" by others, and we were treated with hostility by some naive people during World War II. My mother had been educated in a Christian mission school, and did not hide her love for British and American poetry from me, even in the worst days of the war. Since information about the enemy was censored during the war, my desire to know more about the United States burned even stronger. On the other hand, having experienced the disasters of the carpet bombing of Tokyo and other cities, and anticipating my almost certain and imminent death in the battlefield, I also had some resentment against the "enemy" which was almost visceral in nature. So when I started to study psychology in 1945, I had a very strong ambivalence toward the United States, and just as Berlyne's (1963) writings on conflict and arousal suggest, it was ambivalence that stimulated my interest.

My partner Robert Hess told me once that he had a similar feeling of ambivalence toward Japan. He was in the U.S. Marines during the war, and was stationed as an officer in California, training pilots. Although he himself did not go into the actual combat with Japan, almost all his trainees did. Having been raised in a Mennonite family, he had a conflict between his Christian humanity and the military mission, which made him feel a special concern for the Japanese people he might well have confronted.

A few years after Japan's surrender, I won a Fulbright grant to do my graduate work in the United States, at the University of Illinois at Urbana–Champaign Psychology Department. The wealth, abundance, colorfulness, freedom, and high standards of research in the United States fascinated me as a student, having arrived from amidst the squalor of a totally defeated nation. Along with this admiration for the United States, my personal background also instilled in me then a desire to achieve for the sake of the Japanese people and culture, so that we might some day again measure up to the West.

Because of my personal history, the chance to compare practices of socialization, ethical demands, motivation, and the formation of social behavior between the United States and Japan had a long-standing and strong appeal for me. Although my background did not include training in social developmental research, new trends of the study of cognitive processes in the early 1960s provided me with several opportunities to do cross-cultural studies. After having participated in some cross-cultural studies that involved Japan, I found myself in the position to codirect a project with Robert Hess.

THE CROSS-CULTURAL STUDY
OF FAMILY INFLUENCES

Our cooperation with the Hess research group was conceived at a workshop that took place in November 1971, at the Center for the Advanced Study in Behavioral Sciences in Stanford. For several years, the Japan Society for the Promotion of Sciences (JSPS) and the Social Sciences Research Council (SSRC) of the United States had cosponsored previous United States–Japan cooperative research projects in the social sciences. But most of these projects were fundamentally Japanese studies by American researchers or American studies by Japanese researchers. In order to raise the level of collaboration, the two organizations agreed to organize a joint meeting from which a project would be organized, with researchers from both countries working together as a team for a common goal. Thus a binational workshop on child development and childrearing was planned, with Hess as the American cochair and me as the Japanese cochair. I do not know why the topic of family influences was chosen, but I was approached by Masunori Hiratsuka, then director of the Japanese National Institute of Educational Research, and encouraged to be a chairperson. Jerome Kagan of Harvard was the original cochair of the American side, but since he had to go abroad he nominated Hess as his replacement.

The list of workshop members included B. O. Bushell, Jr., William Caudill, Constance Kamii, Robert LeVine, J. O. Palmer, Halbert Robinson, and Leon Yarrow as the American members, and Tamotsu Fujinaga, Hiroko Hara, Giyoo Hatano, Kazuo Miyake, Shigefumi Nagano, Tsune Shirai, Akira Tago, and Makoto Tsumori as the Japanese members. In retrospect, I think this was quite a powerful assemblage of researchers from both sides. One of the topics discussed at the workshop was the "Chicago Study" that Hess had just concluded.

Bernstein's Hypothesis

The Chicago Study (Hess & Shipman, 1965) was well known for providing evidence that maternal linguistic approaches influenced the cognitive development of children. According to Hess's findings, the degree to which mothers' speech toward children was precise and accurate rather than self-gratifying was correlated with higher school achievement, which supported the hypothesis of English sociolinguist Basil Bernstein (1971).

Bernstein had focused on the question of why many children from lower-class families could not keep up academically and dropped out of school. He believed that the cause of this problem lay in sociolinguistic differences that varied according to social strata, rather than in ability or predispositions. To state his conclusions first, Bernstein (1971) asserted that communication in many lower socioeconomic status families was characterized by a "restricted code," which put their children at a disadvantage when they studied in schools, where an unfamiliar "elaborated code" was prevalent. I will refer to this viewpoint as "Bernstein's hypothesis." Communicating under the elaborated code, one's ideas and meanings are clear and detailed, and are directed such that the other person can understand well. In short, it is an explanatory code.

In contrast, under the restricted code one does not convey one's meanings distinctly, and communicative behavior is directly restrained, as if there were tacit consent to remain silent. The restricted code is characterized by the use of imperatives and informal language.

According to Bernstein, instruction at school is intended to foster understanding, and so as a rule is based on the elaborated code. Children as recipients of this communication must also utilize the elaborated code in order to comprehend their teachers. This approach requires such skills as listening carefully until the very end of a communication, and thinking while listening. However, children raised in an environment dominated by the language of the restricted code are not prepared to function under the elaborated code. This is because under the restricted code one learns to comprehend a signal, to react, and then respond quickly, rather than to try to understand. As a result of this upbringing, many children are not able to learn effectively at schools. According to Bernstein, these pupils lose interest in the subject matter, fall behind intellectually, and eventually become school dropouts.

This theory stimulated considerable interest, and Bernstein himself collected some supportive data, but his data was too indirect to be persuasive. At this point the above-mentioned Chicago Study attracted attention by providing corroboration for Bernstein's hypothesis. The Chicago researchers studied 164 mothers paired with children between age 4 and second grade. They showed that when mothers used the elaborated code in speaking to their preschool children, the children went on to excel academically and in cognitive development. Subjects from four social strata took part in the Chicago Study (from the lower through upper middle classes). Although between-strata comparisons were beyond the scope of that research, we can say that the trends were observable comparing families within the same socioeconomic status groups, clearly supporting Bernstein's hypothesis (Hess & Shipman, 1965).

The Decision to Test Bernstein's Hypothesis in Japan

When this research was presented at the 1971 Stanford conference, the question naturally arose as to whether Hess's Chicago findings would also be true of the Japanese. One of the American participants at the workshop was William Caudill of the U.S. National Institute of Mental Health. He had conducted interesting research on maternal speech with 3- and 4-month-old infants in Japan and the United States (see Schooler, Chapter 8, this volume). One of the main findings of his patient observational research was that American mothers encouraged relatively more verbalization from their babies. Meanwhile, Japanese mothers (1) were less verbal, (2) stayed physically closer to their babies, and (3) tended to touch or tend to their babies more often.

Based on my informal impressions from daily life, it seemed that American mothers indeed spoke with a clearer tone of voice, were more explanatory, and used more words, compared with Japanese mothers. I might have observed a mother in the West explaining plant life to a child at a park quite as if she were giving a lecture, but a Japanese mother would not explain things with such precision. According to Caudill and others, Japanese mothers provided relatively less verbal stimulation. I shall show later that according to our research this is not necessarily always the case, although Japanese mothers' speech was seldom explanatory or instructional.

I and the other Japanese participants at the Stanford conference asked among ourselves, "What was it like in our experience?" and thought back on our own childhoods. Many of us were raised in the urban, educated middle-class, but could not recall that our mothers explained things using the elaborated code. The restricted code seemed more descriptive of everything we university professors and researchers could recall, as well as of our communications with our own children. Along these lines we thought that in parent–child interactions at home, and generally in sociolinguistic terms, Americans might indeed utilize the elaborated code more than did Japanese.

At this point we wondered, "If Bernstein's hypothesis were applied similarly to Americans and Japanese, are Japanese children raised at a relative disadvantage compared with Americans in terms of cognitive development?" An international survey of academic achievement (Husen, 1967) had shown that the mathematics and science achievement of Japanese elementary and middle school children far and away exceeded that of American children. Indeed, their achievement was among the highest in the world. There were also indications that the academic achievement of second- and third-generation Japanese-Americans was at a superior level at primary and middle school levels. Why was this the case?

There seemed to be various possible explanations. One was that Bernstein's hypothesis lacked generalizability outside of Euro-American cultures. Another was that in Japanese schools teaching was not based on the elaborated code, and therefore children did not have to be accustomed to an elaborated code to perform well at school. Still another possibility was that we were wrong to assume that the speech of Japanese mothers was based on the restricted code any more than that of mothers in the United States, and that either there was no actual cultural difference or perhaps the American mothers communicated more under the restricted code. A final alternative explanation was that it was a mistake to assess the restricted code based only on verbal records, as the elaborated code might operate through channels of nonverbal communication.

In the West since the Hellenic Period, demonstration, proof, and refutation ability had been valued, and it was considered important to be able to express oneself clearly and distinctly *(clara et distincta)*. What seemed appropriate from this cultural perspective was none other than the elaborated code. On the other hand, in Japan's culture, which valued elegance and quietness, it seemed less important to exhaust every detail to be "clear." Instead, by obscuring expressions and even being noncommittal or vague, meanings in Japanese communication have become quite refined. In addition, Japanese dialogue can be ritualized (as in tea ceremony), and meanings are accepted without give-and-take or excess information. Within such a culture, it seemed to me that adaptation to education and instruction need not revolve solely on the axis of the elaborated versus restricted codes.

Most of the American participants disagreed with this viewpoint. They asserted that as far as the contents of knowledge learned at school were universal, analytic and distinct communication should also be universal. Therefore, the Americans thought that findings similar to those in the Chicago Study should be replicable in Japan. Only Caudill agreed with the Japanese participants' thinking, in line with his previous statement that American mothers tend to create a physical distance between themselves and their babies, and adjust their position and posture to this distance. According to Caudill, the Japanese mothers maintained continuous physical contact with their babies, and so tended to promote a sense of oneness (Caudill & Weinstein, 1969). Caudill thought that there might be different linguistic and behavioral mechanisms involved in the respective socialization and educational practices of Americans and Japanese.

Formulation of the Research Plan

This debate led to an agreement to use similar methods in Japan and the United States to elicit the truth on this matter, so we for-

mulated a plan for a research collaboration. For several days I con-
ferred intensively with Hess, Shigeo Nagano, and Giyoo Hatano,
and we decided to conduct a 3-year longitudinal study on mothers
and their 3-year-old children. We planned to control for social-class
bias, and to develop equivalent tests and observational methods for
data collection in the Stanford, Tokyo, and Sapporo areas. The
main theme was to be a United States–Japan comparison of the
influence of maternal attitudes and verbal interaction on children's
cognitive development. The SSRC would fund Hess's team, and I
as head of the Japanese side planned to seek funding from the
JSPS. The following year this arrangement was finalized and the
research began.

    The scale of our project was very small in terms of sample size.
The original sample sizes were limited to 76 mother–child dyads in
Japan and 67 in the United States. We had planned to include a
rural subsample in Japan, but when these subjects were eliminated
from the analyses the Japanese sample was reduced to only 58 dyads. Instead of relying primarily on previously developed Western
materials, we developed 15 varieties of tests and observational
methods, and several lengthy maternal surveys. In cases where we
used extant measures, ecologically valid Japanese versions had to
be developed. As a result, this international collaboration required
an exceptionally long period of time. The researchers from the two
countries also had to meet to confer numerous times on the analyses and interpretations of the results. In this sense, the project required an extraordinary amount of effort and was a large-scale en-
terprise, in spite of the small-scale sample. As our general approach,
we decided to try to understand our findings based on a deep and
exploratory analysis of multiple aspects of our limited data set,
rather than on an investigative or multivariate large-scale statistical
approach.

ORGANIZATION AND ADMINISTRATION
OF THE STUDY

Comparisons in "Comparative" Research

I would like to point out various ways in which our plan differed
significantly from that characteristic of most previous cross-cultural
psychological studies. First, we took the stance that it was important
to emphasize a comparison of the structures of interrelated variables within each culture, rather than to focus on direct compari-

sons of observations or test results between Japan and the United States. For instance, it might be appealing and easier for people to understand us if we stated direct comparisons such as that American or Japanese mothers were "better" or "worse." However, it is risky to draw conclusions when something is actually not so clear. For example, past cross-cultural research comparing the cognitive achievement of children in modern Western cultures with that of children in nonmodern societies neglected the cross-cultural meaning of abstract conceptual abilities, and led to inappropriate conclusions. Our research emphasized comparisons of the structures of relationships, so that we might think of the results of various observations in terms of the meaning each has for development.

Development of Materials

The next issue concerned the development of testing and observational methods. Comparisons made in many previous cross-cultural studies had been based on implementing procedures in both cultures based on materials developed in one (usually Western) culture. But as Cole and others (Cole & Laboratory of Comparative Human Cognition, 1983) have indicated, abilities in different cultures develop with different meanings and relative weights. The tests that are developed by researchers raised in Western cultures are weighted with a bias toward abilities that have meaning in their cultures, while they tend to neglect abilities that are meaningful only in non-Western cultures. For instance, in the study of memory materials often utilize meaningless arrays of numbers, and these methods tend to favor American or Japanese children in whose societies such operations are emphasized. But if we study other groups, such as the Ethiopian Badai tribe (Fukui, 1991), stimuli such as the fur patterns of various cattle tend to be more appropriate. Yet psychologists tend not to think about such issues. As stated earlier, researchers are cultural products, too, so we cannot exaggerate the extent to which most testing and observational methods are culturally biased.

American and Japanese researchers from similarly industrialized societies, who have completed training in the same discipline, in a sense share a common culture, that is, their academic field as a social group. This makes it rather difficult to overcome their shared cultural blindness. We were determined to develop comparative methods for both cultures based on the principle of equal status between the collaborators. In actuality, it was not possible to create tests and observational materials, one by one, that were equally appropriate for both cultures, but we kept to the principle that we could maintain a balance by continually checking for bias or appropriateness in each culture.

Let me provide one example. On the block-sorting task used previously in the Chicago Study, it was possible to record and analyze verbal interactions between the mother and child as the mother taught the child how to sort a specified number of blocks. This had been very useful in the Chicago Study, so the American team wanted to definitely include this task. We indeed thought it would be perfect for our research purposes. But Kazuo Miyake of the Japanese team, who had previous research experiences with Southeast Asians, felt uneasy because this task set the numbers of blocks a priori and was basically a structured task with well-defined rules. He felt that this might not be appropriate for eliciting interactions between Japanese mothers and children, and so in addition to this structured task he advocated observations of the mother–child dyad in unstructured interactions. The American team resisted this idea and stated that tasks should be defined clearly, because analyses of communication contents during unstructured interactions would result in wasted data. When we actually conducted the study, we were often puzzled as Japanese mothers taught the task with words even after they demonstrated the task for the children. In addition, when maternal behavior patterns on the block-sorting task were correlated with children's cognitive development at age 6, a higher correlation was found among the American sample. Meanwhile, the correlation between cognitive development and academic achievement and the results of the free-play observations, years later, were more striking for the Japanese sample. Therefore, different observational tasks provided meaningful information in the respective cultures.

Funding Issues

A third characteristic of our research was that the Japanese and American teams operated with separate funding from their two countries. As mentioned earlier, it is difficult to recognize one's own cultural biases, and in working with researchers from another culture one must assert oneself tenaciously in order to achieve satisfying results. Confrontational situations seem to arise naturally in cross-national research, and if the other culture's research team is armed with all the funding, one cannot be aggressive in such a situation. It is not that receiving money from the other side weakens one's attitude, but when one side is awarded the funding they

Mother and 3-year-old son play with action figures in crowded apartment living room, Nagoya, 1996. Daughter's study desk is to the left. Courtesy of Davy Shwalb and Yuka Taniguchi.

are responsible for the public presentation of the results. Even if one is assertive, without the responsibility accorded the side that was awarded the funds, one's persistence will eventually be limited.

THE CULTURAL BIASES OF RESEARCHERS

The fact that researchers are influenced by various cultural factors poses great trouble for collaborative efforts. This is especially true because we researchers are largely unaware of our cultural blindness. As an example, I recall one incident from the Hess–Azuma collaboration, when we were analyzing the results of our childrearing survey. One item concerned how a mother would respond to a child at dinner who refused to eat some vegetables. About a tenth of the American mothers replied that "I wouldn't force the child, and would cook something else," and offered such explanations as "Eating something distasteful is unhealthy" or "A child shouldn't be forced to do things he hates." The Japanese mothers never responded in this way. Meanwhile, about 10% of Japanese mothers responded that they would eventually say "OK, then don't eat it," at which point the child would eat the unwanted food. This second technique was never reported by American mothers.

In trying to analyze the above two types of responses, the American researchers at first wanted to combine both techniques into the same category. But we felt that when a Japanese mother says "OK" she is in fact compelling the child to eat. The American and Japanese teams argued via numerous exchanges of airmail letters, and the matter was finally settled over a lengthy international telephone call. Referring to Doi's (1973) *The Anatomy of Dependence,* we asserted that in Japan mothers do all kinds of things for children due to their strong dependency relationship. As a result, the statement "OK, then don't eat it" has more than a literal meaning, and signifies a cutting off of the *amae* relationship. This in a sense puts great pressure on the child to comply.

We had numerous disagreements like this between the two cultural teams. What often bothered the American side was that just when an issue appeared to be settled, the Japanese side would offer an additional interpretation. From the American standpoint, if there was no immediate disagreement at the meeting it signified a consensus. Yet from our perspective, it seemed impolite for us to contradict our colleagues directly during discussions. At times we Japanese would discuss an issue during a break period or after a joint meeting of the teams, to see if we all agreed. Taken one by one, our cultural differences in communication and behavior seem small, but small differences can accumulate and make it difficult to achieve understanding. In our case, relationships built on trust and personal friendship developed over a period of years in informal settings, such that we could work together productively. It seems to me that the development of such human relationships is a key to successful cross-cultural collaboration.

CULTURES WITHIN CULTURES

Cultural differences exist not only between societies, but also within nations. This is obvious in the case of the United States, yet even within relatively homogeneous Japanese culture there are numerous subcultural groups. The individual and family are both influenced by regional, generational, occupational, and other affiliations, so that even unicultural research is actually cross-cultural research. One particular problem facing researchers in Japan is bias according to one's own social class. Japanese researchers are generally from highly educated and successful families. As a result, we form a subculture that places a high value on education. Additionally, as part of our occupational socialization, we tend to be Westernized. We cannot help but be influenced by our occupational reference group, and in our lifestyles as scholars we also lead a freer existence compared with other occupational classes. Thus, Japanese researchers are in various ways an atypical subcultural group.

When we Japanese study other Japanese, we have a special kind of cultural blindness. During our collaboration with the Hess team, we attempted in as many ways as possible to eliminate biases in our research design and sampling, by forming a rural subsample and a subsample of families whose fathers had lower educational backgrounds. But among the rural families the grandmother rather than the mother was the primary caretaker of the preschool child. Due to this and many other problems, we eventually excluded data from the 16 Hokkaido mother–child dyads from analyses. Thus, our study became a narrower comparison of urban American and Japanese mothers and children. We also became aware then of the fact that our entire research team had been born and raised in the Tokyo area. Perhaps our own upbringing blinded us to sampling and other problems.

THE RESULTS OF THE HESS–AZUMA STUDY: BERNSTEIN'S HYPOTHESIS

It seems appropriate here to conclude with a brief mention of how our study related to Bernstein's hypothesis, since that was the original rationale for our decade-long collaboration. First of all, the research of Caudill and others led us to predict that Japanese mothers would use relatively fewer words, and rely more on nonverbal communication than would the American mothers. This prediction was not confirmed. In teaching situations, there was little difference between the amount of verbalization of American and Japanese mothers—actually, the Japanese mothers were slightly more verbal. In addition, there was a positive correlation, in both cultures, between frequency of maternal verbalization and children's cognitive attainment. Generally, the cognitive performance of children was higher if their mothers spoke more to them. As mothers who spoke more frequently also spoke with more care and detail, our results provided at least some support for the view that the elaborated code facilitates adaptation to school.

On the other hand, some of the findings cast doubt upon the universality of Bernstein's theory. In our study of control strategies, each mother of a 4-year-old child was asked to imagine that her child was engaged in some act that was unacceptable to her, such as drawing pictures on the wall or running around in a supermarket. She was then asked what she would say to stop the child. One of the types of responses to which we paid attention was classified as an "appeal to authority." Instead of giving reasons or telling why it was wrong when a child resisted, the mother might simply send a flat directive message to control or thwart the behavior. This was coded as an appeal to authority, and apparently is a restrictive message. The percentage of such restrictive messages among a mother's total number of messages was correlated with the school achievement of the child 7 years later. This correlation was clearly negative in the United States, as would be predicted from Bernstein's position. But, by contrast, the same correlation was clearly positive in Japan. One possible reason for this is that in Japan, where the mother–child relationship is typically that of symbiotic interdependence, only a mother who feels secure about her relationship with the child could appeal to a directive method that involved potential confrontation.

In addition, we had predicted there would be little social-class variation in Japan, which has been viewed as a single-class, middle-class society. But in our results there was as much social-class variation in the Japanese as in the American data, which tends to support Bernstein's thinking. And surprisingly, when we looked at our follow-up data on the children in upper elementary school, there was actually greater social-class variation in Japan than in America. Could it be that the attitudes and behavior of mothers in the United States lose their significance after the child enters school? In Japan, it appears that the correlation between maternal and child variables persists into the school years. Viewing the above set of findings, it seems that to advance our understanding further we must study the meaning of behavior and communication, going beyond group comparisons of surface cultural differences. Indeed, as we began to fathom the depth of the issues involved, the issue of whether Bernstein's hypothesis "applied to Japan" gradually lost its significance for our research teams.

IN RETROSPECT

As one of the earlier attempts of international cooperation in psychological research, our project had positive educational effects upon the researchers on both sides. There were many wasted moves, overlooked shortcuts, and unnecessary small conflicts and misunderstandings. As far as language and even cultural understanding were concerned, we did not have serious difficulties. I had studied and worked in the United States for nearly 6 years, two other Japanese team members had conducted research in the United States for more than a year, and one member of the American team, Patrick Dickson, spent a full year in Japan early in the study, participating in the activities of the Japanese group. We were motivated by a desire to understand each other's culture and wanted to be open-minded. But as researchers we did not easily compromise on research issues. Often we had to code the same set of protocols with two different coding systems, each advocated by one of the national groups. To settle such matters we had to actually look at both protocols, which gave us a better and understandable profile. Even then the effectiveness of the methods strongly depended on nationality, as often the method advocated by one national group yielded a clearer picture in its own country than in the other country. In retrospect, those experiences in combination with successful efforts to reach mutual understanding were as invaluable as the results we obtained and the reports we wrote.

When Robert Hess knew that he would soon lose his voice due to the ALS that would eventually take his life, he started to take writing lessons so that he could continue to communicate well with others through writing. Quite a remarkable person, he often reflected on his experiences in his writing. In one entry he wrote about a flight to Tokyo with other American project members, as follows:

> We chatted about our sessions scheduled for the next 3 days—a reception, dinners, research discussion. We were particularly concerned about efforts to communicate with our recently acquired Japanese friends. We had discovered that we shared most values where scholarship was involved—respect for accuracy, knowledge, hard work, persistence, and for integrity in gathering and reporting data. We could not match the Japanese, however, in hospitality and agreeableness. At our first conference a year earlier, it became apparent that they tended to agree in face-to-face meeting with any suggestion that we made. We soon came to realize that this was not evasion but an expression of courtesy to my status as the oldest of the group, the American *sensei*. My colleagues hinted that such courtesy, while pleasant, was impractical since after the meetings were over, our Japanese colleagues sometimes suggested changes in procedures or strategies—modifications that they have hesitated to bring up in the conference itself. Lack of candor interfaced with the tough work of making thoughtful detailed decisions when two research groups actually disagreed. I agreed that

this was, indeed, a trade-off but contended that the goodwill it produced among us was a reasonable exchange.

Two months before his death, we got together and talked (Bob used a voice synthesizer at that point). Recalling our meeting early in the study, mentioned in the preceding paragraph, I said that the reason the Japanese group was slow in bringing up counterproposals perhaps was not exactly an expression of courtesy alone. Rather, it was due to our habit of listening. We had been repeatedly taught that if one does not make his mind clean and empty when listening to others, true understanding is impossible. When listening "empty-mindedly" we do not check whether we agree or disagree. Only after all is said do we ponder if we agree or not. Americans, on the other hand, are socialized to listen with a mind full of opinions. Each incoming statement is checked at the entrance, and gets tagged either as "agree" or "disagree" (an idea suggested by Hazel Markus of the University of Michigan). Hess liked this interpretation, and said that he would revise the manuscript of this chapter. To my sorrow and disappointment, he passed away before he could work on it. We had continued our cultural learning more than a decade after the actual research study was over. The same was true for other members of our project, many of whom are now ball carriers in the cross-cultural study of psychological development. This continued learning was unanticipated, but I believe it was the most important product of our collaboration.

REFERENCES

Azuma, H. (1984). Psychology in a non-Western country. *International Journal of Psychology, 19*, 45–55.

Azuma, H., Kashiwagi, K., & Hess, R. D. (1982). *Hahaoya no taido to kodomo no chiteki hattatsu [Maternal attitudes and children's cognitive development].* Tokyo: University of Tokyo Press.

Berlyne, D. E. (1963). *Conflict, arousal and curiosity.* New York: McGraw Hill.

Bernstein, B. (1971). *Class, codes, and control: Vol 1. Theoretical studies towards a sociology of language.* New York: Routledge & Kegan Paul.

Caudill, W., & Weinstein, H. (1969). Maternal care and infant behavior in Japan and America. *Psychiatry, 32*, 12–43.

Cole, M., & the Laboratory of Comparative Human Cognition. (1983). Intelligence as cultural practice. In P. H. Mussen (Ed.), *Carmichael's manual of child psychology* (Vol. 1). New York: Wiley.

Doi, T. (1973). *The anatomy of dependence* (J. Bestor, Trans.). Tokyo: Kodansha International.

Fukui, K. (1991). Ninshiki to bunka: Iro to moyoh no minzokushi [Culture and understanding: Ethnology of color and form]. *Ninchi kagaku sensho [Selected Papers on Cognitive Science], 21.* Tokyo: Tokyo University Press.

Hess, R. D., & Azuma, H. (1991). Cultural support for schooling: Contrasts between Japan and the United States. *Educational Researcher, 20*(9), 2–8.

Hess, R. D., Azuma, H., Kashiwagi, K., Dickson, P., Nagano, K., Holloway, S., Miyake, K., Price, G., Hatano, G., & McDevitt, T. (1986). Family influences on school readiness and achievement in Japan and the United States: An overview of a longitudinal study. In H. Stevenson, H. Azuma, & K. Hakuta (Eds.), *Child development and education in Japan.* New York: Freeman.

Hess, R. D., Kashiwagi, K., Azuma, H., Price, G. G., & Dickson, W. P. (1980). Maternal expectations for mastery of developmental tasks in Japan and the United States. *International Journal of Psychology, 15,* 259–271.

Hess, R. D., & Shipman, V. C. (1965). Early experiences and socialization of cognitive models in children. *Child Development, 36,* 860–888.

Husen, T. (1967). *International study of achievement in mathematics.* New York: Wiley.

Kashiwagi, K. (1984). Japan–U.S. comparative study on early maternal influences upon cognitive development: A follow-up study. *Japanese Psychological Research, 26,* 82–92.

Triandis, H., Botempo, R., Villareal, M. J., Asai, M., & Lucca, N. (1988). Individualism and collectivism: Cross-cultural perspectives on self–in group relationships. *Journal of Personality and Social Psychology, 54,* 323–338.

Maternal and Cultural Socialization for Schooling
Lessons Learned and Prospects Ahead

Sandra Machida

During the two decades when Drs. Robert Hess and Hiroshi Azuma led their cross-national study (1972–1992), many American educators, researchers, and policy makers steadily focused on individual, family, school, and cultural differences that might account for variation in school achievement in the United States and Japan. The Hess–Azuma study (which I will refer to below as the Cross-National Project, or CNP) was a significant contribution to our understanding of maternal and cultural influences on preschoolers' readiness for school and on later school achievement. The study also took place during an era of increasing research interest in maternal factors, the social basis of cognition, and family models suited to study childhood in diverse environments.

This chapter is divided into two sections. The first section of the chapter presents the strengths, contributions, and lessons learned from the CNP in a retrospective analysis. The study provided empirical data regarding parental beliefs, developmental expectations, mother–child interaction styles, and control strategies as predictors of school readiness and achievement. In the second section I focus on directions for future research, including future perspectives on theoretical frameworks and research design. Significant social and cultural changes have occurred in Japan and the United States in the 25 years since the CNP began. Indeed, the socialization ecologies of children have changed, so that current data are needed to examine and test existing models of development and culture.

RETROSPECTIVE ANALYSIS
Strengths
A Strong Collaborative Partnership

One obvious strength of the CNP was the partnership formed by Hess and Azuma. Their collaboration started in Stanford at the conference jointly sponsored by the Social Science Research Council and the Japan Society for the Promotion of Sciences, where they agreed to conduct a longitudinal study as equal partners. The challenges for both Azuma and Hess were clear (Azuma, Chapter 13, this volume; Hess & Azuma, 1990). Their collaboration is particularly noteworthy because this type of partnership between American and Japanese researchers has always been noticeably absent. Many research teams even today are comprised of a clearly identified and dominant American researcher, and a supportive, prominent Japanese colleague. I do not imply that significant findings have not been made by these nonegalitarian types of teams, but rarely do United States–Japan research teams work together as did the Hess–Azuma team. Some of the benefits of this partnership will be discussed below.

An Appropriate Cross-Cultural Comparison

Work in cultural psychology often has contrasted children from nontechnological (non-Western) societies with children from the United States or other Western societies (Rogoff & Morelli, 1989). The CNP allows us a glimpse of variation and similarities in child-rearing practices and beliefs in Japan, a non-Western but technologically advanced society. The study showed how markedly different parenting methods can guide children toward the same goal; that is, parents in both the United States and Japan want their children to learn enough from formal schooling to become productive citizens (Shields, 1989). The CNP made clear that educational achievement was valued by mothers in both countries, yet there were striking differences in what mothers expected, how they used discipline, and how they interacted with their children.

Research Design and Methodology

Another strength of the CNP was its research design as a longitudinal study with multiple instruments, and data collected from mothers, fathers (in the United States only), children, and teachers. Measures included standardized achievement tests given to the children, observations of mothers and their preschoolers performing structured and unstructured tasks, maternal interviews about their childrearing beliefs and expectations, school readiness tests, and achievement ratings by teachers. Azuma and Hess monitored carefully the cultural equivalence of test stimuli, and where differences occurred the research team carefully devised parallel and different scoring protocols. Thus, children's performance was based on a structural framework relevant and sensitive to parenting and children's performance in both cultures.

I should add one note of clarification here. For the sake of convenience, I refer to U.S. mothers and Japanese mothers, but I am referring to those mothers in the CNP only. Azuma (Chapter 13, this volume) has noted that the findings have limited generalizability given the sampling procedures in both countries.

Dissemination of Results

The time frame in which the project was completed and the results published was a third positive point. Data collection period began in 1972, when the children were about 4 years old. Block Sort Task and the Referential Communication Game data were collected in the following 2 years (1974–1975). Because the school years in Japan and the United States begin in different months, school achievement information was collected when children were 11 in Japan and when the children were 12 in the United States. Thus, the time span of data collection was from 1972 to 1980.

Information about the CNP has been steadily published from 1979 to the present. Seven formal conferences (four in the United States and three in Japan) and several informal conferences have been held to discuss their methodology, interpretations, and frameworks (Hess & Azuma, 1990). Since 1979, the CNP has generated at least 14 journal articles (including three in Japanese), three chapters in edited books, and numerous joint conference presentations, as well as articles published in trade publications and newsletters.

To give another example of the painstaking effort and time

needed to report cross-cultural research on children, Beatrice and John Whiting began their Six Cultures Study in 1954. The fieldwork was conducted from 1956 to 1957. Six years later, in 1963, the ethnographies of the cultures were published (B. Whiting, 1963). Twelve years later, in 1975, the Whitings published their quantitative findings in *Children of Six Cultures: A Psychocultural Analysis* (B. Whiting & J. Whiting, 1975). Finally, in 1988, B. Whiting and Edwards published an extension and elaboration of cross-cultural studies which by then were "classics" titled *Children of Different Worlds: The Formation of Social Behavior.* Thus, their project spanned 30 fruitful years. Using the Whitings' work as a benchmark for comparison, the results of the CNP were disseminated relatively quickly. But more impressive than their ability to progress without the fax or E-mail technology we now take for granted was their ability to proceed where there was no road map. There was no precedent for the large-scale, long-term, and long-distance nature of the CNP, so confusion probably occurred more often than was expected.

Publications may be grouped into four content areas: mother–child interactions, maternal beliefs and expectations as predictors, examination of molar variables (socioeconomic status, and historical or religious context), and cultural differences in socialization practices and beliefs. The following list is long and impressive in its breadth of significant developmental issues. First, the results from the mother–preschool child interactions were presented in Dickson, Hess, Miyake, and Azuma (1979) and follow-up data appeared in the article by McDevitt et al. (1987). Conroy, Hess, Azuma, and Kashiwagi (1980) reported variations in maternal control strategies. Other articles concerned the effects of early maternal influences, particularly maternal education on later cognitive development (Kashiwagi, Azuma, & Miyake, 1982; Kashiwagi, Azuma, Nagano, Hess, & Holloway, 1984).

Variations in maternal expectations for mastery of developmental tasks were reported in Hess, Kashiwagi, Azuma, Price, and Dickson (1980). Holloway, Fuller, Hess, and Azuma (1986) reported differences in causal explanations made by mothers concerning their children's math achievement. Examinations of broader and molar variables were conducted by Fuller, Holloway, Azuma, Hess, and Kashiwagi (1986) and Holloway, Fuller, Hess, Azuma, Kashiwagi, and Gorman (1990). Finally, comprehensive overviews of the CNP were provided by Hess et al. (1986) and Hess, Azuma, Kashiwagi, Holloway, and Wenegrat (1987). And as Azuma (Chapter 13, this volume) mentions, many collaborators became cross-cultural researchers as a result of their experiences on the CNP, so that its impact on several members' later publications is an inestimable but enduring result of the CNP. The list of CNP collaborators and contributors is extensive (see Hess & Azuma, 1990, for a list of contributors).

Azuma (Chapter 13, this volume) outlined three examples of how American and Japanese teams examined, confronted, and re-examined results and interpretations. Cultural differences were observed in (1) mothers' understanding of the social context of motivation (i.e., *amae* as a useful construct in explaining differences in student readiness for learning), (2) overstructuring of mother–child interactions with prescribed stimuli and instructions, and (3) the universality of the maternal restrictive code as predictive of lower school achievement. Undoubtedly there were many other differences, but these three differences form the foundation for the study's contribution to our understanding of family and cultural influences on school achievement.

Empirical and Theoretical Contributions

In my opinion, the CNP was most significant in furthering our understanding about family effects (i.e., maternal) in predicting school achievement. Other cross-cultural studies have examined school, classroom, and teaching variables that predict performance in math and reading in the two countries (e.g., Stevenson & Lee, 1990). But the CNP remains the only United States–Japan study that incorporated family data collected during the preschool years—that is, direct observations of mother–child interactions—as robust predictors of school achievement. We can identify five topic areas related to family effects: maternal control strategies, maternal developmental expectations, parent-supported communication skills, achievement-related beliefs, and the social basis of cognition.

Maternal Control Strategies

When mothers were presented with six hypothetical compliance situations, there was variation in their child control strategies (Conroy et al., 1980). U.S. mothers were more likely to resort to their own authority ("Do it because I'm your mother!") while Japanese mothers said they would base their appeals on their own feelings or those of the other people in the situation, sensitizing their children to the social consequences of their actions. Hoffman (1977) referred to this type of reasoning as induction.

Mothers' verbal reports about how they would behave toward their children coincided with their actual behavior in structured and unstructured game tasks with the child (e.g., Hess et al., 1986). The authoritative parenting style (Baumrind, 1971) seems to represent the parenting of their American sample, at least among the mothers whose children later became high achievers. The Japanese mothers, on the other hand, appeared to be warm yet permissive with their preschoolers. Quietly and unobtrusively, the Japanese mothers focused on the socioemotional aspects of the relationship, more than on the successful completion of the experimental task. The researchers attributed the slow and accurate style of children's cognitive performance in part to the Japanese mothers' parenting style.

Maternal Developmental Expectations

The CNP found that Japanese and American mothers had different expectations as to when their children should attain certain developmental milestones and about which milestones were most important. Parents identified their developmental expectations for 38 school-related skills, such as verbal assertiveness, compliance, politeness, emotional maturity, instrumental independence, and social skills.

Japanese mothers expected and valued mastery in areas related to effective participation in groups (e.g., "comes or answers when called" and "waits for turn in games"). American mothers, on the other hand, expected and valued earlier mastery of skills related to verbal expression and leadership skills among peers (e.g., "states own preference when asked"; Hess et al., 1986). Parents expected that their children would attain developmental milestones earlier in domains valued by their cultures. These results parallel work by other cross-cultural developmental psychologists (Goodnow, 1990).

Parent-Supported Communication Skills

Originally, the CNP focused on testing Bernstein's (1971) hypothesis that parental communicative style influences children's school performance. The assumption was that a verbally impoverished childrearing environment would harm children's ability to solve conceptually complex problems. The Referential Communication Task and the Block Sort Task were administered to test Bernstein's hypothesis.

Dickson et al. (1979) reported on the first phase of the study, and found that communication accuracy between mother and child predicted better school readiness and intelligence test performance 2 years later. The predictive power of the communication accuracy on the longitudinal measures remained significant in both cultures even when effects of maternal IQ, socioeconomic status and child verbal/mental ability at age 4 were partialed out. In a follow-up study, McDevitt et al. (1987) reported partial continuity of these effects when the children reached ages 11 to 12. Mother–child communication accuracy predicted performance in vocabulary in the United States and in mathematics in Japan, regardless of the child's verbal/mental ability at age 4, socioeconomic status, or mother's IQ. Hence, the causal links between parent–child interactions and later school performance appeared to be domain-specific and to vary across cultures.

The sociolinguistic environment remains an important focal point as we try to understand children's motivational and school performance. For instance, Tharp and Gallimore (1988) have shown the rich cultural variations of sociolinguistic environments of Hawaiian school children in interactions with peers and teachers. The CNP provided valuable empirical data on the sociolinguistic interactions between mothers and preschoolers.

Achievement-Related Beliefs

Holloway, Kashiwagi, Hess, and Azuma (1986) studied the causal attributions of parents and school-age children in both countries regarding mathematics performance. They found cross-cultural differences similar to those noted in later studies (e.g., Stevenson & Lee, 1990). Japanese mothers and children emphasized effort while American mothers and children emphasized ability. Holloway, Kashiwagi, et al. (1986) found consistency within cultures, but not within families regarding causal beliefs. They concluded that Japanese cultural norms regarding effort and persistence may play a larger role in cognitive motivation than simply as indicative of maternal achievement beliefs. That is, the social organization of families, schools, and cultural institutions all reinforce the beliefs and values of learning at school. Of course, this later contention was beyond the scope of the CNP sample and requires empirical study in future research.

Social Bases of Cognition

The insights gained from the CNP coincide with and reinforce Vygotsky's sociocontextual theory of cognitive development. According to this theory, parents are the more knowledgeable of the partners and guide children in the learning process and in building schemas (Cole, 1992; Vygotsky, 1962; Wertsch, 1985).

Both Japanese and American parents prompt, question, model, encourage, and capture their children's attention, but they seemed to push for cognitive performance in different ways (Hess & Azuma, 1991). Japanese mothers centered on their socio-emotional relationship and the social ramifications of not completing the task, while American mothers more directly provided explicit instructions and information. Many American mothers appeared rather quick and snappy, in comparison to Japanese mothers, who were pensive, ambiguous, and less directive—letting their children listen, think, and make mistakes without threat of embarrassment of failure. Similarly, Stevenson and Stigler (1992) have reported how Japanese first- and fifth-grade teachers also dwell on and ponder a particular math problem from many different angles during a single class period. Their questioning and thought-provoking interactions may promote among Japanese children the metacognitive functions of planning and checking one's work (Wertsch, 1985).

Few believe nowadays that cognitive skills and knowledge simply unfold with age, and yet knowledge and learning is not entirely "self-constructed" from each individual child's encounter with objects and events (Shweder, 1982). The CNP helped refocus our attention on the sociocultural context of learning for Japanese and American children. It demonstrated the important roles of cultural norms (moral responsibility to the group), values (interdependence, self-effacement, reflectivity), and socialization practices (emphasis on affect and relational aspects) on cognitive skills.

Cultural Dissonance: Testing Assumptions

The CNP also helped us to modify several generally accepted assumptions of mainstream psychology and education. It showed us that we need a new vision to overcome our "cultural blindness" (Azuma, Chapter 13, this volume). The results of CNP also tested some of our Western assumptions about childrearing and child development.

The Preeminence of Verbal Interaction

As Azuma noted, it was a point of cultural disagreement that provided the impetus for the CNP. Azuma and his colleagues questioned the applicability of Bernstein's hypothesis to the Japanese. They felt that the hypothesis did not take into account cultural norms that dictate that Japanese mothers communicate with their young children on a nonverbal level. The Japanese team was disturbed and intrigued enough about the mother–child linguistic mechanisms that socialize children toward school readiness that they became involved in the project. As it turned out, social-class variables were a stronger predictor of school achievement in Japan than were mother–child communication measures (Fuller et al., 1986; Kashiwagi et al., 1984).

Controlling the Child

The concept of "parental control strategies" was also found to be based on Western assumptions (Fuller et al., 1986; Hess & Azuma, 1991). As a construct, parental control strategies fit well within a

Mother reads picture book to 3-year-old daughter, who already waits on customers in the family restaurant. Courtesy of Davy Shwalb and Ryoji Tomita.

unidirectional model of parenting wherein, as scholars have assumed until recently, mothers control children. Children were perceived by many in the West as needing direct instruction on how to behave, talk, and think. When observed with their preschoolers, many American mothers asked their children for specific information and made specific requests—efficiently requesting clear-cut and correct answers. Here, mothers seem to be molding the child behavior. Japanese mothers, meanwhile, used modeling and subtly sent messages to their children about their values regarding performance (reflection on problems, careful choice of words and action) and what cultural norms should be internalized (e.g., performance for the sake of the family).

In the CNP, behavioral control by the Japanese mothers avoided direct instruction and overt control, so as not to damage their affective relationship. Hess and Azuma (1991) refer to this process as "osmosis" identification, whereby the Japanese mothers assume that through patience, modeling, and granting of autonomy children will learn self-control. Others have made similar observations of mother–infant interactions (Caudill & Weinstein, 1969; Shand & Kosawa, 1985). In Japan, mothers play a primary role in educating children, but the researchers assume that others also are significant in cognitive socialization—teachers, peers, and television, as well as institutions, such as schools, and *juku* (Peak, 1991; White, 1987). The phrase "maternal control" in Japanese does not recognize the coherent inclusiveness of the numerous social systems that prepare children to internalize cultural norms.

The Dichotomy of Intrinsic–Extrinsic Motivation

Similarly, the dichotomy of intrinsic versus extrinsic motivation fits the Western notion of striving for excellence, yet it is not suitable to describe Japanese notions of motivation (Hess & Azuma, 1991; Holloway & Machida, 1994). Through cultural values, Japanese students internalize a desire to learn, but they are also driven by external pressures such as entrance examinations. Motivation appears to be socially driven, to please and to avoid shaming one's family, to be accepted by peers, and to fulfill dependency needs (Doi, 1973; Vaughn, Chapter 5, this volume).

American concepts of intrinsic and extrinsic motivation assume an individualistic and unidirectional pattern. For extrinsic motivation, sustained effort for children has to be reinforced by a mother, a teacher, and/or an enticing curriculum (Deci, 1975;

Hess & Azuma, 1991). On the other end, intrinsic motivation is seen as based on a personal set of rewards or contingencies. Like cognitive theories of development, theories of motivation place individual children in somewhat of a social vacuum (Holloway & Machida, 1994). Based on one's interests, ability, and perceived competence, children are assumed by psychologists to proceed on their own devices. Yet the lines between intrinsic and extrinsic become blurry when we study cultures like Japan, where motivation is socially driven rather than based on the assumption that children are individualistic. On the Referential Communication Game, Japanese mothers subtly approved of any response made by their preschooler by defining the task as a game rather than a test (Miyake, 1977). Their sustained interest in the task was attributed both to the mothers' external approval, and also to the child finding the game-like task intrinsically satisfying. The CNP provided an initial but important glimpse of the social context as an impetus for motivation.

Ability and Effort

Ability is also a somewhat foreign concept to many Japanese. Teachers are very articulate about how well certain children in their classrooms perform, yet they will redirect the conversation if questions arise concerning a child's ability (Tobin, Wu, & David, 1989). Of course, teachers witness differences in performance, but explain differences primarily in terms of children's lack of effort. Again, the CNP results drew our attention to Western assumptions about causal attributions. Hess and Azuma (1991) have argued that cultural expectations may play a more important role in explaining behavior than personal constructs of ability or effort. In Japan, children are pressed to behave according to specific role prescriptions (e.g., first-born son of a doctor) which may explain more about behavior than personal attributes like ability. In addition, Lewis (1984), in ethnographic observations of classrooms in Japan, reconfirmed CNP results: Socialization for school starts in the preschool years. The press for internalization of school norms and increasing the children's teachability begins long before they enter formal school.

This cultural dissonance by which psychological categories are seen to be culturally specific has refocused our attention on the cultural, political, historical, and philosophical underpinnings of the concepts of effort and ability (Fuller et al., 1986). Why do Japanese play down the importance of ability? Or, better yet, why do

Americans insist on emphasizing ability? Projects such as the CNP show that we are indeed culturally blinded, and that psychologists may be a particularly biased group of thinkers (Azuma, Chapter 13, this volume). We must go beyond research on family dynamics and instructional strategies to understand the causal relationships that underlie school competence. Careful examination of cultural contexts of development are necessary if our field is to become an international science (Harkness, 1992).

DIRECTIONS FOR FUTURE RESEARCH

Changing Ecology of Child Development

Both Japan and the United States are changing rapidly. Japan has a national educational mandate to "internationalize" their educational system (Leestma, 1992). Western values, books, and entertainment are already a part of Japanese culture, and some Japanese values and practices are seen in the United States. American parents concerned with inadequate mathematics instruction in the public schools are enrolling their children in Kumon programmed math tutoring sessions exported from Japan (Ukai, 1994). Many American children have also been introduced to Suzuki music lessons, and thousands of American children take martial arts sessions where they practice discipline and mastery learning along with self-defense skills. In other words, there may be an increasing overlap between the experiences of American and Japanese children.

One change in Japan is in the role of the mother as ultimately responsible for the education of her child. Japanese mothers still have most of this responsibility, but slight changes have been observed. Sengoku, Leiderman-Davitz, and Davitz (1982) reported that Japanese mothers in the 1980s talked with their infants more, bottle-fed more, and allowed the father's participation in infant care, compared with in the 1960s.

Shifts in the United States seem to be in two directions. One shift is in an emphasis on early intervention programs like Healthy Start and Head Start, which place increasing responsibility on community and educational services in supporting children's readiness for formal instruction. Boyer (1991) called for the United States to make a national commitment to helping our youngest children get "ready to learn." Data from the CNP emphasized the importance of mothers in the socialization of children—in getting them ready for school. Yet programs appear to work around the families rather than view them as partners in the promotion of school achievement. Of course, parental support of schools is often mentioned, but only as a passing footnote (e.g., increasing parental input regarding school policies and practices). Parent education about child development is also treated as a footnote, and many policy makers do not consider parents to be the primary socializing agents. Parent's comments are politely acknowledged by school administrators, but their importance is unrecognized. The second American change is a shift in demographics. On the surface, mothers are viewed as primary caregivers for their children; this implies that the mothers are the individuals most responsible for their children's education. However, there are now increasing numbers of fathers, grandmothers, and other relatives who have primary roles in childrearing. As we learn more about ethnic minority children, we can appreciate better the roles of multiple caregivers (Tharp & Gallimore, 1988), and we will need to redefine what constitutes a family. The CNP studied only children in small, intact nuclear families, but simply observing children and their mothers engaged in problem-solving or communication tasks will not unravel the complexity of family influences in 21st-century America.

TESTING AND REFINING
THEORETICAL/EMPIRICAL MODELS
The Contextual Approach

Most theories that have influenced developmental research in the Western world have viewed children as separate from their social and physical environments (Miller, 1993). In views such as Piaget's, cognitive development is constructed by the child's interaction and manipulation of the world. The results from the CNP provided support for a Vygotskian or contextual view of cognitive development. In this view, children are embedded in a social matrix, and development cannot be understood independently from the matrix. Children's thinking moves to higher levels of complexity and functioning, prodded by their parents and other informed experts who build a social-regulated learning environment. The role of language and context for social communication, which helps to guide children's thinking, is important to Vygotskian theory (Vygotsky, 1962). Teaching strategies, including developmentally guided interactions, reflect specific teaching and learning sequences that adults lay out for children. The social guidance provided by parents, teachers, peers, and events/situations are useful in understanding the transmission of cultural skills, including academic skills.

Meaningful Tasks

Family psychologists warn us not to test children with cognitive tasks that are not placed in a culturally appropriate context (Goodnow, 1990; Hess & Azuma, 1990; Rogoff & Morelli, 1989). For instance, Saxe (1988) found that 10- and 12-year old Brazilian children who did not attend school could not do math calculations that required a pencil and paper. But they could calculate in their heads large numbers when observed in the streets as produce vendors. This demonstrates how our evaluations of children's cognitive competence must consider the cultural context of the skills we study. Azuma (Chapter 13, this volume) and his associates recognized, to a certain extent, how culturally inappropriate the Block Sort Task was, so that the Japanese collaborators pressed for the inclusion of an unstructured game. The tasks and the results provided an important insight: The structure of variables that explain school readiness varies across cultures.

The Development of the CNP Team

All cultural psychologists struggle with the emic/etic distinction, that is, the difference between theorizing about the structural significance of observed behaviors or simply observing and recording the behaviors found in each culture. The CNP searched for points of similarity between the cultures. The value placed on academic achievement, formalized school structures, and the importance of families in predicting school performance were all unifying variables. From the emic perspective, both teams were determined to make ecologically valid comparisons and interpretations. The project identified similarities and described cultural differences without making value judgments about better or worse practices. Initially, the project was most sensitive to emic considerations, but seemed to focus on etic-type instruments and procedures. Gradually over time, the procedures and interpretations seemed to reflect the strength of the Japanese team, as they expressed their emic interpretations of the results. In my opinion, their confidence and insights were clear. Extensive interaction, questioning, and discussion were necessary before either team could articulate what made a particular concept of behavior have specific, or different, meanings across cultural contexts. A workable and fruitful process of discovery and integration evolved over time.

A Model for the Study of Diversity

Goodnow (1990) has argued that a model is needed to integrate ideas and empirical data linking parenting beliefs, values, and behavior with child outcomes. The CNP provided empirical data about how cultural context affects development, but we must extend, retest, and refine our models of culture, families, and child development. Harkness (1992) has also challenged us to examine technological, political, and social changes that are changing traditional child ecologies.

Cultural psychologists now go to great lengths to describe development from a positive model. Healthy children are reared in diverse cultural environments, and "cultural imperialism" is avoided. Traditionally, examination of intercultural variations in parenting and development utilized a deficit model (Rogoff & Morelli, 1989). Authoritarian parenting may not be appropriate for middle-class Anglo-American children, but may reflect a strong parenting style for other ethnic groups. With the diversity of children in the United States, we can learn from the neutral approach of cross-cultural psychological anthropologists such as Azuma and Hess about how to study diversity, among ethnic minority children in the United States.

A FINAL NOTE

Bob Hess and Hiroshi Azuma were significant role models for me, as I am now involved in my own cross-national collaborative relationships. Not only did they pique my interest in cross-cultural work, but they provided a framework to guide my interactions with Japanese colleagues. I was aware of the long meetings, stacks of computer printouts, mounds of correspondence, and the friendships that developed over the years between the two CNP teams. I learned from them an important lesson: Conducting cross-cultural research is incredibly tedious, but richly rewarding. I am now involved in a project based on the CNP findings regarding the importance of social context for motivation and school readiness. With Dr. Susan Holloway at Harvard, and Dr. Masaharu Kage at Keio University, I am examining social triggers as well as cognitive factors that may predict children's achievement in mathematics in the United States and Japan. So far, we have benefited from the CNP roadmap and are proceeding as planned. Perhaps one of the most important legacies of Bob Hess and Hiroshi Azuma is the legion of former graduate students who are continuing to conduct careful, thoughtful cross-cultural research that tests assumptions about development. Of course, other valuable lessons have been learned, and the Hess–Azuma partnership and CNP have provided an important light as I continue on my way.

ACKNOWLEDGMENTS

I would like to thank Susan Holloway and Robert Levine for their comments and insights on the historical context of the Hess–Azuma project. In addition, David and Barbara Shwalb provided needed editorial support and patience.

DEDICATION

Robert D. Hess was my mentor during my doctoral studies at Stanford University (1977–1981). Although I never worked on his cross-national study, I associated with his research team and recognized Bob's ability to nurture ideas, instill confidence in graduate students, and build collaborative relationships. Bob was also a dear and inspirational friend for 16 years. With this thought, I dedicate this chapter to his memory.

REFERENCES

Baumrind, D. (1971). Current patterns of parental authority. *Developmental Psychology Monographs, 4*(1), 1–103.

Bernstein, R. (1971). *Class, codes, and control: Theoretical studies towards a sociology of language* (Vol. 1). New York: Routledge & Kegan Paul.

Boyer, E. L. (1991). *Ready to learn: A mandate for the nation.* Princeton, NJ: Carnegie Foundation for the Advancement of Teaching.

Caudill, W., & Weinstein, H. (1969). Maternal care and infant behavior in Japan and America. *Psychiatry, 32,* 12–43.

Cole, M. (1992). Culture in development. In M. Bornstein & M. Lamb (Eds.), *Developmental psychology: An advanced textbook* (3rd ed., pp. 731–789). Hillsdale, NJ: Erlbaum.

Conroy, M., Hess, R. D., Azuma, H., & Kashiwagi, K. (1980). Maternal strategies for regulating children's behavior: Japanese and American families. *Journal of Cross-Cultural Psychology, 11*(2), 153–172.

Deci, E. L. (1975). *Intrinsic motivation.* New York: Plenum.

Dickson, W. P., Hess, R. D., Miyake, N., & Azuma, H. (1979). Referential communication accuracy between mother and child as a predictor of cognitive development in the United States and Japan. *Child Development, 50,* 53–59.

Doi, T. (1973). *The anatomy of dependence.* Tokyo: Kodansha International.

Fuller, B., Holloway, S. D., Azuma, H., Hess, R. D., & Kashiwagi, K. (1986). Contrasting achievement rules: Socialization of Japanese children at home and in school. *Research in Sociology of Education and Socialization, 6,* 165–201.

Goodnow, J. J. (1990). The socialization of cognition: What's involved? In J. W. Stigler, R. A. Schweder, & G. Herdt (Eds.), *Cultural psychology: Essays on comparative human development* (pp. 259–286). Cambridge: Cambridge University Press.

Harkness, S. (1992). Cross-cultural research in child development: A sample of the state of the art. *Developmental Psychology, 28*(4), 622–625.

Hess, R. D., & Azuma, H. (1990). Cross-cultural collaboration in studies of family effects on school achievement. In I. Sigel & G. Brody (Eds.), *Family research* (Vol. 1, pp. 265–288). Hillsdale, NJ: Erlbaum.

Hess, R. D., & Azuma, A. (1991). Cultural support for schooling: Contrasts between Japan and the United States. *Educational Researcher, 20*(9), 2–8, 12.

Hess, R. D., Azuma, H., Kashiwagi, K., Dickson, W. P., Nagano, S., Holloway, S., Miyake, K., Price, G., Hatano, G., & McDevitt, T. (1986). Family influences on school readiness and achievement in Japan and the United States: An overview of longitudinal study. In H. Stevenson, H. Azuma, & K. Hakuta (Eds.), *Kodomo: Child development and education in Japan and the United States* (pp. 147–166). New York: Freeman.

Hess, R. D., Azuma, H., Kashiwagi, K., Holloway, S. D., & Wenegrat, A. (1987). Cultural variations in socialization for school achievement: Contrasts between Japan and the United States. *Journal of Applied Developmental Psychology, 8,* 421–440.

Hess, R. D., Kashiwagi, K., Azuma, H., Price, G., & Dickson, P. W. (1980). Maternal expectations for mastery of developmental tasks in Japan and the United States. *International Journal of Psychology, 15,* 259–271.

Hoffman, M. L. (1977). Moral internalization: Current theory and research. In L. Berkowitz (Ed.), *Advances in experimental social psychology* (pp. 101–110). New York: Academic Press.

Holloway, S. D., Fuller, B., Hess, R. D., & Azuma, H. (1986). Causal attributions by Japanese and American mothers and children about performance in mathematics. *International Journal of Psychology, 21,* 269–286.

Holloway, S. D., Fuller, B., Hess, R. D., Azuma, H., Kashiwagi, K., & Gorman, K. (1990). The family's influence on achievement in Japan and the United States. *Comparative Education Review, 34*(2), 196–208.

Holloway, S. D., Kashiwagi, K., Hess, R. D., & Azuma, H. (1986). Causal attributions by Japanese and American mothers and children about performance in mathematics. *International Journal of Psychology, 21,* 269–286.

Holloway, S. D., & Machida, S. (1994). *The socialization of motivation toward math achievement in first-grade children: Comparison of teachers' and children's beliefs in Japan and the United States.* Unpublished manuscript.

Kashiwagi, K., Azuma, H., & Miyake, K. (1982). Early maternal influences upon later cognitive development among Japanese children: A follow-up study. *Japanese Psychological Research, 24*(2), 82–92.

Kashiwagi, K., Azuma, H., Nagano, S., Hess, R. D., & Holloway, S. D. (1984). Japan–US comparative study on early maternal influences upon cognitive development: A follow-up study. *Japanese Psychological Research, 26*(2), 82–92.

Leestma, R. (1992). Further research: Needs, possibilities, and perspectives. In R. Leestma & H. J. Walberg (Eds.), *Japanese educational productivity.* Ann Arbor, MI: Center for Japanese Studies, University of Michigan.

Lewis, C. (1984). Cooperation and control in Japanese nursery schools. *Comparative Education Review, 28*(1), 69–84.

McDevitt, T. M., Hess, R. D., Kashiwagi, K., Dickson, W. P., Miyake, N., & Azuma, H. (1987). Referential communication accuracy of mother–child pairs and children's later scholastic achievement: A follow-up study. *Merrill-Parlmer Quarterly, 33*(2), 171–185.

Miller, P. J. (1993). *Theories of developmental psychology.* New York: Freeman.

Miyake, N. (1977). *Out-of-code impression on American mother–child interactions.* Unpublished manuscript, Chukyo University, Toyota, Japan.

Peak, L. (1991). *Learning to go to school in Japan.* Berkeley, CA: University of California Press.

Rogoff, B., & Morelli, G. (1989). Perspectives on children's development from cultural psychology. *American Psychologist, 44*(2), 343–348.

Saxe, G. B. (1988). The mathematics of child street vendors. *Child Development, 59,* 1415–1425.

Sengoku, T., Leiderman-Davitz, L., & Davitz, J. R. (1982). *Mother–infant interaction: A cross-cultural study.* Unpublished manuscript, Japan Youth Research Institute, Tokyo.

Shand, N., & Kosawa, Y. (1985). Cultural transmission: Caudill's model and alternative hypotheses. *American Anthropologist, 87,* 862–871.

Shields, J. J. (Ed.). (1989). *Japanese schooling: Patterns of socialization, equality, and political control.* University Park: Pennsylvania State University Press.

Shweder, R. A. (1982). Beyond self-constructed knowledge: The study of culture and morality. *Merrill-Palmer Quarterly, 28,* 41–69.

Stevenson, H. W., & Lee, S. Y. (1990). Contexts of achievement: A study of American, Chinese, and Japanese children. *Monographs of the Society for Research in Child Development, 55*(1–2, Serial No. 221).

Stevenson, H. W., & Stigler, J. W. (1992). *The learning gap.* New York: Summit.

Tharp, R. G., & Gallimore, R. (1988). *Rousing minds to life: Teaching learning, and schooling in social context.* Cambridge: Cambridge University Press.

Tobin, J. J., Wu, D. Y. H., & David, D. H. (1989). *Preschool in three cultures.* New Haven, CT: Yale University Press.

Ukai, N. (1994). The Kumon approach to teaching and learning. *Journal of Japanese Studies, 20*(1), 87–113.

Vygotsky, L. S. (1962). *Thought and language.* Cambridge, MA: MIT Press.

Wertsch, J. V. (Ed.). (1985). *Culture, communication, and cognition: Vygotskian perspectives.* New York: Cambridge University Press.

White, M. (1987). *The Japanese educational challenge: A commitment to children.* New York: Basic.

Whiting, B. B. (Ed.). (1963). *Six cultures: Studies of child rearing.* New York: Wiley.

Whiting, B. B., & Edwards, C. P. (1988). *Children of different worlds: The formation of social behavior.* Cambridge, MA: Harvard University Press.

Whiting, B. B., & Whiting, J. W. M. (1975). *Children of six cultures: A psychocultural analysis.* Cambridge, MA: Harvard University Press.

The Transmission of Culturally Linked Behavior Systems through Maternal Behavior

Nature versus Nurture Revisited

Nancy Shand

INTELLECTUAL/EXPERIENTIAL BACKGROUND

Background as an Anthropologist

My training as an anthropologist was in the Boas–Herskovitz tradition, which asserts that our understanding of cultures must always remain incomplete. I believe that culture is in the eye of the beholder, and that culture as a human perspective is acquired through language, experiences, and training. And after working with three generations of anthropologists I conclude that we still do not understand that which we call "culture."

The concern throughout my own research career has been to describe aspects of human functioning, especially nonverbal behavior and language, in the context of culture. I have also focused on how cultural variation is acquired and expressed, transmitted between generations, and sustained through time (e.g., Shand, 1972). Particularly in my research on Japan, I have sought through objective and replicable procedures to study universal situations wherein variants of culture emerge.

I do not attribute my perspective to any person or school of thought, although I was most influenced by the work of Franz Boas and Melville Herskovitz. Boas, originally a physicist, contributed a theory of cultural transmission and a scientific research strategy to the field of anthropology, which had previously been atheoretical and speculative in its view of culture (Boas, 1928). In his concern for objective detail, meticulous comparison, and probabilistic measures, Boas indeed inspired my lifework. I learned from Boas that to study or even identify another culture is a demanding and intricate task that first involves consummately detailed comparisons. The work of interpreting culture is even more complicated, because historical contacts between various cultures complicate the identification of subject populations.

Experiences Prior to Research in Japan

My chief mentor was Dr. Melville Herskovitz, with whom I studied at Northwestern University, beginning in 1949. Herskovitz (1948) was associated with the concept of "cultural relativism," which suggests that members of each cultural group experience reality in a unique manner. He was a specialist in West African cultures, and had additional expertise on Oceania from the 1930s and 1940s. Herskovitz was also interested then in biological anthropology, but looked with disdain at the evolutionary theory emerging in Leslie White's Michigan group (White, 1959). Both Herskovitz and White were among the principal students of Boas at Columbia University, as were Margaret Mead, Ruth Benedict, and Edward Sapir.

Herskovitz made me his assistant in the early 1950s, so I was closely associated with his informants and students from West Africa, particularly the Tiv, the IBO (the now virtually extinct Christians of Biafra), Yoruba, and other tribal members. Through this exposure to West Africans, I became keenly aware of the variation among human groups. I also became interested then in the relation between culture and personality, and then pursued this interest by studying psychology and working with anthropologist John Gillan at the University of North Carolina. He was heavily influenced by psychoanalytic theory and was conducting fieldwork in Guatemala at that time. In addition, I associated at Chapel Hill with Howard Odum, a sociologist and a leader against the racism that was entrenched in the southern United States in the early 1950s. My exposure to both problack and antiblack cultures of southern whites taught me more about the intricacies and dimensions of culture. After this period I did further graduate studies at the University of London, the London School of Economics, and the London

Institute of Asian and African Studies. In addition, I conducted my own research over the years in North Africa, Lebanon, Egypt, Papua New Guinea, inner-city Chicago, India, and, for the past 2 decades, in Japan.

THE SHAND–KOSAWA COLLABORATION
Rationale for Study of the Japanese

My collaboration from 1975 with Dr. Yorio Kosawa was my first research on the Japanese. I had been well aware of Ruth Benedict's (1946) work, and believe now that her cultural definitions hold true under great scrutiny, even today. She accomplished her research entirely from secondary sources, never having visited Japan or met with Japanese, and wove together substantive data, objectively and carefully ordering it into a meaningful whole. Her accomplishment is not diminished by my own reservations about the "whole" that she called the culture of Japanese-speaking people, or about her collection of details, which described overall and specific dimensions of Japanese culture. Actually, what she and others assumed to be Japanese was really a variant on themes from more ancient Asian cultures, including China and Korea.

My interest in Japan was not based on the work of Benedict, but was derived rather from other influences on my life work. I still prefer to study culture in places such as Papua New Guinea, where purer cultural forms and a less complex "foreign" contact environment still existed in the 1970's. But the convergence of two circumstances led me to focus my thinking on Japan. The first contemporary influence was William Caudill's effort to bring the scientific approach to the elusive entity of culture. The second influence was my own fascination with new knowledge on the biological basis of some behavior, based on contacts with Konrad Lorenz (1966), the imprinting literature and the burgeoning infant development field (Bell & Haaf, 1971). My intent had been to elucidate the relationships between (1) culturally-linked norms of human maternal behavior, (2) maternal behavioral responses linked to hormonally related lactation after childbirth, and (3) corresponding human infant signals.

Prior to my work in Japan I was interested in the interface between biology and culture. I had just completed a study of Caucasian-American breast-feeding women (before, during, and after childbirth), comparing them with a matched sample of bottle-feeding women who had taken lactation-suppressant hormones (Shand,

1981). I used intrasecond time-lapse behavioral analyses to assess the influences of hormones and maternal behaviors that might be culturally linked or override effects of hormone suppressants. In 1975, I decided to use this methodology in a comparative design. Caudill's work suggested Japan as a meaningful site to study the "cultural" versus biological dimensions of mother–infant interactions in relation to those of Caucasian Midwest American mother–infant interactions.

The Nature–Nurture Issue

Anthropological research on culture and personality traditionally emphasized environmental influences on human development (e.g., Whiting, 1963). Caudill (1973) is still cited today by developmental psychologists for his claim that cultural differences between Japanese behavior and Caucasian-American behavior were transmitted from mother to child by the 3rd month of life (Caudill & Weinstein, 1969), and had enduring consequences through 12 years of age and beyond (Caudill & Schooler, 1973). Caudill assumed that biological and developmental differences were randomly distributed in his research samples, and concluded that differences between Japanese and American infant behavior "are learned more than genetic or maturational," although he recognized that "these questions cannot be answered with finality within the limits of our sample" (Caudill & Weinstein, 1969, p. 13).

Cultural groups do exist, although their parameters are still largely undefined, and members consciously or unconsciously do transmit culture to new group members. But our knowledge about mechanisms of cultural transmission and of maturational processes is currently incomplete. Evidence has shown the impact of both *in utero* and external environments, partially linked to culture, on the developing fetus. The early months of life are a critical developmental period for human babies, during which significant changes occur in biochemical and related neurostructures, for example, myelinization of the peripheral nervous system. This same time period is also critical for mothers, as distinctive hormonal changes occur in relation to breast-feeding and other maternal behaviors.

While there is somewhat of a consensus that culture is transmitted to children at a very young age, some of our own research findings raise an additional question: Do characteristics of infants, which may be biologically or genetically based, influence the behavior of mothers, and thus modify culture itself?

The Japan–United States Comparison

The Bicultural Approach

Mother–infant interaction is a useful domain for the examination of developmental hypotheses concerning cultural transmission of forms of nonverbal and language behavior. A comparative design requires two populations with minimal shared origins and comparatively little long-term historic contact, and our choice of Japanese and Midwestern Caucasian-Americans met these requirements. This choice also ensured a measure of confidence that significantly different nonverbal and language behaviors could be interpreted as defining parameters of culture.

Research Technology

In the past, one impediment to vigorous comparative research was the lack of technology required to record the intrasecond minutia of behavior interaction systems wherein culture forms are transmitted between generations. In the 1960s, Caudill was forced to use inaccurate naked-eye stopwatch observation methods, as have other researchers who replicated aspects of Caudill's research (Chen & Takahashi, 1988). Only in recent decades have the technological requirements (e.g., portable cameras for intrasecond time-lapse and stop-frame analyses) for collecting such data become available (e.g., Birdwhistle, 1970; Shand & Kosawa, 1985b). As shown in Figure 15.1, this technology enables us to observe with a degree of reliability impossible in Caudill's time. Technology also allows for repeated viewing, high interscorer reliabilities, and multivariate statistical analyses, which were not feasible for Caudill in the 1960s. As a result, our methods were replicable and allowed for a reliable delineation of cultural parameters.

Changing the Focus of Research

I was originally interested in studying the effects of lactation hormones on maternal behavior in two cultures. But in Japan we could not locate any subjects who took lactation suppression hormone shots, and all but one of our Japanese subjects breast-fed or intended to breast-feed. In America half of our subjects breast-fed and half took the hormones, as sought in the original research design. Thus, our research focus changed when the desired sample was unavailable. We instead concentrated on comparisons of Japanese and American mothers. From the first mother–newborn inter-

FIGURE 15.1. Sequence of photos showing mother kissing baby, a 1-second event that probably would not be recorded using naked-eye observation. Courtesy of Nancy Shand.

actions at the hospital, which varied from moments after birth to 24 hours later, and subsequently at 1 and 3 months, we used intra-second time-lapse filming to get accurate behavioral descriptions. The original samples consisted of 103 Japanese and 104 Caucasian-American first-born children, including equal numbers of boys and girls. The mothers ranged in age from 20 to 30 years, and all were married, lived in middle-class nuclear families, and had at least a high school education.

The Process of Collaboration

I had mastered several methodological and technical problems during a 2-year study in Topeka on bottle-feeding and breast-feeding women, before I first met Dr. Kosawa. Prior to our collaboration, he was not accustomed to studying babies and had not focused on biological aspects of human development. Based on my experiences, biological aspects were certainly as important as cultural factors, and I also brought interests in psychological (not excluding psychoanalytic) perspectives to the collaboration. Kosawa was primarily interested in studying the mothers, and we expanded our research design to include many psychological tests that he added. He and I shared an interest in psychology and psychiatry, so our collaborative work was biological–anthropological–psychological–psychiatric in its origins.

Prior to our collaboration, I had not been to Japan nor experienced Japanese culture. In general, even with so excellent a collaborator as Dr. Kosawa, one should spend substantial time with the population to be studied. Given my focus and interests, I did not believe this was essential initially, and the excellent groundwork provided by previous researchers helped me to understand the relevant aspects of Japanese culture. With a focus such as mine, one might be even better off *not* to submerge oneself in the culture too extensively. A researcher can become so involved in the culture as to lose the perspective needed for objective or neutral observation. The need for prior experiences in the culture depends on the type of research one wants to do. At the interpretive stage, of course, one needs to go and experience the culture.

An additional prerequisite for cross-cultural collaboration concerns the personalities of the researchers. In our case, I found Kosawa's perception of the humor in cultural differences to be a great asset to our partnership. The collaboration always went smoothly, because of his delicacy and resiliency.

RESEARCH RESULTS

Our findings sometimes did not agree with Caudill's, and in some instances reversed his findings. But we acknowledge his enormous contribution to the understanding of cultural transmission, and do not dispute his view that culture via maternal behavior strongly influences infant behavior.

Summary of Findings on Infants and Mothers

We found a significant United States–Japan population difference in spontaneous motor activity level immediately after birth. This finding persisted in measurements at 1 and 3 months of life, as Japanese infants continued to be more active than Americans (Shand & Kosawa, 1985a).

At 3 months we found distinct "Japanese-type" and "American-type" infant behaviors and dyad types (Shand & Kosawa, 1985a, 1985b). But the culture types we found in some ways reversed those described earlier by Caudill and Weinstein (1969). Our research also revealed the presence of distinctive Japanese and Caucasian-American maternal language styles at 3 months (Morikawa, Shand, & Kosawa, 1988). In addition, we observed Japanese mothers to be more field independent and to have less body contact with their babies compared to American mothers (Shand, Kosawa, & Decelles, 1988). Caudill had observed the opposite, that Japanese mothers had *more* of such physical contact. Our finding led us to consider a linkage between cognitive style and maternal behavior toward the baby.

Caudill's research on Japanese infants was the only available scientific data available on another culture, prior to our work, and we were intrigued because he conducted only naked-eye observations. His efforts to study the behavior of 3-month-old infants in contexts of concurrent maternal behavior utilized time-lapse observations, which was a major step in bringing the scientific method into cross-cultural studies. Yet despite Caudill's great achievements, reliance on visual observation may account for some of the discrepancies between our findings. Literally hundreds of movements can be observed in 1 second using cameras and stop-framed film for analysis (see Figure 15.1). In addition, a 15-year time difference in time of data collection probably contributed to differences in our results.

We also knew what Caudill could not have known given the state of infant studies in his own era—that *in utero* and newborn infants could learn from environmental input. Hence, culture is transmittable long before 3 months of age. We first studied mothers in the final trimester of pregnancy. We also filmed both infants and mothers at birth, and infants immediately after birth, and found striking behavioral differences between the two cultural samples. Differences at 3 months could have been the outcome of various factors, including maternal behavior. But at 3 months we assumed that maternal behavior was influenced by the infants' own behavior; by this age each dyad being influenced by both culture and their own biological characteristics. Our extensive analyses of intrasegment films, and other mother and infant measures, consumed several years and are published elsewhere. We will focus below on the preliminary results of our follow-up, which studied the original infant subjects when they were 10 years old.

The Follow-Up Study at Age 10

When the babies we first observed had become 10-year-olds, we taped 40-minute videos of nonverbal tasks and mother-child dyadic language and nonverbal interactions. We are still analyzing these comparative data. We also made academic, personality, and other assessments of both the children and their mothers.

It is already apparent that individual and group differences in activity level were not sustainable through age 10. But the Japanese children still differed significantly in other ways from their American counterparts, displaying greater assertiveness, initiative, and exploratory behavior. At age 10 the findings are as striking as were the results for infancy. The Japanese and Americans, both children and mothers, appear to have distinct behavioral styles.

Our 10-year-old Japanese and American children, and the mother–child dyads, continue to differ in nonverbal behavior as well as in language usage. Differences in maternal behavior may explain some differences in the behavior of the children, but some cultural differences in 10-year-old children's nonverbal behavior and language were significantly correlated with neonate motor-activity level and infant behavior type. Such findings, which may have origins in biological propensities, raise complex questions. For instance, do Japanese infants channel their greater overall motor activity to more specific tasks and focused activities by age 10? Or do Japanese mothers encourage assertiveness in their children? We hope to answer such questions in the ensuing years of analysis and interpretation. We also have used uni- and multivariate analyses of variance, and stepwise regression, to test the value of infant activity level and typology for predicting nonverbal behavior and language style, and dyadic behavior, at 10 years of age. Our initial results are summarized below, and will be published later in detail.

Child Nonverbal Behaviors and Language Style at 10 Years

Overall, cultural differences in 10-year-old children's behavior were striking. Japanese children showed significantly more of every behavior that was a response to environment-based stimuli. They were unabatedly curious, bold to test and explore, lacked inhibition in criticizing their own work, and immediately redid work. In other words, they persevered in answering environmentally presented stimuli and resolving challenges. These findings reverse the direction of culture differences reported by the Japanese government (Umetani, 1985) and by the U.S. Department of Education (Stocking & Curry, 1986). These major studies had unequivocally concluded that Japanese teenage and college youth are (1) *not prepared* according to a Japanese government study (Umetani, 1985), and (2) *less prepared* than American youth (High School and Beyond Study) (Stocking & Curry, 1986) for the future.

How can we explain the "go-getter" approach of our Japanese 10-year-olds? Is this characteristic discouraged during adolescence and in college, after which specific training fits individuals into adult roles? Of course, our data were collected for younger subjects than was the case in either government study, but the discrepancy between these studies and our findings suggest the need for test measures that pertain to the actual environment experienced by youth, and show the limits of the questionnaire-based measures used in the government studies for cultural comparisons. It is also arguable that our samples do not accurately reflect the overall subpopulations. But the consistently significant cultural differences found suggest that our methodological approach should be pursued further.

In addition, findings of significant cultural difference in language usage (regardless of linguistic bias) contrast with media reports of polite reticence and acquiescent behavior among Japanese children. Such behavior is observable, but may be limited to specific public contexts. At any rate, the Japanese 10-year-olds in our sample were better prepared for the future than their American counterparts, in terms of assertiveness and control/mastery of the physical and social environment.

Cultural Comparisons of Dyad Behavior Styles at 10 Years

Overall, mother–child behavior evidenced significant multivariate (MANOVA) effects for culture, and maternal behaviors could be linked to cultural differences in child behavior. We found first that both Japanese mothers and children evidenced more curiosity, going to and manipulating the "Temptation Table" items. The Temptation Table consisted of a set of attractive objects that were located next to the mother and child while they sat during a 10-minute waiting period. Observed during experimental tasks, Japanese dyads persisted at their work after repeatedly expressing dissatisfaction with their Etch-a-Sketch creations, and together they built high-quality symmetrical Lego staircases. In Japanese dyads the children, rather than the mothers, took control of the instruction packets, and ran around the room, exploring, and even taunting the camera, more than did the Kansas children.

The only trend more observable among Americans was that American mothers verbally directed their children's attention to Temptation Table items, usually challenging them to do something. Neither American mothers nor children approached the table or manipulated the items. And they rarely expressed dissatisfaction with their work, or tried to redo the initial Etch-a-Sketch creations. The dyads usually built Lego staircases which were top-heavy, and did not follow through on their work.

In general, the Japanese mothers jumped into the dyadic tasks, leading or following the child, joining together in pursuit of solutions and enjoyment. Japanese mothers and 10-year-olds appeared to enjoy themselves greatly during the video session situations, whereas American mothers and 10-year-olds did not. The American mothers also appeared to put the burden of performance on the children. These mothers were less curious and more readily satisfied with whatever was accomplished on the first try. They were less demanding of themselves and their children, and the American child's behavior mirrored their mothers' disengagement.

Infancy "Predictors": Channeling of Activity Level?

The Japanese children, when they were babies, had significantly higher motor-activity levels than did the Americans immediately after birth, and at ages 1 month and 3 months (Shand & Kosawa, 1985a). But at 10 years, there was no significant cultural difference in overall activity level, and motor-activity level at age 10 did not correlate significantly with infancy period activity level. This led us to ask whether infant motor activity might be channeled into focused activity that is more acceptable or appropriate for 10-year-olds. Such activities might include moving about the room, and going to objects and manipulating them. We scored such behaviors from videotapes of the child when alone and with the mother; such behaviors were more evident among Japanese 10-year-olds.

We tested the null hypothesis using neonatal motor activity (NAL) as the independent variable, and (1) salient single nonverbal behavior scores and (2) factor scores as dependent variables. The only significant multivariate effects of NAL in 10-year-old behavior style (factors) was in its interaction with culture, and these effects show a *developmental reversal* related to culture. Japanese who were *least* active and Americans who were *most* active as infants performed more focused activities at 10 years of age. These subjects (1) persisted, repeatedly redoing their Etch-a-Sketch creations, (2) left their chairs to explore and run about the room, and (3) asserted themselves, going to and manipulating items on the Temptation Table. There is considerable controversy about the usefulness of activity, or any single trait, in developmental studies, so we do not want to overemphasize infant activity level as an predictor of elementary school-age child behavior. Yet our findings suggest such a relationship.

Neonatal Activity Level: Predictor of Maternal Behavior at 3 Months and 10 Years

Among infants, there was a significant gender NAL × gender effect on maternal behavior at 3 months, in both cultures (Shand & Kosawa, 1985a). This finding suggested a feedback loop between neonatal characteristics and maternal behavior, so we examined this feedback concept further in the data at age 10. There were no significant multivariate effects of NAL or interaction of NAL with culture or gender on maternal behavioral style at 10 years of age. Longer term influences of infants on maternal behavior still may occur, but were not observable here.

Infant Type at 3 Months and Child 10-Year Behavior Style

MANOVA and ANOVA were then used to assess the overall and specific effects of 3-month-olds' "infant type," and of culture and gender, on the 10-year-olds' behavior style. According to cluster analyses, 3-month-olds' behavior type was related to children's nonverbal behavior style at age 10. The Etch-a-Sketch and the Temptation Table situations were the most useful contexts for predicting 10-year-olds' behavior from 3-month olds' type. Three infant behaviors were most predictive of age 10: children who as infants spent more time with Hand-to-Mouth, Motor Activity, and Crying at 3 months were more likely 10 years later to persevere, repeatedly starting over on the Etch-a-Sketch task.

The least active infants later, at age 10 years, seldom erased Etch-a-Sketch, even after expressing dissatisfaction, and built symmetrical Lego staircases with mothers. Infant "Talkers," those with the most noncrying vocalizations at 3 months, did not express much dissatisfaction with their Etch-a-Sketch task performance, did not erase/repeat frequently or take much time at the task, and showed little interest in the Temptation Table objects. But at 10 years of age they were outstanding in language.

Dyads at 3 Months and 10 Years

No significant multivariate relation was found between 3-month dyad type and overall dyadic behavior style at age 10, that is infancy dyad type was not a useful predictor. Only two significant univariate effects emerged at 10 years. First, the more Passive dyads at 3 months were most assertive in curiosity 10 years later, with child and mother both going to and manipulating items on the Temptation Table. Second, dyads with highly active mothers and 3-month-old babies who were either Active or "Talkers" (both "American types") appeared 10 years later as mothers who verbally directed the children, although neither mother nor child was particularly assertive.

Infancy Predictors of 10-Year-Olds' Behavior and Language Style

Stepwise regression (using individual scores, not group means) was used to ascertain the best prediction models of 10-year-olds' behavior. Predictor(s) of child behavior style at 10 years were taken from (1) neonate behavior type, (2) 1-month behavior type, (3) 3-months child behavior type and (4) 3-months dyad behavior type.

The results indicated that neonatal, 1-month, and 3-month measures all predict some age 10 variables, but in different domains. Neonates who are either the most Passive or evidenced most Hand-to-Mouth behavior immediately after birth (1) cooperated most with mother to build symmetry into the Lego stairs and (2) expressed most dissatisfaction with their Etch-a-Sketch stairs creations, but did *not* erase them. They also initiated more verbal interaction at 10 years, directing mother's attention to Temptation Table items. Ten-year-olds who had been the most Alert (eyes open) and those who had Grasped more than others as neonates cooperated least with mother in building Lego stairs, and they were more satisfied with, their joint creation of stairs in Etch-a-Sketch. They also seldom verbally directed mother's attention to Temptation Table items.

One-month infant type best predicted both child verbal initiative, directing mother's attention to the Temptation Table, and mother's level of activity in going to, handling, or testing out items. The most Passive (*not* most Active) infant type verbally directed mother more than do children who had been other infant types, and their mothers were more active in relation to Temptation Table items. *Three-month infant type* best predicts child language style 10 years later. For instance, children who as 3-month-old infants were characterized by the most Hand-to-Mouth, and to a lesser extent those who had a diverse repertoire of behaviors, 10 years later agreed with mothers' statements, but rarely gave their own opinions. And the most motorically active 3-month infant type later agreed *least* with mothers' statements.

CULTURAL TRANSMISSION, MOTHERING, AND DEVELOPMENT

Anthropologists for several generations have focused on initiation rites at pubescence, and on the transfer of secret knowledge from specialist to initiate. They have shown that a variety of complex kinship, social-religious, and political-economic systems are transmitted between generations. These systems qualify as aspects of culture, but how are they transmitted? Past anthropological studies have been mainly confined to various stages of adulthood, and have rarely focused on the critical periods of infancy and childhood. The arrival of a new member into the culture group poses the initial opportunity for transmitting culture, including the crucial parameters of nonverbal and prelinguistic behavior. These are received by the infant through selective discrimination of stimuli, usually presented by the mother.

Culture and Motherhood

Japanese recognition of the importance of the mother in transmitting culture and training the child is very old. Doi (1973) and Takahashi (1980) argue that dependency or "symbiotic psychopathology" are important while Caudill and Plath (1966) note that "closeness" (e.g., through sleeping arrangements) set in customary forms enable her to accomplish these tasks. The maternal role traditionally must be performed in the context of the Japanese household, or *ie,* a predominately patrilineal corporate structure that emphasizes the group over the individual (Matsumoto, 1960; Smith & Schooler, 1978). De Vos (1973) argues that the culture dimension of Japanese achievement is characterized by role dedication and the internalization of very high standards of performance.

In contrast, the diverse European roots of the comparatively recent American maternal role may have resulted in an array of often conflicting maternal role expectations. Given this history, we expected substantial differences between modern Japanese and American perceptions of the maternal role, and in a women's confidence in taking on this role for the first time. Indeed, there was a substantial difference between our Japanese mothers and American mothers, particularly in relation to achievement dynamics in the context of culture, even before their children were born (Shand, 1985; Shand & Kosawa, 1980).

To the expectant Japanese mothers in our sample, childrearing was seen as only the beginning of her lifelong role of motherhood within the patrilineal corporate structure. They tended to draw pictures depicting the future in which wife and husband were old persons with grandchildren visiting them. The mother's duty was to bring up a child who is cooperative and meek toward elders, but also motivated to achieve in a highly competitive social order. Thus, Japanese women were well aware of and devoted to the task of cultural transmission.

In contrast, our Caucasian-American expectant women envisioned a temporary maternal role defined as physical care and loving of the child, and terminating (according to their drawings) in adolescence. The American mothers did not express socialization or transmission of cultural values as part of the maternal role (Shand, 1985). Yet all expectant American mothers in our sample were confident about their roles. This might have been related to their lack of stated objectives as mothers, and the wide-ranging options for defining correct American maternal behavior. Japanese mothers faced their maternal role, and its traditionally explicit and rigid rules, with little confidence. In fact, one fifth responded that they had "no confidence," and even expressions of confidence connoted deep reservations.

The Japanese mothers knew their role in cultural transmission, which is demanding, intricate, and significant in the context of Japanese society. Further, they had specific strategies for childrearing, in advance, which revealed their detailed, intimate acquaintance with the role (Shand, 1985). This was frequently expressed in specific phrases, such as "keep the child company," "play together," "stay close to the child," and "always listen to the child's side of the story."

Mother, Infant, and Child Behavior

Our findings of striking, consistent cultural differences between Japanese and Americans, both in dyadic and child behavior in infancy and at age 10, suggest that these Japanese mothers were accomplishing their goals in childrearing. As a result, Japanese 10-year-olds in our sample were more task-oriented, curious, assertive, curious, persistent and self-critical than American children.

The data also reveal a dynamic mother–child relationship in which the characteristics of the infant or child mold maternal behaviors, while the mother shapes the young child. In addition, 10-year-olds' behavior may have roots in earliest infant characteristics and behavior. Still, the origins of these infant characteristics remain unclear: Are they biologically or environmentally based? The infant comes equipped with the perceptual apparatus and motor skills to carry out discriminations and to stimulate maternal behavior. Human infant characteristics at birth include (1) grasping at so slight a stimulus as two hairs in its palm, (2) the ability to focus at 12 to 14 inches, and (3) the stepping reflex, all of which contribute to mother–infant interaction. Whether or not a critical period exists just after birth, our findings suggest that specific infant and maternal behaviors occurring in the first minutes of life may have long-range implications in child nonverbal behavior and language at 10 years.

Differences in maternal behavior at childbirth, as well as at 1 and 3 months, are certainly tied up with cultural forces. How these differences link up at 10 years is the focus of our current work. What is the long-range impact of these differences in behavior of the mothers and children? Certainly the Japanese 10-year-olds and mothers we sampled were very different from their American counterparts. Our goal is to try to understand why some behaviors may be culturally linked and others seem to be sustained from birth through age 10 regardless of cultural group. One impediment to previous examinations of cultural transmission was the lack of explicit dimensions of human interactions that could be considered as parameters of culture. Through objective and accurate measurement techniques, we have sought to delineate some of these parameters.

There are several causal pathways involved in behavioral trans-actions between human infants and mothers. Both bioenviron-mental (Lumsden & Wilson, 1982) and cultural factors are involved in the earliest period of human growth and may contribute in sig-nificant ways to the child's later behavior and cognitive perfor-mance, thereby sustaining the cultural system. The findings summa-rized above support this view. In the coming years we will examine other parameters of culture in our data set, including cognitive style, academic performance and potential for suicide.

Twenty-seven years ago the state of developmental research was described by White (1969) as *An Edifice without a Foundation*. Al-though enormous gains have taken place, and are still taking place in research on Western cultures, the situation has only slightly improved regarding *comparative* research on human development. Caudill's pi-oneering work, and our own efforts, may help provide some of the beginnings of such a cross-cultural foundation for developmental re-searchers and increase the understanding of the impact of various in-teraction systems on the transmission of human culture.

DEDICATION

This chapter is dedicated to the memory of Dr. Hiroshi Wagatsuma. His deep insight into the nature of cultural reality *(which we still are trying to define)*, strongly contributed to the research described here. Wagatsuma was an exceptional and precious person, and was deeply involved in both Japanese and American cultures. We loved and respected him.

REFERENCES

Bell, R. Q., & Haaf, R. (1971). The relevance of newborn waking state to some motor and appetitive responses. *Journal of Child Development, 42,* 69–77.

Benedict, R. (1946). *The chrysanthemum and the sword.* Boston: Houghton Mifflin.

Birdwhistle, R. L. (1970). *Kinesics and context: Essays on body motion communi-cation.* Philadelphia: University of Pennsylvania Press.

Boas, F. (1928). *Anthropology and modern life.* New York: Norton.

Caudill, W. A. (1973). The influence of social structure and culture on human behavior in modern Japan. *Journal of Nervous and Mental Disease, 157,* 240–257.

Caudill, W. A., & Plath, D. W. (1966). Who sleeps by whom? Parent–child involvement in urban Japanese families. *Psychiatry, 29,* 344–366.

Caudill, W., & Schooler, C. (1973). Child behavior and child rearing in Japan and the United States: An interim report. *Journal of Nervous and Mental Disease, 157,* 323–338.

Caudill, W. A., & Weinstein, H. (1969). Maternal care and infant behavior in Japan and America. *Psychiatry, 32,* 12–43.

Chen, S.-J., & Takahashi, Y. (1988). Cross-cultural comparison of mother–infant relationship in Japan and the United States: A critical review. Special Issue: Mother–child relation. *Japanese Psychological Review, 31,* 101–111.

De Vos, G. A. (1973). *Socialization for achievement.* Berkeley: University of California Press.

Doi, T. L. (1973). *The anatomy of dependence* (J. Bestor, Trans.). Tokyo: Kodansha International.

Herskovitz, M. (1948). *Man and his works: The science of cultural anthropology.* New York: Knopf.

Kosawa, Y., & Shand, N. (1995). Perceived self-confidence and perceived importance—Japanese and American children at ten years of age. *Science Reports of Tokyo Women's Christian University.*

Lorenz, K. (1966). *On aggression.* New York: Harcourt, Brace.

Lumsden, C. J., & Wilson, E. O. (1982). Précis of genes, mind and culture. *Behavioral and Brain Sciences, 5,* 1–37.

Matsumoto, Y. S. (1960). Contemporary Japan: In individual and the group. *Transactions of the American Philosophical Society, 50*(Pt. 1).

Morikawa, H., Shand, N., & Kosawa, Y. (1988). Maternal speech to prelingual infants in Japan and the United States: Relationships among functions, forms and referents. *Journal of Child Language, 15,* 237–256.

Shand, N. (1972). *A cross-cultural study of continuities in artistic expression, contact modalities throughout the life cycle, and institutionalized responses to death.* Unpublished doctoral dissertation, University of Kansas.

Shand, N. (1981). The reciprocal impact of breast-feeding and culture form on maternal behavior and infant development. *Journal of Biosocial Science, 13,* 17.

Shand, N. (1985). Culture's influence in Japanese and American maternal role perception and confidence. *Psychiatry, 48,* 52–67.

Shand, N., & Kosawa, Y. (1980). Breast-feeding as cultural or personal decision: Sources of information and actual success in Japan and the United States. *Journal of Biosocial Science, 16,* 65–80.

Shand, N., & Kosawa, Y. (1985a). Culture transmission systems: Caudill's model and alternative hypotheses tested. *American Anthropologist, 87,* 862–871.

Shand, N., & Kosawa, Y. (1985b). Japanese and American behavior "types" at three months: Infant and infant–mother dyads. *Infant Behavior and Development, 8,* 225–240.

Shand, N., Kosawa, Y., & Decelles, P. (1988). Cognitive measures and maternal physical contact in Japan and America. In C. Bagley & G. Verma (Eds.), *The cross-cultural imperative.* London: Macmillan.

Smith, K. C., & Schooler, C. (1978). Women as mothers in Japan: The effects of social structure and culture on values and behavior. *Journal of Marriage and the Family, 40,* 613–620.

Stocking, C. B., & Curry, G. D. (1986). *Postsecondary plans of US and Japanese high school seniors: An introductory comparative analysis.* Washington, DC: USDE Office of Educational Research and Improvement. (ERIC Document Reproduction Service)

Takahashi, T. (1980). Adolescent symbiotic psychopathology: A cultural comparison of American and Japanese patterns and resolutions. *Bulletin of the Menninger Clinic, 44,* 272–283.

Umetani, S. (1985). *Occupational information, placement and choices for the Japanese youths.* Washington, DC: USDE Office of Educational Research and Improvement. (ERIC Document Reproduction Service)

White, B. L. (1969). Child development research: An edifice without a foundation. *Merrill-Palmer Quarterly, 15,* 49–79.

White, L. A. (1959). *The evolution of culture.* New York: McGraw-Hill.

Whiting, B. (1963). *Six cultures: Studies of child-rearing.* New York: Wiley.

Longitudinal Research in a Cultural Context
Reflections, Prospects, Challenges

Per F. Gjerde

Developmental psychology is becoming increasingly concerned with cultural variation, since examination of children in "non-Western" cultures is imperative to achieving a more comprehensive view human of development (Cooper, 1994; Rogoff, 1990; Rogoff, Gauvain, & Ellis, 1984; Stigler, Shweder, & Herdt, 1990.) Knowledge of cultural differences in developmental trajectories remains nonetheless a relatively distant goal, partly due to the absence of longitudinal research—a method that has provided important insights into the development of "Western" children. Given their almost exclusive reliance on cross-sectional methodologies, cultural examinations of children have typically been unable to directly examine development over time. It is within this wider scientific context that Nancy Shand's longitudinal research, conducted in collaboration with Yorio Kosawa, assumes its distinctive importance.

The longitudinal method seeks to map development across circumstances and over time for a period sufficiently long to discern coherent developmental patterns. Although longitudinal designs are useful, even required, to answer essential questions regarding human development, psychologists have often approached this methodology with ambivalence. Longitudinal projects become, by the very demands needed to sustain them, career investments (J. Block, 1993b). Yet if we believe in the essential coherence, or lawfulness of development, longitudinal studies become an essential research tool. Only longitudinal research can yield information about the form or patterning of a developmental function, the different types of behavioral stabilities (see Block, 1971, and Caspi & Bem, 1990, for an analysis of the several meanings of the concept of "stability"), the degree of continuity of variables occurring within individuals over time, the relationship between antecedent conditions and subsequent developmental outcomes, the homogeneity of developmental outcomes emerging from different early circumstances ("equifinality"), the heterogeneity of developmental outcomes deriving from similar early circumstances ("multipotentiality"), and the time of onset and extent to which developmental deviations persist (J. Block, 1993b; Rutter, 1988; Wohlwill, 1973). Longitudinal studies have yielded substantial insights about the coherence of individual development, the long-term implications of early experiences, and the inadequacy of the current, immediate environment to provide a sufficient basis for comprehending development (J. H. Block & J. Block, 1980; Sroufe, 1983; Magnusson, 1988; Bergman & Magnusson, 1990).

Shand and Kosawa have been following a cohort of "Japanese" and "American"[1] children and their mothers for more than a decade. The comments that follow refer mostly to Dr. Shand, since she is the sole author of the chapter included in this volume. This project has over the years made important contributions to our understanding of child development and early mother–child relations in Japan and the United States, and the mechanisms underlying culture transmission (e.g., Shand, 1981, 1985; Sand & Kosawa, 1985a, 1985b; Morikawa, Shand, & Kosawa, 1988). In their research, Shand and Kosawa have applied modern observational techniques to address topics of central interest not only to scholars of cultural variation in development, but also to developmental psychologists more generally. This research has examined maternal influences on long-term development, the relations of early child behavior to later outcomes, infant predictors of maternal behaviors, and the nature versus nurture debate. Shand and Kosawa's emphasis on the mother–child dyad is consistent with traditional descriptions of Japanese family socialization, in which the mother is seen as the central socialization agent and the mother–child bonding as the basis of all human relationships (Lebra, 1984; Tanaka, 1986; Wagatsuma & De Vos, 1984). Thus, maternal practices may relate more strongly to child outcomes in Japan, with its emphasis on the mother–child dyad, than in cultures more strongly characterized by multiple caretaking systems (e.g., Smith, 1980; Tronick, Morelli, & Ivey, 1992; Weisner & Gallimore, 1977). However, the exclusive focus on the mother–child dyad precludes analyses of the interdependence among separate dyadic family relationships (e.g., mother–child and husband–wife) and cannot therefore address indirect parental influences (Gjerde, 1986). In particular, the absence of a systems approach to family functioning may impede closer understanding of the father's role. I will return to this issue later.

While recognizing its multiple contributions, I will focus here mostly on the longitudinal component of the Shand–Kosawa project. In doing so, I recognize that Shand's chapter is a summary/progress report and that important analyses have not yet been completed. My intent is to complement Shand's chapter by outlining several issues that should guide future cross-cultural longitudinal research. First, longitudinal researchers on cultural variation in development must attend to both age- *and* culture-specific manifestations of developmental measures. Second, the selection of variables in a cross-cultural studies should be based on sound theoretical principles and derive from the normative sequence of developmental tasks that children of different cultures encounter as they mature. Third, the construct of culture posited by cross-cultural psychology is often too broad and undifferentiated to be useful in charting individual lives over time. I view culture as constantly changing and as existing in a historical context, not as a static, immutable, and sweeping variable. The ecocultural model (Weisner, Gallimore, & Jordan, 1988; Super & Harkness, 1986), to be discussed later, allows for close analysis of developmental change at cultural, institutional, relational, and individual levels. Fourth, cross-cultural research requires multiple data, multiple contexts of assessment, and multiple informants. My comments on the findings presented in Shand's chapter are interspersed throughout the discussion of these four issues.

CONSTRUCT VALIDITY IN LONGITUDINAL RESEARCH: AGE- AND CULTURE-RELATED MANIFESTATIONS OF DEVELOPMENTAL CONSTRUCTS

Age-Related Manifestations of Developmental Constructs

A comparative longitudinal study must consider, simultaneously, measurement equivalence across both age and culture. As illustrated by Shand's data, close analysis of both the developmental and the cultural aspects of construct validity raises formidable challenges for research design, analysis, and interpretation. The validation of hypothetical constructs is difficult because there is no clear criterion against which their validity can be evaluated. Construct validation is a laborious and never-ending process (e.g., Loevinger, 1957; Cronbach & Meehl, 1955). In their perceptive analysis of data quality in longitudinal research, Bergman and Magnusson (1990) refer to measures for operationalizing hypothetical constructs as "indirect measures." This is because (1) they are inherently "fuzzy" (i.e., cannot be defined unequivocally by a single measurement method); (2) do not reflect merely quantitative differences (i.e., once a score exceeds a certain threshold, its meaning may become qualitatively different); and (3) even if a measure is assumed to reflect the same hypothetical construct at different age levels, the meaning of construct-related behaviors may change with development. Thus, the same construct may have different behavioral manifestations at various ages and, conversely, identical behavioral manifestations may reflect different underlying constructs. A distinctive example of this phenomenon is reported by J. Block, Gjerde, and J. H. Block (1986) in their research on breadth of categorization (i.e., a cognitive style that reflects a preference for broad, or inclusive, versus narrow, or exclusive categories). The behavioral manifestations, moreover, change with age even for constructs known to be relatively stable over time (e.g., aggression; Parke & Slaby, 1983). In sum, one important implication of using indirect measures is the "necessity of seriously investigating the validity of the measures used in each case, because they have only an indirect relation to the theoretical construct they are assumed to measure. The validity cannot be established once and for all" (Bergman & Magnusson, 1990, p. 3). This implication is relevant to the results reported by Shand.

Culture-Related Manifestations of Developmental Constructs

Relations between a hypothetical construct, assessed by "indirect measures," and its behavioral manifestations become even more complex in cross-cultural longitudinal research. This is because the conceptual meaning of a measure, even when administered to same-age children, may index different underlying constructs in different cultures, requiring the researcher to be sensitive not only to the age-appropriateness but also to the cultural meaning of a measure. Although the conceptual definition and the operationalization of a construct may be identical, its psychological implications may nonetheless differ across cultures (Triandis & Brislin, 1984). Takahashi's (1986) analysis of the Strange Situation Procedure used to study attachment patterns in Japan and the United States illustrates how behavior in apparently "objective" experimental situations may exhibit culture-boundedness with infants as young as 12 months old. She interpreted the greater proportion of "insecure" babies found in the Japanese sample in terms of the greater stress caused by the procedure itself among the Japanese babies rather than as indicting actual insecurity of attachment. Jackson (1993) has made a related criticism of this experimental procedure with regard to African-American babies.

Shand's data illustrate how the difficulties involved in interpreting data derived from indirect measures are exacerbated in cross-cultural research. She reports that Japanese babies were more active than American babies immediately after birth, a difference that remained 1 and 3 months later. Although cultural differences in activity level were not observable 10 years later, Shand reports that Japanese preadolescents were substantially more assertive, likely to explore, and likely to take initiative than American preadolescents. In attempting to account for this change, she suggests that either Japanese infants channel their earlier greater motor activity into specific tasks or focused activities or, alternatively, that Japanese mothers encourage greater assertiveness, initiative, and exploration in their preadolescent children.

To evaluate the meaning of these findings obtained a decade apart, we need to examine the psychological meaning of "activity level" and how it may differ both across age/within culture and across culture/within age. One might speculate that activity level in infancy and exploration, assertiveness, and initiative in preadolescence reflect a similar underlying or latent psychological construct: that is, active engagement with the external world, or a relatively low threshold for impulse expression. However, one cannot interpret the meaning of these results across age and culture without further analyses of the correlational network surrounding such findings. As currently reported, the meaning of these findings is equivocal.

Shand interprets her data on 10-year-old Japanese adolescents to indicate that they are better prepared for the future than same-age American children. It is the case, however, that whether or not this behavior pattern indicates that Japanese preadolescents are better prepared for the future than their American peers depends on future social conditions, which themselves are subject to historical change. In this respect, Shand draws too strong conclusions from limited data.

THE NEED FOR MULTIMETHOD, MULTIPLE-CONTEXT APPROACHES TO MEASUREMENT

The Need for a Multimethod Approach

Shand notes that her observer data contradict previous survey data (e.g., Stocking & Curry, 1986). Such discrepancies highlight the importance of using multiple kinds of data (e.g., observer data, self-report data, test data, and life data; see J. H. Block & J. Block, 1980) in cross-cultural research. The convergence between multiple kinds of data is particularly important in cross-cultural research, especially given how difficult it is to establish the conceptual equivalence of even *single* measures across cultures (Triandis & Brislin, 1984). When findings obtained using multiple kinds of data with respect to a construct converge, we can have greater confidence in the findings. Discrepancies raise problems of interpretation, but also provide opportunities for further research.

Compared to observer data and test data, survey data are able to access larger groups of individuals and, by implication, provide information on more representative samples. On the other hand, because survey data are frequently psychologically pallid and subject to socially desirable responses, it is difficult to ascertain their psychological meaning (Gjerde & Shimizu, 1994). The tendency to provide socially desirable responses may in itself be unequally distributed across cultures. For example, Kashiwagi (1986) notes that Japanese adolescents tend to give less positive descriptions of themselves than American adolescents. These responses may not necessarily reflect a "truly" poorer self-image as much as a tendency to observe cultural norms of modesty and reserve *(enryo)*, or sensitivity toward others *(omoiyari,)* presumably major developmental goals for Japanese. Although sometimes prone to distortion, observer data "are able to express the deep structure of behavior by permitting the integrating and contextualizing observer to recognize when a behavior has a certain significance and when it does not" (J. H. Block & J. Block, 1980, p. 59). Although the findings reported by Shand derive from a relatively small sample (a characteristic possibly explaining why Shand and Caudill's data do not converge), they are provocative and cast doubt on the psychological meaningfulness of large-scale cross-cultural surveys of psychological phenomena based uniquely on self-report. As a general principle, evaluation of the structural invariance in patterns of correlations among variables across cultures, based on both different kinds of data and different sources of information, is necessary (although perhaps not sufficient) to establish measurement validity.

The Need for a Multicontext Approach

A limitation of Shand's data is her reliance on a single interpersonal context: the mother–child dyad. Although Japanese culture places great value on this dyad, the exclusive focus on the mother precludes a better understanding of the (indirect or direct) role of the father in Japanese families. Furthermore, it is advisable to study the developmental effects of the family environment in settings other than the family itself (Bronfenbrenner, 1979). The need for studying development in multiple contexts seems crucial when working with Japanese children, because psychological and anthropological sources suggest that Japanese children's behavior is likely to vary according to context (e.g., Lebra, 1976; Peak, 1991).

In addition, Japanese may be particularly aware of their involvement in a multiplicity of social relationships, and that the boundaries between self and other change constantly, depending upon the status of interaction partners.

> These multiple, infinitely graded layers of selfhood are often described in Japanese in terms of two *end points* of a continuum: the *tatemae*, social surface, that which is done to smooth social relations, and *honne*, "real" feeling; *omote*, the front, formal side, vs. *ura*, the back, or intimate side; *soto*, outside, and *uchi*, inside . . . these terms invoke a complex series of graduations along a scale of detachment and engagement, distance and intimacy, formality and informality. (Kondo, 1990, p. 31)

In view of this argument, it seems particularly necessary to follow Bronfenbrenner's (1979) advice to examine behavior in multiple settings before drawing conclusions, because the behavior of Japanese children may be less likely to generalize across settings than the behavior of American children. From Shand's data, we learn that Japanese preadolescents are particularly responsive to environment-based stimuli in the presence of the mother. What we do not know is whether this assertive behavior pattern—which Shand refers to as "control/mastery of the environment" and interprets as indicating that Japanese children are better prepared for the future than their American counterparts—generalizes to situations where the mother is not present, to situations less characterized by *uchi, honne,* and *ura.* In this respect, Shand draws too strong a conclusion from limited data.

WHAT TO MEASURE AND WHEN: THE CONSIDERATION OF AGE-SPECIFIC DEVELOPMENTAL TASKS IN CULTURAL CONTEXTS

A major challenge in longitudinal research is to determine what to measure at each age. This decision should derive from our knowledge of normative patterns of development. Developmental psychopathology defines adaptation in terms of performance on developmental tasks, or stage-salient developmental issues (e.g., Cicchetti, 1993). "Success on these tasks are taken as markers of competence, akin to milestones of psychomotoric development. . . . Some tasks appear to be universal (e.g., attachment to caregivers) while others vary more with culture (e.g., school adjustment)" (Masten & Braswell, 1990, p. 39). Examples of developmental tasks include the formation of a secure attachment relationship in infancy, self-control in the toddler and preschool period, peer acceptance in middle childhood, romantic friendships and identity formation in adolescence, and close intimate relationships in young adulthood (Masten & Braswell, 1990; Sroufe, 1983). Maladaptation may be viewed as failures to successfully negotiate stage-salient developmental tasks. According to this view, "developmental transitions" (such as puberty) are particularly important to examine since the emergence of psychological problems are often associated with how well individuals cope with the challenges posed by stage-salient developmental issues.

This overview of salient developmental issues derives mostly from research on Western children. We need to know more about the sequence of stage-salient developmental issues in other cultures. Some issues (e.g., attachment) can be expected to be relatively universal both in nature and time of emergence; others (e.g., the establishment of peer relations) can be expected to be found with regularity in different cultures but assume salience at different age levels; yet others may be culturally unique or the degree to which they are managed can be expected to have different implications for future opportunity structures. In cross-cultural research, each of these points needs careful consideration. The key is to identify and measure developmental tasks most likely to influence adaptation or opportunity structures later in life.

In addition, even when a certain task, like impulse control, assumes importance in different cultures at the same age level, the mechanisms underlying the eventual mastery of that task may differ across cultures, and longitudinal researchers need to adjust their measurement strategies accordingly. For example, research suggests that examinations in Japan of the development of impulse regulation should pay especially close attention to the transition from home to preschool (Lewis, 1989; Peak, 1991), while in the United States (or in India, albeit in a different and more abrupt manner; Kakar, 1978), family influences might be more influential. Another example: In the United States, the transition to junior high school is an important developmental transition (e.g., Wigfield, Eccles, Mac Iver, & Reuman, 1991). In Japan, however, the long-term implications of this transition may be even more consequential, since Japanese career paths, at least traditionally, have tended to be less flexible than in the United States and perhaps more strongly determined by the quality of the junior high school that a Japanese student attends, an assignment determined by a system of entrance exams. Thus, the psychological circumstances surrounding the transition from elementary to junior high school in Japan require especially close attention, since the manner in which this transition is negotiated may have greater effect on future opportunity structures than in the United States, where differences in educational

Entrance ceremony at a public junior high school. Representatives of the upper two grade levels stand facing the entering class, Aichi Prefecture, 1994. Courtesy of Terutomo Hara.

opportunity structures may derive from other factors (e.g., ethnicity, class, and residence). In sum, even though specific developmental tasks may emerge at similar times, the processes giving rise to successful developmental transitions might differ considerably from one culture to another, dictating different methodological and contextual focuses.

UNWRAPPING "PACKAGED" VARIABLES: THE ECOCULTURAL MODEL OF CULTURE

Cultural longitudinal research should view cultures as changing and multifaceted phenomena that cannot be reduced to broad notions, such as "Japanese" versus "American" or "non-Western" versus "Western." Two issues require our attention: First, longitudinal studies (including the one conducted by Shand and Kosawa) must, like other cultural research, acknowledge the existence of cultural change and intracultural variability. As LeVine (1974) has written, "all cultures, including our own, are in the process of disappearing" (p. 77). Nations, cultures, and ethnicities are historically derived and socially constructed concepts; they are not natural givens but reflect *imagined communities* (Anderson, 1983). National, cultural, and ethnic identity allow for considerable flexibility, interpersonal negotiation, and personal choice, and statements of national continuity and cultural homogeneity are often tainted by ideology (Barth, 1969; Gellner, 1983; Eriksen, 1992; Hobsbawm, 1990; Roosens, 1990). No complex culture is monolithic; each partakes of a measure of both concurrent variability and historical change and permits multiple activity settings that are not always well integrated. As Barth (1991) has noted, culture is "distributive in a population, shared by some but not by others. . . . The most significant structures in culture . . . may not be embedded in its forms but in its distributions, its patterns of *non*-sharing" (p. 134). To view complex cultures as homogeneous, bounded entities is convenient but ultimately illusory. Issues of intracultural variability and change have not received sufficient attention in studies of culture by psychologists. They are particularly important with respect to modern complex societies such as Japan—a nation with a definite, although far from universally accepted, view of itself as homogeneous and middle-class (e.g., Maher & Macdonald, 1994; Yoshino, 1992). De Vos's (1973) comparison of Japanese agricultural and fishing villages provides one example of intracultural variability in Japan. The key issue is to avoid the kind of essentialization of cultures and their descriptions in terms of binary oppositions, so eloquently criticized by Said (1978).

Second, cross-cultural comparisons have typically failed to "unpackage" (Whiting, 1976) culture into separate components, resulting in a downplaying of cultural change and intracultural variation. To the extent that cross-cultural researchers view cultural groups in terms of broad, dichotomized qualities, and as comparably similar and static within each cultural group, they incorrectly view each child as equally representative of his or her culture (Cooper, 1994). They also neglect the insight that culture is distributive (Barth, 1991), and subscribe to the fallible view that children are products of a "thing" called "culture" (see Wikan, 1995, for a strong critique of this position).

> Culture is not a nominal variable to be attached equally to every child, in the same way that age, height, and sex might be. . . . The assumption of homogeneity of experience of children within cultures, without empirical evidence, is unwarranted . . . the method error that follows is to measure culture by assigning it as a trait to all children or parents in a group, thus assuming that culture has uniform effects on every child. (Weisner, Gallimore, & Jordan, 1988, p. 328).

Longitudinal researchers need a differentiated framework for looking at culture that permits shifts between levels of analyses, such as individuals, relationships, and activity settings. The ecocultural model proposed by Gallimore, Weisner, and their colleagues holds some promise in this regard although, in and by itself, this framework is not developmental. However, identifying some of the basic dimensions of ecocultural niches should facilitate examination of intracultural variation and its developmental consequences.

Consistent with Whiting's (1976) proposal to unpackage culture, the ecocultural model posits several interdependent components such as (1) developmental expectations and goals, (2) key socialization agents, (3) communication scripts, and (4) activity settings in which important cultural information is transmitted during daily routines (Cooper, 1994; Gjerde & Cooper, 1992; LeVine, 1974). Below, I briefly describe how Japan and the US differ on these components.

With regard to *developmental expectations* and *interactional scripts*, Japanese mothers are said to promote feelings of interdependency in their children and use the close mother–child bond as an instrument of control (Azuma, Chapter 13, this volume). At least some

Japanese mothers believe that it is difficult to impose discipline unless the child's motivations are fully comprehended. The coveted product is a young person who is *sunao* (compliant, gentle, and cooperative), *otonashi* (reserved, modest, and reflective), and *omiyari* (empathic). (For a rather different and perhaps increasingly valid perspective on Japanese adolescents, see White, Chapter 12, this volume). These developmental goals and values, as well as the means for fostering them, are quite different from the emphasis on verbal assertiveness thought to characterize many American adolescents, males in particular (Gjerde & Cooper, 1992). It has been argued that the Japanese emphasis on interdependence, social integration, and interpersonal harmony continues into adulthood, when Japanese organizations are likely to emphasize emotional attachments and to make extensive use of group participation as a means of social control (Rohlen, 1989).

Key socialization agents also appear different in Japan and the United States. As noted above, the Japanese mother is commonly seen as the key socialization agent, at least during infancy and childhood. The Japanese father–child relationship, on the other hand, has traditionally been viewed as remote (Shwalb, Imaizumi, & Nakazawa, 1987), leading some to refer to Japanese society as "father-absent" (Wagatsuma, 1977). This characteristic has become a source of social concern, since behavior problems appear overrepresented in families with weak father–child ties. One might expect the negative consequences of the long period of mother–child inseparability to become particularly noticeable in adolescence (Lebra, 1984), when, in Western psychodynamic theory, the presence of a salient father figure takes on special importance, as adolescents begin to develop extrafamilial emotional attachments. Such negative consequences are particularly likely to emerge for sons, whose relationship to their mothers is perhaps especially close (Doi, 1973; Gjerde & Shimizu, 1995; Kawai, 1976). However, the father's role in Japan may be changing. In a study emphasizing the importance of studying within-culture variability in Japanese family relationships, Gjerde and Shimizu (1995) documented how our understanding of adolescent competence in Japan is improved by considering the *joint* contribution of mothers and fathers. Shwalb (1995), in his study of the Japanese father–daughter relationship, reports that Japanese fathers experience greatest responsibility for their daughters when daughters attend junior high school.

Differences in *activity settings* between the two countries are less well researched, although Rohlen (1983) has argued that Japanese adolescents, dominated by home and school, live more sheltered and closely supervised lives than their American counterparts and therefore are, as a group, less likely then American adolescents to be exposed to situations offering personal choice. However, some evidence suggests that this situation is changing, at least for some Japanese adolescents (White, Chapter 12, this volume).

This ecocultural description of Japanese development provides a useful background against which to evaluate Shand's results. With respect to one activity setting, the family, Shand writes with insight about the traditional Japanese mother's role and strategies for childrearing (e.g., Shand, 1985, and Chapter 15, this volume). But has this exclusive focus on the mother led Shand to overlook other socialization influences (e.g., fathers, teachers, and peers)? Also, given that American fathers may play a larger role than do Japanese fathers in the socialization of their children, Shand's exclusion of fathers may skew our deeper understanding of the development of Japanese children. If, however, maternal activities are more consequential for Japanese children than for American children (e.g., Kashiwagi et al., 1984), her focus on the mother may capture more fully central socialization processes in Japan than in the United States.

With respect to key socialization agents, the exclusion of the father in Shand's analyses raises additional important questions. As originally noted by Talcott Parsons (1958), the father is more likely than the mother to embody the qualities of the extrafamilial, "nonrelational" world (see also Block, 1971; Youniss & Smollar, 1985). By his symbolic representation within the family of the world beyond (e.g., occupational domains), he becomes an important link between his family and the outside world. However, descriptions of the presumably "absent" Japanese father fail to ask an important follow-up question: If the Japanese father remains absent during his children's adolescence, who then provides the necessary guidance to help Japanese adolescents make decisions about their future? If this role continues to be fulfilled by Japanese mothers, what is the knowledge base that they draw upon to guide their children "cross the bridge" from the family to the world beyond? If the mother does not play this role, who does? Peers? Media? Teachers? Maybe even fathers, however indirectly? Thus, to describe the Japanese family as "father-absent" opens up an array of unaddressed issues. A longitudinal design can address these issues as they gain increasing salience as the child passes through adolescence. Especially during adolescence, it becomes increasingly important to differentiate between, and study the interrelationships among, the different components of the ecocultural model.

CONCLUSIONS AND RECOMMENDATIONS

The Shand–Kosawa collaboration is a research project in progress, and thus the preceding criticisms are preliminary and tentative. Based on the data reported by Shand (Chapter 15, this volume), we look forward to more fine-grained longitudinal analyses of both inter- and intracultural variability in the two countries. My final comments are in the form of recommendations or guidelines for future longitudinal research on culture and development. In consideration of the work by Shand and others on Japanese child development, the following points merit attentive consideration:

1. Researchers should be sensitive to the cultural meaning of measures as they may change with age. In particular, similar behavioral outcomes may derive from different underlying developmental mechanisms or processes in different cultures, and, vice versa, similar developmental mechanisms and processes may result in different behavioral outcomes.

2. Research designs should proceed from a thoughtful analysis of the ecological niches in which children in different cultures develop. These ecological niches may equal the four components of the ecological model, or the three ingredients outlined by Super and Harkness (1986): (a) the physical and social context in which the child develops, (b) the local customs of child care and child-rearing, and (c) the psychology of the caretakers, including parental ethnotheories.

3. Researchers should develop familiarity with how cultures differ in the sequence of developmental tasks and challenges that children encounter. In addition, how do parents' developmental timetables (i.e., their ideas about the ages when particular abilities can be expected to emerge) (Goodnow & Collins, 1990, pp. 28–29) differ across cultures? This kind of theory-driven analysis will help researchers make informed decisions about what to measure at different ages. Researchers must realize that even if apparently identical tasks emerge at similar ages across cultures (e.g., during the transition from elementary to junior high school in Japan and the United States), the developmental implications of how the child copes with these transitions may have different long-term implications in different cultures.

4. Whenever possible, researchers should study constructs from multiple perspectives, using multiple kinds of data, multiple informants, and multiple assessment contexts. As outlined above, the latter is especially important in Japan. Analysis of the convergence among these different components will provide increased in-

formation about the construct validity of measures used cross-culturally.

5. Because culture is not static or homogeneous but is a social construction with "fuzzy" boundaries and considerable within-culture variability, researchers should focus on within-culture variability as much as on between-culture differences, and analyze the structural stability of the variables at each age. The "unwrapping" of culture into its different components also facilitates analyses of how the relative importance of different components change with age.

6. Rather than applying research constructs and instruments derived from one culture to members of another culture, researchers might consider adopting "parallel research" designs (Sue & Sue, 1987). In this three-step design, the first stage involves the identification of potentially universal constructs (e.g., depressive affect). In the second step, researchers develop ways to measure these constructs in a manner appropriate for each culture, and, finally, in the third step, attempts are made to identify both similarities and differences across cultural groups in terms of how these constructs contribute to development.

7. These recommendations are difficult to implement in a single study, even under the best of funding circumstances. So my final recommendation is that researchers interested in culture and development during the first decades of life develop relatively short-term longitudinal studies that focus on specific developmental transitions (e.g., transition to adolescence). This is all the more important because such developmental transitions provide an opportunity to examine developmental processes that direct individuals toward one set of pathways rather than another, often with long-term consequences (Masten & Braswell, 1990). It is also the case that characterological differences are likely to be particularly influential during transitional periods, when "the structuring, role-defining, behavior-directing aspects of a previously stable society or situation are weakened or disappear" (J. Block, 1993a, p. 272). Finally, short-term longitudinal studies may be advantageous because long-term outcomes often derive from a multitude of intervening factors, and distal relationships may frequently have to be analyzed as chains of different, relatively short-term effects (e.g., Rutter, 1988). This latter factor may explain why observations obtained by Shand and Kosawa in infancy seem only weakly related to preadolescent outcomes.

In sum, given the many challenges that await researchers who attempt to conduct longitudinal studies in more than one culture, it is not surprising that relatively few studies of this kind have been undertaken. Perhaps more than any other kind of psychological inquiry, longitudinal studies—because they inherently include a time dimension—of several cultures require attention to the changing historical nature of cultural situations, "to view cultural situations as *always* in flux, in a perpetual historical sensitive state of resistance and accommodation to broader processes of influences that are as much inside as outside of the local context" (Marcus & Fisher, 1986, p. 78). Culture is easily reified by psychologists and often viewed as separate and bounded entities and described in terms of static, dichotomous distinctions (e.g., "individualist" versus "collectivist" cultures or "independent" versus "interdependent" selves) when what exists are "cultures, often subtly grouped, shading into each other, overlapping, [and] intertwined" (Gellner, 1983, p. 49). Although Japanese and Americans may live by only partly overlapping *concerns*—to use Barth's (1993) expression, it is important that we do not reify such notions (e.g., harmony, modesty, amae, individualism, interdependence, hierarchy, etc.) as the essence of the respective "cultures" but look at them for what they are: sets of concerns or worries that people carry with them in their daily lives and which can be expressed, displayed, and negotiated in multiple and often conflicting ways in real interpersonal contexts. It is of key importance that we keep these concerns "embedded in the enigmas, struggles, and indeterminancies of real lives rather than reifying them as 'values' " (Barth, 1993, p. 345). Methodologically, it is essential to examine within-culture variability to avoid the stereotyping that easily results from analyses of between-culture main effects. Both Japan and the US are diverse, heterogeneous countries. Particularly in the case of Japan, however, this fact has long been blurred by the efforts of many Japanese intellectuals' homogeneous characterizations of Japan based on long-existing ideologies emphasizing national distinctiveness and sameness (Yoshino, 1992)—characterizations that make this diversity less immediately apparent and its analysis more difficult. As Befu (1993) recently noted, because "the ethnic Japanese are not only numerically but politically dominant, they are able to impose their ethnic primordality as the official identity of the nation, ignoring divergent primordalities of ethnic minorities" (p. 129). These minorities are then denied cultural citizenship and excluded from most cultural studies. Furthermore, the components of the "ethnic Japanese" need to be more closely examined and greater attention paid to social groups that tend to be "hidden" behind the dominant emphasis on white-collar males and their families, including working women, blue-collar workers, and the elderly. Greater research attention to these later groups will serve to reveal the diverse meanings of what it means to be Japanese.

As outlined at the beginning of this chapter, longitudinal studies are essential if we are to achieve a rich understanding of the nature and course of human development. But, as I have also tried to describe here, to conduct studies that involve more than one "culture" raises complex methodological and conceptual problems. Nancy Shand and Yorio Kosawa should be commended as scholars for their courage in taking up this formidable challenge.

ACKNOWLEDGMENTS

The preparation of this chapter was supported by a grant to Per F. Gjerde and Catherine Cooper from the University of California Pacific Rim Foundation.

NOTE

1. These quotation marks were meant to signify the unstable identities these labels refer to. Here I follow Ivy's argument that each of these names is as much "a discursive construct as an objective referent" (Ivy, 1995, p. 1). Having noted this, however, these quotation marks will be omitted in the remainder of this chapter.

REFERENCES

Anderson, B. (1983). *Imagined communities.* London: Verso.

Barth, F. (1969). Introduction. In F. Barth (Ed.), *Ethnic groups and boundaries: The social organization of cultural difference* (pp. 9–38). Oslo: Norwegian University Press.

Barth, F. (1991). The analysis of culture in complex societies. *Ethnos, 42,* 120–142.

Barth, F. (1993). *Balinese worlds.* Chicago: University of Chicago Press.

Befu, H. (1993). Nationalism and Nihonjinron. In H. Befu (Ed.), *Cultural nationalism in East Asia* (pp. 107–135). Berkeley, CA: University of California Press.

Bergman, L. R., & Magnusson, D. (1990). General issues about data quality in longitudinal research. In D. Magnusson & L. R. Bergman (Eds.), *Data quality in longitudinal research* (pp. 1–31). New York: Cambridge University Press.

Block, J. (1971). *Lives through time.* Berkeley, CA: Bancroft Books.

Block, J. (1993a). Paradox lost. *Psychological Inquiry, 4,* 272–273.

Block, J. (1993b). Studying personality the long way. In D. Funder, R. Parke, C. Tomlinson-Keasey, & K. Widaman (Eds.), *Studying lives through time: Personality and development* (pp. 9–44). Washington, DC: American Psychological Association.

296 · P. F. GJERDE

Block, J., Gjerde, P. F., & Block, J. H. (1986). Continuity and transformation in the psychological meaning of category breadth. *Developmental Psychology, 22,* 820–831.

Block, J. H., & Block, J. (1980). The role of ego-control and ego-resiliency in the organization of behavior. In W. A. Collins (Ed.), *Minnesota symposia on child psychology* (Vol. 13, pp. 51–63). Hillsdale, NJ: Erlbaum.

Bronfenbrenner, U. (1979). *The ecology of human development.* Cambridge, MA: Harvard University Press.

Caspi, A., & Bem, D. J. (1990). Personality continuity and change across the life course. In L. A. Pervin (Ed.), *Handbook of personality: Theory and research* (pp. 549–575). New York: Guilford Press.

Cicchetti, D. (1993). Developmental psychopathology: Reactions, reflections, projections. *Developmental Review, 13,* 471–502.

Cooper, C. R. (1994). Cultural perspectives on continuity and change across the contexts of adolescents' relationships. In R. Montemayor, G. R. Adams, & T. P. Gullotta (Eds.), *Advances in adolescent development: Vol. 6. Personal relationships during adolescence.* Newbury Park, CA: Sage.

Cronbach, L. J., & Meehl, P. (1955). Construct validity in psychological tests. *Psychological Bulletin, 52,* 281–302.

De Vos, G. A. (1973). *Socialization for achievement.* Berkeley: University of California Press.

Doi, T. (1973). *The anatomy of dependency.* New York: Kodansha International.

Eriksen, T. H. (1992). *Us and them in modern societies: Ethnicity and nationalism in Mauritius, Trinidad and beyond.* Oslo: Scandinavian University Press.

Gellner, E. (1983). *Nations and nationalism.* Oxford: Oxford University Press.

Gjerde, P. F. (1986). The interpersonal structure of family interaction situations: Parent–adolescent relations in dyads and triads. *Developmental Psychology, 22,* 297–304.

Gjerde, P. F., & Cooper, C. R. (1992). *Family influences on adolescent competence in Japan and the US.* Proposal funded by the Pacific Rim Foundation, University of California.

Gjerde, P. F., & Shimizu, H. (1995). Family relationships and adolescent development in Japan: A family-systems perspective on the Japanese family. *Journal of Research on Adolescence, 5,* 281–318.

Goodnow, J. J., & Collins, W. A. (1990). *Development according to parents: The nature, sources, and consequences of parents' ideas.* Hillsdale, NJ: Erlbaum.

Hobsbawm, E. J. (1990). *Nations and nationalism since 1780: Programme, myth, reality.* Cambridge: Cambridge University Press.

Ivy, M. (1995). *Discourses of the vanishing: Modernity, phantasm, Japan.* Chicago: University of Chicago Press.

Jackson, J. F. (1993). Multiple caregiving among African Americans and infant attachment: The need for an emic approach. *Human Development, 36,* 87–102.

Kakar, S. (1978). *The inner world: A psycho-analytic study of childhood and society in India.* New York: Oxford University Press.

Kashiwagi, K. (1986). In H. Stevenson, H. Azuma, & K. Hakuta (Eds.), *Child development and education in Japan.* New York: Freeman.

Kashiwagi, K., Azuma, H., Miyake, K., Nagano, S., Hess, R. D., & Holloway, S. D. (1984). Japan–US comparative study on early maternal influences upon cognitive development: A follow-up study. *Japanese Psychological Research, 26,* 82–92.

Kawai, H. (1976). Bosei shakai nihon no eien no shonen tachi [The eternal youth in maternal Japanese society]. In *Bosei shakai nihon no byori [Pathology of the maternal Japanese society].* Tokyo: Chuo Koron-sha.

Kondo, D. K. (1990). *Crafting selves: Power, gender, and discourses of identity in a Japanese workplace.* Chicago: University of Chicago Press.

Lebra, T. S. (1976). *Japanese patterns of behavior.* Honolulu: University of Hawaii Press.

Lebra, T. S. (1984). *Japanese women: Constraint and fulfillment.* Honolulu: University of Hawaii Press.

LeVine, R. A. (1994). Parental goals: A cross-cultural view. *Teachers College Record, 76,* 226–239.

Lewis, C. C. (1989). From indulgence to internalization: Social control in the early school years. *Journal of Japanese Studies, 15,* 139–157.

Loevinger, J. (1957). Objective tests as instruments of psychological theory. *Psychological Reports, 94,* 635–694.

Magnusson, D. (1988). Individual development from an interactional perspective: A longitudinal study. In D. Magnusson (Ed.), *Paths through life* (Vol. 1). Hillsdale, NJ: Erlbaum.

Maher, J. C., & Macdonald, G. (1994). *Diversity in Japanese culture and language.* New York: Columbia University Press.

Marcus, G., & Fischer, M. (1986). *Anthropology as cultural critique.* Chicago: University of Chicago Press.

Masten, A., & Braswell, L. (1991). Developmental psychopathology: An integrative framework for understanding behavior problems in children and adolescents. In P. R. Martin (Ed.), *Handbook of behavior therapy and psychological science: An integrative approach* (pp. 35–56). New York: Pergamon Press.

Morikawa, H., Shand, N., & Kosawa, Y. (1988). Maternal speech to prelingual infants in Japan and the United States: Relationships among functions, forma and referents. *Journal of Child Language, 15,* 237–256.

Parke, R. D., & Slaby, R. (1983). The development of aggression. In P. H. Mussen (Ed.), *Handbook of developmental psychology* (Vol. 4). New York: Wiley.

Parsons, T. (1958). Social structure and the development of personality: Freud's contribution to the integration of psychology and sociology. *Psychiatry, 21,* 321–346.

Peak, L. (1991). *Learning to go to school in Japan: The transition from home to preschool life.* Berkeley: University of California Press.

Rogoff, B. (1990). *Apprenticeship in thinking.* New York: Oxford University Press.

Rogoff, B., Gauvain, M., & Ellis, S. (1984). Development viewed in its cultural context. In M. H. Bornstein & M. E. Lamb (Eds.), *Developmental psychology* (pp. 533–564). Hillsdale, NJ: Erlbaum.

Rohlen, T. (1983). *Japan's high schools.* Berkeley: University of California Press.

Rohlen, T. (1989). Order in Japanese society: Attachment, authority, and routine. *Journal of Japanese Studies, 15,* 5–40.

Roosens, E. E. (1990). *Creating ethnicity: The process of ethnogenesis.* Newbury Park, CA: Sage.

Rutter, M. (1988). Longitudinal data in the study of causal processes: Some uses and some pitfalls. In M. Rutter (Ed.), *Studies of psychosocial risk: The power of longitudinal data* (pp. 1–28). New York: Cambridge University Press.

Said, E. (1978). *Orientalism.* New York: Pantheon Books.

Shand, N. (1981). The reciprocal impact of breast-feeding and culture form on maternal and infant development. *Journal of Biosocial Science, 13,* 1–17.

Shand, N. (1985). Culture's influence in Japanese and American role perception and confidence. *Psychiatry, 48,* 52–67.

Shand, N., & Kosawa, Y. (1985a). Culture transmission: Caudill's model and alternative hypotheses. *American Anthropologist, 87,* 862–871.

Shand, N., & Kosawa, Y. (1985b). Japanese and American behavior types at three months: Infant and infant–mother dyads. *Infant Behavior and Development, 8,* 225–240.

Shwalb, D. W. (1995). *Father–daughter relations as recalled by parents of Japanese junior college women.* Paper presented at the biennial meetings of the Society for Research on Child Development, Indianapolis, IN.

Shwalb, D. W., Imaizumi, N., & Nakazawa, J. (1987). The modern Japanese father: Roles and problems in a changing society. In M. E. Lamb (Ed.), *The father's role: Cross-cultural perspectives* (pp. 247–269). Hillsdale, NJ: Erlbaum.

Smith, P. K. (1980). Shared care of young children: Alternative models to monotropism. *Merrill-Palmer Quarterly, 26,* 371–389.

Sroufe, L. A. (1983). Infant–caregiver attachment and patterns of adaptation in preschool: The roots of maladaptation and competence. In M. Perlmutter (Ed.), *Minnesota symposia on child psychology* (Vol. 16, pp. 41–80). Hillsdale, NJ: Erlbaum.

Stigler, J. W., Shweder, R. A., & Herdt, G. (1990). *Cultural psychology: Essays on comparative human development.* Cambridge: Cambridge University Press.

Stocking, C. B., & Curry, G. D. (1986). *Postsecondary plans of US and Japanese high school seniors: An introductory comparative analysis.* Washington, DC: USDE Office of Educational Research and Improvement.

Sue, D., & Sue, S. (1987). Cultural factors in the clinical assessment of Asian Americans. *Journal of Consulting and Clinical Psychology, 55,* 479–487.

Super, C. M., & Harkness, S. (1986). The developmental niche: A conceptualization of the interface between child and culture. *International Journal of Behavioral Development, 9,* 545–569.

Takahashi, K. (1986). Examining the Strange Situation Procedure with Japanese mothers and 12-month-old infants. *Developmental Psychology, 22,* 265–270.

Tanaka, M. (1986). Maternal authority in the Japanese family. In G. A. De Vos & T. Sofue (Eds.), *Religion and the family in East-Asia* (pp. 227–236). Berkeley: University of California Press.

Triandis, H. C., & Brislin, R. W. (1984). Cross-cultural psychology. *American Psychologist, 39,* 1006–1016.

Tronick, E. Z., Morelli, G. A., & Ivey, P. K. (1992). The Efe forager infant and toddler's pattern of social relationships: Multiple and simultaneous. *Developmental Psychology, 28,* 568–577.

Wagatsuma, H. (1977). Some aspects of the contemporary Japanese family: Once Confucian, now fatherless? In A. S. Rossi, J. Kagan, & T. K. Hareven (Eds.), *The family* (pp. 181–210). New York: Norton.

Wagatsuma, H., & De Vos, G. A. (1984). *Heritage of endurance.* Berkeley: University of California Press.

Weisner, T. S., & Gallimore, R. (1977). My brother's keeper: Child and sibling caretaking. *Current Anthropology, 18,* 169–190.

Weisner, T. S., Gallimore, R., & Jordan, C. (1988). Unpackaging cultural effects on classroom learning: Native Hawaiian peer assistance and child-generated activity. *Anthropology and Education Quarterly, 19,* 327–351.

Whiting, B. (1976). The problem of the packaged variable. In K. F. Riegel & J. A. Meacham (Eds.), *The developing individual in a changing world: Vol 1.* Historical and cultural issues (pp. 303–309). Chicago: Aldine.

Wigfield, A., Eccles, J. S., Mac Iver, D., & Reuman, D. A. (1991). Transitions during early adolescence: Changes in children's domain-specific self-perceptions and general self-esteem across the transition to junior high school. *Developmental Psychology, 27,* 552–565.

Wikan, U. (1995). *Mot en ny norsk underklasse: Innvandrere, kultur og integrasjon [Toward a new Norwegian underclass: Immigrants, culture, and integration].* Oslo, Norway: Gyldendal Norsk Forlag.

Wohlwill, J. F. (1973). *The study of behavioral development.* New York: Academic Press.

Yoshino, K. (1992). *Cultural nationalism in contemporary Japan.* London: Routledge.

Youniss, J., & Smollar, J. (1985). *Adolescent relations with mothers, fathers, and friends.* Chicago: University of Chicago Press.

Conclusions
Looking Ahead

David W. Shwalb
Barbara J. Shwalb

This volume has presented the work of several scholars, mostly Americans, on Japanese childrearing and socialization. Our purpose was to have senior scholars discuss their lifework, and to have "junior" scholars consider through the reaction chapters the implications of this work. We will now first recount several points raised in Chapters 2–16 that have general implications for the study of culture and development. Then we will highlight specific issues that may be the focus of future research. Last, we will consider Doi's (Foreword) question of what outsiders can learn about their own cultures by studying the Japanese. For convenience of referencing, the following subsections about implications and research questions discuss the chapters separately, in their original sequence.

IMPLICATIONS OF PAST RESEARCH
Hara–Minagawa and Chen

Hara and Minagawa showed that a historical perspective on childhood helps us to distinguish between actual traditional behavior and stereotypes of past behavior. For instance, they documented Tokugawa era social-class differences in the responsibilities given to children and adolescents. Next, a comparison of the Hara–Minagawa and Chen chapters reveals that interpretations vary when dealing with historical material. An example of this was their opposing analyses of "the saying that until the age of 7 children are among the gods" (Chen, Chapter 3, this volume, p. 33). A third important point was made by Chen, who cautioned us not to paint "too simplistic a picture" (Chapter 3, p. 37) in the use of dichotomies to compare human relationships across cultures. He gave the example of dependency *(amae),* which is described often as a significant aspect of Japanese childrearing. In Chen's opinion, a focus on dependency has led many to underestimate the importance of Japanese independence training—that is, assuming that if Japanese emphasize dependency they must devalue the "opposite" goal of independence. Together, these two chapters suggest the following: *We should document rather than assume or speculate on the existence of traditions, look for intracultural variations, and avoid cultural comparisons based on simple dichotomies.*

De Vos and Vaughn

De Vos's multidisciplinary approach, extended by Vaughn, showed generational continuity in Japanese socialization for achievement motivation characterized by externally defined goals and a sensitivity to what others feel and think. Vaughn's account was also valuable as a description of how he came to see the value of projective techniques despite his early skepticism. How many other critics of such "outdated" methods have been trained systematically in their use? Before rejecting an old method, Vaughn recommends training in the method to test its usefulness. In sum, their work shows that *we should look for cross-generational continuities, and should carefully test the hypotheses of older generation scholars before dismissing their thinking.*

Lanham–Garrick and Lewis

Lanham and Garrick also stressed the theme of continuity, stating "while material consumption has changed extensively in Japan, the nature of social relations has remained rather stable" (Chapter 6, p. 108). They and Lewis wrote that continuity has been observed for over 40 years concerning (1) respect shown to children, (2) strategies used to control children, (3) emphasis on children's emotional security, and (4) education about morality. Lanham also mentions that she would have used different methods had she been able to visit Japan on multiple shorter trips, which is the nature of many American researchers' contacts with Japan today. Perhaps one should consider the impact of institutional and financial constraints on past and present-day research, and how these impinge on cross-cultural research designs. Overall the Lanham–Garrick and Lewis chapters reveal why *across generations researchers have tended to focus on similar aspects of socialization, although their methods have changed.*

Schooler and Holloway–Minami

According to Holloway and Minami, Caudill's research with Schooler "challenged scholars to question the status quo regarding models of human development" (Chapter 9, p. 164). Holloway and Minami discuss (1) whether socialization research should focus on the parent–child dyad or the individual, (2) whether and how to examine social structural influences, and (3) whether cultural transmission is a unilateral process or a two-way exchange, as examples of how Caudill's work challenges our thinking about child development. Caudill's best known finding was that cultural values fostered a Japanese mother–child relationship style that differed from that found in the United States. The preceding issues show that *comparative research on children forces us to reassess our assumptions about human development, as the nature of relationships and communication may differ between cultures.*

Vogel, Vogel, and White

The Vogels' initial cross-cultural study succeeded, according to White, because they overcame their ethnocentrism and viewed Japanese families and individuals on native terms. Suzanne Vogel's chapter describes various assumptions that she had to question to understand Japanese socialization. These assumptions included that (1) Parsonian (Parsons & Bales, 1955) instrumental roles, such as breadwinner, are more valued than are expressive roles, such as housewife; (2) indulgence is a poor childrearing technique which does not foster healthy child development; and (3) individual fulfillment is the primary goal of human development. Suzanne Vogel's retrospect also revealed how her own personal growth influenced her research interests, her findings, and her interpretations. The Vogels' work shows that *cross-cultural research must also be non-ethnocentric research, and that developmental research can be enhanced by self-awareness of one's own development.*

Azuma and Machida

The experiences of the Hess–Azuma research team reveal that a true dialogue between cultures can further understanding of child-rearing in both cultures. For instance, Hess learned that *amae* is present even in American parent–child and teacher–child relationships, while Azuma observed that cultural group comparisons only skim the surface as we try to understand the "meaning" of mother–

child behavior and communications. But we need do no more than study non-Western-based concepts such as *amae* (Johnson, 1993); the Azuma and Machida chapters both show why we must question every assumption and finding portrayed by Westerners as universal. The equal Hess–Azuma partnership was exceptional even within cross-cultural studies, and while such personal contacts are essential, they are not sufficient to internationalize our field. Azuma's writings indicate why *the social sciences, and the field of human development in particular, require a complete reexamination of what is included in or excluded from our body of scientific knowledge.*

Shand and Gjerde

Shand's work was a counterpoint to Caudill's research, and she tended to view United States–Japan mother–child relations as rooted in genetic population differences in infant temperament. Her collaboration with Kosawa is also a rare example of longitudinal comparative research on development. Gjerde criticizes Shand for limiting her focus to the mother–child dyad, stresses the need for multicontextual research, and notes that behavior observed in public contexts such as classrooms and laboratories may differ from behavior in private settings. Finally, Gjerde questions whether developmental tasks are universal in timing or content, given that school achievement by middle adolescence generally sets one's life course in Japan. The preceding suggests that *we should expand our comparative focus beyond the mother–child dyad, be very cautious about the validity of measures when comparing cultures, and question Western assumptions about developmental stages and milestones.*

RECOMMENDATIONS FOR FUTURE RESEARCH

The preceding findings and interpretations were drawn from Chapters 2–16, and most of the following suggestions were likewise selected from the contributors' pool of ideas for research. We believe their issues should be of central concern for the cultural study of Japanese childrearing in the next generation. As De Vos writes, "Questioning what has been done before is part of science, but global rejection or disregard of past efforts simply changes voices without sequential progression" (Chapter 4, this volume, pp. 76–77.). Therefore to advance this area of study, our agenda for future research builds on a constructive view of past research. At the same time, several retrospects described how scholars changed the focus of their research in midstream, showing that we must be self-critical and open both to reframing our research questions or creating new questions.

Hara–Minagawa and Chen

These two contributions on the historical approach pose numerous research questions. First, while Hara and Minagawa say that historical and social trends affect children's lives, objective data is needed to confirm their interpretations and predictions. For instance, there has been research on the influence of historical events such as poverty and war on Americans' lifespan development (Elder, 1974). Given the enduring psychological significance of Japanese experiences during and in the aftermath of World War II, retrospective studies on historical influences would be perfectly suited for Japan. Similarly, research is needed in Japan on the effects of contemporary life in small nuclear families. Hara and Minagawa relate family demographics to "experiential deprivation" (Chapter 2, p. 23), but this connection must be tested. Second, Hara and Minagawa write that "play, work, discipline, and education were woven together in children's lives, reflecting Tokugawa era beliefs about the nature of childhood" (Chapter 2, p. 17). Future research should consider each of these four factors and their degree of coherence in postmodern Japan. Additionally, Chen advocates a comparative approach in historical studies of child development. In light of Ezra Vogel's (Chapter 11, this volume) remark that family dynamics and entrance examination systems developed along similar lines in Japan, Taiwan, and South Korea, an Asian comparative study of historical effects on child development is warranted. We agree with Chen that United States–Japan comparisons have been too common (as was also noted previously by Sofue, 1992) and that future research should emphasize within-Asia comparisons. At the same time, Azuma's chapter (Chapter 13) shows clearly the potential rewards possible in United States–Japan collaborations, and implies that any imbalance of funding sources might place Japanese researchers in a dominant position within an Asian cross-cultural team.

De Vos and Vaughn

These two chapters gave several examples of how Japanese data confound Western-based psychological theories. For instance, while Witkin's (1969) theory was said to define field independence or dependence as a general trait, the De Vos and Vaughn research found that Japanese youth exhibit high social dependence and high cognitive independence. The Hess–Azuma findings show that De Vos's and Vaughn's research should be pursued further though a developmental approach, which may directly relate social versus cognitive dependence–independence to childrearing and socialization.

Lanham–Garrick and Lewis

Lanham and Garrick recommended comparative studies of how parents use childrearing to help children cope with bullying and other problems. Rather than resurveying parental preferences for disciplinary measures, they also advocated research on the purposes and actual effects of childrearing techniques. In addition, Lewis's chapter reminds us of the need to return socialization research to its original focus: the family. As White (Chapter 12) notes, the same in-depth treatment of family socialization given by the Vogels in 1963 is required in the 1990s. Lewis accurately explains the shift of socialization research from home to school settings, yet the Japanese family is still the primary locus of socialization and identification. In White's words, the "centrality of the family in peoples' lives has changed very little" (Chapter 12, pp. 218–219).

Schooler and Holloway–Minami

In addition to follow-up research on Caudill's hypothesis that the causal direction in family socialization is from mother to child, Schooler's research raises two issues for future investigation. First, psychological studies of women's work roles will be crucial for understanding how Japanese women, men, and families change in the future. As White writes, it is "the new *woman* who is establishing the priorities for the new *man*" (Chapter 12, this volume, p. 214). Second, although Schooler discounted its impact on Caudill's data, he mentioned that the size and layout of American and Japanese homes could impact on maternal and child behavior. Indeed, children's living environments must be investigated intensively (Edgerton, 1971). Finally, Holloway and Minami, citing research on parental belief systems related to childrearing, claim that little is known about meaning making in Japanese families. In their view, the Japanese belief systems of *amae* and *omoiyari* (empathy) were the basis for Caudill's interpretations, and future research should concern how these belief systems are formed.

Vogel, Vogel, and White

In addition to refocusing socialization research on the family, White recommends that new studies should concentrate on phenomena that have evolved over the 33 years since *Japan's New Middle Class* (E. Vogel, 1963) appeared. For instance, she notes that Japanese high school and college entrance examination systems have assumed a central position within the educational system, yet there has been little research on the effects of "examination hell" on adolescent development. We suggest that research be conducted on the direct impact of entrance examinations on socialization, childrearing, and social and cognitive development.

Azuma and Machida

Azuma claims that ethics differ between the two societies, demonstrating fundamental differences between Japanese and American values. Yet Machida suggests that values may be converging among youth in the United States and Japan as we approach the 21st century. Therefore, research should test Azuma's contention that Americans and Japanese have different value systems. The assumption of such differences is part of the rationale for United States–Japan comparisons, but we should consider whether these two cultures are still ideal for comparative research. In addition, Machida offers the concepts of maternal control, intrinsic versus extrinsic motivation, and ability for study between Japan and the United States, because their meanings may differ between cultures.

Shand and Gjerde

Shand's research suggests that infancy is a critical period for the establishment of cultural differences in behavioral styles. Follow-up research on her collaboration with Kosawa should begin by bridging the age gap in their longitudinal study of infants and 10-year-olds. In addition, Gjerde advocated comparative short-term longitudinal studies about developmental transitions, considering the heavy investment necessary for longitudinal research. While Lewis and others have emphasized the smoothness of the institutional transition from Japanese preschools into elementary schools, we recommend the study of the transition into junior high school, where smooth continuity is not the rule (Fukuzawa, 1994). In addition, studies of developmental transitions rather than institutional transitions are welcomed. Lastly, Gjerde cites the Japanese father as a socialization agent who is not well understood but may be increasing in importance.

Research about Comparative Research

This book provided several examples of how relationships among collaborators influence research. To improve future studies on Japanese childrearing and socialization, we recommend an investigation of the research process itself. As Holloway and Minami note, "To the extent that research itself is a process of explicitly constructing and exploring social representations, the actors involved and the process of interaction among them is crucial in determining the final product" (Chapter 9, this volume, p. 172). Therefore, one must study the communication that takes place among cross-cultural researchers. Azuma showed that even bilingual researchers frequently have serious misunderstandings due to cultural differences in values and interactional styles. As one school teacher told us recently, "Even when we understand words we may not understand what is in the heart." When American scholars go to study socialization in Japan, are Japanese collaborators tempted to please them by confirming their American colleagues' expectations? This can occur unknowingly through selective sampling. For example, if an American wants to study the development of prosocial behavior, the Japanese contact might sample schools where such behavior is favored. Or if one were studying Japanese fathering, one might be introduced to a sample of relatively active fathers who are motivated to participate in an "international study." In sum, we must conduct research on precisely what happens when research crosses language and cultural barriers.

WHAT WE CAN LEARN

In his foreword, Doi pondered what Americans studying Japanese culture learn about their own culture. We posed this question recently to several American researchers who had conducted research on Japanese child development, and their responses were extremely varied. As Suzanne Vogel's chapter would predict, what one learns about Japan or one's native culture depends on (1) the background and personality of the individual researcher, and (2) the relationships one forms with individual Japanese. We as outsiders encounter Japan based on our preconceptions, and the biases acquired in our native cultures, and the tinted glasses through which we view Japan are colored by the Japanese people to whom we are closest. One scholar responded to our anonymous minisurvey as follows: "I learned how difficult it is to maintain a multicultural society with equal rights for women and minorities, and that because of this the United States is a marvelous social experiment which is dynamic and interesting to be a part of. I also learned about the strengths and weaknesses of a monoracial, monocultural society such as Japan." Another researcher, who worked with many of the same collaborators as the first respondent, reported that "I found Japanese culture to be impenetrable. Never before did I think there was any virtue to the crass directness of Americans I worked with, but the Japanese refusal to make things plain was very difficult. . . . The differences between public persona and private persona were especially tough. . . . I found it a very intolerant environment—very judgmental." A third was "amazed at the skill and involvement that Japanese express in their interactions with children. . . . Despite all our childrearing theories, we Americans operate in a much less systematic way than Japanese do in relation to children." And yet another scholar had a completely different view, writing that "Tokyo clinicians tell me they are seeing more and more women who are completely lacking in confidence as mothers. These clinicians are worried that the Japanese will raise a generation of girls who know nothing about childrearing!" How can we account for such disparate views of Japanese and American cultures and childrearing among these internationally minded American scholars? Each of the preceding four responses is a different perception of the same overall Japanese "reality." We believe that research by Americans on the Japanese is no more objective than that by native Japanese. It simply provides an additional and crucial set of perspectives (Plath & Smith, 1992) and reflects the intellectual and personal growth experiences of each scholar. We hope the contributors to this book have conveyed their sense of the importance and excitement of having a cross-cultural perspective on human development.

This volume was originally intended for readers interested in culture and development. Yet we hope even "non-cross-cultural" readers will consider a final quotation from Ezra Vogel's chapter, because data collected within the United States are just as much influenced by culture as are Japanese data. Vogel recalled his mentor's advice of 35 years ago as follows: "Ezra, you are terribly provincial. You have never lived in another culture. How could you understand American society without living in another culture? Before you settle down to teaching, you ought to go abroad to a very different culture and live" (Chapter 11, this volume, p. 201). How many graduate school advisers nowadays, particularly in psychology, have the courage or wisdom to give such advice? And how many graduate students would make the sacrifices necessary to follow such a path? A frontier spirit will be necessary if we are to build on the pioneering work presented in this book.

REFERENCES

Edgerton, R. (1971). *The individual in cultural adaptation.* Berkeley: University of California Press.

Elder, G. (1974). *Children of the Great Depression.* Chicago: University of Chicago Press.

Fukuzawa, R. E. (1994). The path to adulthood according to Japanese middle schools. *Journal of Japanese Studies, 20*(1), 61–86.

Johnson, F. A. (1993). *Dependency and Japanese socialization: Psychoanalytic and anthropological investigations into* amae. New York: New York University Press.

Parsons, T., & Bales, R. F. (1955). *Family, socialization and interaction process.* Glencoe, IL: Free Press.

Plath, D. W., & Smith, R. F. (1992). How "American" are studies of modern Japan done in the United States? In H. Befu & J. Kreiner (Eds.), *Othernesses of Japan: Historical and cultural influences on Japanese studies in ten countries* (pp. 201–229). Munich: Iudicium-Verlag.

Sofue, T. (1992). An historical review of Japanese studies by American anthropologists: The Japanese viewpoint. In H. Befu & J. Kreiner (Eds.), *Otherness of Japan: Historical and cultural influences on Japanese studies in ten countries* (pp. 231–240). Munich: Iudicium-Verlag.

Vogel, E. A. (1992). *Japan's new middle class.* (2nd ed.). Berkeley: University of California Press. (Original work published 1963)

Witkin, H. A. (1969). Social influences in the development of cognitive style. In D. Goslin (Ed.), *Handbook of socialization theory and research* (pp. 687–706). Chicago: Rand-McNally.

Author Index

Subject Index